NEITHER MONK NOR LAYMAN

NEITHER MONK
NOR LAYMAN

CLERICAL MARRIAGE IN MODERN
JAPANESE BUDDHISM

Richard M. Jaffe

UNIVERSITY OF HAWAI'I PRESS

HONOLULU

First published 2001 by Princeton University Press
Copyright © 2001 by Princeton University Press
Paperback edition published by University of Hawai'i Press
© 2011 University of Hawai'i Press for preface to paperback edition

Library of Congress Cataloging-in-Publication Data

Jaffe, Richard M., 1954–
   Neither monk nor layman : clerical marriage in modern Japanese
Buddhism / Richard M. Jaffe.
       p.   cm.
   "Originally published in hardcover by Princeton University Press,
Princeton and Oxford, in 2001»—T.p. verso.
   Includes bibliographical references and index.
   ISBN 978-0-8248-3527-9 (softcover : alk. paper)
   1. Buddhist priests—Marriage—Japan.   2. Buddhist priests—Family
relationships—Japan.   3. Marriage—Religious aspects—Buddhism.
4. Buddhism—Japan—-History—1868–1945.   I. Title.
   BQ5355.M37J35 2010
   294.3'61—dc22
                                                2010023145

Printed by Edwards Brothers, Inc.

For my parents

FRANCES AND EDWARD JAFFE

爾者已非僧非俗、是故以禿字為姓

Shikareba, sudeni sō ni arazu zoku ni arazu,
kono yue ni Toku no ji o motte shō to nasu.

I am now neither monk nor layman, therefore
I have taken the name "Stubble Haired."

Shinran, Kyōgyōshinshō

Contents

Chapter 8

Chapter 9

Chapter 10

Figures and Table

Preface

WHILE GATHERING materials in 1989 for a study of Zen Buddhism during the Edo period, I came across a surprising passage in an 1899 compilation of current Sōtō denomination sect law: a regulation that banned the lodging of women in Sōtō temples and reiterated that, as in the past, all Sōtō clerics were to refrain from such unbecoming activities as marriage and meat eating. This intrigued me because like many others familiar with the history of Japanese Buddhism, I had assumed, mistakenly, that the mandatory ban against meat eating and clerical marriage (*nikujiki saitai*) had ended in 1872 as the result of a Japanese government decree ordering all Buddhist clerics to marry. My interest piqued by this contrary evidence, I questioned several scholars of Sōtō Zen who seemed equally surprised (and bewildered) that such a prohibition was part of Sōtō sect law twenty-seven years after the state had abolished the ban against clerical marriage.

Having spent a number of years practicing Zen at the San Francisco Zen Center, including its practice centers Green Gulch Farm and Tassajara, I had long wondered how the distinctive Japanese and, now, American Zen practice of allowing those who were ordained as priests to marry had come about. The founder of the San Francisco Zen Center, Shunryū Suzuki, had pointed out the curiousness of this historical turn in a lecture later incorporated into *Zen Mind, Beginner's Mind*. Suzuki, alluding to Shinran, had stated, "Here in America we cannot define Zen Buddhists the way we do in Japan. American students are not priests and yet not completely laymen. I understand it this way: that you are not priests is an easy matter, but that you are not exactly laymen is more difficult."[1]

Although Suzuki was speaking of the uncomfortable hybridity of Zen in America, it became clear to me through both my personal experience of contemporary established Buddhist (*kisei Bukkyō*) temple life in Japan and the writing of this book that his comments equally reflect the predicament of most Japanese Buddhist clerics—excluding those of the Jōdo Shin and some of the Shugendō denominations—today. As is often the case, in speaking about others, Suzuki was also revealing himself: born in a Sōtō temple in 1904, before the prohibition against lodging women in temples had been lifted, Suzuki was among the first generation of post-Restoration temple sons and the second generation of semi-openly married Sōtō clerics.[2]

---

[1] Suzuki (1970, 133).
[2] For a biography of Suzuki, see Chadwick (1999).

In this book I trace the events leading up to the promulgation of the *nikujiki saitai* measure and the subsequent debate over those practices among the Buddhist denominations that, at least normatively, had previously eschewed open marriage, meat eating, abandonment of tonsure, and the wearing of nonclerical garb by their clerics. In addition, I examine the spread of open clerical marriage among the Buddhist clergy, the denominational response to the spread, and the rise of specifically Buddhist teachings and ceremonies centered on marriage and the family. To better explain the situation of the Buddhist clergy at the start of the Meiji era, I briefly examine the ongoing problem of precept violation by the Japanese Buddhist clergy with particular attention to fornication (*nyobon*), meat eating, and the early modern debate literature concerning *nikujiki saitai*. My main focus is on the period of the most intense and open debate over *nikujiki saitai*, roughly from the promulgation of the decriminalization law in 1872 until the start of the Sino-Japanese War in 1937, the period during which an extensive body of writings concerning *nikujiki saitai* was produced.

The 1872 edict decriminalizing marriage also ended penalties for such other prohibited clerical practices as meat eating, abandoning tonsure, and wearing nonclerical clothing. As a result the debate over clerical marriage was closely tied to those and other previously forbidden practices not even mentioned in the edict, for example, drinking alcoholic beverages.[3] During the late nineteenth and early twentieth centuries, each of those questionable practices was the subject of a debate literature all its own. In much of the early literature debating clerical marriage, these practices are also considered, and to an extent I will examine them. The fight over clerical marriage overshadowed all of these other issues, however, and remained a subject of contention long after meat eating and the abandonment of tonsure were accepted as inevitable. Although these other concerns were also the subject of concern among the clergy, they were never subject to the prolonged, contentious debate that centered on clerical marriage. Unlike such acts as meat eating, alcohol use, or not wearing clerical robes, the repercussions of which are relatively circumscribed, affecting primarily the individual cleric engaged in that activity, the impact of clerical marriage is profound. The acceptance of marriage by the Buddhist clergy entailed not only new attitudes toward what had previously been viewed as fornication. With the spread of open marriage came temple wives and families, phenomena that forced concomitant changes in temple finances, succession practices, and discipleship. Given the magnitude of these transformations, it is not surprising that struggle over clerical marriage was so heated and protracted.

---

[3] See chapter 3 for a definition of the term *nikujiki saitai*.

Although marriage and precept violation had been tolerated prior to the Meiji era, for the first time in the history of the Buddhist tradition the majority of ordained clerics openly married. My aim in describing the struggle over clerical marriage is to provide a clear picture and analysis of one of the most profound, sweeping institutional changes in Buddhist clerical life in the history of the tradition. By closely examining the shift to a married clergy, I believe we can gain a more nuanced perspective of the interplay between official doctrine and actual Buddhist practice and the interaction of often contesting religious regimes among the Buddhist denominations. Additionally, the study will reveal the interaction between the Buddhist clergy and the forces of modernization in late-nineteenth- and early-twentieth-century Japan.

My research is based on the analysis of a wide range of print materials, including government documents, sectarian directives, and the many tracts either attacking or defending clerical marriage that were published from the early Meiji era through the start of the Pacific War in the late 1930s. The boom in newspapers and magazines in the Meiji era made this very much a public debate, with government leaders, journalists, Shintoists, and Christians readily injecting their opinions into the fray. I include materials from all of these perspectives, as well as from different denominations. Efforts to defend clerical celibacy and to advocate clerical marriage crossed sectarian boundaries. In particular, the attempt to rescind the *nikujiki saitai* law and to suppress the spread of clerical marriage engendered cooperation among clerical leaders.

The tracts, articles, and pronouncements concerning clerical marriage are scattered amidst the archives of the Meiji, Taishō, and early Shōwa periods. The lack of primary research on this topic necessitated that I scour these collections for materials related to the *nikujiki saitai* problem. I believe that the materials I have gathered from various collections reflect fairly the various sides of the debate and different sectarian positions with regard to the clerical marriage problem.

Some denominations have been much more public in their airing of the debate over marriage and in their effort to recover the history of this often bitter struggle. Because scholars from the Sōtō and, to a lesser degree, Nichiren denominations have been much more active in investigating and classifying primary documents concerning clerical marriage, information about those denominations has been far more readily available. As a consequence of the unevenness in quantity of materials available, Sōtō Zen and Nichiren loom larger in this book than those denominations that have remained relatively silent about the issue, for example, Tendai, Shingon, Ōbaku, and many of the branches of the Rinzai denomination. Surprisingly, although Jōdo Shin clerics played a central role in the debate during the Edo period, they were largely absent from the controversy that ensued following the decriminalization of clerical marriage in 1872.

The sources used are largely the products of one particular clerical class. The most commonly preserved materials were written by such high-level, well-educated clerics and intellectuals as Shaku Unshō, Fukuda Gyōkai, Nishiari Bokusan, Kuriyama Taion, and Tanaka Chigaku. This is particularly true of the extended tracts either defending or attacking *nikujiki saitai*. These materials have been central to my research, but they fail to reflect the full range of participants in the struggle over clerical marriage in the modern era. As will be seen, by far some of the most important players in the drama were the anonymous clerics, temple wives, and children who remain largely in the shadows, even as they gain partial legitimacy in the eyes of denominational leaders and parishioners. It was this largely silent majority of clerics and their families who forced a reticent leadership to accommodate them. As much as possible I have tried to uncover sources that would provide a sense of these individuals as well as the more elite members of the Buddhist world. To that end, letters to newspapers and petitions to the government have proven useful, but limited amendments to the official statements and tracts. Whenever possible, I have attempted to read between the lines of the elite sources for clues concerning those clerics and their families.

Given how profoundly the acceptance of *nikujiki saitai* affected modern Japanese Buddhism, it is surprising how few scholars have devoted attention to the issue. Pioneering efforts have been made by such scholars as Date Mitsuyoshi, Gorai Shigeru, Morioka Kiyomi, and Takeda Chōshū, each of whom has written articles or book chapters concerning aspects of the decriminalization of clerical marriage and the secularization of clerical life. In addition, during the past decade, a variety of scholars including Ikeda Eishun, Kumamoto Einin, and Hikita Seishun have studied the topic of clerical marriage. In particular, the work of Hikita is noteworthy for its pan-sectarian approach and the range of topics examined. A number of these works appeared as I was working on this project and I have benefited greatly from the leads, as well as the direct advice, many of these authors have provided.

A NOTE ON TERMS AND DATES

Throughout the book I use the words "cleric" and "clergy" as the translation for the Japanese words *sō* and *sōryo*, which commonly are translated as "monk" or "priest." The word monk implies celibacy and, as will be shown, many *sō* were married, even before the Meiji period. By the Edo period, ordained leaders of Jōdo Shin confraternities were considered to be *sō*, but clearly they did not attempt to act as "monks." From a legal perspective, however, they were subject to many of the same requirements as *sō* from other denominations. Neil McMullin has observed the spectrum of meanings for the words *sō* and *sōryo*, noting, "The clergy of some Buddhist schools, especially in the earlier periods, are best called monks. In the late medieval period, however, the period with which this work is mainly concerned, the clergy of many of the Buddhist schools, particularly of the True Pure Land school, were more like priests or ministers than monks: they were not cloistered, and they did not lead communal lives, for most of them were married and had families. Once again, therefore, in order to avoid unnecessary distinctions all Buddhist clerics will be called priests."[4] Although I agree with McMullin concerning the ambiguity of the word *sō*, I have also avoided the use of the word priest because not all *sō* acted in the intermediary religious role on behalf of the laity that the term "priest" implies. As Richard Gombrich has recently noted, "priests, after all, are functionaries who mediate between men and gods."[5] Not all *sō*, therefore, acted as priests. Because "cleric" simply refers to an official religious functionary and "clergy" to that class of individuals, those terms more accurately reflect the full range of meanings of *sō* and *sōryo*. I have opted for "cleric" and "clergy" as the translations for these Japanese terms.

The most central phrase in the book, *nikujiki saitai*, also requires some preliminary clarification. Although literally the four-character compound refers specifically to meat eating and clerical marriage, during the Edo period the Jōdo Shin clergy used it as a sort of shorthand for their distinctive clerical practices. As I will show in chapter 3, precept reformers, critics of the Jōdo Shin clergy, and anti-Buddhist writers viewed Buddhist clerical marriage as illegitimate, referring to it with such terms as *nyobon* (fornication) or *in* (licentiousness). The meaning of *nikujiki saitai* shifted after the promulgation of the 1872 decriminalization measure, when *nikujiki saitai* came to refer also to other practices linked to it in the text of the law, including abandonment of tonsure and clerical robes. Of course, those opposed to those practices used the phrase to connote general clerical laxity; those who favored the adoption of those practices used the compound to signify the cardinal characteristics of a modern clergy. I have uniformly translated the phrase as "eating meat and clerical marriage" and have tried to spell out the wider implications of the term when such an interpretation is mandated by the context. Early uses of the term will be discussed in detail in chapter 3.

Finally, because the Japanese government switched from using the traditional lunar calendar to the Gregorian calendar on January 1, 1873,

[4] McMullin (1984, 12).
[5] Gombrich (1994, 20).

dates during the early Meiji years can be confusing. To avoid ambiguity in referring to dates during the first five years of the Meiji era, I have parenthetically provided Gregorian calendar dates for all events occurring between Meiji 1–5 (1868–1872). I have included the traditional dates to facilitate reference to Japanese source materials, many of which continue to use reign names for dating. Meiji dates prior to January 1, 1873, are abbreviated M. year/month/day, followed by the Gregorian calendar date in parentheses. All conversions to Western dates are based on Yuasa (1990).

Preface to the Paperback Edition

IN THE YEARS since the publication of the hardcover edition of _Neither Monk nor Layman_, my research has continued to focus on developments in Japanese Buddhism from the beginning of the Meiji period until the present. Although my current work is not directly connected with the debate over clerical marriage, as I have read through the writings of various twentieth-century Japanese Buddhists, I have noted the extent to which the interlocking concerns about the legitimacy of Japanese Buddhist precepts and the appropriateness of clerical ordination and Buddhist monastic life for the twentieth century played a role in the thoughts and actions of a wide range of Japanese Buddhists. The desire to find a legitimate basis for ordination and clerical conduct drove such Buddhists as Shaku Kōzen and Kawaguchi Ekai to search in South Asia and Tibet, respectively, for texts, practices, and ordination traditions that would infuse Japanese Buddhism with new life. Ultimately these two adventurers reached radically different conclusions about the viability of unmarried monastic life in twentieth-century Japan. While Kōzen believed that transmitting and following Theravāda's full monastic ordination in Japan would restore the tradition, Kawaguchi returned from his second long sojourn in Tibet and India to renounce, at the age of sixty, his vows as an Ōbaku Zen cleric and, echoing Tanaka Chigaku, who is discussed in detail in Chapter Eight of this book, to deny the very possibility of Buddhist clerical ordination in the twentieth century. Along with numerous other clerics and scholars, ranging from the Tendai cleric Ueda Tenzui to D. T. Suzuki, the writings of these reformers and Buddhist intellectuals demonstrate the degree to which the related issues of the precepts and clerical marriage were on the minds of Japanese Buddhists for much of the twentieth century.

As I suggest in the concluding chapter of this book, the tacit acceptance of clerical marriage by the various renunciant Buddhist denominations in Japan left these organizations with a variety of unresolved doctrinal and practical issues. Since 2001, when the hardcover edition of this book was published, one can find a significant number of publications, particularly in Japanese, concerned with the role of women and temple families in temple life. As recently as January 2010, the Buddhist newspaper _Bukkyō taimusu_ carried a series of articles discussing gender equality for temple wives and nuns within the Sōtō denomination. A stream of books published by working groups of temple wives, nuns, female temple incumbents, and progressive male clerics, for example, _Bukkyō to jendā:_

Onnatachi no nyoze gamon and *Jendā ikōru na Bukkyō o mezashite*, have also been published as part of the effort to transform ingrained discriminatory attitudes towards women—especially temple wives and female clerics—in temple Buddhism. The continued production of this genre of Buddhist literature highlights the fact that, at the start of the second decade of the twenty-first century, Japanese Buddhists still wrestle with the implications of changes in clerical marriage policy wrought within the Buddhist community at the end of the nineteenth.

In the process of publishing the hardcover edition of *Neither Monk nor Layman*, I inadvertently forgot to acknowledge several individuals who assisted me in research or revising the manuscript for publication. I am pleased that the appearance of the paperback edition of the book provides me an opportunity to make amends for my previous oversight by thanking Andrew Bernstein and John Lobreglio, both graduate students at the time, for their careful reading of and thoughtful comments about the manuscript. I also am grateful to Kawahashi Noriko, a scholar of Japanese religion and Sōtō temple wife, for having shared sources and stories about women and temple life that would otherwise have been inaccessible to me.

Richard M. Jaffe
Chapel Hill, North Carolina

_____ *Acknowledgments* _____

GIVEN THE LENGTH of time it has taken me to complete this project and my gregarious personality, it is only natural that I have many people to acknowledge. All of them helped make this a far better book than it would have been otherwise.

I am deeply grateful to my mentors at Yale University. In particular, I thank Professor Stanley Weinstein for his teaching and friendship. He demonstrated a standard of scholarly thoroughness and accuracy, which, while difficult to achieve, is always worth striving to reach. He never failed to share with me all that he has learned during his years of teaching and research. I also express my gratitude to many others at Yale who provided me with guidance. My thanks are due to professors Edward Kamens and William Kelly for sharing their knowledge of Japan with me. The friendship of Morten Schlütter, Ann Lazrove, Yifa, Yamabe Nobuyoshi, Lisa Cohen, and Lucy Weinstein made my years of residence in New Haven pleasant ones. Some of my warmest memories are of our long evenings enjoying New Haven's ambrosial pizza, drink, spirited discussion, and laughter together.

A number of colleagues made useful suggestions about how to make this a better book. Their enthusiasm for the project helped me press on as I wrestled with the chores and trials of junior faculty life. Robert Sharf, Helen Hardacre, Ian Reader, Janine Sawada, Stephen Teiser, and Tony Stewart all spent time reading the manuscript and making what, during my darkest moments, seemed like almost too many suggestions for its improvement. I also extend my gratitude to my departmental colleagues and the administration at North Carolina State University for helping me to find the time and resources necessary to continue my research and writing. The library staff at North Carolina State University provided invaluable help in tracking down obscure materials. Kristina Troost, head of the East Asia collection at Duke University's Perkins Library, generously made that institution's considerable resources freely available to me as well. Brigitta van Rheinberg, Anita O'Brien, Sara Lerner, and David Goodrich provided much needed advice and expertise at various stages of the production process.

Numerous scholars and friends in Japan made it possible for me to complete this project. The late Ishikawa Rikizan encouraged me to pursue the project and taught me a great deal about Buddhism. I also thank Yoshizu Yoshihide, Ishii Shūdō, Kumamoto Einin, Iizuka Daiten, and many others at Komazawa University for their help and hospitality. Scholars and librarians at other institutions in Japan were generous with their time and resources. In particular I am indebted to Tatsuguchi Myōsei of Ryūkoku University for reading Edo period Jōdo Shin materials with me and to Inagaki Hisao for helping to make my study at Ryūkoku possible. Tanaka Ryūichi at Kokuchūkai, the Watanabes at Fukyorain, Kuruma Tamae of Banryūji, and Nakamura Takatoshi of Zendōji all helped me gather photographs and other sources for the book. On my many visits to Japan over more than a decade, Hakushū, Tomoko, Yasuko, Tamami, Nobuyo, and Eshū fed, housed, and laughed with me. It is thanks to their openness and kindness that I now know firsthand what it is like to be part of a temple family.

On the financial front, a variety of grants and fellowships enabled me to work on the book, both in the United States and in Japan. I was the fortunate recipient of support for this work from Yale University, Fulbright IIE, the Bukkyō Dendō Kyōkai (via Ryūkoku University), the Northeast Asia Council of the Association for Asian Studies, and, on several occasions, North Carolina State University. In addition, the Center for International Studies at Duke University provided generous funding for the final preparation of the book manuscript.

The love and companionship that I received from my family were also indispensable. My parents, Edward and Frances Jaffe, and my in-laws, Max and Gloria Maisner, gave me much help and encouragement along the way. My wife, Elaine, read, discussed, and edited these chapters more times, no doubt, than she would have liked. Most importantly, she and my daughter, Zina, provided the love and support that gave me the energy to complete this project.

Reference Abbreviations

BKD	Ono Genmyō, ed. Bussho kaisetsu daijiten
BKJ	Mizuno Kōgen, ed. *Butten kaidai jiten*
DJBT	Inagaki Hisao, ed. *A Dictionary of Japanese Buddhist Terms*
DKJ	Morohashi Tetsuji, ed. *Daikanwa jiten*
DZZ	Ōkubo Dōshū, ed. *Dōgen Zenji zenshū*
GSZ	Mochizuki Shindō, *Gyōkai Shōnin zenshū*
IBJ	Nakamura Hajime et al., eds. *Iwanami Bukkyō jiten*
JIE	Kōdansha, ed. *Japan: An Illustrated Encyclopedia*
JSD	Jōdoshū Daijiten Henshū Iinkai, ed. *Jōdoshū daijiten*
KDJ	Kokushi Daijiten Henshū Iinkai, ed. *Kokushi daijiten*
KKD	Nakamura Yukihiko et al. *Kadokawa kogo daijiten*
MBD	Mochizuki Shinkō, ed. *Bukkyō daijiten*
MBSS	Meiji Bukkyō Shisō Shiryō Shūsei Henshū Iinkai, *Meiji Bukkyō shisō shiryō shūsei*
MKP	Irokawa Daikichi and Gabe Masao, eds. *Meiji kenpakusho shūsei*
MKS	*Meikyō shinshi*
MNJ	Edamatsu Shigeyuki et al. *Meiji nyūsu jiten*
NBJJ	Nihon Bukkyō Jinmei Jiten Hensan Iinkai, ed. *Nihon Bukkyō jinmei jiten*
NBK	Tsuji Zennosuke, ed. *Nihon Bukkyōshi kenkyū*
NJ	Miyazaki Eishū, ed. *Nichiren jiten*
NJTS	Naimushō, ed. *Nihon jinkō tōkei shūsei*
NKD	Nihon Daijiten Kankōkai, ed. *Nihon kokugo daijiten*
NSB	Chikū. *Nikujiki saitai ben*
NSDJ	Aoki Kazuo et al. *Nihonshi daijiten* (Heibonsha)
NSJ	Nichirenshū Jiten Kankō Iinkai, ed. *Nichirenshū jiten*
NSRK	Date Mitsuyoshi, ed. *Nihon shūkyō seido shiryō ruiju kō*
NSSS	Umeda Yoshihiko. *Kaitei zōho Nihon shūkyō seido shi*
OBD	Oda Tokuno, ed. *Bukkyō daijiten*
OBJJ	Ōtsuki Mikio et al., eds. *Ōbaku bunka jinmei jiten*
SDJ	Shimonaka Yasaburō, ed. *Shintō daijiten*
SHS	Shinshū Shōgyō Zensho Hensanjo, ed. *Shinshū shōgyō zensho*
SJ	Kokugakuin Daigaku Nihon Bunka Kenkyūsho, ed. *Shintō jiten*
SJJ	*Shintō jinmei jiten*
SNS	Risshō Daigaku Nichiren Kyōgaku Kenkyūjo, *Shōwa teihon Nichiren Shōnin ibun*
SSD	Okamura Shūsatsu, ed. *Shinshū daijiten*
SSZ	Ōtori Sessō. *Sankō suichō zuki*

STR   Shūkyōshi Kenkyūkai, ed. *Shaji torishirabe ruisan*
SUS   Kusanagi Zengi, ed. *Shaku Unshō*
SZS   Tsumaki Jikiryō, ed. *Shinshū zensho*
T   Takakusu Junjirō and Watanabe Kaigyoku, eds. *Taishō shinshū daizōkyō*
ZGD   Zengaku Daijiten Hensanjo, ed. *Zengaku daijiten*

Ministries and
Other Government Institutions

Daikyōin 大教院 (Great Teaching Academy)
Dajōkan 太政官 (Grand Council of State)
Gaimushō 外務省 (Ministry of Foreign Affairs)
Hyōbushō 兵部省 (Ministry of War)
Jiinshō 寺院省 (Ministry of Temples)
Jingikan 神祇官 (Department of Rites)
Jingishō 神祇省 (Ministry of Rites)
Keihōka 刑法課 (Criminal Law Department)
Kunaishō 宮内省 (Imperial Household Ministry)
Kyōbushō 教部省 (Ministry of Doctrine)
Kyōdōkyoku 教導局 (Office of Doctrinal Instruction)
Kyōin 教院 (Teaching Academy)
Minbushō 民部省 (Ministry of Civil Affairs)
Monbushō 文部省 (Ministry of Education)
Naimushō 内務省 (Home Ministry)
Naikaku 内閣 (Cabinet)
Ōkurashō 大蔵省 (Ministry of Finance)
Sain 佐院 (Chamber of the Left)
Seiin 正院 (Central Chamber)
Shihōshō 司法省 (Ministry of Justice)

NEITHER MONK NOR LAYMAN

CHAPTER 1

Introduction

MORE THAN a century after the decriminalization of *nikujiki saitai*, marriage by Buddhist clerics is now a familiar part of Japanese life. According to a rough estimate made by Kanaoka Shūyū, today approximately 90 percent of the Buddhist clergy in Japan are married.[1] A comprehensive 1987 survey of the Sōtō Zen school, which has been among the most statistically self-conscious of all the Buddhist denominations in Japan, similarly found that more than 80 percent of Sōtō clerics inherited their temples from a family member and that more than 80 percent of them are married.[2] Surveys of other denominations, for example, the Buzan sect (Buzanha) of Shingon, show that as early as the end of the Taishō era there were similarly high proportions of married clerics and patrimonial inheritance of temples.[3] Today the Buddhist clergy universally keep their surnames after ordination, are listed in a household register (*koseki*), and are subject to the same laws as any other Japanese citizen. As with many small, family-run businesses in Japan, temple succession is largely a domestic affair, frequently with great pressure being brought to bear on the son deemed the most likely successor to the father-abbot. Family ties and issues of inheritance have so thoroughly intermingled with the teacher-disciple relationship that potential successors to the abbacy, even if they are already formal disciples, often additionally become a *yōshi* (adoptive son) of the abbot before assuming control of the temple.

In contemporary Japan, marriage and the family have permeated life at all but the small minority of temples that are reserved for monastic training. Again using the Sōtō Zen school as an example, of some 14,000 temples, only 31 remain reserved for strict monastic training.[4] The overwhelming majority of Sōtō temples are inhabited by a cleric and his family. The same ratio between training monasteries and local temples is true for most other Buddhist denominations today as well. Buddhist clerical marriage has become so entrenched in Japanese life that the majority of the laity prefer having a married cleric serve as abbot of their temple. As a 1993 Sōtō denomination survey demonstrated, only 5 percent of the Sōtō

[1] Kanaoka (March 25, 1990, 4).
[2] *Sōtōshū shūsei sōgō chōsa hōkokusho*, cited in Reader (1993, 155, n. 2). The original is unavailable to me at this time.
[3] Hikita (1991b, 280–81).
[4] Foulk (1988, 164).

laity explicitly preferred an unmarried cleric. An overwhelming 73 percent expressed a preference for a married cleric, with the rest of the survey group not expressing a preference.[5] Although I have not seen similar statistics for other denominations, given the broad similarities between the various denominations when it comes to the distribution of married and unmarried clerics, it is likely that this statistic reflects a general Japanese attitude toward the Buddhist clergy.

The presence of the temple wife is now so taken for granted that today, along with the usual Buddhist doctrinal texts, histories, and popular religious manuals found in Buddhist bookstores, one can also find pan-sectarian works like *Jitei fujin hyakka* (Encyclopedia for temple wives).[6] Written by a Buddhist priest, the book is an instruction manual for temple wives, providing basic information concerning the role of the temple in the local community, the training of one's son to be a future abbot, management of the temple cemetery, and basic Buddhist teaching. Similarly, the Sōtōshū Shūmuchō has issued a guidebook for temple families, *Jitei no sho* (Handbook for temple families), in which the denominational leadership describes how the temple family should serve as a shining example of Buddhist domestic life, with the abbot performing Buddhist rituals and sermons, the wife caring for the education of the children and helping with the parishioners, and the children helping in general temple maintenance.[7] By following the instructions provided in this Sōtō-approved manual, those who have "left home" can become the model of Japanese domesticity for their parishioners. Even more recently, the Sōtō headquarters published a retrospective, containing surveys, discussions, and a brief historical sketch, on the temple family in an ongoing effort to establish legitimacy for a practice toward which the Sōtō leadership itself has had a long history of animosity.[8]

The departure of Japanese Buddhism from the monastic and ascetic emphasis of most other forms of Buddhism is striking. The Japanese Buddhist clergy are unique among Buddhist clerics in that the vast majority are married, but they continue to undergo clerical ordination and are considered members of the sangha (*sōgya*) by both the Buddhist establishment and parishioners alike. In such other Buddhist nations as Taiwan, Tibet, Sri Lanka, Thailand, and Burma, those who receive the ten novice precepts or the full set of Vinaya regulations are expected to refrain from sexual relations, marriage, and family life.[9] Some married clerics do exist in Korea and Taiwan, and their presence is largely a product of late-nineteenth-

[5] Odawara (1993, 95–96), also cited Kawahashi (1995, 162).
[6] Arakawa (1989).
[7] Uesuji (1963); see also Reader (1993, 146–47).
[8] "Jizoku: Hyakunen no kiseki" (1994).
[9] On celibacy in Theravāda Buddhism, see Wijayaratna (1990, 89–108). On the precepts in Theravāda, see Bond, "Theravāda Buddhism's Two Formulations of the *Dasa Sīla* and the

and early twentieth-century Japanese missionary and colonial influence. Although indigenous pressure to legalize clerical marriage in Korea came as early as 1910 from such reformist clerics as the Korean Han Yongun (1879–1944), who looked to Japan as an example of successful clerical modernization, his suggestions were largely ignored. It was not until 1926, when the Korean clergy were firmly under Japanese colonial control, that the prohibition against clerical marriage was repealed. In the wake of the Second World War, the procelibacy clerics, with state support, once again asserted themselves in an effort to purge Korean Buddhism of Japanese influence. Having lost control of the majority of temples, today the married clerics are few in number. According to Robert Buswell, whether the rapidly shrinking T'aego order (T'aego chong) of married Korean clerics will survive for another generation remains to be seen.[10] According to Charles Jones, Japanese colonization had a much less drastic effect on Taiwanese Buddhism than on Korean Buddhism; traditional ordination and precept practices continued during the period of Japanese rule, and the colonial authorities never forced clerical marriage on Taiwanese clerics.[11]

The public emergence of the householder cleric in non-Jōdo Shin and non-Shugendō denominations in Japan is a relatively new phenomenon, dating only from the beginning of the Meiji period (1868–1912). Judging from the historical record, it is clear that for much of the premodern period significant numbers of clerics broke the bans on sexual relations and marriage, as Bernard Faure has demonstrated.[12] Nonetheless, such behavior as covert marriage, patrimonial inheritance, fornication, and meat eating was always viewed as transgressive by government authorities and by most of the clerics who set the standards of conduct for the various denominations. Throughout the Edo period (1603–1867), the Tokugawa rulers had attempted, with varying success, to regulate clerical deportment. The array of status regulations backed by the threat of state punishment that the Tokugawa regime adopted had helped to guarantee at least nominal adherence to clerical standards of deportment. Upon ordination, clerics of every denomination abandoned their surname (if they had one; many commoners did not have surnames before Meiji) and received a Buddhist name that they would use for the rest of their life, unless they returned to lay life. Clerics were obliged to observe the precept that prohibited sexual

---

Ethics of the Gradual Path," in Hoffman and Mahinda (1996, 17–42). For an analysis of the varieties of Tibetan Buddhist clerics and a comment on the misunderstood category of so-called married monks in Tibetan Buddhism, see Samuel (1993, 270–89).

[10] On the history of clerical marriage in Korean Buddhism, see Buswell (1992, 25–30). According to Buswell, Han Yongun's arguments, which closely resemble the justifications for clerical marriage advanced by Japanese clerics in the late-nineteenth century, are contained in his *Chosŏn Pulgyo yusillon*, which was published in 1910.

[11] Jones (1999, 93).

[12] Faure (1998).

relations for all ordained clerics. In addition, until 1872 by state law marriage was illegal for any Buddhist cleric, apart from those in the Jōdo Shin or Shugendō denominations. Nor were the clergy to eat meat. The clergy were also expected to wear robes appropriate to their office. Although punishment of clerics by the Tokugawa government may have been sporadic and observance of rules for monastic deportment may have been honored more in the breach than in fact, state support of clerical regulations throughout the Edo period insured that those rules of conduct remained the unquestioned standard of clerical behavior.

The Meiji Restoration radically changed the relationship between the state and the Buddhist clergy. Meiji authorities quickly brought an official end to the Tokugawa state's efforts to regulate clerical deportment. Over a fifteen-year period, as in many modernizing Western nations, the clergy were stripped of privileges peculiar to their clerical status and came to differ "from other men in degree rather than in kind."[13] In short order the Japanese Buddhist clergy were ordered to take surnames, to register in the universal household registration system, and to submit to national conscription. Most problematically, from the perspective of many clerical leaders, in 1872 Meiji officials promulgated a terse law that stated: "from now on Buddhist clerics shall be free to eat meat, marry, grow their hair, and so on. Furthermore, there will be no penalty if they wear ordinary clothing when not engaged in religious activities."[14] Known informally as the *nikujiki saitai* law, this decriminalization measure triggered a century-long debate in the Buddhist world, as clerical leaders and rank-and-file clerics strove to interpret and react to their new legal context.

The formation of the new Meiji order reshuffled the relationship between Buddhist institutions and the state. Beginning with an outright hostility to Buddhism and a prioritization of Shintō, the privileged position of the clergy was destroyed and numerous regulations considered inimical to Buddhism were promulgated. The attacks on Buddhist temples, forced laicizations of the clergy, seizure of temple lands, and abolition of clerical perquisites were the culmination of a growing animosity toward Buddhism that can be traced well back into the Edo period. One manifestation of the state's hostility to Buddhism and the new vision of state-clerical relations was the adoption of the infamous law decriminalizing clerical meat eating, marriage, abandonment of tonsure, and wearing nonclerical garb.

---

[13] Sommerville (1992, 134). Sommerville notes, "The cleric's role had once been as impersonal as a medium's. Now it was bound up with his individual personality, and human personality is inevitably a distraction in worship. Also, with the redefinition of the role to emphasize the teacher rather than the priest, the critical feature was education rather than consecration."

[14] Date (1930, 621).

Of course, neither clerical fornication nor marriage was new to either the late Edo or the nineteenth century. Examples of violation of the clerical precepts prior to the nineteenth century are plentiful; in particular, the sexual exploits of the Buddhist clergy in the premodern and early modern periods are well documented, as Ishida and Faure have recently demonstrated. In chapter 2 I show the pre-Meiji genesis of the clerical marriage problem and discuss the emergence of the term *nikujiki saitai* as the very symbol of clerical laxity. The early modern problem of clerical marriage emerged against the background of the systematization of the status system by the Tokugawa and domainal authorities and the attempt to assert their control over clerical behavior. As part of that effort the ruling authorities issued and sporadically enforced regulations outlawing sexual relations for clerics from the traditionally celibate denominations. The criminalization of once tolerated activities coupled with precept revival movements among many Edo Buddhist schools triggered a reappraisal of clerical behavior by both the Buddhist clergy and their critics. In particular, growing awareness of the *nikujiki saitai* problem must be traced to the problematization of distinctive Jōdo Shin practices by their opponents, a topic that I examine in chapter 3. The intersectarian debate and the voluminous apologetic literature written by Jōdo Shin clerics during the Edo period helped set the parameters for the post-Restoration struggle over *nikujiki saitai*.

The growing controversy over clerical deportment, coupled with attempts by the Meiji regime to forge a more efficient means for surveilling its subjects, resulted in a break with Tokugawa procedures for dealing with the Buddhist clergy. In chapter 4 I describe the abolition of the Edo status system by Meiji bureaucrats and discuss the implications of that unprecedented social change for the Buddhist clergy. In numerous ways, the institutional and social restructuring of the Meiji period proved as transformative of Buddhist life as the outright destruction of temples and property suffered by Buddhism during the suppression of the Bakumatsu and early Meiji years. The policies put into place by the Meiji rulers were often neither well-planned nor consistent, which meant that the Buddhist clergy found themselves responding to a variety of contradictory imperatives. During the early Meiji years government officials wrestled with how to differentiate religion—newly defined in Japanese with the term *shūkyō*—from the state. Government leaders withdrew from active intervention in clerical life, leaving it largely up to the clergy themselves to decide whether the individual cleric or the denominational leaders would set the standards for clerical deportment. At the same time, the boundaries separating the Buddhist clergy from ordinary subjects were erased, as clerics took surnames, registered in the *koseki* system, and became subject to the draft.

Contrary to the picture painted in much of the scholarly literature, the Buddhist clergy were not merely passive spectators to these changes in state policy. By the midnineteenth century, the criticisms of Buddhism voiced for decades in Neo-Confucian, Shintō, and nativist anti-Buddhist literature had been internalized by segments of the Buddhist clergy. The forced opening of Japan by the Western powers, the reemergence of Christianity as a significant presence in Japan, and the violent suppression of Buddhism induced some Buddhist leaders to propose reforms, which, by including the Buddhist clergy in efforts to build a modern Japan capable of competing with the West, would enhance Buddhist clerical prestige. In chapter 5 I discuss efforts of Ōtori Sessō, a Sōtō cleric, and several other clerics to incorporate the Buddhist clergy in a state moral suasion campaign that aimed to strengthen Japanese national identity and to ward off the spread of Christianity. Using his close connections to such important Meiji leaders as Etō Shinpei and Kidō Takayoshi, Ōtori entered government service as the single Buddhist cleric in the influential Ministry of Doctrine. As part of his plan for the revitalization of the clergy, Ōtori proposed the decriminalization of clerical meat eating and marriage. In chapter 5 I also detail the largely unexamined role of the Buddhist clergy in creating Meiji religious policy, their vision of clerical reform, and the confluence of their efforts with the creation of the Imperial Way (Kōdō) as a civil religion embracing Buddhists, Shintoists, and Nativists.

Despite the rather dismissive attitude of most Meiji leaders toward the Buddhist establishment, the leaders of most Buddhist denominations did not sit idly by while new religious policies were being promulgated. This book is intended to expand our understanding of how Meiji Buddhists contributed to the formation of state policies toward religious institutions and how they tried to control what increasingly were categorized by government officials, intellectuals, and some clerics as private, religious concerns. In chapter 6 I demonstrate how those leading the movement to reinstitute strict precept practice within various Buddhist denominations confronted government leaders and clerics of their own schools in an effort to stop the spread of *nikujiki saitai*. Faced with the end to state control over clerical behavior and its transfer from the government to the individual denominations, such Buddhist leaders as Fukuda Gyōkai, Shaku Unshō, and Nishiari Bokusan, whose lives straddled the Edo and Meiji periods, utilized a two-pronged strategy, defending precept adherence to the Buddhist clergy and petitioning the government to continue its regulation of clerical deportment. When that effort failed, they argued that standards of clerical behavior should by determined by denominational leaders, not each individual cleric. In chapter 7 I continue the story, describing how, following the lead of these proprecept clerics, the leadership of the various denominations enacted a series of measures to ensure that their subordinates continued to abide by the ban against meat eating and clerical marriage. These strategies ranged from appeals to the consciences of the rank-and-file clerics to the formation of two distinct clerical classes, celibate and married.

While some clerical leaders sought to renew Buddhism through the enforcement of pre-Meiji standards of clerical behavior, others tried to harmonize Buddhist doctrine and practice with modernist discourses of science, sexuality, individual rights, and nationalism. Far from slavishly copying Western ideas, such Buddhist intellectuals as Tanaka Chigaku, Kuriyama Taion, Kuruma Takudō, Inoue Enryō, and Nakazato Nisshō wove together together Mahāyāna hermeneutics, older nativist anticlericalism, and new scientistic, biological arguments to argue for the dismantling of the prohibitions against clerical meat eating and marriage. Although many of the ideas incorporated into the arguments for *nikujiki saitai*, for example, hereditarian and evolutionary concepts, were of Western provenance, they reached Japan so rapidly that often the implications of these ideas were being simultaneously considered in Japan, Europe, and the United States. In a process similar to that which Frank Dikötter (referring to the changing understanding of sexuality in Republican China) aptly described as "not so much a 'shock of encounters' between 'East' and 'West' . . . but rather the emergence of a plurality of intertwined modernities that have diverse origins and many directions," numerous reformist Japanese Buddhists tried to build the theoretical and practical foundations for a modern, domestic Buddhism.[15]

In the final chapters I consider the proliferation of pro–*nikujiki saitai* literature from the mid-Meiji until the early Shōwa periods against the backdrop of the intellectual and social upheavals in late-nineteenth- and early twentieth-century Japan. In chapter 8 I examine Nichiren cleric Tanaka Chigaku's renunciation of clerical life and his attempt to formulate a new family centered Buddhism. Tanaka's attempt to revitalize a tradition that he argued was almost exclusively associated with funerals led him to found an independent, lay Nichiren organization. In an effort to establish Buddhist foundations for modern family life, he wrote a treatise on the Buddhist couple and argued that monastic Buddhism was no longer appropriate for Japan. He also created a series of ceremonies, including the first Buddhist wedding ritual, in order to bring Buddhism into the everyday lives of his followers. By the start of the twentieth century some Buddhist clerics from the established denominations followed Tanaka's lead. Although these clerics held radically different positions from Tanaka

---

[15] Dikötter (1995, 12).

with regard to clerical marriage, they shared his focus on creating a Buddhist discourse on the family that melded Protestant-style valorization of the conjugal family, Confucian virtues emphasized in such didactic texts as *Onna daigaku* by Kaibara Ekken, and Buddhist ethics. In their heavy emphasis on the conjugal couple, these new Buddhist family teachings departed from older Edo-period tracts on family harmony.

Although many Buddhist leaders contributed to and supported the dissemination of Buddhist family teachings, most did not abandon their opposition to clerical marriage. While explicit denunciation of *nikujiki saitai* was rare after the Meiji era, the literature demonstrates that bureaucratic opposition continued in the monastic denominations well into the twentieth century. In chapter 9 I demonstrate how a new generation of Buddhist clerics advocated the affirmation of *nikujiki saitai*, using arguments based on biologized-medicalized notions of human sexuality and health rather than pre-Meiji moral understandings of the person. I also consider how the rise of social reform movements, statistical analysis, and legions of professional experts fostered growing attention on social problems associated with continued high-level repudiation of clerical marriage by clerical leaders. Ultimately, it was awareness of the social costs of the ongoing resistance to clerical marriage during the late Meiji and Taishō eras that led to a softening of opposition to *nikujiki saitai*. At the start of that period, leaders of most denominations remained doctrinally tied to an anti–*nikujiki saitai* position while begrudgingly making accommodations to the increasing numbers of married clerics. The opposition to clerical marriage by both clerical leaders and some parishioners caused many clerical marriages to remain unofficial. As clerics died, leaving behind widows and children, dispossessed families became a growing social problem for the Buddhist denominations. Embarrassed by reports of destitute widows and children, the leadership of most denominations began to grant de facto recognition to clerical marriage from the mid-Taishō period. Doctrinal affirmation of that practice by the clerical leadership of most denominations never occurred, however. Ultimately, the emergence of a predominantly married Buddhist clergy in Japan was a result of practical problems, rank-and-file clerical choices, and inability to discipline clerics at the local temple level, rather than a deliberate doctrinal shift mandated by Buddhist leaders. As I discuss in the concluding chapter, the contradiction between practice and doctrine that resulted from the partial resolution of the *nikujiki saitai* debate has continued to trouble many clerics until the present day.

CHAPTER 2

Pre-Meiji Precedents

BY THE START of the Meiji period, both critics of Buddhism and many Buddhist clerics themselves generally acknowledged that a significant number of clerics ignored the rules governing clerical behavior. In particular, late Tokugawa and early Meiji authors alleged that the regulations banning sexual relations, meat eating, and alcohol consumption by the Buddhist clergy were frequently and flagrantly being violated. Although many of these allegations are difficult to verify, violations of these regulations and harsh state retributions for those unfortunate enough to be made examples were visible enough to support the general perception that many clerics ignored religious and state sanctions against sexual relations. Particularly during the Edo period, when central authorities attempted to punish and prevent such behavior, the clash between expectations for clerical deportment came into to conflict with popular perceptions about the clergy. By the Bakumatsu and early Meiji periods, those perceptions of the clergy had become assumptions shared by supporters and detractors of Buddhism alike. The prevailing belief that many clerics were guilty of eating meat, marrying, and otherwise abandoning their vows became a crucial factor in the formation of the Meiji government's Buddhist policy and in the reactions of clerical leaders and the public to those policies.

In this chapter I briefly survey the evidence of clerical marriage in the premodern period, the origins of the perceived *nikujiki saitai* problem in modern Japan, and the growing debate over those practices during the Edo period. Separating public perceptions from actual clerical behavior is a difficult task. Distinguishing actual cases of clerical marriage from the use of allegations of corruption for polemical purposes, for example, to attack Buddhism, or, in creative writing, as a literary trope intended to appeal to the prurient interests of readers, is highly problematic. As with any behavior that receives public opprobrium, violators of the proscriptions against clerical marriage, meat eating, and other actions did their best to remain hidden. In addition, much of the historical material concerning the actual conditions of clerical life, particularly in smaller local temples—what Takeda Chōshū has dubbed the "ecosystem of temple life" (*jiin no seitaikei*)—from the ancient through the early modern periods remains relatively unexplored, particularly in non-Japanese scholarship of Buddhism.[1] However, as we shall see, sufficient sources, however fragmentary, convincingly demonstrate that a significant number of clerics were violating the prohibitions prior to the start of the Meiji period. Through sheer repetition, reports of these behaviors became an important influence on those in a position to shape Buddhist policy during the Meiji period and after.

NYOBON, SAITAI, AND PRECEPT ENFORCEMENT BEFORE THE MEIJI PERIOD

In one form or another, the temporal authorities have played an integral role in sangha affairs throughout the course of Japanese Buddhist history. Until very recently the temporal powers in Japan have tried, with varying degrees of success, to use enforcement of the precepts to assert hegemony over Buddhist institutions that in power and wealth often vied with the state itself. State efforts to control the sangha were codified when, following the precedent of Tang China, the court included in the *ritsuryō* codes the *Sōniryō*, a set of regulations specifying state standards for clerical conduct.[2] As in China, the *Sōniryō* used the precepts and Vinaya regulations as the basis for regulating clerical deportment. The extant version of the *Sōniryō* (Statutes pertaining to Buddhist monks and nuns) in the *Yōrō ritsuryō* (Penal code and administrative statutes of the Yōrō period [compiled in 718, promulgated in 757]), for example, stipulated that the Buddhist clergy should abide by the Vinaya regulations and stressed specifically that violation of the four *pārājika* offenses—murder, stealing, fornication, and making misleading statements about one's spiritual achievements—would result in expulsion from the sangha. In addition, several other articles in the *Sōniryō* targeted illicit sexual liaisons by the clergy. Monks were enjoined from staying in convents, and nuns were prohibited from staying in temples. Other regulations prohibited the consumption of liquor and such foods as meat and strong-smelling vegetables, all of which were thought to heighten sexual desire.[3] Thus the rulers of the *ritsuryō* state enforced a variety of monastic regulations. As Nakamura Hajime has noted, by the seventh century "the state functioned not as a patron (*Schutzpatronat*) but as the religious police (*Religions-polizei*) of Buddhism."[4]

[1] Takeda (1976, 9–31). Although studies of life at smaller, local temples—called *minkan jiin* by Takeda—have increased since Takeda wrote the article cited, such studies of the intimate details of clerical life at the local level continue to lag far behind studies of Buddhist doctrine, texts, and large monastic complexes.

[2] Sonoda (1993, 395–97). Sonoda (397) notes that the *Sōniryō* was intended to "make every priest and nun into an efficient agent of support for what has been called Temmu's imperial system."

[3] Ishida (1995, 8–13). See also Tsuji (1944–55, 1:105–9) for a copy of the *Sōniryō*.

[4] Nakamura (1960, 455), cited in Kitagawa (1966, 34).

Despite the fluctuating attempts to control clerical deportment, violations of the various strictures enacted by the temporal and ecclesiastical
authorities were common for most of Japanese history. Reports of
fornication, meat eating, and other forms of clerical disregard for official
standards yield plentiful evidence that violations were widespread and
that the authorities had a difficult time controlling the clergy. Clerical
fornication frequently appears in song, poetry, and other tales, adding to
the impression that clerical meat eating and marriage were entrenched
practices in certain segments of the clerical population.

During the Nara and the Heian periods, violations of precepts and regulations governing clerical deportment were flagrant enough to warrant a
series of edicts directed at the clergy. One edict issued in 798 complained
that the yearly ordinands (*nenbun dosha*) ignored the precepts and abandoned their studies. The authors of the edict continued, "in appearance
they resemble those who have entered the Way; in behavior they are the
same as laypeople" and ordered that all new yearly ordinands be chosen
from individuals thirty-five years or older, who could tolerate the life of a
monk.[5] In 804 another imperial edict lambasted the clergy for their dissolute behavior and their unwillingness to leave behind their wives and
children.[6] On occasion the violations of the ban on relations between
clerics and women were blatant enough to incite punishment from the
authorities. To cite just a few examples, the *Shoku Nihongi* records that
in 812 Ryōshō (n. d.), a Shingon cleric from Yakushiji, was exiled for
fornication to Tanegashima until 833. Similarly, the same text reports
that in 824 two Kōfukuji clerics, Chūgen and Yushin, along with a Gangōji
cleric, Eikei, were all sent into exile for fornication.[7]

There are also indications that from at least the Heian period some
Buddhist clerics married and passed their temples on to their children,
establishing blood-family lineages. The practice was common enough that
during Heian period the rights of a blood child to a deceased cleric's property were legally recognized.[8] By mid-Heian some members of the court
complained that as many as two-thirds of the people claimed to be clerics,
and the bulk of them had families and were amassing personal property.[9]
Ordination also was a popular means to avoid taxes and corvée, a point
that both Kuroda Toshio and Ishida Mizumaro have noted.[10]

Familial inheritance of an abbatial position also served as a means for
those with substantial property to maintain control of private temples
and associated estates. In an essay on the families of clerics in the medieval
period, Nishiguchi Junko has recorded numerous examples of married

---

[5] Ishida, (1995, 39).   [6] Ibid., 40.
[7] Ibid., 41.
[8] Takeshima (1926, 1151–52); Nishiguchi (1987, 188).
[9] *Sanzen seigyō* (914), cited in Kuroda (1980a, 250).
[10] Ishida (1995, 40–41); Kuroda (1980a, 250ff.).

clerics and intrafamilial—particularly father-to-son—transmission of clerical positions. Nishiguchi has found over sixty such clerical lineages among
the Fujiwara, Tachibana, Minamoto, and Taira clans in the fourteenth-
century genealogical collection, *Sonpi bunmyaku*. In many cases the lineage
monopolized a particular monastic office at a specific temple. Family
"ownership" of specific positions appears to have been particularly common among those serving as high-ranking administrators.[11] According to
Nishiguchi, the wives of clerics functioned as guardians and caregivers for
the sons of the cleric and insured that memorial services for the cleric
would be performed after his death. In this regard, Jacqueline Stone has
noted how some Tendai school temples with aristocratic abbots maintained close connections to the noble families that had donated their estates
to the temple. Control of some of those temples was maintained by Dharma
transmission (*jisshi sōzoku*) from father to son.[12] Ishida, Nishiguchi, and
the seventeenth-century Shin scholar Chikū (1634–1718) have all cited
one well-known example within the Tendai and Jōdo traditions, the father-
son lineage of Chōken (1126?–1203), Seikaku (1167–1235), and Ryūshō
at the Agui in Kyoto. Despite the prevalence of clerical marriage and
familial inheritance of temples, the wives of clerics had only marginal
status in the temple or monastery; without a mature son to protect them,
these women frequently lost their right to their husband's property after
his death.

Violation of the strictures against fornication continued throughout the
medieval period. James Dobbins has noted how many of Hōnen's clerical
followers were drawn from the ranks of peripatetic clerics and hermits,
some of whom married and supported families in clear violation of the
precepts and state regulations. Although Hōnen's attitude toward this
outright rejection of the Buddhist precepts was ambiguous—he is said to
have assiduously adhered to them for his whole career as a cleric—his
disciple Shinran chose to marry openly and raise a family, declaring himself
"neither monk nor layman" (*sō ni arazu zoku ni arazu*).[13]

The practice of clerical marriage was not confined to those self-ordained
(*shido*) clerics who were ordained and lived outside of such large monastic
complexes as those on Mt. Kōya and Mt. Hiei.[14] Kuroda Toshio has
described how clerics in these large monastic establishments were stratified into various classes with widely varying standards of deportment.
According to Kuroda, although most of the elite clerics (*gakuryokata*)
were unmarried, large numbers of those who were part of the class of

[11] Nishiguchi (1987, 186–201).

[12] Stone (1995, 28). Ishida (1995, 73–75) provides several examples of blood teacher-
disciple/father-son lineages.

[13] Dobbins (1989, 52–53). For more on marriage among the Shin clergy, see chapter 3.

[14] Dobbins, (1989, 52), points out the prevalence of clerical marriage among this group
of clerics.

clerics who were variously called *zenshū*, *gyōnin*, *shūshi*, or *jinin*, as well as the third class of clerics, the *hijiri*, were married.[15]

By the late medieval period, clerical fornication and marriage appear to have been relatively widespread and accepted. The archive of a *monzeki* of the Daijōin at Kōfukuji, for example, cites an entry recording the pregnancy of the wife (*saijyo*) of the temple manager (*jishu*). As Tsuji comments on this entry in the *Daijōin jisha zatsu jiki*, the very fact that the pregnancy would be recorded in the archive of the *monzeki* is an indication of the openness of clerical marriage at that time.[16] Similarly, foreign missionaries in Japan regularly noted the cavalier attitude of the Buddhist clergy toward the ban against sexual relations. Francis Xavier, for example, writing from Cochin in 1552, complained about the laxity of Japanese clerics in the following passage:

> There are many women within the monasteries. The bonzes say that they are wives of the servants who work the lands of the monasteries. The people frown on this, for it seems to them that so much association with women is bad. The nuns are frequently visited by the bonzes at all hours of the day; and the nuns also visit the monasteries of the bonzes. To the people all of this seems to be very bad. Almost all say that there is an herb which the nuns eat so that they cannot conceive, and another to immediately expel the foetus if they should become pregnant. I am not surprised by the sins committed between the male and female bonzes, even though they are frequent, because people who cease to adore God worship the demon; and when they have him for their lord, they cannot refrain from committing enormous sins. Rather I am surprised they do not commit more than they do.[17]

As the passage clearly shows and as Urs App has noted, in a study of Xavier's perceptions of Japanese Buddhism, Xavier, who had come to Japan in an effort to spread the Catholic faith among the populace, undoubtedly was doing his utmost to discredit the Buddhist clergy in this and many other of his letters. He also was ignorant about differences among the various Buddhist denominations and fails to mention the distinctive practices of the Shin clergy with regard to clerical marriage and meat eating. Thus, for example, in 1549 Xavier described the following group of grey-robed clerics without specifying their denomination:

> Among these bonzes there are some who dress like friars: They are dressed in a grey habit; they are all shaved, and it seems that they shave both their head and beard every three or four days. These live very freely: They have nuns of the same order and live together with them; and the people have a very bad

---

[15] Kuroda (1980a, 253).

[16] Tsuji (1944–55, 6:332). A *monzeki* is a temple whose abbot is a member of the imperial family or a noble.

[17] Francis (1992, 336).

opinion of them, since they think that so much converse with nuns is bad. All the laymen say that when one of these nuns feels she is pregnant, she takes a drug which immediately expels the foetus. This is something that is well known; and from what I have seen in this monastery of monks and nuns, it seems to me that the people are quite right in their opinion of them. I asked certain individuals if these friars committed any other sin, and they told me that they did, with the boys whom they teach how to read and write. These bonzes, who are dressed like friars, and the others, who are dressed like clerics, are hostile to each other.[18]

But while Xavier's charges may be suspect, other domestic sources from the late-medieval period corroborate his statement about widespread fornication. The contemporaneous clerical record *Rokuon nichiroku* noted in an entry for 1549.3.21 that although loss of clerical status is the punishment for meat eating or fornication, the shogunal authorities can do nothing about such practices and so they choose to ignore them. Tsuji has commented that this is yet another indication of the inability of the authorities to control the clergy in the late medieval period and demonstrates that by this time the practices of clerical meat eating and clerical marriage were widespread.[19] Similarly, Sasaki Kunimaro has written that by the Sengoku period (1467–1658) clerical marriage was so widespread that the ruling authorities expected married clerics to contribute corvée. According to Kunimaro, Takeda Shingen (1521–73) offered a special dispensation to the *saitai* clerics of the temple Manpukuji in Yamanashi, thereby freeing them of the usual responsibility for corvée required of married clergy. Kunimaro also cites the *Myōhōji monjo*, which records that Takeda Katsuyori (1546–82) absolved the branch temple Jōjuin of corvée and building tax because it was run by pure clerics (*seisō*), that is, those who were not *saitai*.[20]

THE EDO STATUS SYSTEM AND
THE CRIMINALIZATION OF FORNICATION

The independence of the Buddhist temples, which gave clerics great latitude to determine their deportment, was gradually curtailed by the powerful daimyo of the *Sengoku* period. As daimyo consolidated their

---

[18] The translator, Costelloe, identifies these friars in grey as members of the Shin sect. According to App (1997, 231), they are probably members of the Ji sect. However, Michael Solomon (1974, 408), relates that during the late medieval period most Buddhist clerics appear to have worn black robes, whereas the Shin clergy wore grey ones.

[19] Tsuji (1944–55, 6:332).

[20] Sasaki (1969, 141).

power, they periodically issued temple regulations to the Buddhist institutions within their jurisdiction enjoining the clergy from violating various precepts. Nonetheless, the most powerful of the Buddhist temples—Enryakuji, Honganji, Negoroji, and Kongōbuji—were able to resist the threats of the daimyo. Once the great unifiers of the Japanese state, Oda Nobunaga (1534–1582), Toyotomi Hideyoshi (1536–98), and Tokugawa Ieyasu (1542–1616), broke the military power of large temple establishments at Hiei-zan and the Honganji, the Japanese Buddhist establishment was forced to accept an unprecedented degree of enforcement of religious and secular discipline by the temporal authorities.[21] As both Nobunaga and Hideyoshi consolidated their power over the various large denominations, they moved to enforce stricter adherence to the precepts among the clergy, particularly taking aim at violations of the strictures against sexual liasons and eating meat. In 1584, for example, Hideyoshi issued a regulation for Daitokuji demanding that official discipline be enforced in the monastery.[22] In the same vein, his successor, Toyotomi Hidetsugu (1568–95), promulgated a regulation to all temples prohibiting fornication and meat eating (*nyobon nikujiki*) by the Buddhist clergy.[23] The following year, taking the hint from the Toyotomi rulers, the administration at the Shingon temple Seiwa'in issued a set of internal regulations that echoed the concerns expressed in Hidetsugu's temple rules.[24]

Following their rise to power, the Tokugawas continued the effort of their Toyotomi predecessors, attempting to enforce those aspects of monastic discipline deemed essential for the maintenance of state hegemony over the clergy. And with the destruction of the power of the great monastic establishments, the subjugation of the powerful Shin organizations, and the emergence of a more centralized ruling authority, the Tokugawa and domainal authorities now were in a better position to enforce the standards they decided to set.

Management of the Buddhist clergy became an integral part of the ruling strategy put into place by the successive generations of Tokugawa rulers. While utilizing the clergy to surveil the populace, the state also attempted to enforce its own standard of clerical discipline, which, although rooted in traditional rules of deportment for the clergy, was also dictated by a desire to weaken the power of the Buddhist church and strengthen state control of the clergy. A crucial element in the construction of Edo society was the formalization of the status system (*mibun seido*) by the authorities. As David Howell has summarized,

[21] For a detailed study of the destruction of the military power of the Buddhist temples, see McMullin (1984, particularly 236–83).

[22] Ishikawa (1996, 64–65.)

[23] Tsuji (1944–55, 7:330–32).

[24] Ishikawa (1996, 65).

Status as a legal institution originated in the national unification of the late sixteenth and early seventeenth centuries. Well-known policies like the separation of the samurai from the peasantry (*heinō bunri*), sword hunts (*katanagari*), land surveys, the founding of large castle towns with their merchant and artisan populations, and the compilation of registers of religious affiliation (*shūmon aratamechō*) all contributed to the formal delineation of the samurai and commoner populations as status groups. Furthermore, over the course of the seventeenth century the bakufu and domains institutionalized various other extant social groups, including the court nobility, the Buddhists clergy, and the outcastes as legal statuses.[25]

With all means of open resistance destroyed by the military power of the Tokugawas, even the "home leavers" were unable to escape inclusion in the formal system of status perquisites and responsibilities delineated by the state. The distinctive aspects of Buddhist clerical life—celibacy, vegetarian diet, tonsure, clerical garb, etc.—anchored the Buddhist clergy within the social system and distinguished it from other social groups.

Although we are accustomed to think of Edo society as roughly divided into four social groups—samurai, peasants, artisans, and merchants (*shinōkōshō*)—the predominance of this model is more reflective of the era's dominant Confucian ideology than of actual social reality. Edo society was composed of a complex hierarchy of different classes, including nobles, domain lords, samurai retainers, Shintō clergy, Buddhist clergy, doctors (*isha*), scholars (*gakusha*), and outcastes (*eta/hinin*), in addition to the four groups usually described in histories of the period. These social classes were further differentiated into subclasses. The Buddhist clergy, for example, were stratified into such groups as home-leavers (*shukke*), wandering holy men (*hijiri*), and clerics in the Fuke denomination.[26] Members of the different groups related socially to the four primary classes and to each other according to exacting protocols of behavior.[27]

Throughout the long period of Tokugawa rule, the clergy—both shrine officials and Buddhist clerics—held a special place in society. Like scholars, nobles, outcastes, and others, clerics were not included in the *shūmon aratame* (religious inquisition) system. According to the formal, rigid social status system of the Tokugawa state, clerics were ranked above the mer-

---

[25] Howell (1995, 20).

[26] Kurita (1927, 1:734).

[27] For much more nuanced descriptions of the Edo period status system, see Kurita (1927 1:650–743); Takikawa (1929, 329–37). KDJ (4:585) concludes that there were seven distinct social classes: samurai, peasants, townspeople (merchants and artisans), nobles, Shintō clerics, Buddhist clerics, and outcastes. See also Kodama Kōta (1963, 225–26); Following the comments in Asao (1992, 22), Howell (1995, 20) points out that "the familiar *shi-nō-kō-shō* hierarchy of textbook accounts was a prescriptive rather than a descriptive taxonomy that had no real basis in Tokugawa law."

chants and peasants—and below the samurai. Unlike for most other classes, entrance into the Buddhist clergy depended on ordination, not birth, which also distinguished the Buddhist clergy from the Shintō clergy. Ideally, upon ordination, monks' and nuns' Buddhist names were entered into the clerical registry (*sōseki*) and the monks and nuns ceased to use their secular names. The clerical registries were maintained independently by the head temple of each denomination, and the entire system was placed under the control of the temple magistrate (*Jisha Bugyō*). When in attendance at the local magistrate's office (*bugyōdokoro*), Buddhist clerics were allowed to sit one level higher than commoners.[28] In the "Regulations for the Investigation of Religious Sects and Identification Tags" (*Shūmon tefuda aratame jōmoku*), which the Satsuma domain issued in 1852, the abbots of important domain temples were granted *chakuza* status. This meant that they would be allowed to have an assigned seat and be present at the daimyo's residence when the New Year's audiences of the highest-ranking samurai occurred. *Chakuza* clerics were exempted from carrying wooden identification tags because of their high status and were afforded a rare privilege: such classification placed them on an equal footing with samurai of the second highest ranking in the domain.[29] In recognition of their position outside secular society, the Buddhist clergy were placed primarily under the superintendence of their head temple and the government-sect liaison temple, the *furegashira*. Control of the Buddhist clergy was mediated by the *furegashira* of their denomination.

Although in many cases treated more leniently than commoners, the Buddhist clergy were required to abide by the religious precepts specific to their sect and to maintain proper clerical appearance. Throughout the Edo period, the Tokugawa and domainal rulers issued numerous sets of regulations governing clerical behavior, which became increasingly specific and draconian with time. During the first century of their rule, the Tokugawa authorities promulgated a series of temple regulations (*jiin hatto*) concerning temple administration and other aspects of clerical life. These regulations were issued in two main waves, one beginning in 1601 and ending at the start of the Genna era (1615–24), the other occuring during

---

[28] NSSS, *kinsei*, 133; Kurita (1927, 1:734). Like the Buddhists, Shintō clerics were afforded special privileges. They were allowed to sit at a higher level at the magistrate's office and were permitted to wear swords and to publicly use a surname. As Hardacre (1989b, 14–15) notes, "Buddhist priests inevitably held higher positions and commanded greater administrative authority than shrine priests. Shrine priests were seated lower than Buddhist clerics at village assemblies, and in the minutiae of diurnal etiquette, the lower status of the Shintō priesthood was made abundantly and humiliatingly clear." The subservience of the Shintō clergy to the Buddhist clergy was one of the sources of anti-Buddhist sentiment that exploded in the late Bakumatsu and early Meiji periods.

[29] Sakai (1975, 59–62). According to Sakai (5–6), *tefuda* were wooden identification tags that the Tokugawa authorities required most subjects to carry at all times.

the Kanbun era (1661–73). Ishin Sūden (1569–1633), the Rinzai monk who served as one of Tokugawa Ieyasu's close advisors, oversaw the compilation and promulgation of the first set, which appeared just as Ieyasu consolidated his hegemony. These were aimed at a number of individual denominations, including the Tendai, Shingon, Jōdo, Rinzai, and Sōtō. Although the laws were diverse, addressing a variety of denomination-specific issues, as Tamamuro Fumio has noted, overall they can be viewed as part of an effort to complete state domination of the Buddhist clergy. Thus the bulk of them were concerned with strengthening the head-branch temple system (*honmatsu seido*), creating a clergy that abided by the precepts and was devoted to scholarship and practice, and restraining unaffiliated clerics who remained outside the umbrella of denominational control.[30]

The first several Tokugawa shoguns continued Hideyoshi's policy with regard to the problem of precept infractions. Regulations aimed at the monastic establishments of Taisanji (1609) decreed that areas of the complexes formerly home to married clerics would henceforth be used by "pure clerics" (*seisō*), and those issued for Harunasan (1614) mandated that certain portions of the complex would be off limits to those who were married.[31]

In 1665, under Tokugawa Ietsuna (1641–80), the Tokugawa government issued two more sets of temple regulations for all denominations, the *Shoshū jiin hatto*, as part of an effort to further tighten control of the Buddhist clergy. The *Shoshū jiin hatto* were issued during a period of regulatory efflorence aimed at strengthening Tokugawa control over numerous social activities. In the period leading up to the promulgation of the new set of *jiin hatto* the authorities issued a bevy of laws, including those banning same-sex relations between men (*nanshoku*, 1652); banning kabuki (1652); outlawing the practice of *junshi* (1663), that is, suicide following the death of one's lord; standardizing rules for coinage and a system of weights and measures (1665); and delineating modified *hatto* for samurai (1665).[32]

There were two sets of general *hatto* for temples issued in 1665, one under the seal of the shogun and the second by his senior council (*rōju*). Included among the two sets were those demanding that clerics adhere to denominational liturgy; prohibiting clerics ignorant of ceremonies from being promoted to temple abbot; strengthening the control of the head temples over branch temples; placing all clerics under the jurisdiction of

---

[30] Tamamuro (1987, 25). See Tsuji (1944–55, 8:173–324) for a detailed list and discussion of the *hatto* disseminated by the Tokugawa authorities.

[31] NSSS, *kinsei*, 62; 67.

[32] Tsuji (1944–55, 8:276–277).

state laws and demanding that trangressors be remanded to the authorities; and restricting the luxuriousness of additions and repairs to temples.[33] The group of regulations disseminated by the senior council contained laws requiring that the color and form of clerical robes conform to clerical rank; stipulating that ceremonies performed on behalf of parishioners not exceed the means of those for whom they were performed; banning the use of money to buy contracts guaranteeing abbatial succession; and, most significant for the regulation of clerical marriage, outlawing the housing of women in temples, including relatives. The latter ban contained a significant exemption, however. Recognizing that large numbers of Shin clerics and mountain ascetics (*yamabushi*) had wives, authors of the law allowed clerics from schools that had a tradition of allowing women to live with clerics to continue to do so.[34]

The attempt by the senior council to restrict clerical marriage must, I think, be seen in the broader context of other status-related rules issued by the state. Like commoners bearing swords, men acting as women in kabuki, and clerics wearing robes that did not conform to their clerical rank, clerics residing with women at Buddhist temples threatened the fragile correspondence between social position and behavior. This fear, more than an underlying concern for preservation of the Buddhist precepts, may have motivated the promulgation of the rule concerning women in temples. Another possible aim of the measure, Kita Sadakichi has suggested, was to further weaken the power of the nobles, by curtailing clerical marriage at *monzeki* temples, many of which had been passed on from father to son.[35]

The privileged position held by the clergy entitled them to more lenient penalties for common crimes and necessitated harsher punishment for infraction of the rules governing clerical behavior.[36] If found guilty of a common offense, the offending cleric was subjected to alternative punishments (*junkei*), which, like those meted out to low-ranking retainers, were more lenient than the standard penalties (*seikei*) applied to commoners.[37] If, as was the practice in the Edo period, a group of people including

[33] Ibid., 277–79.

[34] The two sets of general temple regulations are listed in NSSS, *kinsei*, 86–87.

[35] See Kita (1933, 148).

[36] It is important to bear in mind that Tokugawa legal codes were neither static throughout the Edo period nor uniform throughout the various domains. According to Fujii (1987, 58–60), although some domains used the Edo legal codes as the foundation for domain law, others used legal codes that showed marked regional variations. See also Botsman (1992, 2). The subject of law and punishment during the Edo period merits a much more nuanced discussion in the future.

[37] *Seikei* consisted of five standard punishments (*gokei*): whipping, caning, imprisonment, exile, and execution. See KDJ, 5:718 and 8:206.

Buddhist clerics were punished for their involvement with the perpetrator of a crime (*renza*), the clergy were exempted from the punishment.[38] Tokugawa law specified that the Buddhist clergy, along with women and samurai, were not to be caned, a punishment frequently used for petty larceny and other minor crimes.[39] In place of such harsher, corporal punishments, the Buddhist clerics guilty of misusing temple property and other minor crimes were banished from their temple (*tsuien*; *tsuiin*).[40]

By the mid-eighteenth century, the punishments for fornication, adultery, and other sexual transgressions by the Buddhist clergy became increasingly specific and harsh. During the reign of the eighth shogun, Tokugawa Yoshimune (1684–1751), measures to punish clerical sexual transgressions were strengthened. In 1736, for example, a law was issued stipulating that clerics guilty of fornication would be paraded around Edo and then crucified. The regulation also decreed that ordinary clerics guilty of breaking the precepts would be stripped of their robes and either expelled from Edo or banished to an island.[41]

As part of his effort to further shogunal control of society by providing even clearer guidelines for social stratification, Yoshimune continued to restructure various legal institutions and administrative codes as his reign progressed. One important result of Yoshimune's bureaucratic and judicial reforms was the completion of the *Osadamegaki hyakkajō*, a 103-article list of punishments issued in 1742 that was contained in the *Kujikata osadamegaki*.[42] Although a portion of the precedents contained in the new legal code date from before the Kyōhō era (1716–36), the majority of regulations were new.[43] The *Osadamegaki hyakkajō* was never made public, but it served as the guideline for sentencing transgressors for the remainder of the Edo period. The new code became the standard for the areas directly under control of the Tokugawas, but its influence was even more far reaching. The standards expressed in it were adopted by those retainers under the direct control of the Tokugawas and also formed the basis of the legal codes enacted in several other domains. Many of these regulations were only phased out after the start of the Meiji era, when the authorities issued a new set of laws, the *Shinritsu kōryo*, in 1870 (see chapter 3).

[38] Morioka (1984, 374).

[39] *Keimu kyōkai* (1943, 1:594).

[40] According to KDJ, 9:695, *tsuiin* was more severe than *tsuien*. Those sentenced to the former punishment were not allowed to return to their temple before being banished, but those sentenced to *tsuien* were permitted to return temporarily before being expelled.

[41] NSRK, 235.

[42] See Fujii (1987) for a general description of this legal compendium. The *Osadamegaki* is mentioned in Ishida (1995, 155–56); see also Faure (1998, 180; 187).

[43] For a brief description of the legal reforms enacted by Tokugawa Yoshimune, see Tsuji Tatsuya (1991, 425–77).

The *Osadamegaki hyakkajō* set forth a spectrum of punishments for clerics found guilty of sexual transgressions. The inclusion of punishments for fornicating clerics demonstrates Yoshimune's determination to intervene directly in policing the Buddhist clergy to ensure that clerical behavior conformed to clerical status. As with the previous sets of laws, these tougher regulations aimed to eliminate discrepancies between behavior and one's actual place within the status system. Like some other new laws contained in the code, such as those proscribing the unlawful possession of swords, these clerical punishments were part of an effort to bolster the status system, more closely linking punishments and perquisites to social rank.

The punishments for clerical sexual misbehavior codified in the *Osadamegaki hyakkajō* were issued over a period of one hundred years and dealt with a variety of infractions. A precedent dating to 1739 that was contained in the text prescribed that the abbot of a temple guilty of *nyobon* was to be banished (*entō/ontō*), a punishment also given to those guilty of accidental homicide or major organizers of gambling events. Those convicted within Edo were banished to one of the seven Izu islands (Izu Shichitō) or Kōzushima. Those convicted in other jurisdictions, for example, Kyoto or Osaka, were sent to such other islands as Okinoshima and Ikishima.[44] That banishment, a criminal punishment considered second in severity only to the death penalty, would be the sentence for abbatial fornication demonstrates the gravity of that offense in the eyes of the Tokugawa authorities.[45]

A punishment codified in 1721 stated that lower-ranked clerics guilty of fornication were to be subjected to public exposure (*sarashi*).[46] Clerics subjected to this penalty were forced to sit in a kneeling position at a public place—in Edo this meant either at Nihonbashi or at the main entrance to the Shin-Yoshiwara—beneath a lean-to structure that allowed the public to gaze at the criminal. The cleric was clothed in the plain white robe of a humble layperson, and his name, his age, the location and name of his temple, its denomination, and the particulars of his offense were written on a notice board at the site. The shamed cleric was placed on public display in this fashion for three days from eight o'clock in the morning until four o'clock in the afternoon each day. Afterward he was turned over to the *furegashira* temple of his denomination for further punishment, which, judging from several actual recorded cases, consisted of demeaning corporal punishments and expulsion from the temple with nothing more

---

[44] KDJ, 2:413–14; see also Hall (1906, 255). Criminal punishments are described in Article 103 of the *Osadamegaki hyakkajō*.

[45] KDJ, 2:413–14.

[46] Ibid., 6:474; Hall (1979, 793). Umeda gives the date 1746, but this appears to be a typographical error. The date should be Kyōhō 6 (1721), not Kanpō 6 (1742).

than "one umbrella." Hence, the expulsion of precept-breaking clerics from their temple was popularly referred to as *kasa ippon*.[47] (See below for an actual case of *sarashi*.)

The punishment for adultery by a Buddhist cleric, which was codified in 1742, was particularly gruesome. Any cleric, regardless of rank, found guilty of being an adulterer (*mippu*) was subject to decapitation and gibbeting of the head (*gokumon*).[48] After the cleric was paraded through the streets and publicly executed at the execution grounds in Shinagawa or Asakusa, his head was placed on a pillar and displayed for three days.[49]

Following the compilation of the *Osadamegaki hyakkajō*, the Tokugawa authorities continued to tighten their control of clerical behavior. From the mid-eighteenth century until the end of the Edo period, a series of increasingly strident edicts warning against clerical misbehavior were promulgated. For example, the authorities issued statements calling for an end to clerical profligacy, drinking, wearing overly luxurious robes, and fornication in 1788, 1799, 1829, and 1843, respectively.[50] Typical of these warnings was an 1839 edict that called for an end to all illicit activities and ordered clerics in supervisory positions to exhort their subordinates to act in a manner appropriate to clerics.[51]

Even a desultory review of sources for the Edo period suggests that in certain segments of the clerical community, *saitai* remained a common, if covert, practice. A number of Japanese and non-Japanese secondary sources, including those by Tsuji Zennosuke, Hikita Seishun, Ishida Mizumaro, and Bernard Faure as well as compendiums of legal material like the *Shūkyōbu* of the *Koji ruien*, contain long lists of clerical sexual infractions ranging from encounters with prostitutes to long-term covert relationships with one partner.[52] Penal records for the Edo period contain substantial numbers of accounts of arrests of clerics for various types of fornication, ranging from visits to the Yoshiwara to more long-term liaisons, and even, on occasion, for meat eating. The Edo records are a striking contrast to those from the medieval period, which contain almost no cases of clerics receiving punishment for such offenses.[53] Sentences for the most part fell

[47] Fujii (1987, 449–50).

[48] NSSS, *kinsei*, 123. According to the text of the 1790 revision of the *Osadamegaki* contained in NSSS, the sentence of exile was put into effect in 1662, that of *gokumon* in 1742, and that of *sarashi* in 1746. Morioka (1984, 374). Ōhara (1943, 1:685). For a description of *gokumon*, see KDJ, 5:697.

[49] Fujii (1987, 330–31).

[50] A list of some of these edicts is provided in Hikita (1991b, 112).

[51] Tsuji (1944–55, 4:98).

[52] See, for example, Tsuji (1984, 4:96-101); Jingū Shichō (1977, *Shūkyōbu* 2:692–93; 696).

[53] For example, in his catalog of clerical fornication, *Nyobon*, although Ishida lists numerous cases of the authorities punishing clerics during the Edo period, he describes almost no cases of such punishments for the medieval period.

within the range delineated in the *Osadamegaki hyakkajō*. In the records for the Edo period, most of the arrests of the clergy were for fornication (*nyobon*) not for *saitai*, although at times how the illicit relationship should be classified is not clear, because as far as the authorities were concerned, for non-Shin clerics any relationship with a woman was a variety of *nyobon*.

As evidence of the enforcement of antifornication ordinances during the Edo period, several examples can be gleaned from Tokugawa criminal records:

1. In 1671 a cleric from Kanrin Zenkōji was put to death by crucifixion (*haritsuke*) for fornication.[54]
2. In 1738 a cleric guilty of fornication was paraded through the streets of Edo and then crucified.[55]
3. In 1789 Nyozen, a Nichiren cleric from the temple Kōfukuji in Kazusa, was banished for disobeying the orders of the *furegashira* and fornication.[56]
4. In 1660 a cleric named Shōzan and a nun named Seiun were arrested for illicit sexual liaisons (*mittsū*). They were crucified on Manji 3.11.21.[57]
5. In 1684 a cleric from the temple Myōyūji, Ennō, was caught having an affair with a woman and sent to prison, where he died.[58]
6. In 1796 the shogunal authorities launched a raid of the Yoshiwara red-light district in Edo, arresting more than seventy Buddhist clerics. After being pilloried at Nihonbashi—there was no precedent for such a large group of criminals being displayed en masse—they were banished.[59]
7. During the Kansei era (1789–1801) an infamous incident of fornication that later became known as the Enmeiin Incident took place. The Enmeiin was an important temple for the Tokugawa family, particularly the Mito Tokugawa. The former actor and abbot of the temple, Nichidō (age 40), was found guilty of a variety of sexual offenses deemed unbecoming to one with the status of abbot and sentenced to execution (*shizai*) in 1803 by the temple magistrate. His crimes included illicit relations with several women, some of whom served the shogun; sending love letters to other women; lodging women at the temple overnight, under the pretext of performing a wake; and dispensing abortifacients to

---

[54] Hikita (1991b, 122).
[55] Ibid.
[56] Ibid., 123.
[57] Ishii Ryōsuke (1959, 1:444). This case was cited in Tonomura (1995). The case refers to the relationship between the monk and nun as *mittsū*.
[58] Ishii (1959, 1:444–45).
[59] Tsuji (1984, 4:96).

one of the shogun's consorts who became pregnant. The women involved were also subject to various punishments, including house confinement (*oshikome*).[60]

A lower-ranking cleric at the temple, Ryūzen (age 66), was also found guilty of illicit sexual relations with a women in the Yoshiwara district and sentenced to public exposure. Ryūzen was then turned over to the *furegashira* for the Enmeiin, the Sōrinji in Kyoto, where he was punished according to the temple regulations. At the *furegashira*, he was stripped naked, renamed Sanjo, had dried saurel fish stuffed into his mouth, and, with a rope tied around his neck, was led crawling around the perimeter of the temple's main hall three times. He was then chased out the rear gate.[61]

8. In 1824 the Nichiren cleric Kyōze of Myōhōji and four other clerics were punished by public exposure at Nihonbashi for having engaged prostitutes in Shinjuku, Yoshiwara, and elsewhere. They were also accused of meat eating.[62]

9. In the spring of 1830 Ōshio Heihachirō (1793–1837), a police captain serving in Osaka, embarked on a moral purification campaign. He rounded up more than fifty Buddhist clerics for fornication, visiting prostitutes, and lodging consorts disguised as sisters, nieces, and washerwomen in temples. These clerics were banished.[63]

10. In 1830 a cleric described as the abbot (!) of the Chion'in was sentenced to public exposure at the Sanjō bridge in Kyoto for fornication. Afterward he was handed over to the temple for punishment. His punishment, which was similar to that dealt Ryūzen, right down to the dried fish, consisted of his being stripped naked, having a dried fish stuffed into his mouth, and being forced to crawl three times around the perimeter of the monastery's main hall. If he paused or stood up in his demeaning progress around the hall, he was beaten with sticks. He was then led, still crawling, to the rear gate of the monastery, where he was untied and expelled.[64]

11. Tsuji Zennosuke records mass arrests of clerics for breaking the clerical precepts in Edo in 1851.[65]

[60] Ōta Nanpo, *Ichiwa ichigen*, cited in Jingū Shichō (1977, *Shūkyōbu* 2:692–93). A more detailed account is found in Tsuji (1984, 4:96–97). See also Faure (1998, 188) and Faure's source, Ishida (1995, 173). See also KDJ, 2:424; and Fujii (1987, 445–46).

[61] Fujii (1987, 449–50).   [62] Tsuji (1984, 4:97).

[63] Miyagi (1977, 111).

[64] Fujii (1987, 446). This story is based on the account of a pilgrim from Osaka who happened to be visiting the temple when the event took place. Fujii writes that the "abbot" may actually have been a lower-ranking cleric, given his sentence.

[65] Tsuji (1984, 4:96–101).

12. Ōhara Torao estimates that during the period 1610–1866 approximately 221 Buddhist clerics (out of a total of 1,823 exiled prisoners) were sent from Edo to Hachijōjima off the Izu peninsula. Because, as indicated above, many islands in addition to Hachijōjima were used for exile, the number of clerics exiled for fornication during the Edo period was probably considerably higher.[66]

This sampling of cases from among the many recorded by Japanese and non-Japanese scholars suffices to show that the new, tough regulations issued by the Tokugawa shogunate did not eliminate clerical fornication and other violations of the rules of clerical deportment. There is also scattered evidence that in addition to more fleeting sexual liasons, the practice of *saitai* continued at numerous temples, despite bakufu attempts to eliminate the practice. Tamamuro Fumio, for example, asserts that there are a fair number of examples of clerical marriage at temples other than those belonging to Shin clergy or the *yamabushi*, the two groups allowed by the bakufu to continue the practice of *saitai* as they had for much of the medieval period. He notes that in some temple records it was explicitly noted that the temple was pure (*seisōji*), in other words, that the clerics living there were not married.[67]

Chikū, the author of *Nikujiki saitai ben*, offered a number of examples of temples where he claimed that *saitai* was accepted practice as part of his defense of Shin tolerance for clerical marriage. One of the strategies used by Chikū and other Shin apologists was to point out the hypocrisy of those ostensibly celibate clerics who attacked the Shin clergy for practicing *saitai* while they or members of their denomination covertly engaged in similar practices. In an effort to describe how widespread *saitai* was outside the Shin denomination, Chikū claimed that "when we consider the various temples in Japan we find that there are numerous *saitai* clergy."[68] Among those clerics who accept *saitai* he included the shrine priests (*shasō*) at Gion and Buddhist clerics at the Nichiren temple Hokekyōji in Shimōsa. He also listed the Zen temple Kanbōji in Tanba, the Ji temple Shōjōkōji in Sagami, and a variety of meeting places (*dōjō*) in Kyoto, asserting that at the Kanbōji in particular every cleric was *saitai*.[69]

Chikū's claims are made in the heat of his defense of Jōdo Shinshū and must be viewed cautiously. But other evidence from the Edo period substantiates the overall impression given by Chikū that *saitai* was accepted practice at numerous non-Shin temples. Records from 1613 concerning the temple Kinpusenji, a center of Shugendō practice, indicate that of twenty-eight of the Tendai clerics living there, twenty-two were "ordinary

---

[66] *Keimu kyōkai* (1943 1:617).
[67] Tamamuro (1987, 91).
[68] Chikū, *Nikujiki saitai ben*, SZS 59:302.
[69] Ibid., 302–3.

clerics" (*bonsō*). Of the thirty Shingon clerics at Kinpusenji, twenty-three were *bonsō*. Sasaki interprets the term *bonsō*, in this case to mean that the clerics were *saitai*.[70] Records for the Tendai temple Sensōji cited by Sasaki indicate that the stratified structure of the medieval period lasted into the Edo period. The clergy at Sensōji were divided into *shūto*, who were pure clerics that performed services to ensure the peace of the realm, and *jisō*, who were married and served primarily as assistants to the *shūto* clerics. According to documents from 1665, even the supposedly pure *shūto* clerics at the head Tendai temple for the Tōhoku region, Chūsonji in Iwate Prefecture, were married and passed on their position from father to son. The author of the *Sendai Sengakuin monjo*, for example, laments that since the medieval period all traces of the learned clergy had vanished from Chūsonji and that the *shūto* had been using marriage (*saitai*) to maintain their lineages until the present day.[71] According to Sasaki, that practice continued even long after representatives from the head temple for the Chūsonji, the Kan'eiji in Edo, attempted to end the practice of *saitai* at Chūsonji and established the principle in the mid-eighteenth century that dharma succession would take precedence over family ties.[72]

Tamamuro Fumio also provides an excellent example of clerical marriage in a brief article on the subject. Comparing a 1790 census of temple residents at the Kogi Shingon temple Iwamotoin on Enoshima in Sagami Bay with several popular accounts of life at that temple written in 1685 and 1829, Tamamuro has concluded that the official records conceal the actual presence of married clerics at the temple. Although in the census the various cleric's residences (*bō*) list only single clerics as the inhabitants, both popular accounts of the temple state that at least one of the cleric's residences, the Ge no bō, was occupied by a cleric who was married. It is possible that at the time of 1790 census a single cleric lived in the Ge no bō, but it is also clear from the two accounts, separated by over one hundred years, that married clerics lived in that residence.[73]

THE GROWING DEBATE OVER MEAT EATING

Although the primary focus of this study is the spread of clerical marriage in modern Japanese Buddhism, that practice was firmly connected with other infractions of clerical discipline, for example, meat eating, consuming alcoholic beverages, and ignoring protocols for clerical clothing. In particular, as I will show, both the proponents and detractors of clerical marriage

[70] Sasaki (1969, 142).
[71] Ibid.
[72] Ibid., 143. See also Sasaki (1967, 64–66).
[73] Tamamuro (1986, 3–5).

made a long-lived, strong association between that practice and the abandonment of dietary restrictions, especially the taboo against meat consumption. Thus much of the later literature referred to the problem as *nijujiki saitai* as frequently as it addressed the issue of *saitai* alone. As Faure noted in his study of sexuality and Buddhism, "sexual relations were only one aspect of transgression, which also included the breaking of the precepts on alcohol and vegetarianism. Unlike sex, however, the taboo against meat extends to laymen."[74]

Before discussing charges against the clergy for consuming meat and other prohibited foods and drink, it is important to answer the more general question of whether meat was commonly consumed during the periods considered in this study. It is often assumed, particularly in popular writings on Japan, that due to both Buddhist and Shintō attitudes regarding killing of animals, meat—particularly the meat from four-legged animals—was not widely eaten prior to the Meiji period. An examination of the scholarly literature concerning Japanese food customs, however, reveals that the varieties of flesh consumed were far more numerous and that the custom of meat eating was a widespread, if not frequent, occurrence. Such scholars of Japanese eating customs as Kamo Gi'ichi and Harada Nobuo have demonstrated with copious examples drawn from premodern and early modern literature, diaries, and cookbooks that a wide variety of both domestic and game animals were consumed from the Nara period onward.[75] As Susan Hanley has recently summarized, although meat was rarely more than an occasional addition to the pre-twentieth-century Japanese diet, it was not overlooked as a supplement to other sources of protein.[76]

There is also ample evidence that, like the rest of the populace, the Buddhist clergy did eat meat, despite the various prohibitions, both state and religious, against such activity. Attempts by authorities to restrict clerical meat eating and drinking date back to as early as the eighth century. As I noted earlier, the *Sōniryō* regulations contained in the *Yōrō ritsuryō*, which went into effect in 757, contained an article banning the consumption of meat, alcoholic drink, and the five strong-smelling vegetables by the Buddhist clergy. Ishida surmises that the article was probably intended to help curb sexual transgressions by the clergy, because these foods were believed to heighten sexual desire.[77] Nonetheless, even during the Nara period, clerical meat eating was permitted for "medicinal purposes." Several centuries later, with the rise of the various strands of

[74] Faure (1998, 150).

[75] Kamo (1976); Harada (1993). For a summary of Japanese scholarship on the subject see Hanley (1997, 65–67).

[76] Ibid., 67.

[77] Ishida (1995, 11).

the Pure Land tradition in Japan during the thirteenth century, the antimonian dietary practices of some Pure Land clerics came under the scrutiny of the ruling authorities. Complaints about sexual liasons, drinking parties, and banquets where fish and fowl were consumed led the authorities to issue in 1235 a law calling on magistrates to banish from Kamakura any clerics guilty of such offenses. Several decades later another law reiterating the same prohibitions was promulgated as part of the *Kantō shinseijō jō*, which was issued in 1261.[78] The article complained that clerics cavorted with young boys at parties where flesh foods were eaten and strictly banned those activities.[79]

As with marriage and fornication by the Buddhist clergy, complaints about clerics ignoring dietary restrictions were frequent. More often than not, complaints about meat eating were coupled with other charges of clerical profligacy and concupiscence. Thus, for example, one medieval critic of the Buddhist clergy writing in the early tenth century complained that "All of them [the Buddhist clergy] keep wives and children in their homes; they eat fish and meat (*kuchi ni seisen o kurau*). Their appearance resembles monks, but in their hearts they are like butchers."[80] Another source, the fourteenth-century *Kagenki*, contains an entry for 1361.2.27 describing the consumption of rabbit meat at a temple banquet. Similarly, a letter from the Eishō era (1504–21) contained in documents from the Kyoto Shingon temple Kōzanji records how clerics at the temple included rabbits among the year-end gifts that they sent.[81]

Although complaints about clerics violating the prohibitions against meat eating and drinking are common, there are far fewer examples of clerics being punished solely for eating fish or meat. In cases where arrests were made, it was usually as much a result of unseemly deportment as it was the consumption of forbidden foods. An entry dated 1416.6.19 from the *Kanmon gyoki* of Fushimi no Miya Sadafusa Shinnō (1372–1456) records how four or five clerics at the Zen temple Shōkokuji in Kyoto were apprehended for debauchery and consuming fish. As a result, the clerics were banished.[82]

Just as the more stringent scrutiny of the Buddhist clergy by the shogunal authorities brought the awareness of clerical fornication to an unprecedented level during the Edo period, policies put into place by the Tokugawa

[78] Ibid., 97.

[79] Ibid., 98.

[80] *Sanzen seigyō*, 914, cited in Kuroda (1980a, 250).

[81] Harada (1993, 109). Kamo points out that in one passage in the *Teikin ōrai* rabbit is included among a list of game birds used as food and that the counter used for rabbit is *wa*, which is normally used for birds. Because birds and rabbit were both hunted rather than raised domestically, it was permissible to use them as part of even *shōjin ryōri* meals. See Kamo (1976, 182).

[82] Tsuji (1944–55, 6:333).

regime also problematized meat eating by Japanese of all classes and heightened awareness of clerical infractions of the ban against eating meat. On the one hand, Hanley has speculated that meat eating may have become more restricted during the Edo period as land for hunting game disappeared and population pressures forced farmers to use all available land for growing crops rather than raising animals for meat.[83] At the same time, by the late Edo period a constellation of factors, including the systematization of the status system, Buddhist strictures inveighing against meat eating as uncompassionate, and the Shintō notion that slaughtering animals, cooking meat, and using animal hides were impure activities suitable only for the lowest strata of society, combined to raise the actual debate over meat eating to a new level.

During the first century of the Edo period, in particular, a series of shogunal edicts were issued to curb the eating of meat in Japan. Thus, according to Kamo, the *Tokugawa jyūgodai shi* contains an edict issued by the senior councilors to the various daimyo in 1612.8 that bans the killing of cattle and the sale of the carcasses of animals that have died of natural causes.[84] The underlying rationale for the earliest of these measures was not religious, but rather to protect those domestic animals—cattle and horses—that were especially valuable for farming and the military. As Hanley notes, this early restriction was motivated more out of practical concerns for preserving draft animals than by religious reasons.[85]

The official prohibition of the slaughter of animals and, consequently, meat eating, reached its apogee during the reign of the fifth shogun, Tokugawa Tsunayoshi (1646–1709). Unlike the clearly practical restrictions of 1612, Tsunayoshi seems to have been motivated at least partially by religious concerns. Following the advice of a Buddhist advisor, the Shingon cleric Ryōken (1611–87), and perhaps out of grief over the death of his son, Tsunayoshi issued a series of edicts aimed at protecting animals. Beginning in 1685 he prohibited the chaining up of cats and dogs, hunting with hawks, and the use of certain horsehide products, and he limited hunting to specially licensed individuals. At the same time, Tsunayoshi prohibited the serving of fowl and seafood at the Edo castle, ordering that vegetarian fare (*shōjin ryōri*) be served instead. Then in 1687 he promulgated the famous *Shōrui awaremi no rei*, a complete ban on the trapping and killing of all animals, and established a special magistrate for animal affairs, the *shōrui bugyō*. By 1697 the kennels Tsunayoshi had constructed in several locations in Edo, using funds extracted by a tax from the people of Edo, housed over 100,000 dogs.[86] This was not just a measure to ensure

[83] Hanley (1997, 65).   [84] Cited in Kamo (1976, 190).
[85] Hanley (1997, 65–66).
[86] Kamo (1976, 190). See also Tsukamoto (1998, 101–63) for an extensive discussion of Tsunayoshi's attitude toward animals and meat eating.

kindness to strays and to pets. During the early years of the Edo period, dog meat had been a staple food item during the winter months.[87] Tsunayoshi was thus criminalizing what had been a rather common custom. These laws, which proved extremely unpopular, were rescinded by Tsunayoshi's successor, Tokugawa Ienobu (1662–1712), soon after he became shogun in 1709.

Measures specifically restricting or banning meat eating and prohibiting the bringing of fish or fowl into temple compounds also proliferated under Tokugawa hegemony. Even before the beginning of the Edo period, Tokugawa Ieyasu promulgated strictures prohibiting killing of animals at various temples. As early as 1588, rules for the Minobusan region surrounding the monastic complex of Kuonji contained one article prohibiting the killing of animals (*sesshō kindan*) within the Kuonji complex and in the surrounding temple town (*monzen machi*).[88] In 1616 the same prohibition was included in the *hatto* directed at Mt. Minobu and Kuonji by the Tokugawa authorities.[89] Likewise, a government prohibitory notice board (*seisatsu*) erected at the Rengeōin (Sanjūsangendō) in Kyoto in 1651 banned taking life within the temple grounds and ordered that cattle and horses in the vicinity of the temple not be harmed.[90]

The purity of religious sites closely associated with the Tokugawa family was closely guarded through strictures governing the taking of life in proximity to those temples or shrines. In this emphasis on insuring that lands associated with memorializing the shogunal clan not be defiled, we can clearly see how pollution taboos associated with kami worship reinforced the Buddhist prohibition against taking life. Regulations issued in 1654 for the temple Kan'eiji (Tōeizan) in Edo banned all killing within a large, delimited region of the terrain surrounding the temple. The same regulations explicitly banned bringing fish or birds—no doubt because they would end up being slaughtered and eaten—into the temple compound.[91] Another set of regulations issued for the precincts surrounding the Tōshōgū complex on Mt. Nikkō in 1655 also proscribed killing within a large swath of the shrine's territory and, as in the regulations aimed at the temple Kan'eiji, banned bringing fish or birds into a defined area of the shrine lands.[92] Both of these religious complexes, of course, were closely tied to memorializing the founder of Tokugawa rule, Ieyasu, and other

---

[87] Hanley (1997, 65). Hanley does not mention any of Tsunayoshi's measures regarding the slaughter of animals.

[88] NSRK, 321.

[89] Ibid., 343. The date given for the regulations in the NSRK is Tenna 2 (1682), but according to an earlier reference in NSRK (p. 354) and Tsuji (1944–55, 8:176), the regulations for Kuonji were issued in Gen'na 2 (1616).

[90] NSRK, 356.

[91] Ibid., 358.

[92] Ibid., 362.

members of the Tokugawa ruling line as well. Kan'eiji, a Tendai temple constructed in 1625 by Tokugawa Iemitsu (1604–51), contained the Nishi Tōshōgū, a branch of the main Tōshōgū Shrine, and served as one of the two clan temples for the Tokugawa family.

As in earlier periods, people in Japan continued to slaughter game and domestic animals for their meat, despite the move by several shogunal administrations to curb that practice. Evidence of the continued consumption of meat in Japan during the Edo period derives from a variety of sources. For one, reports from foreigners in Japan during the Edo period describe the consumption of meat: the Portugese Jesuit João Rodrigues (1561?–1633) describes the plentiful supply of game and fowl on sale in markets in Kyoto at the beginning of the Edo period, and a report by Don Rodrigo de Vivero Velasco (d. 1636) details how, in addition to a variety of game birds, wild and domestic rabbit, deer, and wild boar were sold in specific parts of Edo. Archaeological finds in the San'ei-chō district of Shinjuku-ku in Tokyo confirm Rodrigo's observations. Along the Kōshū highway (Kōshū Kaidō) connecting the city of Edo with what is now Yamanashi Prefecture, archaeologists have uncovered deposits of animal bones, including those of wild boar, deer, serow, bear, wolf, fox, raccoon dog, and otter, along with those of birds, fish, and shellfish. Given the location of the site—along a major transportation route from the mountains to Edo—Uchiyama has speculated that it may have been a redistribution point for meat that was brought to the capital.[93] Suzuki Shin'ichi has also described the proliferation of specialty shops called *momonji-ya* in the Kanbun era (1661–73) in the Kōjimachi district of Edo. These shops later spread to the nearby Hirakawa area as well. The stores sold a variety of wild game and bird meat as "medicine" (*kusurigui*), even during the height of Tsunayoshi's crackdown on killing animals, when the stores euphemistically were referred to as *Kojimachi no toriya*.[94] Outside of the metropolises, meat eating also continued. At the Suwa Shrine (Suwa Jinja) in Shinano, the shrine officials dispensed amulets, giving the bearer a dispensation to eat venison along with a special pair of chopsticks, while an Edo period cookbook written by a chef in Sendai lists a recipe for beef soup.[95] The diary of one wealthy Edo merchant who visited the previously mentioned Kogi Shingon temple Iwamotoin on Enoshima in 1809 explicitly demonstrates that temple cuisine as well could deviate far from simple vegetarian fare. In his diary the merchant records the daily menu in detail. Although neither meat nor game was served to guests, rice wine, a variety of fishes, including grilled fish, sashimi, several kinds of shrimp, and eel were on the menu. As Tamamuro Fumio has noted, this was perhaps to be

[93] Uchiyama (1992, 299–303).
[94] Suzuki Shin'ichi (1985, 14:986).
[95] NSDJ, *s.v.* "Nikushoku," 5:461–62.

expected in a temple on a small island famous in the Edo region for its fresh seafood.[96]

These various factors—the growing stigmatization of meat eating by some of the Tokugawa authorities, formalization of the status system and the associated stigmatization of those classes affiliated with slaughter of animals, and a growing body of knowledge about the dietary habits of the Europeans—contributed to an unprecedented level of public debate concerning meat consumption by the Japanese during the Edo period. Shintō-ists, Confucians, and various Buddhist denominations argued over the propriety of meat eating for much of the period. As one historian of Japanese food customs has written, "Prior to the Tokugawa period we can say that edicts prohibiting meat eating were frequently promulgated, but there was no general debate about that practice. With the advent of the Tokugawa period, however, meat eating was opposed because it was considered polluting (*kegare*) and, at the same time, the exclusionary attitude toward foreigners who made meat part of their everyday diet grew in strength. Probably in no other period was the issue of meat eating as rancorously debated as in the Tokugawa."[97]

From early in the Edo period through the Bakumatsu era, the debate over the appropriateness of meat eating continued. As early as the mid-seventeenth century, Japanese Confucians like Tan'an defended meat eating and attacked Buddhist vegetarianism, while others, like the Kyoto physician Manase Gensaku (1549–1631), proclaimed the curative powers of meat for a number of illnesses.[98] The Bakumatsu nativist scholar Okamoto Yasutaka (1797–1878), a proponent of meat eating, catalogued a variety of arguments for and against that practice. In an effort to refute those who argued that meat eating was a polluting custom eschewed by the kami, Okamoto turned to several early texts for evidence of meat eating and the use of animal hides in ancient Japan. He concluded that despite the claims that the kami rejected meat eating, the *Kojiki* provided clear evidence that the ancient Japanese ate meat and that the taboo against meat consumption had caused the Japanese to become physically weak.[99]

On the other hand, the growing prominence of meat eating during the latter half of the Edo period sparked an outcry from some Shintoists, scholars, and physicians. Nagoya Gen'i (1628–96) argued that meat consumption was polluting and an unsuitable practice in the land of the kami (*shinkoku*).[100] In a similar fashion, the mid-Edo period nativist scholar

[96] Tamamuro (1986, 5–6).

[97] Kamo (1976, 196). See also Harada (1993, 257).

[98] Tan'an, *Nikushoku ron* (1643?), manuscript held by Kokkai Toshokan; bound with another didactic Confucian text by the same author, *Kunkai hachijō*; Harada (1993, 264).

[99] Kamo (1976, 208).

[100] Harada (1993, 265).

Amano Sadakage (1663–1733) argued against meat consumption because it was polluting.[101] Describing the popularity of meat eating during the Kyōhō era (1716–36), Amano remarked that the practice was widespread even among the Buddhist clergy, who despite restrictions barring the consumption of the five strong-smelling foods and meat, without any scruples drank alcohol, ate meat, and cavorted with women.[102] The debate over meat eating was exacerbated by the spread of Western ideas, particularly the so-called Dutch Learning (*Rangaku*) during the latter half of the Edo period. Opponents of meat eating blamed the importation of pernicious Western customs for the growing popularity of meat. The writer Takada Tomokiyo (1783–1847), for example, described how during the Bunka-Bunsei period (1804–30) shops proffering game—wild boar, squirrel, monkey, etc.—proliferated in Edo. Takada claimed this phenomenon was the direct result of foreign influence. He also argued that the various conflagrations visited upon Edo were due to the wrath of the fire kami angered by the pollution of meat eating.[103] As we shall see when the debate over meat eating during the Meiji period is considered, Takada's fears about angering the fire kami were shared with others, including *yamabushi*, who believed that cooking meat polluted the cooking fires and thus angered the kami.

CONCLUSIONS

The pre-Meiji historical record contains ample evidence that both clerical marriage and meat eating existed at numerous temples in Japan during the Edo period and earlier. The practice of clerical marriage was often covert, particularly at the official level, but for some localized groups of the clergy it appears to have been accepted tacitly as an institutional practice. Similarly, many Buddhist clerics also appear to have accepted the consumption of fish, fowl, and meat. In a provocative essay, Gorai Shigeru stressed the dual nature of the Japanese Buddhist clergy with regard to *nikujiki saitai*:

> It is my opinion that both the Meiji government's decriminalization of *nikujiki saitai* and the Edo bakufu's prohibition of *nikujiki saitai* arose from a misunderstanding of Japanese Buddhism. Because that misunderstanding remains unresolved by the Buddhist clergy and denominations today, it is natural that the debate over *nikujiki saitai* has not been resolved.
>
> The basis for the misunderstanding is that they have not recognized that

---

[101] Kamo (1976, 197).
[102] *Shiojiri*, cited in ibid., 206.
[103] Takada Tomokiyo, *Matsuya hikki*, cited in ibid., 209.

in Japan the clergy are broadly divided into two classes. It is because the ancient *Ritsuryō* government also did not recognize this that the Sōniryō and other laws persecuted the self-ordained clerics. That is, it appears that, almost as far back as the transmission of Buddhism to Japan, *nikujiki saitai* [practicing], half-cleric- half-lay, self-ordained clerics controlled the Buddhism of the people.[104]

In advancing this thesis, Gorai is not unique among scholars. In his brief examination of sources concerning clerical meat eating and marriage, Tamamuro has also found that at least as far as many of the Kogi Shingon clergy are concerned, during the Edo period their way of life differed little from that of the laity.[105] As Faure, following Hori Ichirō's early work on *nikujiki saitai*, has concluded, marriage and familial inheritance of temples were commonplace, particularly among those clerics who staffed clan temples and shrine temples.[106]

On occasion, as conditions permitted, both state and religious authorities sought to strengthen central control of temples by enforcing religious codes enjoining such practices as clerical meat eating and marriage. With the rise of a more centralized, powerful Tokugawa regime, rulers sought to enforce government edicts among various branch temples. This brought both the state and those in charge of head temples in conflict with clergy at temples where such practices as clerical marriage amounted to tacitly accepted, long-standing customs. As Faure has observed, the Edo Buddhist clergy were probably no more decadent than their predecessors. Rather, during the Edo period, the Tokugawa regime increasingly criminalized behavior that had once been tolerated with a wink and a nod.[107] As I have shown in the case of relations between one Tendai head temple, Kan'eiji, and its branch temple, Chūsonji, denominational leaders could meet with resistance from local temples when they tried to end such practices as clerical marriage and familial inheritance of abbacies.

Judging by the frequent arrests of wayward clerics and numerous complaints about married or fornicating monks throughout the Edo period, the effectiveness of these increasingly harsh and specific prohibitions against clerical fornication is questionable. Yet even though inefficacious, the growing criminalization of clerical marriage and the attacks on meat eating from various quarters did raise the *nikujiki saitai* problem to a new level of awareness. At the same time, the formalization of the status system placed all Buddhist clerics on relatively equal footing. Thus from the beginning of the Edo period, both the Shin clergy and the *yamabushi* were

[104] Gorai (1985, 39).
[105] Tamamuro (1986, 7).
[106] Faure (1998, 203); Hori (1966, 374–75).
[107] Faure (1998, 204).

placed alongside all other Buddhist clerics. The large, successful Shin denomination had close ties to the shogun, and its clergy were allowed to engage in activities that were forbidden for most other Buddhist clerics. This was cause for great jealousy and frustration among those Buddhists required to abide by state laws concerning clerical deportment and the Buddhist precepts. As the next chapter will show, the resulting tensions sparked a series of attacks on the Shin clergy, creating a protracted debate over *nikujiki saitai*.

CHAPTER 3

Jōdo Shin Buddhism and the Edo Period
Debate over *Nikujiki Saitai*

AGAINST THE BACKDROP of the systematization of the status system, the increased control of clerical behavior by the Tokugawa and domainal authorities, the sporadic but prominent enforcement of antifornication statutes, and the increasingly vocal contention over meat eating, a sustained debate over *nikujiki saitai* arose among the Buddhist clergy. As shown in the previous chapter, premodern attacks on the Buddhist clergy for violating the protocols of clerical behavior that related to sexual relations and diet were frequent, but it was not until the Edo period that sustained defenses of those practices, not as transgressions, but rather as a legitimate style of Buddhist clerical practice, arose. At the center of that debate was the Shin clergy,[1] the largest and most centrally organized group of what the Tokugawa authorities had referred to in their antifornication temple regulation as those who were "formerly married" (*yūrai saitai*).[2]

The Tokugawas had good reason for approaching Shin organizations—particularly the Honganji branch—with some caution. Over the course of the fifteenth and sixteenth centuries, under the leadership of Rennyo (1415–99) in particular, the Honganji organization had grown massively. Although the large Shin groups were gradually subjugated by the succession of powerful unifiers of Japan—Nobunaga, Hideyoshi, and Ieyasu—the sheer size of their membership made them a force to be reckoned with even after Ieyasu had achieved hegemony.[3] Ieyasu utilized a variety of strategies, including accommodation, alliances, and division, to control the Shin Buddhist clergy and their parishioners. To weaken the Honganji, Ieyasu exacerbated a nascent lineage dispute among the leadership. By offering land for a temple to Kyōnyo (1558–1614), who had been removed

[1] Throughout the book I have chosen to use the more familiar term Shin Buddhism to refer to what was commonly known as Ikkō Buddhism prior to the Meiji period. Although in 1774 a number of sects of Ikkō Buddhism petitioned the Tokugawa authorities for the right to use the name Jōdo Shinshū, the petition was rejected because of protests by members of the Jōdo denomination. The Ikkō denominations were not allowed to use the more familiar name Jōdo Shinshū until 1872. See Tamamuro Taijō (1967, 99–100).

[2] Tamamuro has shown that in official surveys of the clergy only the *yamabushi* and the Shin clerics openly acknowledged the presence of women in their temples. See Tamamuro (1986, 3).

[3] See Amstutz (1997, 21–24).

as head of the Honganji by Hideyoshi in 1593 and was succeeded by his younger brother Jyunnyo (1577–1630), Ieyasu managed to split the organization into two factions, the Nishi and Higashi Honganji, in 1602. Kyōnyo had reached a rapprochement with Ieyasu even prior to the Battle of Sekigahara in 1600, making his wing of the Shin denomination one of earliest Buddhist groups to forge ties with the future shogun. After the founding of the Higashi Honganji, Ieyasu and his successors Iemitsu and Ietsuna remained closely allied with the Higashi Honganji, granting the organization control of important parcels of land, including the site of Shinran's mausoleum at Ōtani in the Higashiyama section of Kyoto. The Tokugawas remained far more circumspect toward the Nishi Honganji, led by Jyunnyo, who, after all, had been placed in power by Hideyoshi. It was perhaps a sign of this lingering suspicion that the head (*monshu*) of the Nishi Honganji was frequently summoned to Edo to appear before the shogun.[4]

Even split into two competing religious organizations, however, Shin Buddhism remained a powerful force that required careful handling by the ruling authorities. The striking absence of any *hatto* specifically directed toward the Shin denomination during the two most active periods of religious legislation during the seventeenth century is indicative of both the caution taken by the Tokugawas with regard to the Shin denomination and their recognition of the centralized nature of Shin's institutional structure. Additionally, the early submission of the Shin leadership to Tokugawa hegemony and the relatively mature head-branch temple organization of the Shin denominations made direct regulation of Shin Buddhism superfluous, at least for the first century of Tokugawa rule.[5] The Tokugawas, while outlawing the lodging of women in temples as a form of fornication for clerics of other denominations, refrained from challenging those longstanding practices by Shin clerics. It was not until the period of the Kyōhō reforms that the shogunal authorities even attempted to rein in Shin clerical excesses by issuing regulations directed specifically at the two Honganji and their branch temples.

Unlike the clerics of most other Buddhist denominations, Shin clerics traditionally had married and had openly practiced father-to-son inheritance of the *dōjō* that served as the centers of Shin religious life. The Shin clergy modeled their behavior after Shinran (1173–1262), who, renouncing his monastic vows, had married Eshinni (b. 1182) around 1207. The relationship between the leader of a congregation and his wife was an important one for the Shin denomination: from the medieval period through the Edo period, most Shin *dōjō* were passed from father to son,

[4] Sasaki Makoto (1970, 191–98).
[5] Ibid., 200.

and the abbot's wife, the *bōmori*, played a crucial role in the daily temple affairs and the religious life of each *dōjō*'s members.[6] In addition, marriage between members of different congregations was a means for forging ties between groups, a strategy that proved particularly useful for Rennyo, who had fathered twenty-seven children with five wives.[7] As I will show in this chapter, the vigor with which Shin apologists defended the practice of clerical marriage demonstrates its continuing importance for Shin Buddhist identity into the Edo period.

With the creation of a more formalized status system and greater state control of religious institutions, for the first time the Shin Buddhist institutions were placed alongside all other Buddhist denominations, as one school among many, subject to control by the shogunal authorities. Yet, although defined as clerics according to the status system and subject to most laws affecting the clergy, the Shin clergy also received a special dispensation from the Tokugawas with regard to certain aspects of their distinctive practice. This did not go unnoticed by clerics from other denominations, especially those with particular interest in reviving strict monastic practice or reinstituting adherence to the full *Shibunritsu* precepts. As a result, the Shin denominations found themselves the subject of attacks from a variety of directions: over the course of the Edo period they were vilified for their departure from standard Buddhist practices and doctrines, as well as their alleged failure to accommodate such popular religious practices as shrine worship. Shin exceptionalism opened them to attack from the new Ōbaku Zen movement, several branches of the Jōdo denomination, and, toward the end of the Edo period, by nativists like Hirata Atsutane (1776–1843).[8]

Most significantly from the perspective of this book, in many of the polemical tracts targeting the Shin clergy, the authors took aim at the Shin practice of allowing clerics to eat meat and to marry. Attacks on the Shin practice of allowing clerical marriage came from at least two quarters during the seventeenth century. One work criticizing the practices of the Shin clergy, *Shinran jagi ketsu* (hereafter *Jagi ketsu*), was produced by a Jōdo cleric. The author's name is unknown, but contemporaneous Shin sources speculate that the work first was circulated by a Seizan sect Jōdo cleric serving as abbot of the Sōjiji in Kishū (Wakayama Prefecture) during the Kanbun era (1661–73). Although the *Jagi ketsu* is no longer extant as an independent manuscript, a detailed refutation of the charges by the Shin cleric Genkaku-bō, *Shinran jagi ketsu no kogi ketsu*, cites at length passages from the *Jagi ketsu*, which enables us to get a sense of the charges leveled

---

[6] See Dobbins (1989, 26–27; 52–53). A detailed account of the seminal role played by the *bōmori* in Shin congregations is given in Endo (1989, 41–79).

[7] Dobbins (1989, 117). On Rennyo, see Solomon (1997, 195).

[8] Hirata's polemic against the Shin denomination is described in Ketelaar (1990, 33–36).

at the Shin clergy.[9] The author of the *Jagi ketsu* asserted that Shinran distorted the teachings of Hōnen by exclusively emphasizing the recitation of the name of Amida and by eating meat and marrying.[10]

The Ōbaku cleric Tetsugen Dōkō (1630–82) also criticized the Shin practice of allowing meat eating and marriage in a series of lectures on the *Ryōgongyō* delivered in 1669. As later described by the Ōtani sect Shin cleric Erin (1715–89), the strife between the Shin clergy and Tetsugen began when Tetsugen delivered a series of lectures in Edo as part of his effort to raise funds for the publication of an edition of the Buddhist canon. While lecturing on the *Ryōgongyō*, a text that stresses the importance of maintaining the monastic precepts, Tetsugen apparently enraged Shin clerics in the audience. In response the Shin clergy entered into a debate with Tetsugen over his interpretation of the text. When a local Edo cleric, Kūsei, was bested by Tetsugen in debate, Chikū (1634–1718), the second head scholar (*nōke*) of the Shin seminary at the Nishi Honganji, was sent to Edo to challenge Tetsugen.[11] Although Chikū arrived too late to debate Tetsugen directly, he devoted considerable energy to defending Shin practice, refuting Tetsugen's interpretation of the *Ryōgongyō* in lectures to Shin clergy and laity and authoring a number of manuscripts answering attacks on Shin practice. Tensions between clerics of the two denominations continued for years, becoming so intense that authorities intervened when members of the Shin denomination confronted Tetsugen while he was lecturing in Kyūshū.[12]

In addition to records of Tetsugen's various lectures on the *Ryōgongyō* and the precepts, there also exist several different manuscripts of a text purportedly by Tetsugen, the *Kōmori bōdanki*, in which the author attacks the Shinshū clergy for eating meat and marrying as well as for a variety of other offenses.[13]

---

[9] A short biography of Genkaku may be found at SSD, 1:472. Although his dates are unknown, his preface to the *Jagi ketsu* was published in 1662, so it is clear he was active during the Kanbun era.

[10] Information on the *Shinran jagi ketsu* is found in the introduction to the *Shinran jagi ketsu no kogi ketsu*, SZS, 59:1–2. The *Kogi ketsu* was written by a Shin cleric who used the name Kikyōshi. BKD, 6:250, suggests he was the cleric Genkaku. See also SSD, 1:1162–63.

[11] Erin, *Shakunan Shinshū sōgi*, SZS, 59:349; Baroni (1994, 196–97).

[12] See Baroni (1994, 196–203).

[13] The manuscript copy of the *Kōmori bōdanki* in my possession comes from the Hayashiyama Bunko in the Ōtani University library. A slightly different manuscript of the text, copied sometime after 1808, is extant in the Naikan Bunko of the Tsuzureko Jinja in Akita Prefecture. The text, with the variant name *Kōmori mōdanki*, is reproduced in full in Ishikawa (1996, 83–96). I will refer to the two texts as the Hayashiyama and the Naikan versions.

The *Kōmori bōdanki* is a highly problematic text in that manuscript copies are extremely rare and contemporaneous descriptions of the debate in Shin sources fail to name the text. Dating the text is difficult. The Hayashiyama version does indicate in the preface that the text is written by Sesshū Naniwa Zuiryū Tetsugen Zenji. Because the Osaka temple mentioned,

The preface to the *Kōmori bōdanki* makes clear the author's personal interest in the doctrines and practices of the Shin denomination. According to the preface of the Hayashiyama version of the text, Tetsugen was the son of a Shin cleric who served as abbot of a large temple in Kawajiri, in the Higo region of Kyūshū. The text states that Tetsugen succeeded his father at the temple at the age of thirteen.[14] Tetsugen claims that his doubts concerning the validity of the Shin denomination's teachings and practices were sparked by an incident in which he and other Shin clerics were ordered to sit at a lower level than other clerics at a memorial service for a domain lord. Tetsugen writes that rather than sitting with the Tendai, Jōdo, Zen, Shingon, or Ritsu clergy, the Shin clerics were seated with the *yamabushi* because they had not taken the precepts like other clerics and they allowed fornication and meat eating. Dismayed by the lower status accorded the Shin clergy, Tetsugen records that he began to investigate the Buddhist canon for the basis for allowing Shin clerics to fornicate and eat meat even though they had been ordained as disciples of the Buddha. Finding no such substantiation of the Shin clergy's distinctive practices, Tetsugen concluded that Shinran was in fact the Evil King of the Sixth Desire Heaven who had disseminated Shin teachings to mislead people.[15] As a result, he left the Shin denomination and eventually became a disciple

---

formerly the Yakushiji, did not have its name changed to Zuiryūji until 1676, the text must have been produced sometime after that date. According to Ishikawa (1996, 75–76) internal textual evidence indicates that the Naikan version was copied from another manuscript after 1808.

Several earlier scholars of Tetsugen have expressed doubts about Tetsugen's authorship of the *Kōmori bōdanki*, and Helen Baroni (1994, 198–99; 203–5), in her article about Shin-Ōbaku tensions, has followed their lead in this regard. On the other hand, Ishikawa (1996), who has provided the most detailed and recent analysis of the text, does not express any reservations about attributing the work to Tetsugen.

Ultimately, whether the text is actually Tetsugen's does not change its significance for our discussion. The *Kōmori bōdanki*, along with the *Shinran jagi ketsu*, should be viewed as representative of the criticisms of Shin clerical marriage and meat eating—both written and spoken—that triggered the production of apologetic literature by Shin clerics and ultimately defined the contours of clerical marriage as an option for the Buddhist clergy. In addition, as Baroni has suggested, even if Tetsugen's lectures on the *Ryōgongyō*, which stressed the importance of the precepts, were not intended as an attack on Shin practice, the Shin clergy perceived them as such and responded vigorously in lectures and apologetic tracts.

[14] The details of Tetsugen's early life are murky, but the different sources agree that he was closely connected with the Shin denomination at an early age. The Naikan manuscript of the *Kōmori bōdanki* states that Tetsugen was the son of a Shin cleric at a large temple in the Owari section of Nagoya. According to the OBJJ, 247, Tetsugen's father was a shrine Buddhist priest (*shasō*) in Higo. At the age of thirteen Tetsugen was ordained as a Shin cleric at a local temple and in 1646 traveled to Kyoto to study under Saigin at the Nishi Honganji. He finally joined the Ōbaku movement in 1655 when he met Ingen.

[15] Erin also writes in the postscript to the *Shakunan Shinshū sōgi* that Tetsugen called the Shin clergy Mara, evil people, and evil hordes in his lectures on the *Ryōgongyō*. Erin, *Shakunan Shinshū sōgi*, 349.

of Mokuan Shōtō (1611–1684), an important early leader of the Ōbaku stream of Zen in Japan. The *Kōmori bōdanki* was written in an attempt to confess and rectify his past errors as a Shin cleric and to alert others to the baseless distortions of Buddhism by the Shin clergy.[16]

Other sources indicate that Tetsugen began to study with Saigin (1605–63), the first head scholar at the Nishi Honganji, in 1646. While at the academy he may have encountered Chikū, who began to study with Saigin sometime after 1648. Tetsugen remained at the academy until mid-1655, when he departed to study Ōbaku Zen with Ingen.[17] Tetsugen's departure from the academy at the Nishi Honganji coincided with its temporary dissolution by the Tokugawa authorities because of the heated sectarian wrangling between Gekkan (1600–74) and Saigin over Saigin's understanding of Pure Land practice and salvation.[18] So bitter was the dispute that, in addition to closing the academy, the authorities exiled Gekkan to Izumo. It seems likely that the dissolution of the academy as well as Tetsugen's disillusionment with Shin teachings played a role in his decision to leave the Shin denomination and study with Ōbaku Zen.

Both the *Kōmori bōdanki* and the *Jagi ketsu* devote considerable space to condemning the Shin practice of allowing meat eating and clerical marriage. The author of the *Jagi ketsu* writes that the Shin clergy are guilty of "not being able to eliminate lust (*in*) or [the desire for] meat."[19] In a similar fashion the author of the *Kōmori bōdanki* rails against the Shin clergy, equating their fornication and meat eating after ordination with the commission of the five gravest offenses (*gogyakuzai*). Tetsugen writes,

> The Ikkō clergy commit the five gravest offenses. Taking the appearance of one who is a disciple of the Buddha, they destroy the essence of the precepts that is the secret wisdom of Buddhism (*emyō kaitai*), therefore they are cutting off the life of the Buddha and killing their father and mother. The Buddha is the compassionate mother of the three realms. Second, taking the appearance of one who is a home-leaver (*shukke*), they fornicate and eat meat, therefore they destroy the sangha (*wagōsō*). Thirdly, defiling the pure precept body of the monk, they are shedding the blood of a Buddha. Fourthly, taking the appearance of a monk but not having a monk's spirit is killing an arhat. Fifthly, one's body is adorned through the practice of the precepts; all give rise to merit and virtue based on [receiving] the ten precepts, but the unrepentant, precept-breaking Ikkō bonzes disturb the monks who conduct monastic ceremonies (*kemosō*). Furthermore they are slanderous, greatly evil people who calumniate the True Teaching, expound on things not in the

[16] Ishikawa (1996, 84–85).
[17] OBJJ, 247.
[18] See Hirata (1979a, 54–55); Baroni (2000, 82).
[19] Genkaku, *Shinran jagi ketsu no kogi ketsu*, 7.

Buddhist sūtras as if they existed, and lead people into the three evil destinies.[20]

Alluding to a passage from the *Butsuzōkyō* in which precept-breaking monks are likened to bats—animals that are neither fully bird nor rodent—Tetsugen writes that the Shin clergy are neither laymen nor Buddhist monks.

> Those of the Ikkō denomination enter into the ranks of the monks, but they are laypeople. However, they shave their heads and wear Buddhist robes. One is called *bhikṣu* because one receives and upholds the precepts. But they break the precepts, so they are said to be laypeople. Thus those of the Ikkō denomination are not monks, they are what Śākyamuni called bats.[21]

DEFENDING SHIN PRACTICE: CHIKŪ'S *NIKUJIKI SAITAI BEN*

The various attacks on Shin practice and doctrine by clerics from other denominations stimulated a steady flow of apologetic works by Shin clerics. These works covered a variety of issues, ranging from the relationship between Shin followers and the state to Shin attitudes toward kami worship. Many of these works focused specifically on defending the Shin practice of allowing clerical meat eating and marriage. During the two and a half centuries of the Edo period, Shin scholars produced more than thirty apologetic texts mounting a defense of meat eating and clerical marriage by the Shin clergy.[22] The earliest of these defenses by Saigin was written in 1655, more than a decade before Tetsugen's lectures on the *Ryōgongyō*. This work served as a template for many of the later works defending Shin practice. In his capacity as a Shin scholar, Saigin wrote the *Kyakushō mondō shū*, a pointed defense of the loyalty of Shin clerics and parishioners to the Tokugawa rulers and an extended justification for the practices of meat eating and marriage by the Shin clergy.[23] Although not solely concerned with the defense of *nikujiki saitai*, Saigin's extended justification of those practices served as template for many of the later works devoted to that topic.

One of the most detailed and frequently reproduced defenses of Shin practice was provided by Chikū, who, as mentioned earlier was the second Head Scholar at the Nishi Honganji and a disciple of Saigin. As noted

[20] Ishikawa (1996, 86–87).

[21] Ibid., 93. The author of the *Kōmori bōdanki* attributes the quotation concerning bat-monks to the *Nehangyō* but Ishikawa writes that (p. 59) no such passage is found in that text. The passage is found in the *Butsuzōkyō*, T 15:788c. See also Faure (1998, 155).

[22] A very thorough catalog of many of these texts is found in Ishikawa (1996, 66–70).

[23] Hirata (1979b, 24–31).

by Erin, Chikū lectured widely on a variety of texts, but his defense of clerical meat eating and marriage was a leitmotif running through his talks.[24] In 1702 he wrote a work defending Shin practice, *Kattō besshi*, and his lectures on the topic of *nikujiki saitai* were recorded in a number of texts, entitled variously *Nikujiki saitai kikigaki*, *Nikujiki saitai ben*, and *Nikujiki saitai ron*.[25]

The *Nikujiki saitai ben* was a direct reaction to the attack on Shin tolerance of meat eating and clerical marriage that was launched by other denominations during the early Edo period. Curiously, however, neither the *Kōmori bōdanki* nor Tetsugen was mentioned explicitly in Chikū's text, and, from internal evidence alone, it is impossible to determine which of the texts was composed first. Nonetheless, the rhetorical devices employed in the introductory passages of Chikū's work bear an uncanny resemblance to those found in preface of the *Kōmori bōdanki*. As noted above, the *Kōmori bōdanki* begins with a summary of how slights suffered by the young Tetsugen because of the Shin clergy's low status vis-à-vis that of Buddhist clerics from other denominations led him to search the Buddhist canon for support for the Shin acceptance of *nikujiki saitai*. In a similar vein, Chikū began his defense of Shin practice by mockingly describing the arising of his doubts about meat eating and clerical marriage within the Shin denomination: "I think that it is difficult to comprehend and accept that in our school we practice *nikujiki saitai* while wearing robes, cloaking ourselves in surplices, and residing in monasteries. When I was young, from the time I read one or two texts I harbored this doubt. If one reads the *Nehangyō*, the *Daibon hannyakyō*, or the *Ninnōkyō* and the *Kegonkyō*, one does not find [such behavior]."[26]

Like the author of the *Kōmori bōdanki*, Chikū also detailed how such practices had affected the place of the Shin clergy within the Edo status system. Both authors took the worldly prosperity and formal status of the clergy as indicative of the truth of their interpretation of Buddhist doctrine and practice. Chikū's description of the place of the Shin clergy within the Tokugawa status system, however, stands in stark contrast to the picture given in the *Kōmori bōdanki*, in which Tetsugen claimed that the practice of clerical marriage by the Shin clergy had led to their insultingly low status.

---

[24] Erin, *Shakunan Shinshū sōgi*, 349.

[25] See Ishikawa (1996, 67). The various versions of the text that I have obtained are essentially the same in content and share the characterstics of material that was delivered originally as lectures. The texts are composed in very colloquial language and contain internal evidence that the material was presented over a period of several days in lecture format. One manuscript of the *Nikujiki saitai kikigaki* is owned by the Ryūkoku University Library as well as the very similar *Nikujiki saitai ron*. Unless otherwise indicated, all references to the *Nikujiki saitai ben* are to the version found in SSZ, 59:293–318 (hereafter NSB).

[26] NSB, 293a.

In the *Nikujiki saitai ben* Chikū painted a radically different picture of
the Shin schools. Feigning incredulity and resentment, he claimed that
despite violating the accepted standards of clerical deportment, the Shin
clergy had not received the sort of divine or worldly retribution as predicted in such texts as the *Daibon hannyakyō*. Despite a variety of textual
warnings of punishment for precept-breaking clerics, the Shin denomination had prospered and its clergy had been afforded a special relationship
with the court and the Tokugawa authorities.

> If one looks at the *Nehangyō*, the *Bonmōkyō*, or the *Ryōgakyō*, one will see
> that these sutras all enjoin those who are ordained to give up the four acts of
> taking life, stealing, licentiousness, and lying. Therefore one would expect
> one who has been ordained to refrain from *nikujiki saitai*. However, two-
> thirds of the people of Japan now follow the school of our founder, and
> those who pray to be reborn in the Pure Land are numerous. What does the
> Brahma King do about this? Is Indra blind? They agreed in the presence of
> the Buddha [to punish such transgressors], so why do they not censure these
> things? Why didn't the kings and great ministers split the head of Shinran
> into seven pieces and drive him to another cosmos? I grew angry and resentful
> that not even the Four Great Guardian Kings understood that this teaching
> had spread to two-thirds of Japan and that many sentient beings had been
> led astray.[27]

Chikū then elaborated in great detail all of the ways in which the Shin
denominations had prospered, using this portrait of the wealth, strength,
and close ties with the ruling authorities as evidence that Shin practice
was being rewarded, not punished. Describing special dispensations from
the authorities for temple rebuilding at the Nishi Honganji and at the
Tsukiji Honganji in Edo, Chikū mocked his critics, asking why, if they
were so evil and decadent, they were being rewarded in this fashion. He
mentioned how the heads of other denominations fawningly visited the
head of the Nishi Honganji, gladly sitting in a separate room from him
for an audience. He also noted other special treatment from the Tokugawas.

> Our school was given license to oversee three hundred *koku* worth of temple
> lands. On top of that, on occasion [the head of the Honganji] leaves the
> capitol for Edo. He enters the *chūjakumon* in his palanquin, comes up along-
> side the entrance platform, and gets out.[28] He goes directly to the entrance
> platform. He does not touch the ground at all. When all others go to be in
> attendance at the castle, they get out of their palanquins and walk about 1½
> *chō*.[29] In general, if we look at the form of their visits, excluding the members

[27] Ibid., 293b.
[28] The *chūjakumon* was one of the entrances to the central compound of Edo Castle.
[29] One *chō* approximately equals 109 meters.

of the three branches of the Tokugawa family, the rest of the people, including even the heads of the other Buddhist schools and the *monzeki* abbots, have to dismount outside the *chūjakumon*. The head of our school alone does not once trod upon the ground. He is greeted by the shogun's aids. There are almost no examples of one being treated in this special manner by the shogun.[30]

After a detailed description of Shin prosperity, Chikū provided a vivid description of decrepitude, poverty, and corruption within other monastic Buddhist denominations, the implication being, of course, that such dire conditions were a direct result of practices that were invalid for the current age. Although it is difficult to assess the veracity of many of Chikū's claims about Edo Buddhist institutions, he nonetheless provided a fascinating survey of the changing economic and social conditions at large Buddhist temples, including the phenomenon of selling local specialties as a means of temple livelihood.

First, when I went to Yamato, the main hall at the Tōdaiji had reached the point of collapse and even the Buddha was soaked by the rain. When I went to see the Saidaiji, it had become wretched and disordered. The monks rolled balls of medicine that was called *hōshintan*.[31] There was also [a residence for] the nuns called the *gosho*. There the nuns made small dolls for a living. They were in such a pitiful state. When I went to see the Yakushiji the hall was in ruins and the Yakushiji Nyorai was soaked by rain. All of the roof tiles had fallen down. When I went to see Gyōki's Gangōji, the hall was in ruins and was wrapped with straw matting. It was a pitiful thing. Although there is separate hall where the monks live, now they spend their days raising barley and other things. When I went to see the Daihannyaji, it had become so disordered that I could not bear to look at it twice. Only the foundations were left. When I went to see the Fujiidera in Kawachi, all of the hands had fallen off of the thousand-armed Kannon and there also was no one there to make the repairs. When I went traveling here and there, I only saw wretched things. The Kenninji in Kyoto was also mere foundation stones. Amidst the ruins of the lecture hall (*godō*) a thicket of cedar and pine grew wildly. The Tōji as well was mere foundation stones.

Furthermore, the stone and metal lamps of important monastic compounds are put up for sale in town, and people of means from Kyoto and Osaka purchase them. They use the [top of the] lamps as water containers in front of their verandas or as stepping stones in their gardens. The metal lamps are used for illuminating their toilets.

Well, it indeed is ridiculous. In spite of the fact that these temples were constructed by leading teachers, they are totally in ruins. I have felt the regret

[30] NSB, 294b–95a.
[31] According to the NKD, 9:76c, Saidaiji was famous for its Hōshintan medicine.

and sadness of the pitiful desolation of these places. I have been maddened by it and have cried hot tears. I am consumed by anger—can't the Four Guardian Kings see these horrors? Don't they know about this?[32]

Having established for his audience the infirmity of various non–Shin Buddhist institutions, Chikū launched into an extended, tripartite justification of *nikujiki saitai*. He began his defense of Shin practice by cataloging a variety of precedents drawn from Buddhist literature or, in the case of Japan, alleged eyewitness accounts of legendary and historical Buddhists who either ate meat, engaged in sexual relations, or married. The next portion of Chikū's defense centered on an "investigation of the sources," that is, a compilation of examples drawn from various canonical sources, for example, Vinaya and sūtra literature, of tolerance for *nikujiki saitai*. Finally, in the third section, Chikū attempted to provide doctrinal justification for *nikujiki saitai* by "explaining the principles (*dōri*)." It was in this section of the text that Chikū marshalled various Shin interpretations of the precepts, skillful means, and the decline of the Buddhist teaching to account for distinctive Shin practices.

In the first section, Chikū listed those illustrious Buddhists who either ate meat or had relations with women, in order to establish precedents for Shin practice, prove early tolerance of those customs, and demonstrate the hypocrisy of Shin critics. He provided a variety of examples, beginning with a description of such supposedly fallen monks as Kumārajīva (J., Kumarajū) (343–413), Kuiji (632–82), Myōichi (728–98), Jōzō (891–964), Chōken (1126–1203), Nichiren (1222–82), and Seikaku (1167–1235).[33] Using several widely accepted Buddhist biographical sources to justify his allegations, Chikū wrote that all of these great monks had sexual relations with women and fathered children, but they continued to be revered as great Buddhists.[34]

Chikū painted a tawdry picture of Buddhist temple life during the early Edo period, claiming that meat eating and clerical marriage were widespread among the clergy. Accusing his critics of hypocrisy, he described marriage at such temples as the Nichiren temple Shōchūzan (Hokekyōji) in Shimōsa, the Zen temple Kanbōji in Tanba, and a number of important Ji temples, including the Ji head temple, Shōjōkōji in Fujisawa, the Mieidō (Shinzenkōji), and various *dōjō* scattered throughout Kyoto.[35]

---

[32] NSB, 296a–b. Later in the text, Chikū provides many more examples of how clerics of other denominations have been forced to resort to the sale of various *meibutsu*—miso, dried rice, medicine, bamboo shoots, and nori—for support. See ibid., 315a–b.

[33] The charge against Nichiren is based on allegations made in the Tendai text, *Kindan Nichiren gi*, by Shin'yō (d. 1656). See Shin'yō, *Kindan Nichiren gi* 3:15r–l. For more on the text see NSJ, 66.

[34] NSB, 300b–302a.

[35] Ibid., 302b–303a.

Although in many cases it is difficult to assess the veracity of Chikū's claims, some scattered external evidence supports his assertions. One such example is his description of Seikaku's lineage. The case of Seikaku, a leading disciple of Hōnen (1133–1212), was particularly valuable for Chikū's defense of Shin practice, given that Seikaku's *Yuishinshō* was an important work for both the Jōdo and the Shin traditions. Shinran frequently copied this influential commentary on Hōnen's teachings and Pure Land faith and eventually wrote extensive notes about it in his *Yuishinshō mon'i*. Seikaku, an ardent defender of Hōnen, also remained a key intellectual figure for clerics in the Jōdo tradition. Although revered by Jōdo clerics—some of whose members had attacked Shinran and the Shin denomination in works like the *Jagi ketsu*—Seikaku was, according to Chikū, part of a long-standing lineage of married clerics, which, in its practice of father-son transmission of the teaching, resembled Chikū's Shin denomination. Chikū asserted that "Seikaku was married just as his father Chōken. Seikaku's son was named Kōshō and his son was Kenjitsu. Kenjitsu's son was named Kenki. One generation after the next engaged in *nikujiki saitai*."[36] This claim is not unique to Chikū. A similar description of the lineage is found in the *Sonpi bunmyaku*, a Muromachi period (1333–1568) work.[37] According to Nishiguchi Junko, who made use of the *Sonpi bunmyaku* in her study of the families of medieval clerics, the first member of the lineage described by Chikū, Chōken, was the brother of Fujiwara no Sadanori. Sons of both Chōken and Sadanori became successive abbots of the Agui in Kyoto. Nishiguchi noted that having their descendants serve as abbots of the temple allowed the family of Chōken and Sadanori to control the abbacy of the Agui for many generations. Recorded in a genealogical record like the *Sonpi bunmyaku*, by Chikū's day it must have been commonly accepted that a familial lineage had controlled the Agui.

Another case where coincidentally we have evidence that echoes Chikū's claims is his indictment of the Nichiren temple, the Hōkekyōji in Shimōsa, as a place that tolerated illicit clerical marriage. Chikū seems to be recording generally accepted information in this particular instance. One century after Chikū wrote his defense of clerical marriage, the anonymous author of the *Ukiyo no arisama* described how authorities rounded up and punished several clerics, including one nun, from subtemples within Hōkekyōji for carrying on sexual relationships with each other and with laywomen in the area.[38] Could it be just coincidence that Chikū accused the clerics at Hōkekyōji of illicit activity, or was Chikū giving voice to salacious rumors about life at that temple complex that were already circulating in clerical circles by the start of the eighteenth century?

[36] Ibid., 302a.
[37] See Nishiguchi (1987, 195; 200).
[38] Ishida (1995, 182).

Following his listing of various precedents for Shin practice among past and contemporaneous Buddhists, Chikū then proceeded to cite a variety of Buddhist textual sources in which meat eating and sexual relations are not condemned. He drew examples from sutras and Vinaya texts that describe the use of animal fat as medicine, permit the eating of fish and meat, or call for the laity to honor even clerics who have broken their monastic vows. Chikū stressed inconsistencies within the canon by contrasting texts produced in different periods of Buddhist history or by placing passages with a dispensationalist tenor alongside those condemning precept infractions. For example, he cited one passage from the *Shibunritsu* in which the consumption of meat that is pure in three ways (*sanshū no jōniku*) is permitted, and another from the *Daishūkyō* in which the widespread marriage of the clergy is predicted.[39]

> [I]n Volume 42 of the *Shibunritsu* the eating of various types of fish is permitted. On page 6 of the same volume, it is permitted for ill monks to eat beef. Again, in the same volume, meat that is blameless in three ways is also permitted. Again, in the *Daishūkyō* it states, "Five hundred years after my death, all of my disciples will eat meat and will marry. When there is no gold then silver is a priceless treasure, . . . when there is no iron then lead is a treasure. In accordance with a thing's rarity it grows in value. In other words, the period of the Imitative Teaching, is inferior to the period of the true Teaching, and the Last Age of the Teaching is inferior to the period of the Imitative Teaching. Although during the Last Age of the Teaching all the priests will be referred to as having no precepts, if they sincerely instruct others, they will achieve merit ."[40]

After providing a long list of similar passages from a variety of canonical sources, Chikū reached the conclusion that there is no universal, unchangeable restriction against *nikujiki saitai* within the corpus of Buddhist writings. For Chikū, the eating of meat and the marriage of Buddhist clerics are merely manifestations of compassion, of skill in means that allow the

---

[39] A variety of restrictions exist in the *Vinaya* regarding what type of meat may be eaten by the Buddhist clergy without violating the precepts. Meat may be classified as pure according to either a threefold, fivefold, or ninefold scheme. The threefold classification is common to the other two and includes the following restrictions: the meat must not come from an animal the cleric sees being killed, an animal he hears being killed, or an animal he has reason to suspect was killed specifically for him. In addition to these general restrictions, certain specific types of meat are proscribed—for example, the authors of the *Vinaya* of different schools universally enjoined the eating of meat from elephants, horses, snakes, and humans. For an interesting discussion of the issues surrounding the consumption of meat in Indian Buddhism, see Shimoda (1989, 1–21) and Shimoda (1990, 98–110). I would like to thank Professor Yoshizu Yoshihide of Komazawa University for referring me to Shimoda's research.

[40] NSB, 303b–304a. Ellipses in the sūtra citation are Chikū's. The *Daishūkyō* (T 13:1–409) is alternatively called the *Daijikkyō*.

clergy to reach out to and help sentient beings. Chikū concluded his investigation of the sources by noting that the prohibition of marriage or meat eating is not consistent in the texts. Rather, depending on the time and the type of person who is the target of the teaching, the precepts are sometimes advocated and sometimes relaxed. In either case, these are examples of skillful means being used to lead sentient beings to the Buddhist teaching.[41]

After establishing the existence of precedents for Shin practice and demonstrating the centrality in Buddhist sources of adjusting monastic practice to accord with the spiritual disposition of people, Chikū provided an extended doctrinal justification of Shin tolerance for *nikujiki saitai*. Emphasizing the notion that skillful means rooted in compassion should be the foundation of all clerical activity, he detailed Shinran's abandonment of his monastic vows and marriage to Eshinni (b. 1182) and the continuation of that tradition within the Shin denomination. In this section Chikū gave examples from classical sources—both Buddhist and secular—in which regulations are abrogated to preserve the spirit that underlies those rules, including Mencius's scolding of a disciple about the need to override protocols of etiquette in order to help people in distress, and the legendary story of Benkei (?–1189) feigning disrespect for a disguised Minamoto Yoshitsune (1159–89) in order to deceive their foes about his lord's true identity. In all these ways, compassion takes precedence over mere rules and regulations. Summarizing this point, Chikū wrote,

> when we help those who are in the mud, we cannot help that person unless we, too, get muddy. If we stand on the shore, how are we to help one caught in the stream? To help those sentient beings who are now trapped in the mud of the five defilements (*gojoku*) and whose stomachs are filled with the waters of lust and delusion, one must suppose that one cannot help if one does not also get one's own body dirty with the five defilements and does not enter the water of love of wife and child.[42] In this way our Patriarch [Shinran] entered the mud of the five defilements and mixed with all sentient beings so that we might in this life achieve birth in the Pure Land.[43]

Chikū portrayed Shinran's marriage and his abandonment of his clerical vows as an act of pure compassion. Without entering the world in this manner, Shinran would not have been able to reveal the path to the Pure Land. Chikū wrote that Shinran was no mere mortal human being. Rather, Shinran entered the world willfully to save sentient beings from suffering. For this reason, Chikū warned, Shinran's and, therefore, the Shin denomi-

---

[41] NSB, 304b.

[42] The five defilements are: defilement of period (various natural and human-generated catastrophes arise); defilement of view; defilement by evil passions; defilement of sentient beings (people's karmic fruit is inferior); and, defilement of life (life span is short).

[43] NSB, 306b–307b.

nation's *nikujiki saitai* is not the same as that of ordinary precept-breaking clerics.

To prove this point, Chikū recalled Shinran's life story, concentrating on the apocryphal tale of Kujō Kanezane (1149–1207) asking Hōnen that a cleric be sent to marry his daughter and head his Pure Land confraternity. According to this story Hōnen was miraculously aware of a dream that Shinran had during a hundred-day retreat at the Rokkakudō. In Shinran's dream the bodhisattva Kannon told him that should Shinran succumb to sexual desire, Kannon would become Shinran's wife and be ravished by him.[44] Hōnen, secretly aware of this dream, then asked Shinran to assent to Kanezane's request for a disciple of Hōnen's to marry his daughter and join his lay Pure Land confraternity. When Shinran protested to Hōnen that after years of devoted practice this would be an extremely bitter fate for him, Hōnen took a brush and inkstone and wrote out the words that Kannon had spoken to Shinran during Shinran's retreat at the Rokkakudō. Astounded that Hōnen knew what had transpired at the Rokkakudō although he had not breathed a word of it to anyone, Shinran relented and renounced his monastic vows.

> For three years after having been told by Kannon, "if the believer, because of the fruition of karma . . . ," Shinran held the words in his heart, not saying a word of them to anyone. But, somehow Genkū Shōnin perfectly remembered these words and was able to write them without error. Is this not incredible? The reason for this is that in the Pure Land Hōnen Shōnin is Mahāsthāmaprāpta (Seishi) bodhisattva, our Shōnin (Shinran) is Amida Nyorai, so without anything being said or explained, [Hōnen] understood this perfectly. Shinran accepted Denka's directive and became *saitai*. Because Kannon said, "I will become Tamajo . . . ," Kujō Denka's [Kanezane's] daughter the honorable Tamahi, when seen from the perspective of Kannon's instructions, is no ordinary person either. For that reason Shinran did not say no. Within the day Zenshin [Shinran] Shōnin was recommended to Denka, and they returned to his mansion in the same vehicle. Until now, no one from the other schools or sects has known this explanation of Shinran's *nikujiki saitai*. Because they do not know [what is explained above], those of other schools think that Shinran married because of his own private inten-

---

[44] The same tale of Shinran's retreat in the Rokkakudō is found in the *Shinran muki* and the *Godenshō* (*Honganji no Shōnin Shinran denne*) by Kakunyo. According to Kakunyo's description, on the ninety-fifth day of his retreat, Shinran had a dream in which Kannon appeared to him and said, "If the believer, because of the fruition of karma, is driven by sexual desire, / Then I shall take on the body of a beautiful woman to be ravished by him. / Throughout his entire life I shall adorn him well, / And at death I shall lead him to birth in Pure Land." Dobbins (1989, 23–24). The *Godenshō* makes no mention of the marriage to Kanezane's daughter Tamahi, but the Edo period Takada-ha biography, *Shinran Shōnin shōtoden*, written in 1715, does contain this complete story. See Bloom (1968, 12–13).

tions. Because Kannon herself became the spouse and guided all sentient beings, promising that they would achieve return to the Pure Land, the *nikujiki saitai* of our school is different from the ordinary.[45]

According to Chikū, because Shinran was a manifestation of Amida, the clerical marriage of the Shin denomination is not the same as that of other schools. Shinran's teachings are completely in harmony with people's spiritual capacity and the nature of the current age, which is the period of the Final Teaching. As a result, Shin clerics do not covertly fornicate and eat meat while pretending to eschew those practices, unlike the clergy of other denominations, whose emphasis on celibacy is inconsonant with the age. Chikū concluded that it was precisely because Shin clerics are at ease, unburdened by the regrets and hypocrisy of other clerics, that they are able to attract a following that includes two-thirds of the Japanese people.

In advancing these arguments, Chikū was following the lead of his teacher, Saigin, who in the *Kyakushō mondō shū* had presented a defense of Shin clerical marriage that had emphasized that the marriage of the Shin clergy was a manifestation of the spirit of *wakō dōjin*, that is, hiding one's brilliance and assuming the same form as a layperson. This was done to reach out to and rescue sentient beings mired in ignorance and guilty of the worst offenses. But, as Hirata Atsushi has noted with regard to Saigin, this sort of argument marks a departure from Shinran's intent in renouncing his monastic vows, becoming "neither monk nor layman." Rather than being a provisional means willfully adopted by Shinran to save sentient being, Shinran's marriage and abandonment of his vows was a profound acknowledgment of his frailty and inability to practice.[46] Chikū did argue in part that one must as a cleric embrace *nikujiki saitai* because celibate monastic practice is no longer possible. However, his crowning argument, following an interpretation that had been part of mainstream Shin thought since Kakunyo (1270–1351), portrayed Shinran's embracing of *nikujiki saitai* as a willful act of compassion made by a manifestation of Amida, not as an admission of failure by a flawed human being.[47]

It was precisely the success of the Shin clergy in attracting a lay following, derived from their consonance with the needs of people living during the age of the Latter Dharma more than anything else, Chikū contended, that sparked the harsh criticisms of *nikujiki saitai* from the clerics of other denominations. Unable to restrain themselves from covert fornication with women, or, even worse, when that is impossible, with

---

[45] NSB, 310b–311a, The notion that Shinran is an avatar of Amida and that Hōnen is a reincarnation of Mahāsthāmaprāpta Bodhisattva can be traced back to Kakunyo's *Shinran Shōnin denne*. See Solomon, (1974, 405–406).

[46] Hirata (1996, 113–14).

[47] For a discussion of this trend in biographies of Shinran, see Dobbins (1990, 179–96).

other men or boys, the critics from other denominations were nothing more than hypocrites destined for hell.[48] Having seen the Shin school grow in size and receive special treatment from the court and the shogun, these clerics lashed out in jealous anger. In the end, they were only trying to fill their own bellies, nothing more: "Because their stomachs are growing thin, they slander us and deceive our parishioners. They curry favor in all sorts of ways and dispatch their monks who come with their gifts and greetings. They go in and out of homes, regaling the parishioners and use insincere flattery while criticizing our school in an exaggerated fashion."[49]

Like the poor seen at the rice market in Osaka, whom wealthy traders allow to pick up bits of rice that spill on the ground, Chikū wrote, these clerics who criticized the Shin school, failing to reflect on the shortcomings of clerics of their own denomination, should be allowed to steal a few parishioners from the prosperous Shin denomination. They deserved pity, nothing more.[50]

Chikū, while vigorously defending the Shin clergy, was clearly aware that certain actions by Shin clergy and devout parishioners could incite the clerics of other denominations to attack the Shin clergy. He thus warned Shin clerics to refrain from actions that would be construed negatively by the laity and clerics from other denominations. Noting that Shinran renounced his monastic vows for altruistic, not selfish, reasons, Chikū stated that even if the Shin clergy are no different from the laity in their practice, they must not act in self-serving ways that bring disrepute on the denomination. Recounting the story of a devout layman who urinated on a *torii* at the temple Tennōji to show his disregard for all miscellaneous practices, Chikū warned his audience to be respectful toward the kami and Buddhas. He also instructed his followers not to engage in activities that are unsuitable for a cleric, for example, hunting and fishing, even if the Shin clergy are technically the same as the laity (*zaike*).

Expressions of concern about the behavior of the Shin clergy are fairly common in this genre. Similar warnings against engaging in activities that are not suitable for clergy are also found in Saigin's *Kyakushō mondō shū*.[51] In addition, in 1722 rules for the Tsukiji Honganji clergy stated that even if they lived in a manner that was the same as the laity, they were not to take part in activities like fishing that were inappropriate for a monk (*shamon*), even if they were invited to do so by their lay compatriots.[52] Following another government warning about unseemly behavior by the Buddhist clergy in 1788, the leaders at the Nishi Honganji sent another directive to its clerics reminding them that Shin clerics of all rank,

[48] NSB, 315b.
[49] Ibid., 316b–317a.
[50] Ibid., 317a–b.
[51] Hirata (1996, 136, n. 23).
[52] NSRK, 415.

not just abbots, were allowed to practice *nikujiki saitai*. But, the directive admonished, even if they were permitted to marry and eat meat, they were to avoid the pleasure quarters, lest they be punished by the head temple.[53] Judging from these texts, it appears that having been granted the status of clerics by the authorities, while being allowed to marry and live like the laity, required that the Shin clergy be circumspect in their actions, lest they anger their critics and the authorities. The Nishi Honganji leaders issued similar warnings, this time particularly aimed at those clerics in training (*shokesō*), in the wake of a crackdown on illicit clerical activities by Ōshio Heihachirō in Osaka in 1830.[54]

The attacks on clerical marriage and the warnings aimed at Shin clerics also catalyzed an effort to codify the position and behavior of the Shin temple wife. Starting in the mid-Edo period, the Shin clerics produced a number of didactic texts directed at the temple wives. Works like *Bōmori hōgo* by Sōboku (1719–62) and *Bōmori kyōkai kikigaki* by Tokuryū (1772–1858), which was reprinted in the Meiji and the Taishō periods, specified the unique position of *bōmori* for Shin congregations and set the protocols to be followed in dealing with the parishioners and managing the temple.[55] Sōboku, for example, warned Shin temple wives to remain frugal in their dress, to raise their children with care, to be diligent caretakers of the temple in their husband's absence, and to receive all gifts from parishioners, no matter how small, with equanimity.

Throughout the Edo period, attacks on Jōdo Shin practices continued. As late as 1849, Hirata Atsutane lashed out angrily against Shin clerical marriage, criticizing the legendary story of Shinran's retreat at the Rokkakudō as a self-serving fabrication used to justify dissolute behavior.[56] Shin scholars continued to defend their distinctive practice of allowing their clergy to practice *nikujiki saitai*, and a number of these works were reissued during the Bakumatsu and early Meiji eras.

THE ORIGIN OF THE TERM *NIKUJIKI SAITAI*

In much of the Edo period literature defending distinctive Shin practices, meat eating and clerical marriage were referred to by the four-character compound *nikujiki saitai*. That phrase, as we shall see, also was used widely in Meiji publications to signify the general secularization of the clergy and more specifically to denote the practices of eating meat and marriage by the Buddhist clergy. It was only during the Edo period, how-

[53] Hirata (1996, 107–8).
[54] Ibid., 124–26.
[55] Sōboku, *Bōmori saisoku no hōgo*; Tokuryū (1898); Ikai (1911). For a summary of Sōboku's text, see Chiba (1977, 73–86).
[56] Ketelaar (1990, 34–35).

ever, that the term came into widespread use, particularly in the numerous apologetic works of the Shin clergy and in more popular works that
recorded the life of the clergy and other townspeople.

The first half of the compound is not particularly problematic; *nikujiki*
can be translated simply as "eating meat." The pronunciation *nikujiki*
rather than the more conventional *nikushoku* is the *go-on* reading of the
two-character phrase used by Japanese Buddhists. The use of this reading
thus indicates that this is a Buddhist compound. Again, in the *Kōjien* we
are told that *nikujiki* is a Buddhist term that refers to the eating of such
blood-polluted (*namagusai*) foods as the meat of birds, animals, and fish.[57]
The more common pronunciation of the term, *nikushoku*, has a broader
meaning, referring simply to the eating of animal flesh without the pejorative tint associated with the Buddhist term *nikujiki*.

The latter half of the compound, *saitai*, I have uniformly translated as
"clerical marriage." The Japanese meaning of the two-character compound is ambiguous. The *Kōjien*, for example, defines *saitai* simply as "to
have a wife" (*tsuma o motsu koto*).[58] The example sentences for the term
given in the *Nihon kokugo daijiten* date from the late medieval period or
later, and all but one of them seem to have a Buddhist context, which
suggests that originally the term may have referred specifically to the marriage of the Buddhist clergy.[59] This is the interpretation given in the *Kadokawa kogo daijiten*, which states that the term *saitai* "particularly means
those people included in the class of those with the appearance of a cleric
or living in a temple for whom having a wife is permitted."[60] In a similar
vein, the fifteenth-century *Setsuyōshū* defines *saitai* as being laicized
(*genzoku*).[61] Thus although today the word *saitai* certainly does mean
marriage in general, the term more specifically in a Buddhist context indicates clerical marriage.

The combination of the two elements into the four-character compound
nikujiki saitai appears to be fairly recent: I have found no instances of the
phrase being used prior to the start of the Edo period. Of course, arguments based on lack of evidence are notoriously risky, but the compound
nikujiki saitai appears to have been first used regularly in Shin apologetic
literature aimed at countering the criticisms of the Ōbaku and the Seizan
Jōdo clergy. Many of these works used the term *nikujiki saitai* in their
titles. This is particularly true for the closely related set of texts by Chikū,
including *Nikujiki saitai kikigaki*, *Nikujiki saitai ben*, and *Nikujiki saitai
ron*.[62] Numerous other later Shin authors, for example, Ekū (1644–1721),

---

[57] Shinmura (1991, 1946). See also IBJ, 630; MBD, 5:4023.

[58] Shinmura (1991, 1946).   [59] NKD, 4:1267a.

[60] KKD, 2:608c–d.

[61] NKD, 4: 1267a. The *Setsuyōshū* (also read Setchōshū) was a mid-fifteenth century
Japanese-language dictionary.

[62] A thorough list of these works is provided in Ishikawa (1996, 66–70).

Enchō (1685–1726), Kōgan (1757–1821), and Reiō (1775–1851), also used the phrase in the titles of their apologia. The term appears to have entered into wider usage around the time of the Edo debate between the Shin clergy and their opponents.

As in the case of *saitai*, the dictionary example sentences used to illustrate the four-character phrase all date from at least the Edo period. In the *Nihon kokugo daijiten*, for example, one source is the late Jōdo Shin biography of Shinran, the *Takada kaisan Shinran Shōnin shōtō den*, compiled in 1715. The second source given is the popular work, *Ukiyodoko* by Shikitei Sanba (1776–1822), which was published between 1813 and 1823. Mochizuki, in his encyclopedia of Buddhist terms, gave an extended entry for *nikujiki saitai*, but, tellingly, the actual phrase did not appear in any of his citations until he wrote about the Shin clergy during the Edo period. Although meat eating and marriage are mentioned in various ways, the precise formula in question occurred only in Mochizuki's Edo sources.[63]

The fact that the term *nikujiki saitai* is of late provenance and first arose in the context of Jōdo Shin sectarian writings helps us refine our understanding of the problematical term *saitai*, for I believe that the context in which the term first regularly appears will make clear what was intended by that term.

In their numerous responses to the attacks leveled against them by critics like Tetsugen, scholar-clerics at the Nishi and Higashi Honganji academies were loath to define their practice of marriage as *nyobon*. In the process of defending themselves, these scholars frequently recast the terms used by their critics, for example, *nyobon nikujiki* or *in*, with the less denigrating four-character phrase *nikujiki saitai*. As we have seen, in the *Kōmori bōdanki* Tetsugen described the relationship between the Jōdo Shin clergy and women as *nyobon*, which I have chosen to translate as "fornication." Like most non-Shin clerics, he considered *saitai* a variety of fornication. By not using the term *saitai* to describe the marital relationship of the Shin clergy, the authors of the *Kōmori bōdanki* and the *Jagi ketsu* withheld any recognition of legitimacy for Shin marriage.

Shin clerics naturally did not refer to the practice of clerical marriage as either *nyobon* or *in*, the manner in which critics of the Shin denomination wished to define it. Shin authors chose instead to replace those terms with more positive ones. In responding to the charges raised in the *Jagi ketsu* and the *Kōmori bōdanki*, Shin authors uniformly substituted the word *saitai* for the offensive terms *nyobon* and *in*. It was in the context of their rebuttal to hostile charges about Shin adherence to the Buddhist precepts that they regularly began to use such four-character compounds as *nikujiki saitai*. In responding to the charges raised in the *Jagi ketsu*, for example, Genkaku wrote that such false charges were raised because "they consider

---

[63] MBD, 5:4023–24.

only that our great master [Shinran] permitted clerical marriage and meat eating (*saitai jikiniku*). They are ignorant about what happened in the past."[64] Genkaku thus described Shin practice as *saitai*, not *nyobon* or *in*.

In one of his lengthiest defenses of clerical marriage, Chikū pointed out that the relationship between the Shin cleric and the *bōmori* differed from that between clerics of other schools and women because it was an open marital relationship. Chikū wrote, "in our school, one has one wife (*tsuma*), and she is made the *bōmori*."[65] According to Chikū the Shin marital relationship is permanent and visible, which distinguished *saitai* from the furtive licentious liaisons so commonly practiced by the clergy of other schools. Chikū referred to the partner in the *saitai* relationship as *tsuma*, a wife, as opposed to a casual liaison or a concubine.[66] A variety of Shin apologetic texts make clear that the Shin clergy considered the *bōmori* a wife. Genkaku also stressed the long-term, marital character of the relationship between the *bōmori* and the Shin cleric, pointing out that the cleric has sexual relations only with his *tsuma*; to desire any other woman would be to contravene the intentions of the Buddha.[67] In addition, as Chikū and Genkaku stressed, the relationship was not fleeting or licentious. It is crucial to remember that *saitai*, as far as its supporters were concerned, did not mean casual sexual relations between a cleric and women, for example, visits to the prostitutes of the Yoshiwara.

As I have shown, political, legal, and social changes throughout the Edo period raised the issue of *nikujiki saitai* to a new level of attention. Those attempting to discipline the clergy, be they clerical leaders or government officials in charge of temple policies, tried to eliminate these practices, even though in many instances they had been long accepted by the local clergy. However, given the frequency with which the shogunal authorities issued laws calling for an end to clerical fornication, the attempt to eliminate these practices was a miserable failure.

With the transformation of the legal and social landscape during the Edo period, common clerical behavior had been criminalized, in effect creating the problem of *nikujiki saitai*. The same political and social changes that led to a crackdown on fornication among the Buddhist clerics of most of the denominations also resulted in a major shift for the Shin

[64] Genkaku, *Shinran jagiketsu no kogi ketsu*, 8. In the passage that follows Genkaku goes on to list a number of examples of clerics who had relations with women as a defense of Shin practice.

[65] NSB, 308.

[66] According to Edo law, a woman could be a *tsuma* only if her name was entered as a *tsuma* in her husband's *ninbetsuchō*. Without such registration a woman would be regarded only as a common-law (*naien*) wife (*mekake*), regardless of the length or status of her relationship with her husband. Such usage of the term *mekake* differs from the modern one in which the term has come to refer to a concubine. See Ishii (1990, 148).

[67] Genkaku, *Shinran jagiketsu no kogi ketsu*, 11.

clergy. As members of the Tokugawa social order, Shin clerics were subject to most of the same laws as the clerics of other denominations. But Tokugawa law allowed the Shin clergy to marry, and scholar clerics from other, competing denominations attacked the Shin exceptionalism with regard to the precepts, creating an ongoing debate over the legitimacy of *nikujiki saitai*.

As hostility toward Buddhism from Shintoists, nativists, and others increased to a critical level in the waning years of Tokugawa rule, charges of precept infractions, particularly fornication and *saitai*, became a common pretext for closing temples and forcefully laicizing clerics. The issue of clerical marriage, which had plagued the Buddhist world throughout the Edo period, became even more damaging as anti-Buddhist elements took control of religious policy. With the rise of the new, even more powerful and centralized Meiji state, and in the wake of some of the most violent attacks on the Buddhist clergy in Japanese history, it was left to both government officials and temple leaders alike to resolve what by the end of the Edo period had become the "*nikujiki saitai* problem." The efforts to control the deportment of the Buddhist clergy and to extirpate covert sexual liaisons during the Edo period had been part of a larger structure of social and legal controls of Buddhism. With the waning of Tokugawa hegemony and the rise of the Meiji state, the old system of laws affecting clerical life was dismantled. As we shall see in the next several chapters, the debate over *nikujiki saitai* became even broader and more contentious as a result.

CHAPTER 4

The Household Registration System and the Buddhist Clergy

FROM THE last decades of the Edo period through the early years of the Meiji era, the Buddhist clergy were confronted with the most violent assault on Buddhist institutions in Japanese history. Over the course of the Bakumatsu era, Buddhism was increasingly attacked from a variety of perspectives by Confucians, Shintō clergy, Nativists, and political economists. In domains like Mitō and, later, Satsuma, where anti-Buddhist sentiment ran the strongest, daimyo experimented with measures that limited entrance into the Buddhist clergy, closed temples that were abandoned or without a resident cleric, outlawed Buddhist funeral ceremonies, and forcibly returned clerics, particularly those guilty of "offenses," to lay life.

With the total collapse of the Tokugawa regime and the rise of the new Meiji state in 1868, anti-Buddhist measures that had been restricted to specific domains became national policy. The Meiji Restoration temporarily brought such hard-line Shintō and Nativist scholars as the lord of Tsuwano han, Kamei Koremi (1825–85), and Kamei's advisor, Fukuba Bisei (1831–1907), to positions of power in the newly established Department of Rites. Seeking to provide an ideological foundation for the new government, Meiji leaders distanced themselves from the Buddhist institutions that had given support to the Tokugawa government. Instead, they turned to Shintō, in particular the worship of those kami associated closely with the imperial family, to supply the religious underpinnings for their claim to power. To create a Shintō free from the "foreign" influence of Buddhism, Meiji leaders issued a series of laws aimed at removing all Buddhist elements from sites associated with kami worship, thus ending the centuries-long fusion of veneration for the Buddhas and worship of the kami. When the series of edicts calling for the separation of the kami and the Buddhas (*shinbutsu bunri rei*) triggered an explosion of anti-Buddhist violence (*haibutsu kishaku*, literally, abolish the buddhas and destroy Śākyamuni), government officials stood by idly as temples were trashed and looted. Although the exact number of temples destroyed may never be known, Tamamuro Fumio estimates that of the approximately 200,000 Edo period temples, only 74,600 were left after the early years of the Meiji era.[1] Only

---

[1] Tamamuro (1997, 504–5).

in 1871, after armed uprisings by Jōdo Shin partisans and the failure of the Shintō clergy to conduct a proselytization campaign on their own, did officials move to quell the physical attacks on Buddhist clerics and temples.[2] The destruction of temples was massive.

The Meiji Restoration marked a turning point in the relationship between the state and the Buddhist clergy. Between 1868 and 1884 Meiji government leaders almost totally reconstructed state policy concerning clerical status, the definition of the Buddhist clergy, and Buddhist institutional structure. As a result of those changes, the Buddhists who attempted to reform their religion in the wake of the Meiji suppression were in a totally different legal position from pre-Meiji clerics. Changes in the legal status of the Buddhist clergy and the reorganization of Buddhist institutional hierarchy brought about an almost total rupture between pre- and post-Restoration Buddhism. Like the forced separation of Buddhism and Shintō, the dissolution of special Buddhist clerical status and the division between the laity and the clergy by Meiji officials were crucial elements in the emergence of modern Japanese religious consciousness. The decriminalization of *nikujiki saitai*, an attempt by the Meiji government to end the unsuccessful efforts of the Tokugawa rulers to eliminate precept infractions, must be understood in the context of the broader social and legal changes affecting the clergy during the Meiji era.

During early Meiji, state decisions concerning general social policy wrought sweeping changes in the legal status of all Japanese subjects, regardless of their occupation or social class. For the Buddhist clergy, the modifications brought about by the new government policy erased many of the boundaries between lay and clerical life, necessitating a radical reconceptualization of their role in society that sparked years of heated debate within the Buddhist establishment. The decriminalization of clerical marriage, which was the most contested and visible of all new government regulations, and the diverse Buddhist response to the new regulation must be seen in light of such broader actions as the implementation of a uniform civil code that transformed the legal status not only of the clergy, but of all Japanese subjects as well. As part of the network of modifications in social structure instituted under the banner of such slogans as the "unity of the four classes" (*shimin dōitsu*) and the "equality of the four classes" (*shimin byōdō*), the clergy were stripped of their exceptional status and ceased to be considered those who "had left home and abandoned secular life" (*shukke datsuzoku*). As a direct result of their incorporation into the

---

[2] Ketelaar (1990, 3–86) has described in detail the period of anti-Buddhist violence. Briefer studies of the suppression of Buddhism and early Meiji religious institutions are Grapard (1984, 240–65); Collcutt (1986, 143–67); Hardacre (1989b, 27–31, 42–59); Thelle (1987); and Davis (1989, 304–39). Two important translations from Japanese on the subject of Buddhism in the Meiji era are Kishimoto (1956) and Murakami (1980).

household registration (*koseki*) system, they were methodically exposed to the same legal treatment as any other Japanese subject.

Restructuring of Buddhist institutions and their relationship with the central government also had important implications for the clergy. In some instances, these changes circumscribed the range of responses open to the Buddhist clergy as they struggled to accommodate themselves to their new role in society. Buddhist adaptations to the new position of the clergy in society were complicated by government-mandated changes that solidified the hegemony of the head temples over the branch temples while allowing clerics new freedom to define their practice, thereby intensifying already existing differences within the Buddhist community. The intrasectarian wrangling that characterized Buddhism from early Meiji until the beginning of the Pacific War—for example, the attempt by some members of the Sōjiji sect of the Sōtō denomination to form an independent denomination, the secession of the Kōshōji sect from the Nishi-Honganji, the struggle between "pure" and "common" clerics in the Shingon denomination, and the ongoing debate in several denominations over clerical marriage—was greatly exacerbated by official policy that vacillated between intervention in and withdrawal from sectarian affairs. No description of post-Meiji changes in Japanese religious life or Buddhist thought can be complete without taking the institutional restructuring of Buddhism and the new position of the clergy in Japanese society into account; these changes may well have had a more profound impact on the Buddhist clergy than the actual violence inflicted on the Buddhist church by anti-Buddhist zealots.

THE JINSHIN KOSEKI SYSTEM

The restructuring of religious institutions and changes in clerical status are intimately connected with one of the most pivotal of all legal changes during the Meiji period, the establishment of the new household registry law. The Jinshin Koseki Law was completed in May 1871 and fully instituted by the summer of the Jinshin year, 1872, for which the law has been named. By adopting the new code, Meiji political leaders hoped to replace the older, primarily temple-based systems of household registration that had been developed during the Tokugawa era with a homogeneous national structure for determining the number of households, the size of the population, and other census information. The Jinshin Koseki Law was a central piece of Meiji social policy and was considered an essential mechanism for the maintenance of social control. As noted by Fukushima Masao and Toshitani Nobuyoshi, the purpose of the law was to accurately determine the number of households nationwide and to effectively regulate family morality.[3] Government leaders intended to use the new law to record information concerning an individual's genealogy, provide proof that a given individual was not a vagrant or criminal suspect, and keep a record of marriages, births, and posthumous names (*kaimyō*).[4] Formulated just prior to the abolition of the domain system and the establishment of a network of nationwide prefectures, from the very start the Jinshin Koseki Law was conceived of as embracing the whole state. As stated in a communication from the Grand Council of State to the Tokyo prefectural authorities, "household registration is the foundation of governance—among the various governments [in the world], none have not originated with this."[5] Fukushima Masao has emphasized that government leaders considered the reformation of the household registration system "preparation for the establishment of centralized authority" and saw the institution of the new procedures as an indispensable first step toward the enactment of a number of crucial programs.[6] Meiji leaders were convinced that the creation of a powerful army and modern industrial development depended on having a precise assessment of the nation's population and tax base.[7] So central was proper registration to the maintenance of domestic peace and the extension of benefits to all subjects that the architects of the system believed those who managed to slip through the net of state registration verged on not being legitimate subjects.[8]

From the perspective of those who designed the new law, the old Edo system, or, more accurately, patchwork of systems, contained too much variation in the way the individual domains had chosen to register individuals, and too many social groups were excluded to allow for the efficient tracking of people. During the chaos of the Restoration, large movements of people to urban areas and civil unrest caused by demobilized troops spurred the leaders of the Restoration to create more effective means of maintaining order. Control and pacification of the vagrant population, particularly in large cities and other strategic places, was a primary goal of the new registration system.[9] In addition, the creation of an efficient, draft-based modern army like that of the Western powers required an accurate record of the location of all eligible subjects. Such pressures impelled the Meiji leaders to establish a new registration system as soon as possible. The household registration system maintained its pivotal role in

---

[3] Fukushima (1959a, 1:Kaidai, 49).   [4] Ishii (1981, 291).

[5] Ibid., 21.   [6] Fukushima (1967, 21).

[7] Ibid., 20–21.

[8] Fukushima (1959a, 1:Sect. 2, 32–33).

[9] According to Dani V. Botsman (1992, 18–23), the problem of vagrancy and homelessness had reached crisis proportions by the second half of the Tokugawa period. Authorities resorted to detention, relocation, and the creation of work colonies for the homeless to ameliorate the problem.

government policy for most of Meiji and served as a means for spreading the reach of the new regime throughout Japan. The diffusion of the new system was laden with meaning, symbolizing the pacification of the nation and the transition from the old order to the new.[10]

The new household registration law departed from the Edo system in several crucial respects. First, the Jinshin Koseki Law ended the use of separate registries based on social class. The authors of the law claimed that the Edo system had failed because the classes were treated separately, people were not registered according to their residence, and thus there was no means to obtain information about those who had been overlooked by the system.[11] To correct that defect, the law said that all subjects were henceforth to be registered at their place of residence. The term used for subjects, *shinmin ippan*, was the legal parlance for the people of Japan (*kokumin*) and was explicitly defined in an interlinear note included in the law as "peers (*kazoku*), samurai (*shizoku*), soldiers (*sotsu*), shrine officials, Buddhist clerics, and commoners."[12] The new law actually helped create a sense of being a Japanese subject by universally including in the registration system all residents of the realm.

The principal of universal registration had major implications for Buddhism. The clergy were, for the first time, defined as *kokumin* alongside all other social groups. In this respect, the Jinshin Koseki Law marks a qualitative departure not only from the Edo religious inquiry census registers (*shūmon aratame ninbetsu chō*), but also from the Kyoto prefectural registration system that had served as the prototype for the Jinshin code. Under the Kyoto system, which many prefectures had adopted shortly after the Restoration, the clergy, while included in the general household registration system for the first time, had been registered separately from commoners and other classes.[13]

The second important difference between the Jinshin Koseki Law and the Edo registers is that the new household registration system was to be administered directly by central government officials. This innovation also had substantial implications for the Buddhist clergy. One of their primary responsibilities during the Edo period had been their involvement in the temple registration system. They had worked closely with the Tokugawa bakufu, helping the shogunate extirpate Christianity by ensuring that all families were registered as parishioners of a Buddhist temple.[14] With the

[10] Fukushima (1967, 23).

[11] Fukushima (1967, 21). The complete text is found in Fukushima (1959a, 1: Sect. 2, 33).

[12] Toshitani (1959, 341).

[13] Fukushima (1967, 77–78). Ketelaar (1990, 70) briefly mentions the incorporation of the clergy into the *koseki*.

[14] For more on the Edo registration system, see Tamamuro (1986, 80–90); Ōishi (1959, 1–92); and Ishii (1981, 135–286).

institution of the new registration bureaucracy, the Buddhist clergy were replaced in this role by a hierarchy of central government officials that devolved from the pinnacle of bureaucratic authority in the Grand Council of State, through the Ministry of Finance, to the regional governments, to the ward registrar (*kochō*), each of whom had jurisdiction over wards (*ku*) comprised of approximately one thousand households, and, finally, to the family head (*koshu*).[15]

A third distinctive feature of the Jinshin Koseki system was the close linkage among the formation of State Shintō, the establishment of an official shrine hierarchy, and the registration system. This involved the prioritization of shrine membership over temple membership and marked a shift from Buddhism to Shintō as the central religious component of the registration system. As noted earlier, the main feature of the *shūmon aratame chō* was the requirement that every household be attached to a particular temple parish as proof that no Christians lived in the household. As the Meiji government attempted to deal with the continued presence of Christians in Urakami, pro-Shintō, Nativist factions led by Fukuba Bisei pushed for the institution of mandatory shrine registration in place of obligatory temple-parish membership. Subsequently, a provisional law requiring shrine registration in the Kyūshū region was adopted in 1869. A similar requirement was later incorporated into the Jinshin Koseki Law. Article 20 of the law stipulated that every six years, at the time of renewal of the household registration, officials were to certify that each subject possessed a protective amulet (*mamorifuda*) from their tutelary shrine.[16] In effect, as part of the ongoing effort to stifle the spread of Christianity in Japan, a system of guaranteeing temple membership was replaced by a system of ensuring each individual was a shrine parishioner through a process known as shrine parishioner inquiry (*ujiko aratame*). This system, which required ascertaining that each subject possessed a talisman from their tutelary shrine by checking every sixth year, proved exceedingly difficult to institute, and its emphasis on individual shrine membership ran counter to the household-centered nature of much early Meiji family law. As a result, although Meiji authorities continued requiring until 1884 that the name of the local shrine be recorded in each person's

---

[15] Fukushima (1967, 171–72; 176–79; 191–93).

[16] Fukushima (1959a, 1: Sect. 2, 36). The law detailing procedures for *ujiko shirabe* are found in the District Shrine Law (*Gōsha teisoku*), which became effective in the late summer of 1871. See ibid., 56–57 for the additional laws covering the *ujiko shirabe* system. Shrine registration is briefly described in Hardacre (1989b, 83–84). According to Takagi (1959, 336), although a *gōsha* was established in each district, there was no explicit requirement that the talisman specifically come from the district shrine. In fact, the regulation stated that even though a district shrine had been designated, the *ujiko* affiliation of parishioners would remain the same, that is, they would not become *ujiko* of the district shrine.

household registry, the state soon abandoned practice of shrine parishioner inquiry.[17]

As in the *shūmon aratame* system, the suppression of Christianity had been one motivation for the establishment of the new household registration code. Despite the connection between State Shintō and the early Meiji household registration system, the religious character of the new registration organization was minimal. Takagi Hiroo has observed that control of the Jinshin system remained in the hands of bureaucrats, not the clergy: the authors of the Jinshin Koseki Law took careful steps to ensure that the ward registrar rather than shrine officials maintained control of registration and shrine membership. To this end, the law required that a certificate from the ward registrar be presented to the shrine priest before the legally required talisman could be given to an immigrant to the shrine parish or a newborn. Without authorization from the local authorities one could not become a shrine parishioner. Thus, the central government even mediated the relationship between shrine officials and parishioners.[18] Furthermore, the architects of the new registration code were far less exclusive in their commitment to and reliance on Shintō than the Edo officials had been with regard to Buddhism. Pragmatic in their willingness to use whatever means of control were available to them, the authors of the Jinshin household registration law continued to demand a Buddhist institutional affiliation for every household while adding a Shintō registration requirement. The Edo practice of recording the parish temple for each household continued along with shrine registration until the dissolution of the Doctrinal Instructor (Kyōdōshoku) system in 1884.[19]

JINSHIN KOSEKI LAW AND CLERICAL STATUS

The changes in the laws governing household registration had major implications for the Japanese clergy and were a crucial component in the construction of the Doctrinal Instructor system. Haga Shōji, summarizing the implications of the Jinshin law for the Buddhist clergy, notes that the new household registration laws were fundamental to the construction of a modern state. At the same time, the principles underlying the registration system were applied to control of the clergy, resulting in the elimination of the old system of religious status (*shūkyō mibun*) and its supplantation by the new Doctrinal Instructor system.[20] Because of the importance the establishment of the household registration system held for the clergy, I

[17] Takagi (1959, 329–35).
[18] Ibid., 330–31, 336–37 .
[19] Fukushima (1959a, 1: Sect. 2, 42). See also Takeda Chōshū (1976, 158–63).
[20] Haga (1985, 114).

shall begin by sketching the broad contours of what was truly social engineering undertaken by the Meiji government and discussing the implications of those changes for the Buddhist clergy.[21]

For the Buddhist clergy, the end to their control of the *shūmon aratame chō* and their exclusion from ordinary registration procedures signaled the loss of many of the perquisites they had enjoyed from the start of the Edo period until early Meiji. During the first decade of the Meiji period the government systematically abolished most of the privileges that Tokugawa law had granted to the Buddhist and Shintō clergy and removed many of the state regulations that had been used to bolster clerical discipline. The removal of the Buddhist clergy from their important role within the temple registration system and the elimination of their special status under the law reflect the atmosphere of official disdain or even outright hostility toward the clergy and, perhaps more importantly, the growing effort by the Meiji founders to differentiate religious from state institutions. The Buddhists were not the only group to lose their perquisites under the Meiji regime; the Shintō clergy and even the samurai, despite some stubborn resistance, were merged into the household registration system and stripped of many privileges as well. Such changes are indicative of an overall strategy aimed at constructing a Japanese citizenry relatively undivided by status distinctions and directly controlled by the central government. As David Howell recently noted, in the course of this large-

---

[21] Several pioneering secondary sources in Japanese on the effects of the establishment of the Jinshin Koseki Law on the Buddhist clergy have been published. The earliest Japanese study of this problem is found in Date (1930, 147–52). See also Takeda Chōshū (1976, 151–70). The most detailed research concerning clerical status is by Morioka Kiyomi. See Morioka (1984; 1986; 1995).

In addition to the aforementioned secondary works, in both this and subsequent chapters I have made extensive use of memorials to the government (*kenpaku*) and the *Shaji torishirabe ruisan* (A Compendium of investigations into shrine and temple affairs; hereafter, STR). This work, which, as the name would imply, is broadly concerned with religious matters, is a compendium of early Meiji documents consisting of private inquiries from the clergy and local officials to government ministries, interministry correspondence, and ministerial responses to those inquiries. It provides the signed drafts, ministry responses, and local petitions to the government concerning religious matters, making it an invaluable primary source for the study of early Meiji Buddhism and Shintō. See Shūkyōshi Kenkyūkai (1964, 1–3). Professor Morioka Kiyomi pioneered the use of the *Shaji torishirabe ruisan* in the study of Meiji religion and cited in his articles many of the documents that I use. I thank him for suggesting that I examine this collection thoroughly. Lack of pagination in the original documents prevents more precise citations. Reference numbers for the STR are based on volume numbers provided in Shūkyōshi Kenkyūkai 1964.

There appears to be a good deal of overlap between the contents of the *Kōbunroku*, a similar collection found in the Kokuritsu Komonjokan, and the STR. Many of the documents concerning the abolition of special *koseki* regulations for the clergy discussed below, for example, are also found in the *Kōbunroku*. Sakamoto Koremaru and Haga Shōji have used the *Kōbunroku* extensively in their research on Meiji religion.

scale transformation from Edo to Meiji "the intermediate autonomies—of village community, of status group, of alien ethnicity—that had ordered relations between the early modern state and individual Japanese disappeared, replaced by a single geography that directly tied subjects to the state without the encumbrance of mediating groups and identities."[22]

Although the most violent suppression of Buddhism occurred prior to 1872, at first the central government did little to change the legal status of the clergy, and many of the Edo period restrictions governing clerical deportment remained in effect. According to the Shinritsu Kōryō, the new criminal code established in early 1871, clerics guilty of stealing, gambling, or fornication were to be punished by whipping and forced laicization. At least one Buddhist leader, Shaku Unshō (1827–1909), who saw such penalties as an aid to his attempt to revive strict precept practice, welcomed the harsh penalties for clerical offenses.[23]

The first glimmering of change in the Meiji government's policy concerning the status of the clergy may be found in some of the prefectural household registration laws that served as the partial basis for the construction of the new nationwide registration code. The most influential of those prefectural systems was instituted by Kyoto officials who, following the lead of the Chōshū domain, replaced the old temple-based registers with a system administered by the prefectural authorities.[24] The establishment of a standardized system provided a useful model for the new Meiji regime, and the reforms undertaken in Kyoto were soon instituted in all areas directly administered by the central authorities, including Tokyo Prefecture. The Kyoto household registration law went into effect on Meiji 1/10/28 (December 11, 1868) and was gradually amended during the following months to create separate household registers for Buddhist (*jiseki*) and Shintō clergy (*shaseki*), as well as for nobles, samurai, and other classes that had been placed in separate registers in the original code.

The Kyoto registration system, in forcing all subjects, including the clergy, to register with the prefectural census authorities, was a major departure from the Edo registration system. As the Kyoto registration code was adopted by other regional governments and the central government, the partial incorporation of the clergy into the household registration system spread to other parts of Japan. The new law, although revolutionary in its inclusion of all subjects in separate registries, remained heavily indebted to the Edo system in its treatment of the clergy. For one thing, the Kyoto government continued to place households in registries accord-

[22] Howell (1995, 23).

[23] Shaku Unshō approvingly mentions the special penal code for clerics in a petition protesting the decriminalization of clerical marriage. See Shaku Unshō, "Sōritsu no gi," in MKP 2:945–46. Information concerning the Shinritsu Kōryō is found in KDJ, 7:951 and Kumagai (1987, 77–78).

[24] Fukushima (1967, 20–21).

ing to class and to afford each group different legal privileges based on class. The notion of unifying all subjects under a universal system, a distinguishing mark of the Jinshin Koseki Law, is not found in the Kyoto registration code. Furthermore, the Kyoto registration law neither required clerics to take a family name nor attempted to register clerical families, which were still illegal for all denominations apart from the Jōdo Shinshū. Finally, and this was the most significant feature of the Kyoto code as far as the clergy were concerned, the operative information for each cleric remained the place and date of ordination—preordination status, birthplace, and date were not recorded. Under the Kyoto registration system, the government continued to recognize that ordination was legally valid and that joining the Buddhist community had the power to change one's birth status and sever family ties.

The special registration procedures for the clergy were gradually abolished as the new registration system was constructed, in a piecemeal manner, from 1871–1876. From its inception, the Jinshin Koseki Law abandoned the *shūmon aratame chō* system and the traditional Edo class structure. The Edo system was replaced by six new classes: nobles (*kazoku*); samurai (*shizoku*); soldiers (*sotsuzoku*: lower-ranking samurai or retainers, who later were incorporated into either the *shizoku* or the commoner classes); *shikan* (Shintō priests, including *miko*); Buddhist clerics, including nuns (*sōryo*); and commoners (*heimin*). The architects of the new law again adhered to the earlier Kyoto and Edo models in their maintenance of the two distinct clerical classes. As in the Kyoto registration system, the permanent domicile (*honsekichi*) for each cleric was the place of ordination, not the actual birthplace. In addition, all residents of a single temple—abbot, attendants, and disciples—were regarded as part of a single household under the new law. Thus, at the earliest stage, the Jinshin registration code maintained state recognition of the legitimacy of ordination.[25]

THE CREATION OF THE DOCTRINAL INSTRUCTOR SYSTEM

Government policy regarding clerical status quickly changed over the next few years as the leaders of the Meiji regime responded to both internal and external pressures. Modifications to the Jinshin Koseki regulations concerning the clergy went hand in hand with the creation, maturation, and abolition of the Doctrinal Instructor system, which was established on Meiji 5/3/14 (April 21, 1872).[26] The close chronological correspon-

[25] Morioka (1984, 376).

[26] For a detailed account of the rise and fall of the Doctrinal Instructor system, see Ketelaar (1990, 87–135) and Hardacre (1989b, 42–59).

dence between the institution of the Jinshin Koseki Law and the formation of the Doctrinal Instructor system was no mere coincidence. Indeed, the various changes in registration procedures for the clergy were an integral part of the creation of the Doctrinal Instructor system.

The Doctrinal Instructor system was a Meiji government response to a variety of concerns. Sakamoto Koremaru has pointed out that the dilemma facing the Meiji leadership in the early 1870s was to stem the spread of Christianity internally while convincing the Western Powers that some degree of domestic religious freedom for all Japanese, including Christians, had been granted.[27] Following the Restoration, Meiji leaders had continued the Tokugawa ban on Christianity, fearing its foreign, liberalizing influence. However, throughout the early years of the Meiji period, Japanese government officials came under increasing pressure from the European and American powers to liberalize their policy toward Christianity as a precondition for the renegotiation of the unequal treaties that had been concluded between Japan and the Western Powers at the end of the Bakumatsu era. Forced by outside pressure to decriminalize and, eventually, legalize Christianity, government leaders strove to develop a policy of religious and political indoctrination that would bolster support for the emperor, and hence the new government, and check the Christian threat.

One important element of the Meiji leadership's response to these concerns was the development of a corps of national teachers who would reliably inculcate the people of Japan with respect for the nation and the imperial family. In an effort to realize this goal, during the first several years after the Restoration, Meiji leaders had tried to employ a corps of Proselytizers (Senkyōshi) drawn exclusively from the ranks of Nativist scholars and Shintō clerics and administered by the Department of Rites and, later, the Ministry of Rites. However, unaccustomed to preaching, riven by sectarian differences, and inefficacious as propagandists for the new regime, the Proselytizers soon fell out of favor with other government officials.[28]

To invigorate the dissemination of national teachings, the Meiji leadership broadened the scope of potential teachers to include the Buddhist clergy. This would enable the state to capitalize on the talents of the Buddhist clergy, who, due to their greater experience in teaching and proselytizing, would perhaps make better evangelists than the shrine priests. The leaders also began to experiment with the creation of a new ministry that would oversee the corps of instructors and manage both shrine and temple affairs. A Sain proposal for the creation of a new ministry, the Ministry of Temples (Jiinshō), and the incorporation of the Buddhist clergy into state

---

[27] Sakamoto (1983, 50–51).

[28] For more on the Proselytizers, see Ketelaar (1990, 96–99) and Hardacre (1989b, 29–30, 44).

efforts to promulgate a National Teaching (Kokkyō) argued that combining the Proselytizers with the Buddhist clergy and ordering both groups to instill the people with state teachings would help ward off the malificent influence of Christianity and the spread of "republican government" (*kyōwa seiji*).[29]

Thus government officials—despite differences between the pro-Shintō, vehemently anti-Christian faction of Etō Shinpei and Kuroda Kiyotsuna and the more moderate group represented by Shimaji Mokurai (1838–1911), Inoue Kaoru (1835–1915), and Mori Arinori (1847–1889), all of whom viewed the decriminalization of Christianity as inevitable—were able to agree upon a more embracing policy toward the Buddhist clergy. To manage the Buddhist clergy as national teachers, officials created the Ministry of Doctrine (Kyōbushō) in 1872 and, using the web of shrines and Buddhist temples, established a series of Great, Middle, and Small Teaching Academies (Dai/Chū/Shō Kyōin) where the National Teaching would be taught to the doctrinal instructors and promulgated to the public. Those clerics who through examination qualified as doctrinal instructors were to disseminate to the people the Three Standards of Instruction (Sanjō no Kyōsoku):

1. Comply with the commands to revere the kami and love the nation.
2. Illuminate the principle of heaven and the way of man.
3. Serve the emperor and faithfully maintain the will of the court.[30]

The start of the Doctrinal Instructor system marked the beginning of the gradual separation of National Teaching and rite (*saishi*), which could be used in state functions, from religious doctrine (*kyōhō*), which was gradually being defined as a private, religious concern. According to Sakamoto, "Shintō (*Shinkyō*), Confucianism, and Buddhism were all religious doctrines, but Amaterasu Ōmikami and the Three Sacred Objects (*sanshu no jingi*) were the necessary basis for clarifying the relationship between the sovereign and the people and for supporting the Great Way of loyalty and filial piety (*chūkō no daidō*)."[31] Those elements of Shintō that were seen as essential for the justification of imperial rule were held to transcend mere doctrine. Underlying the creation of the Ministry of Doctrine from its inception was the germ of what would mature into the government's separation of Sect Shintō, Buddhism, Christianity, and the

---

[29] The passage cited is from a Meiji 4/10/4 (November 16, 1871) proposal by the Sain for the establishment of a Ministry of Temples. The original is found in the *Kōbunroku* and is quoted in Sakamoto (1983, 50–51).

[30] Ketelaar (1990, 106).

[31] Sakamoto (1983, 52). The Three Sacred Objects, which symbolize the imperial throne, are the sword (Ame no Murakumo no Tsurugi), the jewels or *magatama* (Yasakani no Magatama), and the mirror (Yata no Kagami).

New Religions from State Shintō, with State Shintō teachings and, particularly, rites being defined as "areligious" (hishūkyō). With the institution of the new system, Meiji officials attempted to create a state clergy that drew from but superseded all other clerical groups and an official state doctrine that transcended all sectarian teachings. As I will show below, in creating the new system, the ministers transferred many of the privileges previously given to the Buddhist clergy—the right to teach publicly, to conduct funerals, to become an abbot—to those whom the state recognized as doctrinal instructors.

Given the importance the kami and the imperial household held for the members of the Sain and the government leadership in general, it is not surprising that despite the acceptance of Buddhism into the campaign to disseminate the National Teaching, Buddhism and Confucianism remained in a secondary position in relationship to Shintō. As Ketelaar has explained, the Buddhist clergy officially participated in the campaign as doctrinal instructors, not as Buddhist clerics per se. On occasion this entailed shedding the most important symbols of Buddhist monasticism and the donning of Shintō robes.[32] Some prominent Buddhist leaders, including Ōtori Sessō and Hanazono Sesshin (1808–77), as well as government officials and Shintō clerics accepted the subordination of Buddhism to Shintō. Ōtori, a leading Buddhist member of the Ministry of Doctrine, exhorted his fellow Buddhists to "explain to every household and teach every person the goal of a rich [nation] and powerful [military] (fukyō), and fully instruct them to take refuge in the Way of the Kami (Shintō)."[33] For many other Buddhist leaders, most significantly Shimaji Mokurai, however, the structure of this new Shintō-centered National Teaching quickly came to be seen as an infringement of the rights of the Buddhist clergy to practice and teach their religion. These tensions played a significant role in the dissolution of the ministry in 1877.[34]

THE DISSOLUTION OF CLERICAL PRIVILEGES

As part of the attempt to create a corps of doctrinal instructors, who were in effect unpaid government officials, bureaucrats at various government offices, including the Ministry of Finance, the Ministry of Doctrine, and the Sain, systematically dismantled whatever vestiges of clerical exceptionalism remained in civil and criminal law. By the mid-1880s decisions concerning religious matters had been drastically privatized and made

[32] Ketelaar (1990, 122–23).

[33] The memorial is contained in Fujii (1934, 7:445). It has also been anthologized in Yasumaru and Miyachi (1988, 30).

[34] Ketelaar (1990, 122–30).

voluntary: they were to be worked out and enforced by sect authorities and members rather than the government. The government retreated from involvement in what it now defined as purely sectarian concerns.[35]

As indicated earlier in this chapter, prior to the Meiji period Buddhist ordination had been a rite of passage that allowed the ordinee to actually change his or her status. Following ordination, the cleric was distinguished from ordinary subjects by differences in name, dress, diet, census registration, and deportment. These differences were instantiated not only in sect regulations, but also in secular law. Following the institution of the new household registration system and the inception of the Doctrinal Instructor system, the distinctions became increasingly problematic for the government and were seen as hindrances to the uniform enforcement of the various registration requirements, the gathering of exact census data, the draft, and the mobilization of the Buddhist clergy as doctrinal instructors. Many of the clerical distinctions supported by state law were also seen as outmoded customs that prevented the full modernization of Japan and the building of a strong nation.

Although the reincorporation of the Buddhist clergy into the *koseki* may be understood as part of the government's anti-Buddhist program, the Buddhists were not the only group to lose their legal perquisites during early Meiji, a period of enormous social reordering. The changes in status forced upon the clergy were part of a concerted effort by the central government to abolish the Edo period status system, rationalize the tax system, and professionalize the military. The changes affecting the clergy are best understood when seen alongside a number of other laws dissolving similar restrictions governing other groups, for example, the laws allowing commoners to use surnames in public (1870) and samurai voluntarily to cut off their top knots, wear ordinary clothing, and go without swords (1871); the abolition of the *hinin* and *eta* classes (1871); and the ban on the wearing of swords by samurai in public (1876).[36]

Under the banner of equality of all subjects (*shinmin dōitsu*), the samurai classes and the Shintō clerics underwent changes in status as significant as those endured by the Buddhists. Despite the relative ascendancy of the pro-Shintō and Nativist factions immediately following the Restoration, the Jinshin Koseki Law and the various addenda to that act steadily eroded the legal position of the Shintō clerics. Such Meiji officials as Konakamura Kiyonori argued that the Buddhist clergy be afforded the same treatment as the Shintō clergy, who since July 1871 had been forced to register as *shizoku* in the general household registration system. Likewise, despite resistance from members of the *shizoku* class, Meiji leaders ended the separate registries for the samurai and nobles, and in 1876, after much

[35] For an excellent, detailed description of these changes, see Haga (1985, 114–38).
[36] Takeda Chōshū (1976, 158–63).

struggle, promulgated the *taitō kinrei*, which forbade all but the military, police, and government officers to bear swords. This measure proved almost as unpopular among *shizoku* as the decriminalization of clerical marriage was among Buddhists. The similarities between government measures concerning the clergy and those dealing with the nobles and samurai are indicative of the more general trend away from Edo period status distinctions and toward the professionalization of a number of different spheres of social life—religion, the military, and government.

Some of the first steps in the process of clerical disestablishment subsequent to the institution of the new household registration law involved the dissolution of those laws and customs that had differentiated the clergy from ordinary subjects. One of the earliest measures, the *nikujiki saitai* law, promulgated on Meiji 5/4/25 (May 31, 1872), lifted restrictions against clerical marriage, meat eating, and the wearing of nonclerical garb by the Buddhist clergy. The straightforward edict from the Grand Council of State read, "From now on Buddhist clerics shall be free to eat meat, marry, grow their hair, and so on. Furthermore, they are permitted to wear ordinary clothing when not engaged in religious activities."[37]

自今僧侶肉食妻帯蓄髪等可為勝手事但法用ノ外ハ人民一般の服ヲ着用不苦候事

(*Ima yori sōryo nikujiki saitai chikuhatsu nado katte tarubeki koto. Tadashi hōyō no hoka wa jinmin ippan no fuku o chakuyō kurishikarazaru sōrō koto.*)

In several respects, the adoption of this regulation by the Grand Council of State accompanied a shift in the nascent government's religious policy. For one thing, as Ketelaar has noted, this new law, "in spite of its seemingly innocuous phraseology, in fact disguises a radical change in the conception of the relation between public, Imperial law (*Ōbō*) and the Buddha's law (*Buppō*) as contained within the priests' religious vows." As such it marks the end to state enforcement of religious law and signals the increasing privatization of religious concerns.[38] The close linkage of several crucial elements of state policy—the Jinshin Koseki Law, the registration of Buddhist clerics, and the decriminalization of clerical marriage—is readily visible in the Grand Council of State's Edict 26, issued on January 22, 1873, which extended the *nikujiki saitai* law to Buddhist nuns. "From now on nuns may freely grow their hair, eat meat, marry, and return to lay life. Furthermore, those who return to lay life should notify the ward registrar after reentering a household registry."[39] Ishikawa Rikizan has suggested that giving equal treatment to nuns with regard to the decrimi-

---

[37] NSRK, 621.
[38] Ketelaar (1990, 5–6).
[39] NSRK, 636.

nalization of clerical marriage was part of the government effort to extend the Jinshin Koseki Law into every nook of Japanese society.[40]

The debate over clerical marriage and, on a smaller scale, the matters of meat eating, clerical dress, and tonsure that arose following the promulgation of this law caused deeper divisions within the Buddhist community than any other issue. Unlike the Buddhist reaction to new legislation concerning other aspects of clerical life, the struggle over clerical marriage has continued in fits and starts until today. Because this particular law was so strongly contested by the clergy and had enormous impact on the development of Buddhist doctrine and practice in the early modern period, I shall examine its adoption and the subsequent debate surrounding it in detail in the next several chapters. Let me merely note here that the decriminalization of clerical marriage was part of a general trend in state policy to dismantle the special legal supports for sect regulations and replace them with laws governing all subjects. Several months later, in July, the Grand Council of State ordered all Buddhist clerics to follow the same mourning procedures as ordinary subjects, thereby ending yet one more outward sign of clerical status.[41]

THE PROBLEM OF CLERICAL NAMES

Another stumbling block to efficient registration of the Buddhist clergy was the clergy's customary abandonment of surname (*myōji*) and birth status following ordination. Upon joining the clergy, each ordinee received a new Buddhist name (*kaimyō* or *hōmyō*) and gave up his or her secular name.[42] Ordinees who had been a noble or samurai abandoned the use of a surname after ordination.[43] As part of the state's effort to end status

[40] Ishikawa (n.d., Sōtōshū ni okeru, 3–4).

[41] KDJ, 12:284–85. The mourning system established in 1684 by the famous Bukkiryō had set up separate prescribed periods of mourning and mourning dress for commoners and *bushi*. If one's mother or father died, for example, one was to wear mourning attire for thirteen months; the death of one's wife required one to wear mourning clothes for ninety days. The regulations remained in force, with numerous minor emendations, until 1874, when the Grand Council of State abolished the separate mourning regulations for nobles and forced all subjects to abide by the customs for commoners set forth in the Edo period Bukkiryō.

[42] See, for example, IBJ, 107; 730. The name received after ordination and receiving the precepts (*jukai*) is called either the *kaimyō* or the *hōmyō*. In the Jōdo Shin sect, where the precepts are not conferred, the new name is called the *hōmyō*. The word *kaimyō* also refers to the name conferred on those who have died without having received one during their lifetime. The posthumous name is known as the *gyakushu hōmyō*. See also MBD, 5:4643–44.

[43] During the Edo period, only nobles and samurai officially had been permitted to use surnames. See Toyoda (1971, 135–54); Morioka (1986, 130–32). According to Asao Naohiro (1992, 11), some commoners, particularly the wealthy, did have surnames, but they were not allowed to use them for official business. See Asao (1992, 11).

distinctions and in preparation for the institution of the Jinshin Koseki system, the Grand Council of State in the autumn of 1870 issued a proclamation that ended the ban on the use of surnames by all nonsamurai.[44] The Buddhist clergy were free to ignore that rule, but in the spring of 1872 the Ministry of Doctrine required members of the sacerdotal lineages (*hōshuke*) of the Jōdo Shinshū head temples, that is, the abbots of the Nishi and Higashi Honganji, Bukkōji, Senjuji, Kōshōji, and Kinshokuji (Nishigori-dera), to join the *kazoku* class and to adopt surnames. The Ministry of Doctrine further stipulated that "the temple name [*jigō*] should be used in sectarian affairs, the surname should be used in private affairs."[45] Thus, for example, Morioka points out that the abbot of the Higashi Honganji, who had formerly used only the name Higashi Honganji Kōshō, was henceforth to use that name only in religious affairs; at all other times he was required to use the secular name Ōtani Kōshō.[46] Whereas prior to the Meiji period the entire identity of the sacerdotal family had been tied to the temple—in effect the temple was the analogue for the secular family—now there was a separation between the sacerdotal family and the temple as an institution. Writing about the implications of these new regulations for the Jōdo Shinshū in 1900, Inoue Hōchū of the Higashi Honganji lamented, "Following the Restoration, the family register (*zokuseki*) for the Buddhist clergy was established. The one body of the Higashi Honganji was divided in two, becoming the Honganji and the Ōtani family. Thus, the character of the temple was drastically altered."[47] The surname law for the Shin sacerdotal families represents an attempt by Meiji leaders to distinguish the head temples as religious institutions from the inhabitants of the temple, that is, the various heads of the Shin sects and their families. This trend continued in the increasing distinction that was drawn within the various Shin sects between the residence of the abbot of the head temple and the temple proper and between objects belonging to the head temple and the personal possessions of the abbot and his family.[48]

On Meiji 5/9/14 (October 16, 1872), the Grand Council of State broadened the requirement for clerical surnames, issuing Proclamation 265, which mandated that all Buddhist clerics adopt a surname and register it with the government by the end of the year.[49] The new law, which some Buddhists felt undermined the unity of the sangha, was controversial and met by a variety of reactions from the Buddhist community, ranging from acceptance to some creative attempts to minimize its impact.

At least one member of the Buddhist clergy supported the surname requirement and urged his compatriots to accept the regulation. Provisional

---

[44] Iinuma (1988, 20).   [45] Morioka (1978, 578).   [46] Ibid., 578.
[47] Cited in ibid., 578.   [48] Ibid., 579.
[49] NSRK, 622; Miyachi (1988, 449). See also Morioka (1995, 9); "Sōryo myōji shintei no ikken" (1913, 56–57).

Minor Instructor (*Gon Shōkyōsei*) Ugai Tetsujō (1814–91), an important member of the Jōdo sect and a fervent anti-Christian, wrote a brief treatise entitled *Shamon seishi ben* the same month the new law was promulgated.[50] After briefly—and selectively—tracing the frequent use of surnames, court ranks, and other appellations by the Buddhist clergy in China and Japan, Ugai argued that the Japanese are far superior to those in other countries in their reverence for the deceased and for lineage. Claiming that family lineage (*shizoku keitō*) is fundamentally important for human morality, Ugai concluded that if our ancestry "becomes confused, the difference between noble and base is lost and the ancestral hierarchy is altered. How, then, will we be different from the beasts?" At the end of his proposal, Ugai cited customary biographical style of the lives of eminent monks genre to argue against the abandonment of surnames. He exhorted his fellow Buddhists not to cling to the outmoded custom of not using a surname, while raising the customary inclusion of secular names at the beginning of each biography in the collections of traditional biographies as proof of past Buddhist reverence for family lineage and precedent for complying with the surname requirement.[51]

One proposal, written by an anonymous group of doctrinal instructors shortly after the enactment of the new law, urged the abbot of each sect's head temple to adopt the surname of the founder of that sect. All clerics residing at that temple were also to assume that name, so that they could constitute a unified household. The authors of the proposal suggested, for example, that clerics residing on Mt. Hie take the name Mitsu, Saichō's preordination surname, and that those at Mt. Koya take the name Saeki, after their founder, Kūkai. If one moved to another temple, one should change one's surname to that of the new temple's founder.[52]

Some members of the Buddhist clergy believed that the acceptance of a secular surname by the clergy would be harmful, for the practice would

---

[50] According to the law establishing the office of *kyōdōshoku*, there were fourteen grades of *kyōdōshoku*. The highest, Grade 1 (*ikkyū*), was *daikyōsei*, and the lowest, *gonkundō*. *Gon shōkyōsei* was Grade 6 (*rokukyū*). See Miyachi (1988, 447).

[51] "Sōryo myōji shintei no ikken" (1913, 56–57). Many contemporary clerics continue to emphasize the role of Buddhism in the preservation of family lineage. For example, in Reader (1991, 42): "The view that the ancestors are the transmitters of life and benefactors of the living is repeatedly emphasised in Buddhist writings. The Sōtō priest Sakai Daigaku talks of the blood of the present generation as being bestowed to it by the ancestors, while Kamata Shigeo states that Buddhism itself is a gift passed on through the generations by the ancestors."

[52] "Sōryo myōji shintei no ikken" (1913, 56–57). In STR, 155, "Anjōji Ryūtō kengonsho shintatsu tensho," Ryūtō introduces the same proposal for reference in his petition. Although the first proposal is not dated, Ryūtō's petition to the Kyōto prefectural government is dated Meiji 5/10 (November 1872), so the proposal must have been submitted sometime between the promulgation of the new law, Meiji 5/9/14, and the time Ryūtō wrote his petition. Ryūtō does not mention to which of the six grades of doctrinal instructors the authors of the document belonged. For a brief discussion of the petition, see Morioka (1995, 10–11).

reveal the cleric's preordination societal status to the entire community, and that would undermine the leveling effects of ordination. Shaku Ryūtō (d. 1891), a Shingon cleric from the temple Anjōji, argued in his petition to the governor of Kyoto Prefecture, Nagatani Nobuatsu, that the proposals proffered by Ugai and the group of doctrinal instructors undermined the significance of entering the Buddhist clergy. In his attempt to defend the abandonment of surnames by Buddhist clerics, Ryūtō ignored the long-standing practice of family inheritance of certain temple ranks and property that I have noted in the previous chapters. Instead, he highlighted the supposedly separate, world-renouncing nature of clerical life. Ryūtō stressed that although surnames served to tie together generations and to distinguish an individual's origins, upon entering the Buddhist community the ordinee leaves behind his family, abandoning all connection with the management of the family's wealth and lineage. "The true spirit of the Śākya family is to abandon secular name, office, and home and take the tonsure, don a cleric's robes, and, with a heart that is lighter than a drifting cloud, to be like flowing water." Ryūtō wrote that as a disciple of the Buddha (*Busshi*, literally, a child of the Buddha), the cleric should honor the lineage of his teacher without regard to the nobility or humbleness of his own secular family. The transmission of the precepts from teacher to disciple forms the basis for dharma lineage. Ryūtō suggested that to best preserve the unique harmony of the sangha, all clerics should take as their surname the name Shaku, Japanese for Śākya, the tribe of Gautama Buddha. In the period of enlightenment (*bunmei*), Ryūtō concluded, "we must understand the differences between the laity and the clergy and should clarify their paths. Therefore, those who take the name Shaku (Śākya) must not be ashamed to transmit the true meaning of the Shaku family and to be called a descendant of the Buddhas and the Patriarchs." Ryūtō observed that the word for the Buddhist community, *sōgyaya* (usually the transliteration of *saṅgha* is written *sōgya*), means "those who have gathered together" (*wagōshū*), because immediately after ordination, all people, whether kings, ministers, or members of any status, are equally subject to the Buddhist precepts.[53]

[53] "Anjōji Ryūtō kengonsho shintatsu tensho." Ryūtō became a *gon shōkyōsei* Doctrinal Instructor in 1876. According to Zürcher (1972, 1:281; 2:343, n. 213), the practice of adopting the religious name Shi began with Daoan (312–85). Prior to Daoan's time, Chinese monks adopted the surname of their master—if the teacher was not Chinese this meant they went by their teacher's ethnic appellation, for example, Dharmarakṣa (Ch., Fahu, c. 266–308) took the name Zhu ("the Indian," J., Jiku), the ethnic designation for his teacher, as his religious surname. Other clerics of his day continued to use their secular surname even after ordination. The same historical information about Buddhist names is given in the "Shamon seishi ben" by the Jōdo sect cleric Ugai Tetsujō. See "Sōryo myōji shintei no ikken," 56–57. According to Mochizuki (1957, 3:2145–46; 4:3842) and Zürcher (1972, 1:281), Daoan's practice became widespread after it was apparently confirmed by a passage in the *Zoichi agongyō* (*Ekkottarāgama*) that stated all who became monks took the name Shaku.

Ugai's argument for the acceptance of surnames by the Buddhist clergy made no sense, according to Ryūtō, because the clergy have absolutely no connection with secular lineage. "You should know that disciples of the Buddha (*Shakashi*) maintain the continuity of the dharma lineage by means of the wisdom of the *dharmakāya* (*hosshin no emyō*). This requires only that the genealogy of the precept transmission (*kaimyaku*) be ascertained."[54]

Ryūtō also criticized—for logical reasons and because it compromised the otherworldly nature of the Buddhist community—the suggestion contained in the doctrinal instructors' proposal that clerics take the surname of the temple founder. He argued that if clerics were to change names as they move from temple to temple, it would totally violate the purpose of the surname, which is to maintain continuity across the generations. Buddhist clerics, unlike all other subjects, have left their parents and have no imperative to ensure the unbroken succession of their descendants. The plan offered by the doctrinal instructors also would pose a problem for clerics who resided at temples that have been founded by parishioners. If they were to take the founder's name, in this case a layperson's, as their own, Ryūtō argued, they would be liable to mistake the temple for their own property and temple property as their private means. Ryūtō was not unique in his concerns about the disposition of temple property; as Buddhist clerics married, took surnames, and were forced to return their names to the secular household registration system, clerics and government officials were forced to clarify whether the state, the parishioners, the head temples, or the abbots and their families owned the temples and their contents.

Much to the chagrin of some at the Ministry of Doctrine, a number of clerics apparently came to the same conclusion as Ryūtō and took such Buddhist names as Shaku and Jiku as a form of resistance to the new requirement. Some other prominent clerics used a strategy similar to Shaku Ryūtō's to select their surnames: Shaku Unshō, Shaku Sōen (1859–1919), Shaku Shugu (1866–1920), and Shaku Kōnen (1849–1924), to name a few. A directory of doctrinal instructors ranked Grade 6 or higher lists three more clerics taking the surname Shaku.[55] Adopting a slightly different strategy, the famous precept advocate Fukuda Gyōkai (1809–88) reputedly made the Buddhist term *fukuden*, "field of merit" (Sk., *puṇya kṣetra*), the basis for his surname.[56] In an ill-fated attempt to prohibit such blatant attempts to undermine the surname requirement, officers at the ministry proclaimed on April 9, 1873, that a surname should be based on an

---

[54] "Anjōji Ryūtō kengonsho shintatsu tensho."

[55] Sakamoto (1987, 373).

[56] Masutani (1942, 125). Masutani also briefly discusses the government edict that ordered clerics to take surnames, pointing out that this measure amounted to an end to government recognition for ordination.

individual's family origins, and, therefore, those who had taken the names Shaku, Jiku, or Futo (the Japanese transliteration of Buddha) should immediately change them. Either because of continued opposition from the clergy or perhaps reflecting just how divided the Ministry of Doctrine was, or both, the new prohibition was repealed just five days later.[57] Officials at the Grand Council of State did continue to demand that if Buddhist clerics who had taken any of the above names reregistered with their family, they would have to have the same name as the househead.[58]

CHANGES IN CLERICAL REGISTRATION
AND THE ASSAULT ON THE ORDINATION SYSTEM

By the end of 1872 the legal position of the clergy had been severely eroded. The government had ended the ban on clerical marriage, meat eating, and the wearing of civilian clothing, and the Buddhist clergy also had been forced to assume secular names and follow ordinary mourning customs. Over the next year, the government extended the decriminalization of *nikujiki saitai* to nuns, abolished all criminal statutes concerning clerical fornication, and eliminated court ranks (*ikai*) for all Buddhist clerics.[59] The diminished status of the Buddhist clergy spawned confusion, as different ministries wrestled with the problem of applying the new regulations to affairs within their jurisdiction.

Beginning in the autumn of 1872, as part of its effort to create a corps of nonsectarian government doctrinal instructors drawn from the ranks of the Shintō and Buddhist clergy, as well as from a variety of popular entertainers, officials at the Ministry of Doctrine began to investigate procedures that would "abolish separate registries for the Buddhist clergy and register the clerics with all other subjects (*shimin*)."[60] Vice Minister (Shō) Kuroda Kiyotsuna (1830–1917) and Undersecretary (Tayū) Shishido Tamaki (1829–1901) of the Ministry of Doctrine proposed to the Seiin in January 1873 that the Buddhist clergy be given the same treatment as the Shintō clergy, who since 1870 had been forced to register in the regular household registration system as samurai. The two officials pointed out the inconsistency in the treatment of Shintō and Buddhist clerics and offered

---

[57] See Ministry of Doctrine edicts 16 and 18 in NSRK, 649. Although the law specifically mentions the name Futo, I know of no clerics who adopted that surname.

[58] Ibid., 677.

[59] Miyachi (1988, 452). Grand Council of State Edict 23, issued on January 19, ended clerical court ranks. The law concerning nuns, Grand Council of State Edict 26, the law concerning nuns, was issued on January 22, 1873. See also Morioka (1984, 380) for information about the end of criminal statutes for clerical fornication.

[60] Haga (1984, 121). The passage quoted in Haga comes from the *Dajōruiten*, vol. 2, fascicle 270, and is dated Meiji 5/8.

the concrete suggestion that separate registries for the Buddhist clergy, the *sōseki*, be abandoned.[61] In a draft edict appended to their letter, they recommended that all Buddhist clerics be returned to the general registration system as either samurai or commoners, depending upon their preordination status.[62]

The Buddhist leadership did not ignore these government moves to revamp the registration code for the Buddhist clergy. The possibility of such radical changes in registration procedure posed a grave threat to the clerical leadership, and they made various attempts to sway officials from enacting such measures. In late autumn 1872, while various proposals to end the separate registration procedures were under discussion by officials at the ministries of Finance, Doctrine, and Justice, a group of leading Buddhist clerics lobbied at the Ministry of Doctrine against the abolition of the old registration system and submitted a petition signed by the chief priests (*kanchō*) of all the Buddhist denominations.[63] The petition shows that the new registration procedures were problematic for the Buddhist clergy in several respects. For one thing, the petitioners feared that Buddhist clerics and laity alike would construe the dissolution of separate clerical registration procedures as the forced laicization of the entire clergy. In addition, with the clergy at a particular temple no longer registering as one group, cohesion at the temple would disappear and the resident clerics, lacking any legal connection to the temple, would fight over the disposition of temple property. Like Ryūtō, who worried that the adoption of surnames by the clergy would lead to theft of temple property, the authors of the petition expressed the fear that the new procedures would sever the close ties within the "temple family," that is, between a teacher and his disciples. The authors also expressed concerns that some clergy, abandoning their calling, would mistakenly treat temple possessions (*jūmotsu*) as their private property.[64] To prevent these types of problems at the temples, which after all were teaching academies and therefore central to the government's proselytization efforts, the authors suggested that the officials at the Ministry of Doctrine inform the appropriate authorities that the Buddhist clerics should determine their permanent domicile based upon their current temple. The petitioners also suggested that a cleric who moved should be allowed to transfer registration.

---

[61] According to Sakamoto (1983, 47–68), Shishido, who replaced Fukuba Bisei as minister, was a member of the more moderate Chōshū wing of the Ministry of Doctrine. Kuroda belonged to the strongly pro-Shintō Satsuma faction.

[62] "Sōryo henseki ken Seiin gian." Morioka (1995, 14). The most recent, detailed discussion of the changes in the registration system is found in Morioka (1995, 113–20).

[63] Hanazono (1974–83, 11:222).

[64] *Jūmotsu* refers to items in a Buddhist temple that are used for practice—in other words, things that belong to the temple rather than to individual clerics living at the temple. This includes items ranging from brooms and dishes to works of art, sculpture, and other valuable

Over the course of the next year, a consensus favoring Kuroda and Shishido's proposal was built within the government. In May 1873 the Nativist scholar Konakamura Kiyonori (1821–95), who was then serving in the Ministry of Doctrine, elaborated on the ministry's position concerning clerical status in a response to a letter of inquiry from the Ministry of Justice primarily concerned with various aspects of the legal disposition of temple property. Konakamura noted that temple abbots were in charge of temple affairs and so more closely resembled the shrine priests than lay households. Despite the fact that the Shintō clergy were government officials and the Buddhist clergy were not, the Buddhist clergy were allowed to use their ordination location as their permanent domicile while the Shintō clergy were required to use their birthplace for that purpose. Konakamura argued that because both groups were acting as doctrinal instructors and were involved with the management of shrine or temple affairs, they were in essence serving in the same capacity and should be treated equally. With regard to household registration, Konakamura contended that, unlike in the past, becoming a "home leaver" (*shukke*) had lost much of its meaning because now the clergy could grow their hair, marry, and serve as doctrinal instructors. There was no longer any reason for allowing them to claim their place of ordination as their permanent domicile. Rather, like all other subjects, the Buddhist clergy should be registered based on their birthplace and the status of their birth family.[65]

Officials at the Ministry of Justice and the Ministry of Doctrine were not the only ones to perceive a contradiction between the new civil code and the vestiges of clerical exceptionalism with regard to registration procedures. Some of the staunchest advocates for controlling clerical registration and, if at all possible, reducing the number of subjects entering the Buddhist clergy were to be found at the Ministry of Finance.[66] Undersecretary of Finance Inoue Kaoru and Secretary of Finance (Ōkurakyō) Ōkubo Toshimichi viewed the continued existence of large numbers of Buddhist clerics as detrimental to the economic well-being of Japan and attempted to use the registration system to curb the growth of the Buddhist clergy. In their 1871 inquiry directed to the Seiin, Ōkubo and Inoue argued that Japan could not support the large number—according to their rough

---

property. See IBJ, 400, and MBD, 3:2393. Judging from the mid-seventeenth-century entries in the MBD, the improper sale of temple artwork for an individual cleric's private purposes was a problem prior to the Meiji period. In the previous chapter I showed that Chikū also complained about the trade in temple properties.

[65] "Shihōshō yori sōryo no gi ni tsuki kakariai."

[66] Established in 1869, the Ministry of Finance was expanded in 1871 and gained responsibility for those areas of government formerly handled by the Ministry of Civil Affairs. In addition to overseeing such financial matters as taxation and coinage, the officials at Finance acquired broad jurisdiction over a number of domestic affairs, including management of the household registration system and the census.

estimate, 50,000—of Buddhist clerics because the clergy failed to perform any productive labor. The only solution to the problem was for the government to manage ordinations more carefully. The Seiin responded positively to the inquiry, and on Meiji 4/10/12 (November 24, 1871) the Grand Council of State issued an edict that required the careful examination of all ordination candidates by the regional authorities. Only upright individuals who planned to pursue a course of sectarian studies would be allowed to be ordained.[67]

Despite the effort to control ordination more tightly, the bureaucrats in charge of the household registration system continued to find the existence of separate registration procedures for the clergy to be a hindrance to total enforcement of the new registration code. Now that the government had eliminated most of the distinctions between the Buddhist clergy and the laity, officials at the Ministry of Finance argued that little reason existed to continue the ordination system at all. An inquiry into the matter of clerical registration submitted on September 9, 1873, by Councillor (Sangi) Ōkuma Shigenobu of the Treasury to Prime Minister (Dajōdaijin) Sanjō Sanetomi (1837–91) expressed this position in detail. In his recommendation, which the prime minister forwarded to Shishido and Kuroda at the Ministry of Doctrine for their opinion, Ōkuma expressed his concern about the confusion caused by the continuation of special registration procedures for the clergy. Echoing the point made by Konakamura, Ōkuma wrote that the Buddhist clergy had ceased to differ from the rest of the populace in any significant way. In sum, because the clergy used a surname, married, and ate meat, they were no different from ordinary subjects. But, because of the continued existence of a registry for the clergy, the *sōryo koseki*, they were sometimes entered into the registration system twice, causing unnecessary confusion for those in charge of the system. Ōkuma therefore suggested that "to continue to use the term *shukke tokudo* is meaningless." He went on to advocate the abolition of the clerical ordination system and the inclusion of the clergy in the general household registration system.[68] Bureaucrats at the Ministry of Doctrine and the prime minister agreed with Ōkuma, and new household registration regulations for the clergy were enacted early the next year, on January 20, 1874.[69]

Judging from the tone of Ōkuma's inquiry, it is obvious that those at the Ministry of Finance viewed the new regulation as the legal laicization

[67] The inquiry, *Shimin shukke no gi ni tsuki ukagau*, is cited in Sakamoto (1987, 13–14). The Grand Council of State edict is found in Miyachi (1988, 443).

[68] "Sōryo henseki no gi ni tsuki." The STR copy is the most complete, but the same passage is also cited in Morioka (1986, 133; 1995, 14–15). A slightly different version of the same document is found in Fukushima (1967, 111, note 6).

[69] Miyachi (1988, 460). The clerical registration law also is found in Fukushima (1959a, 1:Part 2, 52–53). The draft version of the law is found in "Shihōshō yori sōryo no gi ni tsuki kakariai."

of the entire Buddhist community. The new requirements marked a departure from the Jinshin Koseki Law in several crucial respects. First, the amendment to the registration law abolished separate registration for the Buddhist clergy. All clerics were to register as one of the three classes of subject; those who were currently in the clerical registry were to return their name to the secular household registry and assume whatever social status—noble, samurai, or commoner—to which that entitled them. Religious affairs could be conducted as before, but the conduct of temple affairs would now be regarded as no different from any other occupation. The Buddhist leaders' petition protesting the new household registration laws, mentioned above, did not go entirely unheeded by the officials in charge of drawing up the regulations. Provisions were made so that clerics who did not wish to reregister with their family would be able to do so. Finally, temple abbots would be treated as samurai, even if they were registered as commoners.

On July 10, 1874, the Grand Council of State further clarified the registration procedures: those who returned to their family registry would assume the status of their family. Those whose former status was unclear or who did not wish to register at their original domicile could choose a new permanent domicile, but regardless of their former status, they would be registered as commoners. Buddhist clerics were given three choices for registration: they could return to their preordination domicile; start a new, permanent domicile at their current location; or, after starting the new permanent domicile, they could apply to transfer to a third location. In addition, as Konakamura had previously recommended, apart from those members of the Jōdo Shin denomination who previously had been registered as nobles, all members of sects that allowed familial inheritance of temples (seshū)—that is, Jōdo Shin and some Shugendō clerics—would be registered as commoners.[70]

After the sudden institution of the registration requirement, clerical procrastination, evasion, and overall confusion were widespread. In 1875 the Home Ministry complained of disorder resulting from clerics choosing to make their permanent domicile locations other than the one at which they were currently residing.[71] In addition, the slow pace with which the Buddhist clergy registered hints at just how difficult it was for the new government to achieve anything approaching uniform enforcement of the measure, particularly outside the metropolitan centers. As long as four years after the passage of the new requirements, some prefectural governments were complaining about the lack of uniform registration by the Buddhist clergy. The authorities in Ehime Prefecture, for example, who

[70] Fukushima (1959a, 1:Part 2, 53); Miyachi (1988, 462–3). Although Shugandō was abolished in 1872, its clerics were absorbed into the Tendai and Shingon denominations.
[71] Fukushima (1959a, 1:Part 2, 53–54).

had first issued an edict calling for compliance with the new household registration code in April 1874, were still admonishing the Buddhist clergy in 1878 that they must register by August 15 of that year.[72] The central government, while able to issue laws and regulations at will, proved far less effective in enforcing them at this early date.

The new household registration requirements for the Buddhist clergy were tantamount to the end of all official recognition for the ordination ceremony. Over the next few years, entrance into the Doctrinal Instructor system replaced sectarian ordination as the route for becoming a state-sanctioned Buddhist cleric. Although the draft version of the law contained in the response from the Seiin to the Ministry of Finance had pointedly stated that "from now on the system of ordination is abolished (*shukke tokudo no sei o haishi*) and all Buddhist clerics must register as one of the three classes of subject," this passage was dropped from the registration regulations promulgated in January and July 1874.[73] Just four days after the edict was issued, the officials at the Ministry of Doctrine sent an inquiry to the Grand Council of State: "[T]he new edict states that they [the Buddhist clergy] should reenter the secular registry and that the management of religious affairs should be regarded as an ordinary occupation. Should we not consider the clerical registry to have been abolished and that which is known as ordination (*tokudo*) to be nonexistent?"[74]

The bureaucrats at the Grand Council of State answered affirmatively on February 14. The new law concerning clerical registration in effect ended any change in legal status for those who were ordained. In an effort to distinguish between the abolition of official recognition for ordination and the proscription of that system, the statement issued by the Grand Council of State stipulated that "the ceremony known as ordination that is conducted for private religious purposes is not specifically prohibited."[75] That is, ordination was henceforth to be regarded as a matter involving only the ordinand and his or her denomination. Although ordination was no longer under government jurisdiction, individuals were still free to take monastic vows. The denominational ordination ceremony, however, would no longer confer any legal benefits on the ordinee. Most strikingly, during the brief period from 1876 to 1879, Buddhist ordination per se no longer even entitled the ordinee to be called a monk or nun (*sōni*) or to change his or her name.[76]

The abolition of ordination as an officially recognized ceremony enabled the Ministry of Doctrine and, following the abolition of that ministry in 1877, the Home Ministry to assume almost complete jurisdiction over the

---

[72] Ibid., 396.   [73] "Sōryo henseki no gi ni tsuki."

[74] The letter of inquiry is contained in NSRK, 677. See also Date (1930, 149) and Morioka (1986, 135–36).

[75] Date (1930, 149).   [76] Miyachi (1988, 471).

admission of individuals to the Buddhist clergy. The approval process for
doctrinal instructors was closely intertwined with the newly minted policy
concerning clerical registration and ordination and was one of the nodes
whereby registration policy, the Doctrinal Instructor system, and sectarian
practice intersected. While such ministries as Justice, Finance, and Doctrine had ceased to recognize the official validity of ordination, Ministry
of Doctrine bureaucrats remained in charge of approving all doctrinal
instructors and thus had the power to define who was an official member
of the Buddhist clergy. Officials from the Grand Council of State declared
on December 16, 1876, that only those who were candidates for doctrinal
instructor or higher would be publicly recognized as a Buddhist monk or
nun.[77] A complementary regulation held that only those who were at least
doctrinal instructor candidates (kyōdōshoku shiho) could become an
abbot.[78] As a result of these two measures, anyone publicly recognized as
a Buddhist cleric or abbot was ipso facto at least a candidate for doctrinal
instructor. Many Buddhist clerics, for example, an abbot's disciples, often
were not doctrinal instructors, however. Therefore, ordained disciples
living at a particular temple and studying with a master were not, in the
government's eyes, officially monks or nuns. The government thereby
further vitiated the ordination ceremony: official recognition hinged on
the rank of the cleric in the state hierarchy, not the taking of vows under
the aegis of a master.[79] Just as importantly, these measures also enabled the
government to assert full control over who became the abbot of a temple.

The abolition of official recognition for the ordination system and
increased government jurisdiction over the abbatial appointments by
means of the Doctrinal Instructor system obviated the need for direct control of ordination. Because ordinees who were not doctrinal instructors
were not considered monks or nuns, there was no longer any need to
examine directly potential entrants into the Buddhist order. Rather, by
examining candidates for doctrinal instructor on matters of National
Teaching, for example, the Three Standards of Instruction cited earlier,
bureaucrats could control those who were officially considered monks or
nuns. The five-year period following the establishment of the Ministry of
Doctrine saw a steady dilution of laws that demanded formal requests
from all desiring to enter the Buddhist clergy. Between 1872 and 1874
government authorities moved from requiring all potential ordinands to
undergo state examination to abolishing all state examinations and licenses

[77] Ibid., 471.

[78] Date (1930, 151–52). The rank of *shiho* was established on Meiji 5/8/20 (September
22, 1872) was established for every class of doctrinal instructor from Grade 7 to Grade 14.
On December 28, 1873, separate classes of *shiho* were abolished, and all were to simply be
referred to as *kyōdōshoku shiho*. The chief priest of each denomination appointed the *shiho*
for that denomination. See Nitta (1987, 153–54). See also Sakamoto (1987, 62–63).

[79] Morioka (1984, 381).

for ordinands.[80] The separation of ordination as a private matter, which did not require state oversight, from entrance into the corps of doctrinal instructors, which necessitated state oversight, therefore reinforced the separation of sectarian concerns from state teaching.

Official recognition of one's status as a member of the Buddhist clergy was not a trivial matter. Following the promulgation of the edicts concerning ordination, local officials further questioned the legal status of those Buddhist clerics who were not doctrinal instructors and attempted to circumscribe greatly their claim to any privileges specifically reserved for those officially considered Buddhist clergy. According to an 1874 emendation to the Conscription Law of 1873 (Chōheirei), only those who were candidates for doctrinal instructor or higher would be entitled to draft deferments. Other ordinees, like any other subject, would be eligible for military service. On April 28, 1874, the government further restricted the rights of the Buddhist clergy, prohibiting preaching by anyone who was not at least a candidate for doctrinal instructor. When local officials from Wakayama in 1877 inquired whether unrecognized clerics legally could change their names after the ordination ceremony (since 1872 name changes for commoners were forbidden, with notable exceptions including the Buddhist clergy), officials at the Home Ministry responded that such persons could not because they were not actually clerics. Niigata prefectural officials in October 1878 asked whether those who, even if ordained, were not at least apprentice doctrinal instructors should be allowed to lecture, wear clerical garb, or conduct funerals and other clerical business. In response, officials at the Home Ministry specified that although in accordance with earlier laws, only doctrinal instructors could conduct sermons and funerals, other clerical business could be performed by those not considered full-fledged Buddhist clerics.[81] Similarly, in August 1881, when the complete ban on collecting alms (takuhatsu) by the Buddhist clergy was partially lifted and alms gathering before noon was permitted, only those ranked as candidates for doctrinal instructor or higher were allowed to participate.[82]

Meiji census figures give us a sense of the numbers involved in these changes in status (see fig. 1). The Nihon zenkoku kosekihyō provides information concerning the number of clerics between the years 1872 and 1876, and the Meiji Taishō kokusei sōran contains partial data on the clergy from 1877 through the Taishō period. After the period of anti-Buddhist violence, the number of monks, nuns, and their disciples declined from 122,882 in 1872 to 97,980 in 1875. The number dropped precipitously to 36,194 in 1876, however, following the redefinition of male and female Buddhist clerics as only those who were doctrinal instructors or

---

[80] Miyachi (1988, 439; 461; 467); Morioka (1984, 379); Morioka (1986, 136).
[81] NSRK, 711–12.   [82] MNJ, 2:398.

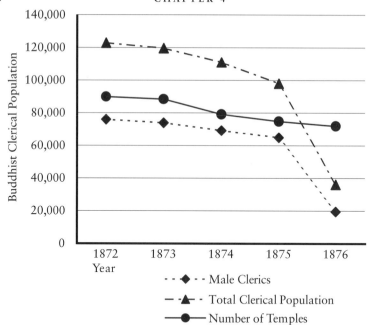

Figure 1. Buddhist Clerical Population and Number of Temples, 1872–76.

candidates for doctrinal instructor. By contrast, between 1875 and 1876 the number of temples declined from 74,784 to 71,962, a loss of only 2,822 temples, far too few to account for the massive change in the number of monks and nuns.[83] Thus the redefinition rendered 61,786 (63 percent) of those who had formerly officially been considered Buddhist clerics ordinary students who were subject to the draft and unable to conduct sermons or funerals. The Ministry of Finance had accomplished its goal, which was severely to curtail the number of clerics. When partial statistics—the number of abbots (*jūshoku*)—become available again for 1882, the number has risen from 19,490 in 1876 to 56,945, close to the 64,881 in 1875, when abbots were described merely as *sō*.

The legal redefinition of who was a monk and the importance of becoming a doctrinal instructor sometimes led to comical inversions of status for the Buddhist clergy. One such case involved the Rinzai cleric Tairyū Bun'i (1827–880) and his student at the monastery Shōgenji, Seishū Shusetsu (1849–1921). In 1872 Tairyū and Seishū traveled to Tokyo to

[83] Statistics for Meiji 5–9 (1972–76) are from NJTS, vol. 1. (There is no pagination for the censuses.) The Meiji 5–9 censuses provide statistics for monks (*sō*), nuns, their disciples, and family members. Statistics for Meiji 15 (1882) are from *Meiji Taishō kokusei sōran*, 681, which lists only the number of abbots (*jūshoku*). Similarities in the numbers lead me to conclude that by *sō* the Meiji census takers meant abbots. See also Collcutt (1986, 163).

undergo the doctrinal instructor examination concerning the Three Standards of Instruction established by the Ministry of Doctrine. Unlike Seishū, who was well-educated and acquainted with issues of government policy, Tairyū seemed unable (or unwilling) to memorize the fine points of the National Teaching requisite for the examination. When the two were examined in Tokyo, Tairyū continually responded to questions about the Three Standards, "I don't know." He would have failed the examination entirely, writes Katō, but for the intervention of Ogino Dokuon, who at the time was the head of the Great Teaching Academy. When the teacher and student returned to Shōgenji, the master had been given the rank of assistant reader (*gonkundō*, one of the very lowest), while his student was a senior lecturer (*daikōgi*). Upon arriving at his quarters, the dispirited Tairyū supposedly remarked, "Aaah, if Dokuon and Tekisui don't shape up soon, Buddhism is finished."[84]

THE END OF THE DOCTRINAL INSTRUCTOR SYSTEM

Intersectarian disputes, the gradual diminution of concern on the part of government leaders about the spread of Christianity, and the emergence of a consensus within the government to grant Japanese subjects a limited degree of religious freedom in the Meiji Constitution, which was promulgated in 1889, comprised the primary reasons underlying the dismemberment of the Ministry of Doctrine in 1877 and the dissolution of the Doctrinal Instructor system in 1884. The attempt by the Ministry of Doctrine to use religious leaders of all persuasions to disseminate the pan-sectarian National Teaching had evinced signs of fracturing from the ministry's very inception. The pro-Shintō faction led by Etō Shinpei had quickly dominated the new ministry and had promoted a series of policies that restricted the freedom of the Buddhist clergy to teach anything but national dogma. As the inferior role of the Buddhists within the ministry became clear, some Buddhist members of the promulgation campaign had begun to agitate for withdrawal of their school's participation. Given Jōdo Shinshū's traditionally strong opposition to the worship of kami, it is not surprising that the Nishi-Honganji monk Shimaji Mokurai led the move to secede. Deeply influenced by his tour of the United States and Europe, Shimaji began criticizing the Doctrinal Instructor system as early as 1872, commenting that the proper separation of public instruction and private religious teaching was being abrogated. By 1875 most of the Shinshū had withdrawn from the Great Teaching Academy, and the academy itself was closed later that year.[85]

---

[84] Katō (1998, 157–58).
[85] For more on the closure of the Daikyōin, see Ketelaar (1990, 60–67).

Sectarian squabbling, which began almost from the founding of the Ministry of Doctrine, also helped persuade the Meiji leadership to withdraw from direct involvement in sectarian doctrinal concerns. The Pantheon Dispute (*Saijin ronsō*) between the Ise and Izumo factions of Shintō and the intrasectarian struggle between the Kōshōji sect and its head temple, the Nishi-Honganji, proved to be intractable.[86] Although the Ministry of Doctrine lasted until 1877, following the abolition of the Great Teaching Academy, officials from the Home Ministry increasingly tried to distance Shintō religious functions and clergy from state ceremonies. In the process, state support of all shrines at the prefectural level or below was prohibited, and Shintō clerics were forbidden to receive joint appointments as local government officials. Subsequent to the temporary resolution of the Pantheon Dispute in 1881, a distinction was drawn between those who would oversee state rites and those who were purely religious doctrinal instructors from various Shintō sects. The latter would be treated the same as the Buddhist clergy, that is, as purely religious clergy (*tanjun no shūkyōsha*).[87]

Preparations for the adoption of a constitution forced government leaders to clarify the extent to which the government would remain involved in sectarian matters and how much religious freedom would be granted to the individual religious denominations.[88] After much discussion, including a suggestion from Inoue Kowashi (1843–95) that the central government continue to grant ordination certificates (*dochō*) to the Buddhist clergy, the staff of the Home Ministry determined that the nation was ill-served by continued direct government intervention in sectarian matters.[89] In July 1884 a Home Ministry inquiry to the Grand Council of State asking for permission to dissolve the Doctrinal Instructor system argued that "although we have experienced many problems as a result of state intervention in religion, we have not yet seen any benefits." On August 11, 1884, the Grand Council of State abolished the system. The responsibilities of the doctrinal instructors devolved to the indivdual denominations, under the watchful eyes of the chief priests.[90]

The constellation of edicts surrounding the abolition of the Doctrinal Instructor system forms another juncture at which may be glimpsed the

[86] For more on the Pantheon Dispute, see Hardacre (1989b, 48–51); KDJ, 6:171; Nakajima (1972, 26–67). The dispute over the enshrinement of Ōkuninushi no Mikoto in the Office of Shintō Affairs was between the Izumo and Ise factions. On Kōshōji, see Kashiwahara (1990, 47–49).

[87] Sakamoto (1983, 66).

[88] Hardacre (1989b, 114–32); Abe Yoshiya (1969, 57–97); Nitta (1987, 147–98); Thelle (1987, 115–17).

[89] Nitta (1987, 155). A letter of opinion written by Inoue on March 17, 1884, and addressed to Minister of the Interior Yamagata Aritomo contains this suggestion. See Yasumaru and Miyachi (1988, 68–70).

[90] Takagi (1959, 7: 23).

complex intermingling of several different issues confronting the Meiji leadership. Once again, regulations governing clerical status, registration law, and the status of Christianity in Japan shifted in concert. As the drafters of the constitution agreed in 1884 upon the limited guarantees for religious freedom that were eventually incorporated into Article 28 of the Meiji Constitution, measures originally undertaken to prevent the spread of Christianity became superfluous. In the same year officials abolished the Doctrinal Instructor system, ended the requirement that shrine and temple affiliations be recorded in the household registries, and lifted the ban on independent funerals (*jisō*).

Direct control of the Buddhist clergy was also relaxed. Following the abolition of the office of doctrinal instructor, officials of the Home Ministry continued to exercise indirect control over the Buddhist denominations and Shintō sects by shifting responsiblity for administration of the clergy from government ministries to the new Chief Priest system. On June 5, 1872, just days after the inception of the Ministry of Doctrine, government officials established the Chief Priest system. The new system was built upon the head-branch temple organization that had been used for most of the Edo period to give ministry officers a conduit for controlling the clergy of the various denominations. The Chief Priest system replaced the administrative temple (*furegashira*) system, which had been in effect for most of the Edo and early Meiji periods. In the late summer of 1871, following the dissolution of the feudal domains and the creation of the prefectures (*haihan chiken*), the government had abolished the administrative temple system. The responsibilities formerly handled by the administrative temples, including, for example, the transmission of government regulations to branch temples and the forwarding of requests from temples to the appropriate ministry, were transferred to the ward registrars (*kochō*).

The Buddhist chief priests were chosen by members of each school from among the abbots of the head temples, a method that made continuity with the older *honmatsu* system possible and thereby minimized resistance from the Buddhist leadership. The chief priest was to be responsible for rectifying the regulations of the denomination and reforming clerical behavior. The Ministry of Doctrine on Meiji 5/10/3 (November 3, 1872) consolidated the various sects and announced that one chief priest would be chosen from among the top two highest ranks of doctrinal instructors for the following seven main denominations: Tendai, Shingon, Jōdo, Zen, Jōdo Shin, Nichiren, and Ji. Of course this left many sects without a chief priest and forced very different sects (*ha*) within each denomination—for example, the five sects of the Shin denomination—and separate denominations together under the jurisdiction of one chief priest. For instance, Ōbaku, Rinzai, and Sōtō Zen denominations were unified under the leadership of one chief priest. In addition, a number of smaller Buddhist schools, for example, Kegon and Hossō, as well as the smaller sects with independent head temples, were forced to merge into the seven recognized schools.[91] This proved untenable, however, and in March 1884 each sect was allowed to elect a chief priest if it chose to do so.[92] By the end of 1884 the Home Ministry had recognized nine chief priests for Shintō and thirty-five for Buddhism.[93]

As the government loosened its grip on religious affairs in the latter half of the 1870s, much of the responsibility held by officials at the Ministry of Doctrine and the Home Ministry devolved to the chief priests. To ensure continued discipline among the clergy and obedience to the chief priest, Home Ministry officials redefined their stance toward non-doctrinal instructor ordinees, ordering them in 1879 to abide by the doctrine of their denomination for the rest of their lives.[94] Ordinees who were not candidates for doctrinal instructor were also once again allowed to deliver sermons.

With the final abolition of the Doctrinal Instructor system, Home Ministry officials planned to oversee the internal affairs of the religious organizations by retaining the power of approval over sectarian institutional structure (*shūsei*) and by treating the chief priest of each sect in the same manner as officials appointed by the emperor (*chokuninkan*).[95] According to the law abolishing the Doctrinal Instructor system,

> From now on, the office of Buddhist and Shintō doctrinal instructor is abolished. All appointment of abbots and advancement of teachers shall be entrusted to the chief priests. Furthermore, we resolve the following articles:
>
> 1. There must be no irresponsible advocacy of either secession or amalgamation among the various sects. There also must not be any intersectarian feuding.
>
> 2. Each sect of Shintō and each Buddhist denomination should elect a chief priest. If a group of Shintō sects wish to choose jointly a chief priest, or if various sects of the Buddhist denominations wish to have their own chief priest, that will be permissible.
>
> 3. The chief priest should establish the regulations in accordance with the institutional structure and regulations (*kyōki*) of their denomination, be it Shintō or Buddhist, and must obtain the approval of the secretary of the interior (*naimukyō*).[96]

---

[91] Kashiwahara (1990, 51); NSRK, 634.

[92] NSRK, 675.

[93] Nitta (1987, 195, n. 47). NSSS, *kindai*, 132–40, has a detailed chart showing the evolution of the various denominations and sects during the early modern period. See also Kashiwahara (1990, 51); NSRK 627, 634; and Ikeda (1998, 13–18).

[94] Haga (1985, 130–31).

[95] NSSS, *kindai*, 157.

[96] Miyachi (1988, 481–82). The draft is cited in Nitta (1987, 171–72).

The edict went on to specify that the chief priest of each Buddhist sect would be responsible for institutional structure, temple regulations (*jihō*), the status and titles of teachers and clergy, the appointment of abbots and the advancement of teachers, and the preservation of archives and valuable artwork contained within the sect's temples. With the promulgation of the edict that established the office of chief priest, for the first time in almost three hundred years the Buddhist clergy were freed from almost all direct state intervention in internal sectarian affairs.

The new system did not totally staunch the ongoing diminution of clerical perquisites. Laws passed in July and August 1884 clarified that all those clerics who had served as doctrinal instructors would continue to be treated with the same status they had held as doctrinal instructor. At the same time, government officials at several ministries continued to erode any exemptions that the clergy had held ex officio as doctrinal instructors. Most significantly, in 1884 the Buddhist clergy who had been doctrinal instructors lost their exemption from the draft, and in 1889 all clerics, including Shintō, were forbidden from holding either national or regional elected office.[97]

CONCLUSIONS

Between the Meiji Restoration in 1868 and the promulgation of the imperial constitution in 1889, the leaders of the Meiji state embarked on an ambitious but far from unified program of modernization. Pressed by the Western Powers to end the prohibition of Christianity, Meiji officials sought an ideological and ritual framework for the construction of a modern nation-state. Along the way, they experimented with a variety of relationships between the state and what came to be defined during that same period as religious institutions—shrines, temples, churches, and religious communities. One result of this reorganization was the partial disestablishment of those organizations that the leadership defined as "religions" (*shūkyō*). At the same time these religious organizations, including the Christian churches, were freed from most state intervention, and subjects were allowed to choose among such competing religious communities as the various denominations of Buddhism, Sect Shintō, the new religious organizations, and Christian denominations.

No doubt there is much that is familiar in the attempt to free government from sectarian squabbling, while confining religion to the private realm. As José Casanova has observed, this process is fundamental to the emergence of modern society. "To say that in the modern world 'religion becomes

[97] Nitta (1987, 176); NSSS, *kindai*, 164.

private' refers also to the very process of institutional differentiation which is constitutive of modernity, namely, to the modern historical process whereby the secular spheres emanicipated themselves from ecclesiastical control as well as from religious norms. Religion was progressively forced to withdraw from the modern secular state and the modern capitalist economy and to find refuge in the newly found private sphere."[98] As a result of this process of differentiation, ordination, the precepts, and doctrinal problems were forced into the "private" realm.

Casanova has pointed out that this bipolar public-private distinction can be misleading because the modern social order actually consists of three realms: governmental, personal or private, and a public, nongovernmental arena intermediate between the first two that is variously labeled "civil society" or the "social."[99] Strictly speaking, the "privatization of religion" in Meiji Japan refers to the process by which the state ended its intervention in certain aspects of religious life, for example, setting standards for one who would undertake the ordination ceremony or determining what precepts they would follow. Although ordination became private in the sense that the state ended official recognition for the ceremony, the ceremony remained public in that it continued to be mediated by religious denominations that gave it legitimacy. As we will see in later chapters, much of the struggle over *nikujiki saitai* centers on whether the state (government officials), the denomination (clerical leaders) and parishioners, or the individual (the ordinand) would set the standards for clerical behavior.

To muddy the waters even further, we must also remember that in Japan prior to the end of the Pacific War the disestablishment of these religious communities was never complete. Leaders of the Meiji regime kept a hand in religious affairs, albeit indirectly, by insisting that all denominational regulations be approved by the appropriate authorities and that clerical members of the denominations abide by the orders of sectarian leaders. According to the new Chief Priest system instituted in 1884, the leader of each religious community was an imperial appointee. The recognition given to the Buddhist denominations in the form of the awarding of posthumous imperial titles, Great Teacher names (*daishigō*) and National Teacher names (*kokushigō*), also continued to tie most established Buddhist denominations directly to the court. Throughout the Meiji and Taishō periods, the court continued to issue these honorific titles for important founders of the various denominations. During the modern era, Great Teacher names were bestowed upon Dōgen, Nichiren, Hōnen, Shinran, Rennyo, Ippen, Kanzan Egen, Ingen, and others.[100] These imperially recog-

---

[98] Casanova (1994, 40).   [99] Ibid., 42.

[100] KDJ, 5:646–47; 8:751. About two-thirds of the *daishigō* listed in the *Kokushi daijiten* were issued after the start of the Edo period. About half were issued in the post-Edo period.

nized founders and teachers remained central to the sectarian identities of each of these groups, even as the denominations established their modern Kanchō-centered structure.[101]

The differentiation of secular and religious in Meiji Japan remained incomplete in another sense. In place of a state Buddhism or Shintō subject to absolutist control, the Meiji leadership attempted to separate imperial rituals derived from the myth-histories of Japan and shrine worship from the elements of Buddhism and Shintō they had deemed religious. They thus created State Shintō, which was viewed as an areligious part of civic life, but which effectively was a community cult coextensive with the Japanese state. Unlike the various religious communities in Japan, participation in which was now voluntary, adherence to the community cult of emperor-centered State Shintō was mandatory. Changes in the registration procedures for the Buddhist clergy showed that not even those who "left home" could opt out of this cult. While an individual was free to become a Christian, a Buddhist, a Shintoist, or even a member of a new religious association, the one thing that was absolutely forbidden was disrespect for the symbols of State Shintō or the emperor. Although the violation of religious precepts was no longer a crime, committing lèse majesté was another matter.

The changes in the Buddhist clergy's legal status and registration requirements, which occurred in tandem with the creation of State Shintō, had several important implications. According to Date Mitsuyoshi, the loss of special status was one of the most momentous recorded changes in the concept of the Buddhist clergy.[102] The changes in clerical status made it increasingly difficult for the clergy to argue that ordination meant "leaving home" or that as clerics they were free of responsibilities to their secular families and the state. After early Meiji, the Buddhist clergy, just like all other Japanese subjects, officially had a surname, belonged to a household, had an occupation, and bore such civic responsibilities as military service. The abolition of their special status also meant that those who violated the law would now be treated as commoners or, in the case of temple abbots, as samurai.[103]

The abolition of the separate registries for the clergy had other important repercussions. Takeda Chōshū has succinctly stated that this in effect meant that henceforth, "Whether one was ordained and became a Buddhist cleric or one left the clergy to return to lay life, escape from the household (*ko* = the *ie*) of the Household Registration Law was impossible." In effect, Takeda, concludes, "The fact that the Buddhist clergy, just like other lay

[101] Haga (1994, 241–42).

[102] Date (1930, 147; 149).

[103] NSRK, 694. Response of the Ministry of Justice to an inquiry from Mizusawa-ken officials. Mizusawa-ken was located in the area that now comprises Iwate and Miyagi prefectures.

people, had a family—concretely speaking, they possessed a household registry and a surname—meant that 'home leavers' (*shukke*) became 'those at home' (*zaike*). This surely was 'laicization' (*kizoku* = *genzoku*) although legally speaking, that which was called '*kizoku*' did not refer to this process."[104] Due to the growing equivalence between the household and the *ie,* the reincorporation of all Buddhist clerics into a household registry, and hence an *ie,* amounted to their legal laicization. This was especially true for those who, perhaps hoping to maintain noncommoner status, chose to return their name to their preordination family's register.

The decriminalization of *nikujiki saitai* was part of a complex of actions undertaken by the Meiji authorities in an effort to eliminate Edo period status distinctions and to facilitate the ability of the state to track all subjects through the household registration system. But government leaders were not the only ones who believed there were benefits to be reaped from allowing limited freedom of religious choice and decriminalizing those practices. Support for the new emperor-centered community cult of State Shintō, the disestablishment of religion, and the end to criminal penalties for precept violations also found support among some important members of the Buddhist denominations, Shintō clerics, and Nativist scholars. In the next chapter I will examine in detail their role in the decriminalization of *nikujiki saitai.*

---

[104] Takeda (1976, 169ff.). The term *kizoku* refers to the voluntary renunciation of one's clerical vows in order to return to lay life. *Genzoku*, on the other hand, indicates that one has been forcibly ejected from the clergy because of some transgression. See ZDJ, 201–2; OBD, 241.

CHAPTER 5

Passage of the *Nikujiki Saitai* Law: The Clergy and the Formation of Meiji Buddhist Policy

THE 1872 decriminalization of clerical meat eating, marriage, and several other associated practices was an integral part of the social reforms that ended most special legal treatment for the Buddhist clergy. As discussed in the previous chapter, the various measures enacted by the Meiji regime, although resisted by many members of the Buddhist clergy, did find some support even among Buddhist reformers. Ugai Tetsujō, for example, supported the requirement that the Buddhist clerics take surnames. Similarly, Shaku Unshō viewed the dissolution of the old religious inquiry census system as an opportunity for the clergy to return to their true calling, Buddhist practice and teaching, instead of becoming involved in government administration.

But the Buddhist clergy were even more involved in the creation of Meiji religious policy than is commonly assumed. State officials did not unilaterally draft religious policy and force compliance from the clergy. Rather, the creation of such measures resulted from a complex interaction among elements of the Buddhist clergy, Shintoists, and intellectuals with a variety of perspectives. In addition, modification of the stern anti-Buddhist edicts was not solely a result of outside pressure from such Buddhists as Shaku Ryūtō, Shaku Unshō, and, most importantly, Shimaji Mokurai; it was partially shaped from within the government by individuals sympathetic to Buddhism. Even at the peak of anti-Buddhist hostility, some leading Buddhist clerics remained both confidants and colleagues of many leading politicians. Buddhists like Shimaji and the little-known Ōtori Sessō, whom I will discuss in this chapter, had close ties with numerous influential members of the government. In addition, some officials, such as Shimada Mitsune (1827–1907), were devout lay Buddhists. It was thus forces inside the government as well as outside that helped temper anti-Buddhist hostility and develop a religious policy that recognized the importance of Buddhism for the construction of a new state teaching and the education of the masses.

This is not to say that the Buddhist leadership universally accepted the religious policies advocated by influential Buddhist clerics and laymen. During the Bakumatsu and Meiji eras, the Buddhist clergy held a multiplicity of views as to how best to respond to the anti-Buddhist violence, the opening of Japan, and modernization. As we have already seen, many of the measures supported by one segment of the clerical population, for example, the assumption of surnames or the end to clerical responsibility for household registration, were stiffly resisted by other Buddhist clerics. The deep divisions within the Buddhist community at the start of the modern era became manifest in the debate concerning the Meiji government's Buddhist policy and the decriminalization of clerical meat eating and marriage.

One of the great ironies of the passage of the *nikujiki saitai* law was the role played by Buddhist reformers in supporting its formulation and enactment. Buddhist supporters of the decriminalization of clerical meat eating and marriage backed many of the changes in the status system and played an important role in the establishment of a new ministry to oversee religious affairs. They viewed the creation of the Ministry of Doctrine in 1872 as a victory for Buddhism. The ability of some Buddhists to influence government leaders and their general sympathy for much of the state's religious policy demonstrate the extent to which state religious policy was not unilaterally determined by anti-Buddhists. The creation of that ministry and the formulation of its policies were the products of compromise and negotiation among a variety of concerned parties, including the Buddhist leadership, Nativist and Shintō leaders, and government bureaucrats.

ŌTORI SESSŌ AND THE ESTABLISHMENT OF THE MINISTRY OF DOCTRINE

One of the most important Buddhist clerics involved in both the establishment of the Ministry of Doctrine and the decriminalization of *nikujiki saitai* was the relatively obscure Sōtō school monk, Ōtori Sessō (1814–1904). Although little has been written about Ōtori in the various studies of Meiji Buddhism, I believe that it is not an exaggeration to say that with his entry into the government in 1872 he became one of the most influential Buddhist clerics of the early Meiji period.[1] Ōtori was the most highly placed member of the Buddhist clergy to advocate a shift in government religious policy from the suppression of Buddhism to the incorporation of the Buddhist clergy into the Doctrinal Instructor system in order to combat the spread of Christianity. Without Ōtori's support as a member of the Ministry of Doctrine, it is not clear that Buddhist attempts to join the

---

[1] Ikeda Eishun (1994, 31–48) has provided one of the best and most recent accounts of Ōtori's role in Meiji Buddhism. See also Jaffe (1991, 89–92) and Jaffe 1990, 470–81); Hardacre (1989b, 69). Brief biographies of Ōtori can be found in KDJ, 2:664 and the *Shintō jinmei jiten* (1986, 69–70).

state proselytization campaign would have been as successful as they were. While serving in the Sain and, later, in the Ministry of Doctrine, he helped effect changes in state religious policy that continue to have an impact on Japanese Buddhism to the present day.

Certainly Ōtori was not a brilliant doctrinal scholar and advocate on a par with Fukuda Gyōkai, Shaku Unshō, Shimaji Mokurai, or other leading Buddhist intellectuals of the day, but his name appears frequently in documents concerning state-church relations in Japan. In fact, it is almost impossible to avoid Ōtori as one searches through the documents concerning early Meiji religious policy. Over the course of the Meiji period, he appears, Zelig-like, in a variety of roles—Buddhist cleric, government official, shrine priest, and chief priest of Ontakekyō. At the height of the suppression of Buddhism he remained the confidant of such leading Meiji political figures as Ohara Tesshin (1817–72), which enabled him to contribute to the formation and tempering of the Meiji government's religious policy.[2]

Ōtori exerted considerable influence within the Sōtō school as well, having served as a member of the committee that sought to arrange a compromise between the Eiheiji and Sōjiji factions of the school. He also was one of the five candidates for chief priest of the Sōtō school in 1872, although eventually he withdrew from the election. Even more importantly, perhaps, was the influence exerted by his disciples who contributed to the compilation of the *Tōjō zaike shūshōgi*, one of the proto-texts that developed into the centerpiece of modern Sōtō teaching, the *Shūshōgi*.[3] In addition, one of Ōtori's leading disciples, Aokage Sekkō (1832–85), became the abbot (*kanshu*) of Eiheiji in 1883.[4]

Originally from Higo (present-day Kumamoto in Kyūshū), Ōtori was ordained at the age of six by Tetsuran Mutei (d. 1843), a Sōtō school monk in the dharma lineage of Manzan Dōhaku (1635–1714) and acquaintance of the Miyachi family. After sixteen years of study under Mutei, Ōtori went on a pilgrimage during which he studied with the illustrious Sōtō scholar-monk Kōsen Mujaku (1775–1838) for several years.[5] Ōtori finally received dharma transmission (*shihō*) from Mutei in 1838.[6]

Several years after the death of his teacher, Ōtori began a series of abbacies that placed him in close contact with a variety of important Bakumatsu political leaders. From 1846 until 1872 Ōtori served as the abbot of the

---

[2] For a brief biography of Ohara, see KDJ, 2:903.

[3] Ikeda (1990, 342).

[4] Eiheijishi Hensan Iinkai (1982, 2:1350–51). Aokage had entered the Buddhist clergy under Ōtori's teacher, Tetsuran. Following Tetsuran's death, Aokage became a disciple of Ōtori's and received transmission from him.

[5] NBJJ, 256.

[6] KDJ, 9:27. These details about Ōtori's career have been gleaned from the SSZ; Hattori (1938); Kobayashi (1936); and Ōtori (1936).

clan temples (*bodaiji*) of the Toda (Ōgaki domain), the Matsudaira (Fukui domain), and the Ii (Hikone domain). During this time he became the confidant of Ohara Tesshin, a principle retainer (*hanshi*) for the Toda family who was to become one of Ōtori's closest friends and supporters. He also met a number of reformers who later played a role in the establishment of the Meiji regime, for example, domain reformer Matsudaira Yoshinaga (1828–90) and his Confucian–scholar advisor, Yokoi Shōnan (1809–69).

Ōtori's assumption of the abbacy of the temple Seiryōji in Hikone in 1867 placed him in proximity to Kyoto at a crucial juncture in Japanese history. As the Tokugawa government weakened, Ōtori was called upon by his former lord, Matsudaira, to come to the capitol to discuss with a group of influential samurai the problem of the growing Christian presence in Japan following the forced opening to the Western Powers. After meeting with Matsudaira, Ōtori was visited by a number of leading radical patriots (*shishi*) and antibakufu court nobles, most notably Kido Takayoshi (1833–77), Ōkubo Toshimichi (1830–78), and Iwakura Tomomi (1825–83).[7]

Soon after the Restoration, Ōtori began to use his connections in an effort to effect the reform of the Buddhist clergy and ameliorate the harsh suppression of Buddhism. Echoing the concerns expressed in the Charter Oath of Five Articles (*Gokajō no seimon*) in 1868, which set forth the official policy of the "unity of Shintō rites and rule" (*saisei itchi*), he submitted a memorial to the throne in the spring of 1868. The memorial was one of the earliest petitions calling for the formation of a national teaching based on the three main traditions in Japan—Shintō, Buddhism, and Confucianism.[8]

In the memorial, Ōtori expressed grave concern over the growing presence of Christianity in Japan. Unlike during the Edo period, when such strict measures as having the Buddhist clergy superintend all funerals and mandatory universal temple registration kept Japan free from pernicious Christian influence, pressure from the West now had forced Japan partially to open itself to the foreign religion. He cautioned against suddenly allowing the practice of Christianity without proper preparation, lest the people be moved to rebellion. However, the increased contact with the West, he believed, would make the continuation of the prohibition against Christianity impossible. Although in some ways similar to the situation that had faced the Tokugawas, the latest foreign intrusion into Japan,

---

[7] Kido mentions in his diary (1932) his frequent meetings with Ōtori during 1868 in his diary. Though he does not say what they discussed, the two men seem to have been friends—certainly Ōtori's claim to have influenced Kido is plausible.

[8] Shidankai (1972, 7:183). The interview with Ōtori was originally published in the September 17, 1896, edition of the journal. Volumes 7–231 of the journal were titled *Shidan sokkiroku*. Ōtori's petition is found in SSZ, 2:7r–8l, and Hattori (1938, 34–36).

along with the Restoration, Ōtori claimed, had brought the dawn of a new age. Furthermore, because the Protestant Christianity now entering Japan was not the same as the Christianity that had entered Japan in the past, a new approach was required. Rather than try to uphold an outdated ban, the government must strive to inculcate the people with the indigenous Japanese faith.

The strongly anti-Christian tenor of Ōtori's petition was common in Buddhist tracts and memorials written during the late-Bakumatsu and the early Meiji periods. In the wake of numerous attacks on Buddhism by Nativist scholars and economic theorists, many Buddhists responded with a flurry of apologetical writings that strove to protect the teaching from its detractors. Typically, these works attempted to capitalize on the growing fear of Protestantism and foreigners, calling for the protection of the nation (*hokoku*) and "opposition to the evil religion." By so doing, Buddhist leaders no doubt hoped to redirect the hostility toward Buddhism, so rampant at the start of the Meiji period, toward Christians, both foreign and domestic. In the words of Notto Thelle, "Buddhist apologetics was more and more characterized by a strong anti-Christian zeal. After the opening of Japan hardly any apologetic work was published that did not include a criticism of Christianity. The rejection of Christianity became the primary duty of the Buddhist world."[9]

To prevent rebellion and chaos, Ōtori wrote that the state needed to use the three teachings of Shintō, Buddhism, and Confucianism. This had been the formula for success in the past. "Our ancestors established the nation using Shintō as the essence (*tai*) and Confucianism and Buddhism as the function (*yō*). They relied on these three teachings to support the customs of the people and thereby bring peace to the state (*kokka*)." In this regard, Buddhism had much to offer the new regime, because it made "goodness and compassion primary, thereby providing succor to the multitude."[10] Ōtori later explained in an interview that although both Confucianism and Buddhism originally were imported traditions, through the long expanse of Japanese history they came to aid the government in conjunction with Shintō like the interdependent legs of a tripod. It was the presence of these three teachings that enabled Japan to maintain its sovereignty until the Meiji period, because the tripartite national religion had penetrated into the very marrow of the Japanese people and had taught them the proper relationship between lord and vassal.[11]

Ōtori's contention that Shintō was the essence, that is, the most privileged of the three traditions, was becoming, out of necessity, a more common

---

[9] Thelle (1987, 26).
[10] SSZ, 71.
[11] *Shidankai* (1972, 7:183).

viewpoint, even among fully committed Buddhists. Along with Ōtori, a number of influential clerics attempted to justify state support of Buddhism by emphasizing its close relationship with Shintō or by declaring its subordination to Japan's "indigenous" tradition. The stalwart Shingon monk Shaku Unshō wrote a petition to the government early in 1869 in which he argued that Buddhism and Confucianism were indispensable auxiliaries for explaining Shintō. Buddhism was an important doctrine, he said, because, just as is taught in Ryōbu Shintō, Shintō is made manifest through the principles of Buddhism. When the people lose faith in Buddhism, he warned, they also begin to doubt the kami (*shinmei*).[12] Similarly, in the spring of 1869 Takaoka Zōryū and Ugai Tetsujō submitted a petition arguing for an end to the suppression of Buddhism. They contended that Buddhists generally agreed that "Shintō is the indigenous path (*koyū no michi*) of Japan; Confucianism and Buddhism are auxiliary teachings and should be practiced alongside it. All these teachings make impartiality their trunk and benevolence and compassion their root."[13]

Although Ōtori stressed the importance of these teachings for governance, his petition was highly critical of the clergy. According to him, during the long period of peace under Tokugawa rule, all clerics, not just the Buddhists, had become indolent and decadent. However, his harshest and most detailed criticisms were reserved for the Buddhist clergy. In keeping with the spirit of Article 4 of the Charter Oath, which exhorted that "the corrupt customs (*rōshū*) of the past shall be abandoned and everything based on the just laws of heaven and earth," and Article 5, which called for knowledge to be sought all over the world in order to further imperial rule, Ōtori wrote,

> the clergy today lack practice and education. At this time, if they are not made to reflect on themselves and to return to fundamentals, then how can they have the ability to meet the disciples of the foreign faith and denounce them? Superintending the disposal of corpses and managing the household registry are secondary; learning and morality are fundamental. If the secondary is abandoned and the fundamental grasped, then the Buddhist teaching will be able to flourish and we can allow the foreign religion entry. They overly concern themselves, however, with outward appearances and do not awaken to the spirit of the times (*jiki*). Taking rules that cannot be followed and forcing them on people who are incapable of following them is to create a laudable but unenforceable law. This cannot be ignored.[14]

In the memorial, Ōtori accepted the common anti-Buddhist polemic that the Buddhist clergy were decadent and ignorant, stating that they lacked both education and diligence. He believed that at the same time,

---

[12] NBK, 253; Tsuji (1949, 84).   [13] NBK, 4:306.
[14] SSZ, 2:7l–8r.

the special position of the clergy had led them to concentrate on the more mundane and lucrative jobs of administering funerals and overseeing the household registry system, thus precipitating their indolence and moral lassitude.

Ōtori, using a phrase redolent with Buddhist connotations and also evocative of the Meiji push for modernization, accused the clergy of being ignorant about the disposition of the age (*ji*) and human spiritual capacity (*ki*). As a result, the sect leaders forced their students to follow outdated religious regulations, asking weak people to follow impossible laws. Just as Chikū had resorted to the notion of the decline of the teaching as one justification of Jōdo Shin *nikujiki saitai*, Ōtori also remarked on the dissonance between Buddhist practice and the modern age. Ōtori's attempt to bring Buddhist practice into harmony with modernity and human capacity, as I shall discuss later, remained central to most subsequent arguments in favor of clerical marriage. The appeal to *zeitgeist* as the rationale for reforming the Buddhist clergy must also have resonated with many in the Meiji leadership who conceived of their main task as the modernization of a backward nation.

In the petition, as in much of the "preserve the Teaching" (*gohō*) literature, emphasis was not placed on the soteriological efficacy of Buddhism. Rather, Ōtori argued that it was the ability of the Buddhist clergy to act as educators and proselytizers that made them important to the nation. If strict adherence to outdated codes of behavior hinders the ability of the clergy to perform such tasks, then those regulations must be changed. Ōtori's defense of the faith is pragmatic, grounded in the ability of Buddhism to support the state.

The project outlined by Ōtori in his petition, with its recommendations for the mutual support of the three faiths, reformation of Buddhism, and the repelling of Christianity, reflects concerns that were central to the early Meiji pan-sectarian movement. The platform developed by the leaders of the new Buddhist organization, the Shoshū Dōtoku Kaimei, at one of its early meetings in 1869, for example, called for the study of such topics as the inseparability of the secular and Buddhist law; the interdependence of Shintō, Confucianism, and Buddhism; the study and refutation of Christianity; the elimination of evil clerical practices; the establishment of new schools; and proselytization among the common people.[15] In addition, like Ōtori, many members actively lobbied for the right for Buddhists to participate in the activities of the promulgation campaign undertaken by the Ministry of Rites.

---

[15] A detailed description of the Shoshū Dōtoku Kaimei is found in Tsuji (1949, 83–166). The eight topics for study are on pp. 96–97. Kashiwahara notes the connection between earlier *gohōron* literature and the platform of the Shoshū Dōtoku Kaimei in Kashiwahara and Fujii (1973, 546).

Despite Ōtori's relatively well-placed connections, however, the petition had little immediate effect on government religious policy; within days after the proclamation of the Charter Oath, the government renewed the Tokugawa prohibition of Christianity and called for the strict separation of the kami and the Buddhas in places of worship, which sparked off a wave of violent attacks on Buddhist temples and clergy. Although one year later the government did institute a plan to shore up public morality along the lines of Ōtori's request, participation in the Great Teaching Promulgation Campaign was at first limited to Shintō priests. Ōtori's desire for a Buddhist role in the campaign was not realized until 1872, when the government allowed Buddhists to join the movement as doctrinal instructors.

According to Ōtori, reaction to his memorial was mixed, but he attributed the later formation of the Office of Doctrinal Instruction (Kyōdō-kyoku) and the tempering of *haibutsu kishaku* by the government to the influence of his petition. In a later interview, he claimed that after the memorial was submitted, a number of his more influential friends and Meiji leaders, including the imperial tutor Akizuki Tanetatsu (1833–1904), Matsudaira Yoshinaga, Ōkubo Toshimichi, Hirosawa Saneomi (1833–71), and Kido Takayoshi, threw their support behind his effort to end the excesses of anti-Buddhist violence, reform the clergy, and provide a secure place for Buddhism in the new government.[16] Both Kido and Ōkubo, however, disagreed with Ōtori's contention that the normalization of relations with the Western Powers would inevitably lead to the legalization of Christianity, and they argued for continued prohibition of the foreign faith. Ōtori countered that such considerations were secondary and, in any case, ultimately out of Japanese control. The crucial task was to shore up both Shintō and Buddhism and to use these teachings to educate the populace in order to prevent the spread of Christianity. When, in 1868, trouble with the Urakami Christian community flared again, Kido became convinced that only a national teaching, including Buddhism, could slow the spread of Christianity and, in its wake, civil disorder.[17]

Soon after submitting the petition, Ōtori found himself increasingly drawn into government service. Beginning in 1868, at the behest of the government, he tried unsuccessfully to mediate the thorny dispute between the Eiheiji and Sōjiji wings of the Sōtō denomination over control of the

[16] *Shidankai* (1972, 7:173–89). Note that, like Yokoi Shōnan, Hirosawa was assassinated in 1871.

[17] For a description of the Urakami Christian incident, see Abe (1968–69, 9:297–300). In 1865 Christians in the Nagasaki region tried to make contact with French Catholic missionaries. Then in 1867, members of the Urakami Christian community refused to give donations for the repair of the local Buddhist temple or to participate in Buddhist funerals, thus threatening the livelihood of the local clergy. This resulted in the execution of their leaders in 1868 and the exile of more than three thousand Christians to other provinces in 1870–71. See Thelle (1987, 36–37).

denomination.[18] Then on Meiji 2/5/3 (June 12, 1869), Ōtori was invited to serve as commissioner (*goyōgakari*) in the newly created Office of Doctrinal Instruction, a precursor to the Ministry of Doctrine. Office of Doctrinal Instruction officials were to oversee the state's proselytization efforts and direct the corps of official proselytizers. As shown in the previous chapter, the formation of the Office of Doctrinal Instruction and the creation of the Ministry of Doctrine marked a shift in state policy toward the Buddhist clergy. By 1869, government leaders had reached a consensus that the best plan for preventing the spread of Christianity was to create a solid national teaching and to include the Buddhist clergy in efforts to disseminate it among the people. According to Ōtori's account, the Office of Doctrinal Instruction, created in Meiji 2/3 (April–May 1869), would be better able to oversee state religious policy than the old Ministry of Rites.[19]

The new office was headed by Soejima Taneomi (1828–1905) and included such prominent members as the Confucian scholar Ono Jusshin (1824–1910); the Chōshū-born, Nativist scholar and student of Hirata Atsutane, Inō Hidenori (1805–77); and Akizuki Tanetatsu.[20] That Ōtori, a Sōtō cleric, should be included in an organization intended to oversee the exclusively Shintō proselytizers demonstrates how well regarded he was in government circles. His inclusion in the Office of Doctrinal Instruction also shows that as early as 1869 government leaders were beginning to consider incorporating the Buddhist clergy in the promulgation campaign and that Buddhists had not been entirely shut out of positions of influence despite the generally anti-Buddhist climate at the time. As the sole representative of the Buddhist clergy in the office, Ōtori argued that Shintō alone could not stop the spread of Christianity in Japan. Most other members of the office, however, were openly hostile to Ōtori's position, and the very first meeting reportedly degenerated into a shouting match. The dispute over religious policy became so bitter that Ōtori even claims that anti-Christian partisans, believing that he was advocating the introduction of Christianity, planned to have him assassinated.[21] After little more than a month serving in the new office, Ōtori withdrew from his post. The office itself was abolished on Meiji 2/7/9 (August 16, 1869), not long after his departure.[22]

[18] Hattori (1938, 46–47). For more information on the Eiheiji-Sōjiji dispute, see Dumoulin (1990, 333–34; 411–12); Sakurai (1966, 46–48); Bodiford (1993, 81–84).

[19] *Shidankai* (1972, 7:184).

[20] According to Hattori (1938, 56–57), Ono Jusshin (Sekisai) was Ōtori's most vocal opponent in the Office of Doctrinal Instruction. The impetus underlying the formation of the Office of Doctrinal Instruction is discussed in Sakamoto (1979, 92–93). For more on Ono Jusshin's role in the Office of Doctrinal Instruction and the formation of state religious policy, see Haga (1984, 15–19); Sakamoto (1993, 84–89).

[21] *Shindankai* (1972, 7: 184–85).

[22] Nihon Shiseki Kyōkai (1973, 2:296) Ōtori (1936, Nov. 19, 8).

ŌTORI'S SECOND PETITION AND
THE DECRIMINALIZATION OF CLERICAL MARRIAGE

Ōtori remained in relative seclusion during 1870 at a hermitage near Lake Biwa. By 1871, however, Matsudaira and Ohara Tesshin were urging him to return to Tokyo to take part in the pro-Buddhist activity in the capitol. Upon his return to Tokyo in the summer of 1871, Ōtori was met by a contingent of Shin, Jōdo, and Shingon clerics that included the Shin clerics Shimaji Mokurai and Akamatsu Renjō (1841–1919) and Ugai Tetsujō of the Jōdo school. The group urged Ōtori to submit another petition to the throne calling for Buddhist participation in the movement to promulgate the National Teaching to the populace, and he decided to do so.

The effort to win state acceptance of Buddhist participation in the proselytization effort had been growing since Ōtori had submitted his memorial in 1868. Clerics from the Nishi Honganji, Shimaji in particular, had been vocal advocates for the inclusion of Buddhists in the promulgation effort. In 1870 the Nishi Honganji had petitioned for the formation of a separate government bureau to deal with temple affairs. In response, the Jiinryō was established later that year. Shimaji, in an 1871 petition, personally argued for a more effective government office to oversee the reformation (*risei*) of the clergy. In a tract remarkably similar to Ōtori's 1868 memorial, Shimaji described the repression of Christianity under the Tokugawa regime and the differences between the past and present Christian threat. He then called for the employment of a reformed Buddhist clergy in the campaign to ward off the spread of Christianity. He noted the general failure of the Jiinryō to accomplish Buddhist reform and suggested the establishment of a new bureau to supervise Buddhist affairs.[23]

Ōtori submitted a second petition to the government shortly before January 1872. The document covered much the same ground as his 1868 memorial but also included several specific new proposals for reforming the Buddhist clergy. Ōtori stated that the only purpose of his petition was to enable the clergy to expound on Buddhism in order to prevent the spread of Christianity. The new government policy of unifying Shintō rites and doctrine (*saikyō itchi*) was easily accepted by the upper classes, Ōtori wrote, but the ignorant masses, long accustomed to Buddhism, will be confused by too rapid a change in doctrine. The imminent entry of Christianity into Japan would only further lead people astray, thereby compounding the problem. For this reason, it is essential that Buddhists reform their teaching and put themselves in a position to "explain to every household and teach every person the goal of a rich [nation] and powerful [military] (*fukyō*), and fully instruct them to take refuge in Shintō."[24]

---

[23] See Shimaji, *Kyōbushō kaisetsu seigansho*, in Yasumaru and Miyachi (1988, 131–34).
[24] Yasumaru and Miyachi (1988, 30). See also Fujii Jintarō (1934, 7: 445).

In his 1868 memorial, Ōtori had already accepted the primacy of Shintō in relationship to both Confucianism and Buddhism.[25] The second petition went a step further, straightforwardly acknowledging that Shintō provides the foundation for the national polity and calling on all Buddhists to expound that principle to the people. It also appended three concrete suggestions for reforming the Buddhist clergy:

1. The Buddhist clergy erect lofty goals and contradict Heavenly Principle (*tenri*). They establish rules that suppress human emotion (*ninjō*) and are unsuitable for noble positions and superior vision. The clergy are also human beings and we desire that they teach in a more humble and kinder fashion.
2. Today's most urgent business is as I have described it above. We should provide funds to send clerics to the West so that they will be enlightened and know themselves and others.
3. The Buddhist clergy should cease all corrupt practices, learn about the state of affairs in the world, and subsequently begin sectarian study and teach that which creates harmony among the people.[26]

Ōtori's ties to the new government and influence on state religious policy were greatly enhanced when, on Meiji 4/10/5 (November 17, 1871), he received an order to serve in the Sain, a new government institution involved in the drafting of legislation. The same day, Ōtori was also instructed to return to lay life during his tenure in the Sain. According to his own account, "I received an order from the court to return to lay life and at the same time I was instructed to serve in the Sain. The intent of this order was to allow me to argue for my memorial on the legislative level. Although the order was irksome, I took up the post because it was an imperial command."[27] Hattori claims that Ōtori was initially reluctant to comply, but when Kido, Iwakura, and Etō Shinpei—who argued that this would be the most effective way to ensure the adoption of his suggested reforms—arranged for the Sain to order him to leave the clergy, he finally assented.[28]

The Buddhists were not the only ones to recognize the failure of the early efforts by the Ministry of Rites to reach the populace or to call for the employment of the Buddhist clergy in the proselytization effort. In a petition submitted to Iwakura Tomomi in Meiji 4/9 (autumn 1871), for example, Ōhara Shigetomi (1801–79), who had served as governor of the Ministry of Criminal Law (Keihōkan) and, in 1869, chief secretary of the

---

[25] Sakamoto (1983, 54) states that Ōtori's petition to the Sain describes the dominant sentiment of the Ministry of Doctrine, which, far from regarding Buddhism and Shinto equally, held that Shinto was the fundament of the Japanese state.

[26] Yasumaru and Miyachi (1988, 30).

[27] *Shidankai* (1972, 7:185).

[28] See ibid.; Nihon Shiseki Kyōkai (1973, 2:296); Hattori (1938, 64–65).

Shūgiin, called for a new direction in state religious policy.[29] In his memorial, Ōhara continued to advocate the superiority of Shintō, calling for all subjects to be registered at their tutelary shrine at birth and annual investigation of shrine membership. In addition, he wanted to mandate that every household install an altar (*kamidana*) for kami worship. He explicitly stated that the Buddhist clergy should be required to carry amulets from their local shrine and be permitted to visit the main compound at Ise Shrine.[30]

Despite this strongly pro-Shintō stance, Ōhara also recognized the failure of the exclusively Shintō proselytization program and called for new measures to improve efforts to spread the National Teaching, which he called the Imperial Way (Kōdō), to the masses. Like Ōtori, Ōhara believed that Confucian and Buddhist teachings might prove useful in this regard, so Confucians and Buddhists should be employed along with the Shintō clergy in the dissemination of the National Teaching. While vigorously rejecting Christianity, Ōhara went so far as to suggest that the Japanese people be allowed at least limited freedom of religious choice, allowing those who are inclined toward Confucianism or Buddhism to follow those teachings. He attempted to distinguish various religions (*hōkyō*)—a category that included Confucianism, Buddhism, and Shintō—from a common national cult, the Imperial Way, shared by all subjects. If leaders tried to force religious teachings that contravened custom on the people—an allusion to the old, exclusively Shintō policy—it would only increase their mistrust. Although he believed Buddhism and Confucianism to be inferior to Shintō, Ōhara recognized the utility of these teachings for reaching the ignorant masses. He asserted that "Confucianism and Buddhism are aids; the Imperial Way embraces both of them." Rather than force the people to follow the Imperial Way, he urged the state to educate them to respect the kami, revere their ancestors, and understand the nature of the imperial nation. Once they had been properly instructed in these principles by teachers who, through their deportment, set a proper example, the people would gladly embrace the Imperial Way.

Even though he tolerated an auxiliary role for both Buddhism and Confucianism, Ōhara believed that various "evil customs" (*heifū*) of those traditions contradicted the Imperial Way, leading people astray. To remedy this problem, he suggested that these deviant practices be eliminated. Instead,

> there should be a uniform law for the Imperial Nation regarding marriage, meat eating, tonsure, and dress. Those who do not conform should be punished. If people are allowed to choose whatever style of dress they prefer,

[29] For a brief biography of Ōhara, see KDJ, 2:681.
[30] Yasumaru and Miyachi (1988, 19–20).

the Confucians will wear Confucian dress, the Buddhists will wear Buddhist robes, some will wear British styles and others Asian styles. If each dresses according to his preference, we will be unable to fix a standard for Japanese clothing. An imperial edict to reform standards of dress and to rectify (*isshin*) customs should be promulgated.[31]

Like Ōtori's petitions calling for the incorporation of a variety of teachers into the state's proselytization efforts, Ōhara's petition called for a shift in state policy with regard to the Buddhist clergy. The petition also marked a clear shift from the exclusive Shintō policy to a more inclusive one that centered on the Imperial Way and embraced, albeit reluctantly, other strands of Japanese religious life. Many of the linkages we have seen in Ōtori's petitions were also present in Ōhara's. In particular, Ōhara connected effective education of the ignorant masses to the rectification of various "evil customs." Achieving that goal required, in Ōhara's opinion, strict rules regarding all aspects of dress and deportment. Whereas in matters of belief—that is, doctrine (*hō*)—differences could be tolerated by the state, in matters of action and outward appearance, uniformity must prevail. Ōhara's petition therefore may be read as a call to orthopraxy rather than orthodoxy.

As a member of the Sain, Ōtori's ideas concerning the reform of the clergy and their role in the new proselytization effort were quickly circulated at the highest levels of government. He also became directly involved in the construction of state policy underlying the creation of the Ministry of Doctrine in 1872. His second petition was appended to a Meiji 4/12/12 (January 21, 1872) proposal concerned with the transfer of the sacred mirror from Ise to the court in Tokyo and the establishment of the Ministry of Doctrine.[32] The document contained recommendations from a variety of government organs and individuals, including the Sain, the Ministry of Rites, and the Grand Council of State. The following month Grand Minister of State Sanjō Sanetomi (1837–91) circulated the proposal among officials at the ministries of Foreign Affairs, War, and Education. In this manner, Ōtori's suggestions for the Buddhist clergy were placed in the context of overall state religious and educational policy. His proposals were viewed in the highest echelons of the Meiji government as one component of the plan to stem the spread of Christianity and quell discontent among the general populace by incorporating Buddhists and Confucians in an effort to spread the National Teaching.

The document circulated by Sanetomi marked a shift from previous government religious policy, trading blatantly anti-Buddhist, anti-Christian measures for a conciliatory approach. According to the proposal, the Min-

---

[31] Ibid., 20–21.
[32] The complete memorial is ibid., 23–30. See also Fujii Jintarō (1934, 7:435–46).

istry of Rites was to be replaced by two bodies: the Ministry of Doctrine, which would oversee the affairs of not only Shintō but all religions in Japan (*zenkoku shokyō*), and the newly formed Bureau of Rites (Shikiburyō), which would be responsible for all state rites.[33] Thus government leaders now began to accept the idea of a distinction between state and religious teachings (*chikyō/shūkyō*), as Shimaji had recently proposed.[34] As a result, the officials initiated the process of separating state rites, doctrinal matters, and education, placing them, respectively, under the jurisdiction of the Shikiburyō, the Ministry of Doctrine, and the Ministry of Education.

The proposal also recommended granting Japanese subjects limited religious freedom, contending that Buddhism and Confucianism did not necessarily contradict the desires of the kami and that the people should be free to choose their faith as they saw fit. The authors concluded that the Christianity currently entering Japan was not to be feared as it was in the past. If people wished to follow that faith they could do so. The various authors of the proposal were careful to stress, however, that any doctrine or religion that harmed the national polity would be strictly prohibited.[35]

The Ministry of Doctrine was established on Meiji 5/3/14 (April 21, 1872), under the direction of Etō Shinpei and Ōgimachi Sanjō Sanenaru (1820–1909). Through the recommendation of Etō Shinpei, Ōtori was appointed a commissioner in the new bureau with the specific intent of having him serve as an expert on Buddhist affairs.[36] Although clearly the shift in religious policy resulted from the confluence of numerous forces, for Ōtori the creation of the Ministry of Doctrine amounted to the realization of his vision for Buddhism in the new nation. "At last the gist of my petitions had been enacted," he later reflected. "Finally a Great Teaching Academy uniting the two teachings of Shintō and Buddhism was established."[37]

During the first part of 1872 officials at a variety of ministries enacted measures to create a corps of doctrinal instructors and a nationwide system of academies (*kyōin*) for the promulgation of state doctrine. That year proved to be an extraordinarily busy one for the production of new regulations concerning the clergy, religious institutions, and the organs of government that would administer them. In the laws and institutions created at this time, one can trace the enactment of the proposals made by Ōtori, Ōhara, and the Sain. Perhaps reflecting concern that the diet of the populace be improved and that outmoded food taboos be abandoned, the court

[33] Yasumaru and Miyachi (1988, 27).

[34] Shimaji's distinction between areligious *chikyō* and *shūkyō* is discussed in Haga (1984, 13–14). See also Ketelaar (1990, 124–25).

[35] Yasumaru and Miyachi (1988, 25–27).

[36] Matono (1968, 632). See also Tokoyo (1988, 383).

[37] *Shidankai* (1972, 7:185–86).

started off the year portentously, announcing in the influential *Shinbun zasshi* newspaper on Meiji 5/1 (February 1872) that henceforth the ban on meat eating at the court would be lifted. Meat—beef and lamb regularly, and, pork, venison, and rabbit occasionally—henceforth would be part of the imperial menu.[38] In a similar vein, while standardizing state doctrine, bureaucrats at the Ministry of Doctrine attempted to modernize the clergy by ending practices it deemed superstitious, such as the prohibition against women entering the sacred precincts (*nyonin kinsei*) of shrines and temples. Other exceptional practices of the Buddhist clergy, for example, special mourning procedures, also were ended. Standardization of state doctrine and rites, which had begun the previous year, continued with the codification of the Three Principles on Meiji 5/4/28 (June 3, 1872).

According to several secondary sources, it was in this context that Ōtori proposed the decriminalization of *nikujiki saitai*. He recommended this step as part of the broader ministry effort to modernize and systematize all religious organizations. Although primary resources other than Ōtori's vaguely worded second petition are lacking, secondary accounts by Hattori Masao, Matono Hansuke (a biographer of Etō Shinpei), and Mishima Chūshū (1830–1919) suggest that Ōtori was one of the primary advocates of the new law. According to the accounts of Hattori and Matono, Ōtori recommended the lifting of the ban to Etō, who in turn brought the suggestion to the secretary of the Ministry of Doctrine, Ōgimachi Sanjō Sanenaru.[39] After a brief discussion within the ministry, the ban on clerical marriage was officially lifted by the Grand Council of State on Meiji 5/4/25 (May 31, 1872) (see chapter 4). Matono notes that Ōtori recommended that the prohibition be terminated because, contrary to the original intent of the law, it had only led to more corruption among the clergy. Hattori further explains that Ōtori believed that the clergy were no longer capable of adhering to the the strict regulations of the *nikujiki saitai* law. As Ōtori had written in his 1868 memorial, the sect leaders took rules that could be followed and forced them on people who were incapable of following them. Rather than preventing fornication, marriage, and meat eating, the law made criminals of a significant portion of the Buddhist clergy, which prevented them from participating effectively in the government effort to inculcate state teachings among the populace.

The relaxation of laws regarding clerical deportment found vigorous support from at least one Buddhist cleric outside the government, the Tendai cleric Ugawa Shōchō of the temple Senkōji in Ōzone, Niihari Prefecture (now Ibaraki and Eastern Chiba Prefecture). Seven months after the decriminalization law was issued (Meiji 5/11/27; December 27, 1872)

[38] MNJ, 1:540. See also Harada (1993, 17–18).
[39] See Hattori (1938, 62–64); Matono (1968, 632). Mishima writes of the proposal in his epitaph for Ōtori. See Kobayashi (1936, *furoku*).

Ugawa wrote a lengthy petition to the government that called for the mandatory marriage of all Buddhist clerics. Although considerably more explicit and detailed than Ōtori's writings, the overall thrust of Ugawa's petition reflects similar concerns about the condition of the Buddhist clergy.[40] Like Ōtori, Ugawa believed that the most important tasks facing the Buddhist and Shintō clergy were the repulsion of Christianity and the pacification of the people. To help the government achieve these goals, Ugawa called for compulsory marriage and meat eating for all Buddhist clerics; examination of all clerics and the return to lay life of those deemed unfit; limitation of the number of temples; elimination of all separate Buddhist denominations; and unification of dress, liturgy, rules, and doctrine for all Buddhists.

Ugawa's petition began by noting the general failure of the newly launched proselytization campaign incorporating the Buddhist clergy to calm domestic unrest and instill loyalty to the new regime in the people. The policy was inefficacious, argued Ugawa, because stubborn, backward Buddhist clerics filled the villages and selfish, conniving Shintō clerics incited people in every hamlet to riot. Although there were a few good clerics, they were despised and ignored by the majority. Ugawa suggested that those clerics of outstanding learning be selected from the masses of clerics, and that those who failed to meet stringent standards be removed from the clergy and returned to productive life as farmers.

One of the sources of the failure of the proselytization effort, according to Ugawa, was the disparagement of the Buddhist clergy by the Shintō clergy. "Those Shintō clerics who are employed in proselytization all praise themselves and condemn others and vilify Buddhism. They exclusively advocate respect for the kami but fail to advocate the great matters of patriotism, obedience to the emperor, and respect for the will of the court."[41] Ugawa recommended that the Shintō clergy be given strict orders to desist from attacking the Buddhist clergy and that, like the Buddhist clergy, they be purged of individuals who lacked the qualities necessary for serving as efficient proselytizers.

Ugawa also urged officials at the Ministry of Doctrine to clarify the intent of the *nikujiki saitai* law that had been adopted just months before he submitted his petition. It is important to understand, he urged, that the world had entered the Last Age of the Teaching and that people were of inferior spiritual disposition. As a result, the Buddhist clergy were unable to uphold the precepts. Although nothing could be done about the decline in human nature, the clergy would continue to have the potential to serve the nation if they would abandon their fixation on trivial matters of individual morality (*nairin*). Ugawa wrote,

[40] Tsuji (1949, 219).
[41] Ibid., 221.

How can one embrace trivial matters of internal morality and abandon the crucial matters of important policy? Therefore Buddhist clerics who are ignorant of doctrine, deluded in practice, and without learning or understanding should be removed from the clergy. Clerics of great character should not be bothered with matters of the personal precepts. They must only resolutely and diligently exert themselves to the utmost on behalf of the nation (*kuni*), advance to destroy the [opposing] great armies, aid the imperial government, respectfully preserve the intentions of the emperor, and unite the hearts of the people.[42]

Ugawa's appeal to the Ministry of Doctrine bore an uncanny resemblance to Ōtori's earlier petitions, particularly with regard to the combination of several different requests for the government. As in Ōtori's second petition, the decriminalization of *nikujiki saitai* was placed in the context of support for the nation. Expounding on what he felt was the rationale for each part of the *nikujiki saitai* measure, Ugawa wrote that marriage would enable the clergy to understand human morality (*jinrin*). Like Fukuzawa Yūkichi and members of the government who viewed meat eating as essential for having a strong, virile populace, Ugawa encouraged the clergy to increase their vigor by eating meat.[43]

Although the government had moved in the correct direction by decriminalizing clerical marriage and other related practices, Ugawa believed the law was too vague to be fully effective. Differing interpretations of the decriminalization measure led to protracted debates among the Buddhist clergy. Some clerics, ashamed to openly marry, continued to have surreptitious affairs. To end the confusion, Ugawa urged the court to clarify the intent of the law and reissue an order that all clerics should eat meat, marry, grow their hair, and wear Western clothing.[44]

Ugawa also believed that the Buddhist clergy could be effective proselytizers only if they served as examples for the people. For Ugawa, an essential element in being a teacher to the people was proper clerical dress and deportment. In a rather cryptic sentence, he contended that letting the Buddhist clergy wear Western clothing and short-cropped hair would allow them to "investigate principle to the utmost." Echoing the sentiments of some Meiji officials, he wrote that the proliferation of schools and temples was wasteful of national resources. To remedy the problem he called for the reduction of the number of temples and an end to the use of gold leaf and other precious materials in Buddhist images. He also suggested that all Buddhist clerics adopt uniform dress and liturgy in order

---

[42] Ibid., 221–2.

[43] On early Meiji attitudes toward meat eating, see Harada (1993, 17–18).

[44] Tsuji (1949, 221–22). A similar complaint about lack of compliance with the decriminalization measure was written by Suzuki Kiichi on January 2, 1874. Suzuki noted that the clergy still were not openly marrying and urged them to do so. See Hikita (1991b, 167).

to end the biased parochialism so rampant among the partisans of various competing denominations. The overall goal of his petition was to enable the Buddhist clergy to play a significant role in the forging of a rich nation and a powerful army.[45]

THE CLERIC AS DOCTRINAL INSTRUCTOR

It is well known that at the start of the Meiji period anti-Buddhist, pro-Shintō individuals played a crucial role in the formation of the new government. The participation of Buddhist clerics and laymen sympathetic to Buddhism in shaping state religious policy has often been underemphasized or forgotten. Throughout the early years of Meiji, Ōtori served as confidant and colleague to many leading politicians, and we have seen that they often agreed with him on the importance of Buddhism for the construction of a new state teaching and the education of the masses. Modification of the stern anti-Buddhist edicts was not solely a result of outside pressure from such Buddhists as Shimaji (who, although not a member of the government, also had close ties with influential leaders); it was partially shaped from within the government by individuals at least partially sympathetic to Buddhism. The countless, often contradictory, shifts in religious policy partially reflect the struggle within the government among Restoration Shintōists (Fukuba and Kamei), pro-Buddhists (Ōtori, Kido, and Shimada Mitsune), and pragmatists concerned with "a rational order, not a divine one" (Etō and Saigō).[46]

This is not to say that those in government who sought to utilize the Buddhists and those who lobbied for their inclusion in state proselytization efforts were willing to accept the Buddhist clergy as they were. Ōtori, Ōhara, and Ugawa all accepted the characterization of the Buddhist clergy as backward idlers who needed to be reformed before they could serve a useful function in the new society. Rather than viewing the decriminalization of *nikujiki saitai* law as an attempt to deal a final blow to a religion nearing extinction, Ōtori and Ugawa believed that the regulation would help transform monks who were out of step with the times into dynamic subject-clerics ready to serve the nation. For Ōhara and clerics like Ōtori, being a doctrinal instructor, that is, a proselytizer for the central government, and providing support for the Imperial Way took precedence over their affiliation with a particular denomination. From this perspective, Ōtori's postclerical career as government official, director of the Great Teaching Academy, shrine priest, and, finally, chief priest of Ontakekyō is not so strange. Over the same period, he continued to serve as a doctrinal

[45] Tsuji (1949, 223–24).
[46] Ketelaar (1990, 67–68).

instructor, rising from middle instructor (*chūkyōsei*) to provisional major instructor (*gon daikyōsei*), the second highest rank. From the time he entered government service, Ōtori devoted himself to the Imperial Way, trying to staunch intrasectarian tensions in various Buddhist and Shintō denominations. Underlying all of his efforts was the belief that the national interest overrode petty sectarian concerns.[47]

The decriminalization of meat eating, clerical marriage, and other previously forbidden clerical practices resulted from the intersection of concerns for Buddhist clerical reform with the attempt to create an effective corps of instructors to disseminate the National Teaching. The government's effort to modernize and standardize clerical deportment was supported by a coalition that included intellectuals, Buddhist clerics, and state officials. The petitions of Ōtori, Ugawa, and Ōhara all gave voice to concerns that resulted in the end to state enforcement of clerical discipline. What these diverse camps shared was the belief that distinctive Buddhist practices like the prohibition of meat eating and marriage or mandatory tonsure and wearing of robes hampered the dissemination of the National Teaching and the strengthening of Japan. If the government's reforms were to succeed, the evil customs of the past would have to be eliminated.

In the end, the decriminalization of clerical meat consumption and marriage was construed by its supporters as an extension of the Charter Oath's imperative that Japanese subjects abandon all "corrupt customs"—in this, case, vegetarianism and celibacy. It was thus seen by clerics like Ōtori and Ugawa as an attempt to revitalize and reform the Buddhist clergy. But the power of the Charter Oath's articles lay precisely in their vagueness, and there was more than one way to interpret which practices were decadent. In contrast to Ōtori and Ugawa, in the eyes of most high-ranking Buddhist leaders, clerical meat eating and marriage were precisely the "corrupt customs" that the clergy needed to extirpate if they were to rescue Buddhism from irrelevance.

---

[47] For a description of Ōtori's post–Ministry of Doctrine career, see Jaffe (1995, 125–29).

CHAPTER 6

Horses with Horns: The Attack on
Nikujiki Saitai

THE NEW LAWS relaxing regulations regarding clerical deportment as well as the announcement that meat would be eaten at the court were met with considerable resistance from different factions of the clergy. One early violent incident occurred a little more than one month after the court announced that meat would be part of the imperial menu. On Meiji 5/2/ 18 (March 26, 1872), a group of ten members of the Onatake confraternity (Ontakekō), dressed in white, forced their way into the imperial grounds. The purpose of their incursion into the palace was to present the emperor with a petition demanding an end to the pollution of the sacred islands of Japan by such barbaric practices as meat eating, which they argued were the result of evil foreign influence. In the ensuing scuffle with the guards, four of the *Ontakegyōja* were killed, one was severely wounded, and the rest were taken into custody. Occurring soon after the start of the policy to abolish the old domain system, the incident was misconstrued by the British diplomatic corps in Japan as an attempt to stage a coup d'état.[1]

Buddhist clerical protest against the decriminalization of *nikujiki saitai* was even more persistent and widespread. Soon after the promulgation of the measure by the Grand Council of State, meetings were held by clerics throughout Japan to protest the decriminalization, and a group of representatives was sent to Tokyo to protest directly to the Ministry of Doctrine. According to a firsthand account by Kuroda Kiyotsuna, vice minister of the Ministry of Doctrine, soon after the promulgation of the *nikujiki saitai* law a delegation of clerics visited the ministry and was met by Ōgimachi Sanjō, Ōtori, and a third official, Takagi Hidenori. On spotting Ōtori, the clerics screamed at him, "You corrupt priest (*maisu*)!" An uproar ensued, but Takagi finally interceded to explain the government's rationale for decriminalizing *nikujiki saitai*, and order was restored. Takagi compared the new law to the *sanpatsu dattō rei*, which had made voluntary the bearing of swords and wearing of top knots by the samurai. The Buddhist clergy were overly attached to form at the expense of true spiritual cultivation, Takagi remonstrated. The government was concerned because so many clerics ignored their duty to the state and neglected moral cultivation while busying themselves with trifles of demeanor. The govern-

---

[1] See "Ontake gyōja kōkyo shinnyū jiken," in Yasumaru and Miyachi (1988, 168–77).

ment therefore desired for the clergy to train themselves morally and, in accord with the age, work on behalf of humanity (*jindō*). According to Kuroda, the contingent of clerics thereupon left the ministry peacefully.[2] Matono writes that after the incident Ōgimachi Sanjō met with Fukuba Bisei and other members of the ministry to discuss the problem and then recommended to Etō that the law be repealed. Etō, however, refused to take such a step, fearing that it would set a bad precedent. Etō reportedly replied, "Though we have not yet issued many laws, already we hear voices of protest. If we were to repeal the law immediately, this would diminish the authority of the government. Even if the law were in error we could not repeal it. We have even less cause to change the law when, as in this instance, it is correct."[3]

After the initial shock of the new law abated, the chief priests of a number of other Buddhist schools, while waging intrasectarian fights to prevent the spread of clerical marriage within their own school, turned to petitions in order to persuade government officials to return more control over clerical deportment to the schools. Some of these letters to the government were from the individual leaders of various denominations, but the most influential of them were signed by representatives of each school. The cooperation of teachers from all the schools opposed to the decriminalization of *nikujiki saitai* proved crucial in forcing Ministry of Doctrine and Home Ministry officials to clarify and modify the decriminalization law.

The pan-sectarian organization founded in 1869 for the revitalization of Buddhism, the Shoshū Dōtoku Kaimei, provided the venue for much of the activity that aimed at achieving the repeal of the new law. Among those involved in the early opposition to the law were some of the most powerful clerics in the Buddhist world, many of whom were also leading members of the Shoshū Dōtoku Kaimei. They included Fukuda Gyōkai (1809–88, Jōdo school, head of the Great Teaching Academy); Ugai Tetsujō (Jōdo school, abbot of Chion'in); Morotake Ekidō (1805–79, Sōtō school, abbot of Sōjiji); Ogino Dokuon (1819–95, Rinzai school); Shaku Unshō (Shingon school, Omuro sect); Arai Nissatsu (1830–88, Nichiren school, chief priest); Takaoka Zōryū (1823–93, Shingon school); and Murata Jakujun (1838–1905, Tendai school, chief priest).

Members of the Shoshū Dōtoku Kaimei for the most part saw the persecution of Buddhism as just punishment for what they considered a largely corrupt Buddhist clergy. This was particularly true of Fukuda Gyōkai and Shaku Unshō, two of the staunchest opponents of clerical marriage. In the words of Winston Davis, Fukuda's and Shaku Unshō's emphasis on "praxis came to function virtually as a theodicy for persecu-

[2] Matono (1968, 636).
[3] Ibid., 634.

tion."[4] For many precept advocates in early Meiji, the emphasis on correct practice not only provided direction for the reform of Buddhism, it also implied that deviation from such practice was the origin of the suppression. Other members of the Shoshū Dōtoku Kaimei also linked adherence to the Buddhist precepts to the revivification of Buddhism and viewed the decriminalization of *nikujiki saitai* as a stumbling block to Buddhist reformation.

Although the fury of anti-Buddhist repression and pro-Shintō sentiment in high government circles had left the Buddhists in a strategically weak position, they doggedly pursued bureaucrats in the Ministry of Doctrine for a number of years and ultimately were able to wrest a degree of autonomy in the maintenance of clerical deportment. The shifting understanding of the bounds of state intervention in sectarian affairs naturally followed the contours of the important discussion of the separation of religion and the state (*seikyō bunri*) that was at its most heated from 1870–1875. Over the course of the debate the sectarian leadership skillfully used the evolving understanding of freedom of religion and shifts in state religious policy as a justification for continued resistance to the decriminalization of clerical marriage. In this chapter I examine the early petitions and tracts protesting the *nikujiki saitai* law, focusing on pan-sectarian efforts to sway government leaders and the various doctrinal arguments that were marshalled against the decriminalization measure.

Apart from the petitions by Ōtori, Ohara Shigetomi, and Ugawa Shōchō advocating clerical marriage, I have found few documents promoting *nikujiki saitai* during the first decade after the promulgation of the new regulation. Virtually all the literature on the subject is opposed to *nikujiki saitai* until the 1890s, when Tanaka Chigaku began work on his tract in favor of clerical marriage. Such works as Fukuda Gyōkai's *Sessō tōmon*, however, use a dialogue format that allows us to glimpse some of the arguments in favor of allowing *nikujiki saitai*. When examined along with other major tracts opposing clerical marriage that were published in 1879—Uan Dōnin's *Dan sōryo saitai ron*, Ueda Shōhen's (1828–1907) *Sōhiron*, and Shaku Unshō's petitions to the Sain—these works allow us to glean some of the main arguments in favor of clerical marriage circulating among members of the Buddhist community and the wider public.[5]

---

[4] Davis (1989, 312–13).

[5] See MBSS, 6:171–74; 7:228–32; Uan (1999, 78–86). In the introduction to *Dan sōryo saitai ron*, Furuta Shōkin states that little is known about Uan Dōnin, the author of the work. Kumamoto Einin and Shibe Ken'ichi have suggested that Nishiari Bokusan (a.k.a. Nishiari Kin'ei, 1821–1910), a vocal Sōtō school opponent to clerical marriage, was the author. Nishiari used the similar pen name Uan Rōnin on occasion. He became the chief priest of the Sōtō school in 1902. See ZGD, 977; Kumamoto (1991, 106; 110, n. 9).

FUKUDA GYŌKAI AND THE PRECEPT REVIVAL MOVEMENT

Fukuda Gyōkai was one of the most important Buddhist leaders in the movement to rescind the decriminalization of clerical marriage. A Jōdo cleric who in early 1872 was the abbot of the temple Ekōin, Fukuda was an influential member of the Shoshū Dōtoku Kaimei and served as editor-in-chief for the publication of the *Dainihon kōtei daizōkyō* (also known as the *Shukusatsu daizōkyō*). After 1873 Fukuda was the abbot of the temple Zōjōji, an important Jōdo temple that also served as the site of the Great Teaching Academy.[6] Along with the Shingon cleric Shaku Unshō, Fukuda was one of the most visible leaders of the movement to "preserve the Teaching" through the resuscitation of Buddhist discipline as exemplified in the ten good precepts (*jūzenkai*) for the laity and the ten major precepts (*jūjūkai*) for the clergy.

In his emphasis on the ten good precepts, Fukuda was heavily influenced by Onkō Jiun (1718–1804), the Edo period Shingon cleric who had played an important role in reviving interest in the ten good precepts as the core of pan-sectarian Buddhist practice in Japan.[7] Like Jiun, Fukuda contended that adherence to them was fundamental to all Buddhist practice. Fukuda stressed that "the precepts are the foundation of the Threefold Training (*sangaku*). Meditation and wisdom do not exist without relying on the precepts. The clergy and the laity alike should observe them. This is why they have been preserved and kept from corruption in the past and the present."[8]

Fukuda was careful to distinguish between three separate groups of the ten precepts: ten good precepts for the laity; ten novice precepts; and ten prohibitory precepts for the bodhisattva (*bosatsu*). Fukuda stressed that it was essential not to confuse the three sets. According to his analysis, the ten good precepts are secular, tainted precepts (*seken uro no kai*) and are therefore the same as secular morals. Adhering to these precepts would enable the individual to be reborn as a god, king, or emperor but will not in itself result in enlightenment. Whereas the precepts for the laity merely prohibited illicit sexual activity, in the two sets of precepts for the clergy, all sexual activity was forbidden.[9]

---

[6] The main sources for biographical information on Fukuda are Tsunemitsu (1968, 1:130–10); Masutani (1942); Ikeda (1976a, 81–92); Staggs (1979, 1:82–94); Davis (1989, 304–39).

[7] So close is the association of Fukuda with Jiun that at the Fukyoraian, a private chapel in Shizuoka dedicated to the preservation of Fukuda's memory, a portion of Fukuda's bones are interred along with hairs from Jiun's beard. The memorial stūpa also contains the teeth of Tokuhon Gyōjya (1758–1816), a famous peripatetic Edo period Jōdo cleric. See Izuya Denpachi Shinkō Zaidan (1999, 4).

[8] See *Jikkai ryakutō*, GSZ, 336–337.

[9] Ibid., 336–39. For a detailed discussion of Fukuda's view of the precepts, see Jaffe (1995, 136–40).

Figure 2. Fukuda Gyōkai

Although the three groups of precepts were different, Fukuda warned clerics against treating the precepts for the laity and for novices dismissively because all were similar in their ultimate aim. By elucidating a difference between the three types, he distinguished the practices of the laity, novices, and clergy while advocating a body of fairly uniform rules that transcended the distinction between these three segments of the Buddhist community. As I will show below, this distinction played an important role in Fukuda's attack on clerical marriage.

Fukuda's insistence that these sets of precepts be kept distinct and his adamant opposition to clerical marriage should be viewed in the context of the ongoing struggle within the Jōdo denomination to determine which precept tradition to follow for ordination ceremonies. Since the fifteenth century a distinctively Jōdo set of the precepts, described in the *Jōdo fusatsu shiki*, had become an increasingly significant alternative ordination tradition within the denomination. By the start of the Edo period, this ordination had adherents in such influential temples as the Chion'in in Kyoto and the Zōjōji in Edo, and its proponents pushed to make it the standard for Jōdo ordinations. Purported to be a set of precepts handed down solely within the Pure Land tradition, the *Jōdo fusatsu shiki* contained a particularly ambiguous interpretation of the precept forbidding all sexual relations and contended that if one was unable to adhere to all ten major precepts, then following four of them—not killing, not lying, not stealing, and not slandering the Three Jewels—would suffice. Although the text lost influence during the Edo period, proponents of the *Jōdo fusatsu shiki* continued to follow the tradition into the Meiji period. It was at that time that Fukuda worked to completely eliminate the use of that tradition for Jōdo ordinations.[10] His opposition to the alternative ordination tradition, with its lenient interpretation of the third precept, may well explain his attempt to bring Jōdo understanding of the precepts more in line with that of the Tendai and other non-Jōdo traditions, a trend that, according to James Dobbins, had dominated Jōdo denomination since the mid-Edo period.[11]

GYŌKAI AND THE SUPPRESSION OF BUDDHISM

While Ōtori, Ugawa, and Ōhara had all come to view the Buddhist insistence on celibacy and other aspects of clerical deportment as a corrupt customs that prevented the Buddhist clergy from actively serving society, Fukuda and the proponents of celibacy had an entirely different interpretation of clerical corruption. Like the proponents of the *nikujiki saitai* law, Fukuda and like-minded clerics accepted the overall characterization that Buddhism had become hopelessly corrupt and agreed that the Buddhists had only themselves to blame for the violent attacks on their institutions. But unlike Ōtori and others, Fukuda and his supporters felt that true reform of the clergy required even more stringent enforcement of the precepts, not a relaxation of the laws governing the clergy.

Like Shaku Unshō and Takaoka Zōryū, Fukuda stressed that the suppression of Buddhism was in large part a result of clerical deviation from orthodox practice. According to Fukuda, some aspects of the suppression of Buddhism, for example, the loss of landholdings, were actually fortunate because they forced the clergy to return to a simpler, more austere practice. He vigorously criticized his fellow clerics for lapses in behavior

---

[10] This summary of the *Jōdo fusatsu shiki*'s role in the Jōdo denomination is based on Dobbins (1995, 17–21).

[11] Ibid., 25.

and placed the blame for the persecution of Buddhism at the feet of those who had ignored the rules of proper clerical decorum. Thus, the elimination of clerical ranks and the diminution of temple lands benefited the clergy by forcing Buddhist clerics to give up desire for wealth and fame.[12]

Fukuda clearly expressed this sentiment in the *Shakumon shinki sansaku,* an 1879 elaboration of the agenda of the Shoshū Dōtoku Kaimei. In his proposal Fukuda remarked that although no order had been given to destroy Buddhism, the violent suppression was similar to the three major suppressions that occurred in China. He explained that there were six different reasons for the destruction of Buddhism: (1) the Shintō clergy had been oppressed by the Buddhist clergy and were now repaying them for years of bitterness; (2) the Confucians detested the Buddhist clergy and now had joined forces with the Shintō clergy; (3) the Christians had entered Japan and confronted the Buddhist clergy; (4) the Buddhist clergy were indolent and Buddhist doctrine was lifeless—their living quarters were luxurious, their clothing beautiful, they were proud of their court ranks, but they did not understand compassion or charity; (5) the officials were envious of the clergy's wealth and would deprive them of it; and (6) the Buddhist clergy were guilty of five errors. Those errors were: (1) preoccupation with clothing, food, and lodging; (2) attachment to their parishioners; (3) regarding their precept documents (*kaiken*) with contempt and not of their own accord restraining their inappropriate behavior; (4) overattachment to the doctrines of their own school and failure to appreciate the good in the doctrine of other schools; and (5) concern solely with superficialities and failure to apply themselves to learning and practice.[13]

To resolve these various problems and revive true Buddhist practice, Fukuda proposed a variety of measures to the members of the Shoshū Dōtoku Kaimei. Included among his suggestions were a number of temple fiscal reforms to help further clerical education, which he considered the most important task facing the Buddhist leadership. He exhorted the clergy to listen to the orders of their superiors and also stressed that those at the lower levels of clerical society were to follow the traditional regulations of Buddhism and to concentrate on scholarly matters. If they purged themselves of past evils, they would be able deal with whatever fate brought their way, no matter how terrible it was.[14]

One of the primary sources of Buddhist decrepitude was the lack of clerical discipline. In another, five-part proposal for the Shoshū Dōtoku

[12] *Kyōhō shihi,* GSZ, 391–92.

[13] Fukuda Gyōkai, *Ekōin Gyōkai Shakumon shinki sansaku,* in NBK, 4:350–51. A summary of the work is provided in Tsuji (1949, 108–9). See also Staggs (1979, 1: 78). The three suppressions of Buddhism took place under Dao Wudi of the Northern Wei, Wudi of the Northern Zhou, and Wudi of the Tang. See DKJ, 1:179; MBDJ, 2:1637–39. The *kaiken* was a document proving that one had received the precepts.

[14] NBK, 4:356; Tsuji (1949, 109).

Kaimei composed the following year, Fukuda apportioned blame for this moral lassitude to the clerical leadership and the subordinate clerics. Clerical discipline was lax because those in charge of the head temples tolerated corruption at lower levels of the sectarian establishments. The answer was for the leaders to enforce strictly sectarian regulations and for subordinates to abide stringently by those rules. Government officials should also be asked to cooperate in the effort. Fukuda went on to detail thirteen reasons for abolishing temples, including overabundance of temples in a particular area, the presence of profligate, shiftless, or criminal clergy, and lawsuits concerning temple landholdings or borders.[15] In this document, the broad contours of Fukuda's plans for Buddhism are very clear. He believed that an emphasis on scholarship and the traditional precepts would save Buddhism from destruction. He also viewed insubordination and lack of discipline among the lower-ranking clergy as one of the prime sources of the degeneration of Buddhism.

Fukuda's position with regard to the destruction of Buddhism was a radical, uncompromising one. In the first section of *Dōtokuron*, he emphasized that the age required the protection of the spiritual, not the material, aspect of Buddhism. Buddhists should not defend their sectarian concerns, temple property, clerical ranks, or emoluments because these are human-constructed and, ultimately, ephemeral things.[16] Similarly, in the *Shakumon shinki sansaku* Fukuda suggested that the clergy should not bemoan the loss of temples, pagodas, ample food, or court ranks. Rather, they should only be saddened that the suppression of Buddhism robbed both gods and humans of the path of ultimate good.[17]

Fukuda steadfastly maintained the superiority of Buddhism to all conditioned teachings and firmly rejected the positions presented by the fictional opponent in *Dōtokuron*, who put forth notions of the church-state relationship consonant with what rapidly was becoming the standard Buddhist paradigm for the Meiji period. In his insistence on the supramundane character of Buddhism, Fukuda dissented from the dominant Buddhist interpretations of the interdependent and subservient relationship between *Buppō* (Buddhist Law) and *Ōbō* (Kingly Law). According to Fukuda, Buddhism was not, as Ōtori, Ugawa, and others had contended, first and foremost a means for stabilizing the nation and bolstering imperial rule. Invoking arguments that Buddhist apologists in China had used to defend Buddhism, Fukuda claimed that unlike Confucianism and Shintō, which were concerned only with the present life, Buddhism also provided for past and future existences. In response to the auxiliary charge that Buddhism was useless for the state and therefore should be abolished—an

[15] Tsuji (1949, 109–10).
[16] *Dōtokuron*, GSZ, 408.
[17] NBK, 4:352.

argument that closely resembled the position advocated by officials in the Ministry of Finance—Fukuda wrote that although Buddhism was not useless for governance, that was not its primary concern. The practice of Buddhism produced humanity and justice (*jingi*) and therefore served as the basis for a well-ruled nation, but this was merely a by-product of Buddhist practice. To overemphasize Buddhism's utility at the expense of true practice was a mistake because "Buddhism was not a Way that was expounded for the sake of ruling the nation. The ability to rule people today is only a side effect of the Buddhism. It is not the true essence of Buddhism."[18]

As far as Fukuda was concerned, even those worldly activities that had become most central to the support of the clergy were superfluous. When, for a short time at the height of the suppression of Buddhism, Buddhist funerals were banned, Fukuda did not, unlike the majority of Buddhist intellectuals, view this as a hardship. In *Sessō tōmon* he responded to the suggestion that the clergy should depend solely upon the performance of funerals for their livelihood by pointing out that although the *Shibunritsu* monastic code made provisions for services for deceased clergy, it contained no mention of funerals for the laity. Nonetheless, he complained, funerals had become the primary means of support for the clergy, as if such mortuary ceremonies were their fixed occupation. "Ultimately, as clerics we have forgotten to wait for our own deaths and instead wait for the deaths of our parishioners. We have forgotten to cultivate good ourselves; instead we work for the good of the deceased."[19]

In this regard his position resembled that of another prominent precept advocate of the Meiji period, Shaku Unshō. Like Fukuda, Unshō was a staunch advocate of strict adherence to the precepts and the disengagement of the Buddhist clergy from such worldly matters as the management of the *koseki* system. Eventually Unshō was unable to abide the overwhelming emphasis in the Shoshū Dōtoku Kaimei on support for the state's proselytization efforts, so he withdrew from the organization, although he continued independently to petition the government to enforce the traditional precepts and end the harsh anti-Buddhist measures.[20]

By drawing a stringent distinction between the Buddhist path and worldly and governmental concerns, Fukuda placed himself at odds with most of the members of the Shoshū Dōtoku Kaimei and most of the leading clerics of the Jōdo school.[21] In a number of important respects, Fukuda's

---

[18] *Dōtokuron*, GSZ, 410.   [19] *Sessō tōmon*, GSZ, 181.

[20] Ikeda (1976a, 66). In SUS 3:13–14, Unshō recorded his discussion of the *koseki* system with Ugai.

[21] Ikeda (1976b, 50). Staggs (1979, 1:80) cites Tamamuro to the effect that both Shaku Unshō and Fukuda Gyōkai resigned from the Shoshū Dōtoku Kaimei because of their dissatisfaction with the worldly emphasis of the organization. I have been unable to locate Tamamuro's statement, however.

recommendations stand in stark contrast to those of Ōtori Sessō and such members of the Shoshū Dōtoku Kaimei as Ugai Tetsujō. Like Ōtori, Fukuda blamed the clergy for indolence and lack of learning. But he did not see Buddhism primarily as a bulwark against Christianity and as a support for imperial rule. Buddhism's contribution to pacification of the populace was nothing more than a by-product of its main purpose, which was liberation from the world of desire. Unlike Ōtori and others in the Ministry of Doctrine, Fukuda did not believe that the revitalization of Buddhism depended on abolishing precepts that were out of step with the time. For Fukuda, the renewal (*isshin*) of Buddhism meant the restoration (*fukko*) of past practices. There was no need to adapt Buddhism to the age. What was required was to return the clerical community to what Fukuda believed were the high standards of the past.

FUKUDA'S OPPOSITION TO THE *NIKUJIKI SAITAI* LAW

Fukuda and Unshō were two of the most steadfast, vociferous opponents of the government's decriminalization of clerical marriage. Their attacks on clerical marriage began soon after the adoption of the new law. Throughout the early years of Meiji, Unshō and Fukuda spearheaded the efforts to force the government to rescind or at least modify the *nikujiki saitai* law in order to preserve clerical discipline. Despite their general opposition to the mixing of secular and Buddhist concerns, Fukuda and Unshō did not hesitate to ask for continued government enforcement of the prohibition against *nikujiki saitai* after the Ministry of Doctrine promulgated the new law in 1872.

Fearing the repercussions from the loss of government support for the precepts, Fukuda began mobilizing the chief priest of each denomination to work for the repeal of the law. In a letter he warned them that acceptance of the new law would lead to the spread of five evils in the clerical community: it would (1) throw the basic precepts of Buddhism into confusion; (2) create a foundation for the destruction of Buddhism; (3) destroy the chastity of the monks; (4) dissolve the distinction between clerical and lay behavior; and (5) vitiate proselytization efforts. In an 1888 preface to several documents related to the *nikujiki saitai* law, Fukuda compared the promulgation of the decriminalization measure to the violent repressions of Buddhism in both India and China and described how many clerical leaders believed the issuance of the law spelled the beginning of the end for Buddhism.[22] Consistent with his position that the Buddhist clergy themselves rather than the government were the source of their predicament, Fukuda placed ultimate responsibility for the passage of the law on the

[22] GSZ, 449.

clergy, who after hundreds of years of decadent behavior had left the court without any other way of enacting clerical reform. He urged the chief priests to spare no effort in creating a strategy to end the crisis that was engulfing Buddhism.[23]

At the same time that he attempted to garner the support of the heads of the other Buddhist schools, Fukuda submitted to the chief priests a petition that he had written and planned to send to the Ministry of Doctrine. The petition was one of the most important defenses of the Buddhist ban against meat eating, clerical marriage, and the wearing of ordinary clothing outside of religious contexts. Fukuda began by expressing the clergy's surprise over the sudden relaxation of the traditional state ban on *nikujiki saitai*. After noting the confusion rampant among the clergy, he asked the officials to consider the following problems with the new regulation:

1. Allowing the clergy to freely eat meat, marry, and grow their hair signaled a complete relaxation of the precepts and would lead weak humans astray, hindering the proselytization efforts of the Buddhist clergy.
2. By abolishing the practices that distinguish the Buddhist clergy and the laity the new law would lead to confusion and trouble.
3. The clerics who eat meat, marry, etc., would be dwelling alongside clerics who uphold the precepts and would be treated the same. This would create confusion at temples, where religious rites were conducted. As there were no rules governing this unprecedented situation, it would result in great trouble at the temples.
4. Temples were built using pure donations (*shōjōzai*) from parishioners. Supporting meat-eating, fornicating individuals with those donations contradicted the intentions of the parishioners, who would cease to use the temples.
5. As there were no provisions prohibiting those who eat meat and marry from living in the temples, there would be a confusion of the pure and impure, which would have a deleterious effect on the teaching of Buddhism.
6. Relaxing the rules of deportment would make it almost impossible for Buddhist leaders to control younger clerics, who by nature were more disposed toward committing sexual transgressions.
7. The Buddhist sūtras record that carnivorousness exists only in lower realms, not in the realm of the gods or higher. Similarly, according to Buddhist cosmology, sexual desire only exists in the realm of desire (*yokkai*), not in the realm of form (*shikikai*) or

---

[23] GSZ, 450–451.

beyond. As a teaching for all three realms of existence, Buddhism depended on upholding the precepts governing meat eating and sexual relations.[24]

Fukuda concluded his petition by noting that "Lords and fathers proscribe disloyalty or unfiliality by vassals and sons. Because the delusions of sentient beings cause profound pain to the Buddhas, they established precepts to prevent error and stop evil. If one modifies the precepts by making them voluntary, under the pretext that during the Last Age those who can uphold these [precepts] are few, one misunderstands the intent of the Buddha's teaching and vitiates the transmission of the teaching. This is something that all of the schools lament."[25] He ended by rhetorically asking why ministry officials would want to throw Buddhism into confusion by adopting such a law when they had just consented to Buddhist participation in the state's proselytization efforts.

The petition was signed by "the chief priests of all the schools." It therefore presented the common concerns of most of the leading members of the Shoshū Dōtoku Kaimei. Clearly Fukuda was not alone in his dismay over the spread of *nikujiki saitai* among the clergy—both Takaoka Zōryū and Arai Nissatsu, prominent participants in the Shoshū Dōtoku Kaimei, had independently condemned clerical violation of the precepts. Zōryū, for example, complained that the public lodging of women and nuns in temples for pure clerics (*seisōji*), eating meat, and entertaining prostitutes were the underlying causes of lay derision of the clergy.[26]

In his petition Fukuda stressed the confusion that the decriminalization measure would sow in the Buddhist community. The sharp distinction between the clergy and the laity was crucial for the health of the Buddhist community. There was no room in the clergy for those who are neither fully laity nor completely clergy. The *nikujiki saitai* law, by allowing some clerics to follow a less stringent set of regulations, would pit "pure" clerics against "impure" ones. This in turn would discourage the laity, whose generous donations made in good faith were to support the Buddhist clergy, not those who belonged to this half-lay, half-clerical group.

Fukuda stressed the relationship of the clergy with the parishioners and the role of clergy in the state's proselytization efforts. The goals of the Buddhist leadership and the Ministry of Doctrine had much in common. By weakening control of the lower-ranking clergy, the decriminalization would vitiate the attempt by the Shoshū Dōtoku Kaimei to improve the quality of the clergy through education.

Fukuda was adamant in his insistence on adherence to at least the novice precepts by all members of the Buddhist clergy. He believed that it was

---

[24] These points are a paraphrase of the petition, *Kyōbushō e kengen*, GSZ, 451–53.
[25] Ibid., 453.   [26] Takaoka, NBK, 4:401–2.

impossible for one who did not follow at least the ten precepts for novices to be considered anything but a lay person. "Sexual desire (*in'yoku*) creates attachment in the Three Realms. Eating meat hinders the action of great compassion. Therefore these things are proscribed for novice home-leavers and above."[27] Clearly the clerics who failed to abide by the minimal standards of clerical practice should return to lay life rather than remain in the community of clerics in some nebulous half-lay, half-clerical status. In *Sessō tōmon*, Fukuda referred to a chapter of the *Hōshakukyō* in which a contingent of five hundred monks who cannot endure monastic life are ordered by the Buddha to return to lay life and cease living off lay donations.[28] This, according to Fukuda was in conformance with the Buddhist teaching. From this perspective, he wrote, "today's edict means that those who absolutely wish to return to lay life should be free to return to lay life. In no way does it mean that they should remain among the clergy and eat meat and marry." The purpose of the decriminalization law was to allow failed clerics to leave the Buddhist order. Like Ōhara Shigetomi, Fukuda expressed a fear of clerical "cross-dressing," asserting that "we should place the edict on a par with the law that prohibits men from dressing as women and women from dressing as men, actions which would presumptuously throw customs into confusion and destroy what is proper. In what way is a Buddhist cleric who acts like a lay person different from men and women wearing each other's clothing? If the one is wrong, how can we say that the other is correct? If this one is correct, then the other should not be considered wrong."[29]

No doubt the influx of Western styles of dress and behavior and the uncertainty created by the massive social changes of early Meiji contributed to the sense of instability with regard to many aspects of Japanese life. Ōhara argued for one standard of behavior that would be followed universally by Japanese subjects; Fukuda, on the other hand, called for more exacting differentiation between members of different classes of subjects. Like Ōtori, Fukuda also agreed that it made no sense to force those who were incapable of following the precepts to do so. The end result of such

[27] *Kyōbushō e kengen*, 453.

[28] The *Hōshakukyō* is an abbreviation for the *Daihōshakukyō*, T 11:#310. The passage cited by Fukuda is found at T 11:643. In that passage, the monks leave the clergy because they do not wish to receive lay donations after having committed impure acts. Those who return to lay life are criticized by other members of the sangha, but the Buddha defends their actions as being in accordance with the Buddhist teaching.

[29] *Sessō tōmon*, GSZ, 177. The work is so named because the dialogue between the clerics takes place on a day in which a snowstorm leaves them the time for such discussion. As with Ōhara Shigetomi, Fukuda stressed the importance of proper dress and the need to distinguish clearly between classes of subjects by reference to standards of dress and deportment. The desire to maintain strict boundaries between lay and cleric, men and women, etc., reflects the dominant attitude of the status system that had been in use throughout the Tokugawa period.

rigidity was hypocrisy and pretense. However, there was no place in the Buddhist clergy for those unable to uphold the precepts. Fukuda resolved the problem of ambiguity in the *nikujiki saitai* law by advocating the maintenance of the firm division between the laity and the clergy.

Following the precepts, Fukuda continued, was an unconditional requirement of one who took the tonsure. Those who abandoned the ban on *nikujiki saitai* had no recourse but to return to lay life because "When the cleric leaves his home and takes the tonsure he follows the example of the Buddha entering Mt. Daṇḍaloka. By not eating meat he obeys the proscription set forth at the assembly in Laṅkā (Ryōgae) and manifests the great compassion of the bodhisattva.[30] This is the behavior of a member of the Buddhist clergy. Chapter 31 of the *Daichidoron* says that 'upholding the precepts shall be your inner essence (*shō*); the tonsure and robes shall be your outward appearance'."[31]

For Fukuda, absolutely no alternative existed for one who wanted to be an ordained Buddhist cleric. Alluding to the folk etymology of the highly pejorative Japanese word *baka*, that is, one so stupid he or she cannot distinguish a horse from a deer, Fukuda fulminated against those like Ōtori or Ugawa who argued that matters of clerical deportment were mere trifles. "We know that those who take the tonsure and wear robes are Buddhist clerics; we know that those who eat meat and marry are lay people. There are no horses with horns, no deer with manes, no lay people who shave their heads and wear robes, and there are no Buddhist clerics who eat meat and marry. Is there any difference between pointing at a person who grows his hair, eats meat, and marries and saying, 'That is a Buddhist cleric,' and pointing at a horse and saying, 'That is a deer'?"[32]

The *nikujiki saitai* law was ambiguous because it did not clearly state what would be the status of those clerics who opted for marriage. Fukuda wanted all clerics who failed to abide by the novice precepts to leave the clergy. As far as he was concerned, those clerics who lived in temples and ate meat or married were at best thieves. This contention grew out of his understanding of the relationship between the parishioners and those who staffed their temple. Fukuda noted in his petition to the Ministry of Doctrine that the temples depended upon the donations of the parishioners

---

[30] Chapter 8 of the *Laṅkāvatāra Sūtra* (*Ryōgakyō*) concerns meat eating. There are three extant Chinese translations of the sūtra, by Guṇabhadra (T 16:#670), Bodhiruci (T 16:#671), and Śikṣānanda (T 16:#672). See, for example, T 16: 561–64. Unlike many earlier sūtras, which allow for the eating of certain types of meat, the *Laṅkāvatāra* calls for the complete proscription of meat eating by the clergy.

[31] *Sessō tōmon*, GSZ, 177; the *Daichidoron* passage is found at T 25:293b.

[32] *Sessō tōmon*, GSZ, 177. I would like to thank Stanley Weinstein for pointing out the connection between this passage and the folk etymology for the word *baka*, which actually is a variant phonetic compound derived from the Sanskrit word *moha*, meaning ignorance.

for their existence. But those donations were intended to support the disciples of the Buddha, not their wives or children. In *Sessō tōmon*, Fukuda elaborated on this point as follows:

> [A] monk lives in a Buddhist temple to gain protection from the elements; he wears the Buddha's robes for protection from the cold and the heat; he eats the Buddha's food to avoid hunger and thirst. Is it not due to following the Buddha's regulations and upholding proper clerical deportment that one is allowed to spend his whole life of one hundred years living amidst the Three Jewels? In a temple does one store food for one's wife and child; does one keep money for the purchase of pigs and sheep? The system of law holds that using one spoonful of water or one handful of salt for that which has no connection with the Three Jewels is a form of thievery. This is why there is no law [explicitly] governing eating meat or marriage in the Vinaya. This is the reason that, if one wishes publicly to accept the current law about meat eating and marriage, one should not remain within the Buddhist community.[33]

THE PROBLEM OF *MAPPŌ*

One of the main arguments in favor of clerical marriage that several anti–*nikujiki saitai* works confronted is that the decline of the Buddhist teaching during the Last Age of the Teaching (*mappō*) rendered strict adherence to the precepts of the past impossible. A natural explanation for the supposed degeneracy of the clergy and for more lenient clerical rules was found in the doctrine of the decline of the Buddhist teaching. The notion that during the Last Age of the Teaching no one would be capable of upholding the precepts was a common feature of Japanese Buddhist thought. As early as the late Heian, the probable date for the composition of the *Mappō tōmyōki*, a seminal statement of Japanese *mappō* thought, important segments of the Japanese Buddhist community argued that the world had entered the Last Age of the Teaching, which made adherence to the precepts impossible.

The doctrine of decline evoked two radically different responses from the Buddhist clergy, as Jan Nattier has described in her work on pan-Asian Buddhist notions of the decline of the Dharma. One approach has been to call for renewed vigor and strictness in practice to counter the prevailing trend. The other tack, which Nattier has labeled "dispensationalism," has been to claim that the change in the spiritual disposition of the age requires an entirely new teaching. More often than not, the new teaching involves a simplified practice that is supposedly more accessible to people living during the age of decline. Much of the history of Japanese Buddhism,

---

[33] Ibid., 178.

including the debate over *nikujiki saitai*, may be seen as a conflict between these alternative responses to *mappō*.[34]

In the *Mappō tōmyōki*, for example, the unknown author clearly takes the latter approach. The author accepts that by his day the world was already at the extreme end of the period of the Imitative Teaching (*zōbō*). He also claims that at the end of the period of the Imitative Teaching and in the Last Age of the Teaching, Buddhist clerics who can uphold the precepts will be as rare as "a tiger in the marketplace." According to the author, during the period of decline the laity should revere those clerics who cannot uphold the precepts, because "there are no other merit-fields" available to whom to give offerings.[35] The "dispensationalist" approach to *mappō*, as represented in the *Mappō tōmyōki*, played a fundamental part in the thought of the great Kamakura reformers Hōnen, Shinran, and Nichiren and without doubt is among the most significant doctrinal strategies in Japanese Buddhist history. As shown in chapter 3, Chikū and other Jōdo Shin authors used this strategy during the Edo period.

In the *Dōtokuron*, Fukuda's fictional opponent turned to the theory of decline to argue for the decriminalization of clerical marriage. The interlocutor presented the quintessential dispensationalist argument. "Today is not the first time it has been said that the Threefold Training—precepts, meditation, and wisdom—are essential areas of study for all Buddhists. However, the world has entered the last period (*gyōki*), and it is as if all traces of the Threefold Training have been swept away. Even if it is often said one should study these three things, "study" means to learn these things in letter only. Practice and awakening are set aside in a corner unused. This is extremely lamentable." The interlocutor claimed that the Threefold Training would be impossible in the last five hundred years of the teaching. During that time ordinary people would be unable to go beyond mere imitation of true practice.[36] Similarly, in the *Sessō tōmon*, we find the naive young novice lamenting that the days of great yogis like Siddhārtha, Mahākāśyapa, or Pārśva are over and that the three poisons are far more potent than during Śākyamuni's lifetime.[37]

The solution presented by the young cleric, while not as radical as that found in the *Mappō tōmyōki*, called for greatly lowered expectations for

---

[34] Nattier (1991, 137–39).

[35] Rhodes (1980, 91, n. 25; 92).

[36] *Dōtokuron*, GSZ, 411. The Threefold Training includes morality, concentration, and wisdom.

[37] *Sessō tōmon*, GSZ, 161. Mahākāśyapa was renowned for his adherence to the twelve ascetic practices and became the head of the Buddhist order following the death of the Buddha. Pārśva, a Sarvāstivāda monk and the supposed teacher of Aśvaghoṣa, was one of the twenty-four great Indian transmitters of the teaching described in the *Fuhōzō innen den* (T.50:314b). He vowed not to lie down until he achieved enlightenment. The three poisons are greed (*ton'yoku*), anger (*shinni*), and delusion (*guchi*).

clerical behavior. Given the weaknesses of those who practice today, would it not be preferable for all to abandon any attempts to follow the Three-fold Training and instead engage solely in an easy practice such as the *nenbutsu* of Hōnen and Shinran or the *daimoku* advocated by Nichiren? This is the meaning of preaching Buddhism in accordance with the spiritual capacity of people (*taiki seppō*).[38]

In response to these arguments, Fukuda admitted that the world had long since entered the Last Age of the Teaching, but he did not despair that true practice and adherence to the precepts were impossible. Although conditions might make practice and realization more difficult, individual effort would bring results. Fukuda disputed the claim that his contemporaries were less capable of true practice than the masters of old. Even in the past, during the lifetimes of these illustrious monks, evil forces of great power, for example, the evil Devadatta, who tried to kill his cousin Śākyamuni, and the patricidal Ajātaśatru existed. In fact, Fukuda wrote, Śākyamuni lived toward the end of a cosmic period when the human lifespan had declined to one hundred years. For this reason, "If in the ancient period people's afflictions had been weak, then could these rebellious sins have occurred? If we speak about the difference between the ages on the basis of the five defilements, Śākyamuni's lifetime was no different than today."[39]

Of course, Fukuda did not contend that the current age is exactly the same as the time of Śākyamuni. It was necessary for him to explain the abundance of wise men and sages, arhats, and great bodhisattvas during Śākyamuni's lifetime and the scarcity of the same during the present day. He attributed this "striking" discrepancy to two causes: the awesome karmic power that resulted from Śākyamuni performing meritorious actions lifetime after lifetime, and the conditions created by Śākyamuni's miraculous spiritual powers. Fukuda admitted that as one enters the Last Age the influence of these two causes grows weaker, changing the nature of the Three-fold Training and making enlightenment through any of the Three Vehicles more difficult. "The change in the nature of the Threefold Training and the distancing of the Three Vehicles from awakening is due to the gradual diminution of the influence of the two factors over time. You should not doubt that the power of an arrow from a crossbow will weaken at the end of the arrow's flight. It is not due only to the strength or weakness of the passions."[40] The weakening of the influence of the two aforementioned factors accounted in large part for the difference in number of great practitioners during Śākyamuni's time compared with the Meiji era.

Fukuda's concern with the problem of practice in the Last Age was not unique. The question of the Last Age of the Teaching and the inability of

[38] *Sessō tōmon*, GSZ, 162.   [39] Ibid., 165; Ikeda (1976a, 89).
[40] *Sessō tōmon*, GSZ, 166.

the clergy to adhere to the strict discipline of early Buddhist monasticism runs through much of the literature defending the ban on *nikujiki saitai*. Although a member of the Sōtō school—in which the doctrine of the decline of the teaching had played a relatively minor role—Nishiari Bokusan felt it imperative to address similar concerns about the spiritual capacity of his fellow clerics. In a letter to Sōtō clergy of Miyagi Prefecture, where Nishiari practiced, he responded to claims of inherent moral weakness:

> The Dharma does not spread by itself. It is necessary for people to spread it. There is no period of the true, imitative, or last age of the teaching. These periods change in accordance with the flourishing or weakening of the spiritual capacity of human beings. Therefore the Buddha said, "As I have preached over and over on Vulture Peak, if you practice my teaching, the Absolute Body of the Tathāgata will be present without extinction." The current decline of the teaching is totally due to human beings. Certainly if in one school there were to be a person of great talent, that school would overwhelm all the rest. [41]

According to Nishiari, the decline of the Buddhist teaching only occurs if the clergy fail to perform their duties with care. In his letter he urged his fellow clerics to practice with diligence, paying close attention to such duties as morning and evening religious services, caring for the temple altars, and cleaning the temple compound. If one does these things, then naturally people will take refuge in the Three Jewels and will support the cleric and his temple financially. [42]

Given the relative importance of *mappō* thought in the Jōdo school compared with the Sōtō or Shingon denominations, it is natural that Fukuda would find it necessary—and more difficult—to refute in detail the argument that *nikujiki saitai* was unavoidable in the *mappō* period. In addition, because Fukuda promoted the ten good precepts as the foundation for rebuilding Buddhism, it was essential that he counter claims that the precepts and the Threefold Training were no longer relevant to practitioners in the Meiji period. Hōnen's ambiguous attitude toward the precepts and the practice of the Threefold Training compelled Fukuda to stress those aspects of Hōnen's teaching that best supported his own emphasis

[41] Nishiari (1875, 1–2.) The paper reprinted Nishiari's letter urging adherence to traditional Sōtō discipline by his fellow clerics in Miyagi Prefecture. Nishiari is clearly echoing Dōgen's *Bendōwa*, in which Dōgen responds to a question about the possibility of practice in the Last Age by saying, "in the scriptural schools they emphasize names and forms, but in the true teaching of the Mahāyāna there is no division of the teaching into the True, Imitative, and Last periods. It is said that all who practice will attain the Way." DZZ, 1:742. See also Stone (1985, 38). Dōgen did not entirely dismiss the notion of *mappō*, however, for on occasion he referred to various problems inherent to living in the Last Age. See Weinstein (1973, 79).

[42] Nishiari (1875, 1–2).

on those practices.[43] While conceding that the world indeed had entered the period of the Final Teaching, he continued to advocate the cultivation of the precepts, meditation, and wisdom. In *Sessō tōmon*, for example, he highlighted the severity of Hōnen's initial training on Mt. Hiei and Hōnen's disciplined recitation of the *nenbutsu* (invocation of the name of Amida Buddha)—up to seventy thousand recitations each day. Rather than stressing the exclusivity of the *nenbutsu*, Fukuda emphasized that Hōnen had received the Perfect, Sudden Precepts (*endonkai*) from his teacher, the Tendai monk Eikū (d. 1179?), and had carefully observed the precepts for his entire life. In the *Dōtokuron*, Fukuda softened the emphasis on the exclusive recitation of the name of Amida and called attention to the diversity and severity of Hōnen's training. He wrote that Hōnen's denials of his ability to adhere to the precepts, meditate, or achieve wisdom were a result of Hōnen's profound humility, not a description of his actual practice. Hōnen was, after all, the descendant of such illustrious monks as the Pure Land patriarchs Nāgārjuna and Vasubandhu (according to Fukuda and the Jōdo tradition) and teacher to such high-ranking, learned clerics as Kenshin (1130–92) and Myōhen (1142–1224). Because such great clerics were all capable of benefiting from the practice of the Threefold Training, Fukuda contended that Pure Land practice does not necessarily exclude adherence to the precepts.[44] He thus concluded that it would be foolish to stress Hōnen's statement that "the Threefold Training are without benefit" to the exclusion of the other aspects of his teaching.[45]

In *Sessō tōmon* Fukuda described how the practice of *nikujiki saitai* deviates from true Buddhist and, specifically, Jōdo practice. In particular he stressed the importance of the precepts for the Jōdo tradition and Hōnen's warning against precept infraction in his *Seven-Article Pledge* (*Shichikajō no kishōmon*).[46] According to Fukuda, eating meat or marrying were problematical for a Jōdo cleric because those who engaged in such acts contravened the *Pledge* that was recited every day in Jōdo temples as part of the morning liturgy. Those wayward clerics destroyed the perfect-sudden precepts and made light of the precept lineage into which they had entered. As a result, all of the benefits of taking the precepts were lost. Furthermore, "When the Buddhist clergy act improperly in public they make light of those who have received the precepts and mock the people throughout the country."[47]

---

[43] On the ambiguity in Hōnen's attitude toward the precepts, see, for example, Katsuki (1974, 24–25). See also Furuta (1958, 94–103), who points out on pp. 98–99 that Hōnen referred to observance of the precepts as the "great basis of the Buddhist teaching" and also as a "miscellaneous practice" (*zōgyō*). See also Dobbins (1995, 14–18).

[44] *Sessō tōmon*, GSZ, 169–70.

[45] *Dōtokuron*, GSZ, 411.

[46] See Dobbins (1989, 17).

[47] *Sessō tōmon*, GSZ, 179.

BUDDHIST COSMOLOGY AND THE DEFENSE OF CELIBACY

In a number of the texts attacking the *nikujiki saitai* law, the authors' arguments are rooted in the acceptance of traditional medieval Buddhist cosmology. Like the Tendai cleric Entsū (1754–1834), the most prolific modern defender of Buddhist cosmology, Fukuda, Nishiari, and Unshō all continued to argue for a literal understanding of three-realm, Sumeru-centered Buddhist cosmos and elements of Buddhist eschatology during the last quarter of the nineteenth century.[48]

Fukuda, in particular, was an ardent proponent of the Sumeru-centered Buddhist cosmology. In 1878, responding to a ban issued by the Ministry of Doctrine against teaching that cosmology, Fukuda published the short tract *Shumisen ryakusetsu*, in which he set forth the scriptural basis for the traditional Buddhist understanding of cosmography. In this work, Fukuda attempted to show that this cosmology was of import because it provided the basis for the Buddhist understanding of causality.[49] Unlike, Entsū, who attempted to use astronomical data to empirically prove the validity of the Buddhist cosmology, Fukuda based his defense solely on a literal interpretation of sūtra passages and on claims that this understanding could be verified through developed spiritual faculties.[50]

Fukuda used his fundamentalist interpretation of cosmology to support his advocacy of vegetarianism and celibacy for the Buddhist clergy. In his first petition to the Ministry of Doctrine, he had argued that there was a qualitative, moral difference between the three realms of existence (*sangai*)—that is the realms of desire (*yokkai*, Sk. *Kāma-dhātu*), form (*shikikai*, Sk. *rūpa-dhātu*), and nonform (*mushikikai*, Sk. *arūpa-dhātu*)—with regard to meat eating and sexual relations. He wrote that the activities of meat eating and sex are found in the desire realm but do not occur in the higher realms. Fukuda appeared to take it for granted that this cosmology was accepted by his readers—the officials at the Ministry of Doctrine—and argued that because Buddhism is a teaching that aims to save beings in all three realms, it was inappropriate for Buddhist clerics to eat meat or have sexual relations. To do so, as mentioned earlier in this chapter, would render them incapable of saving beings outside of the desire realm. No doubt this reference to traditional Buddhist cosmology had little attraction for those at the Ministry of Doctrine, whose policies increasingly aimed at spreading Western scientific cosmology and extirpating outmoded "superstitions."

---

[48] For a detailed description of Entsū's defense of Buddhist cosmology, see Okada (1997).

[49] Fukuda, "*Shumisen ryakusetsu*," in MBSS, 90–93.

[50] Okada (1997, 168–69). According to Okada, Entsū's attempt to utilize empirical, scientific data to verify Buddhist cosmology made him one of the earliest "modern" Japanese Buddhists.

The same reliance on traditional cosmology can be seen in Nishiari's *Dan sōryo saitai ron* (Refutation of clerical marriage). Based on his reading of the *Kojiki*, Nishiari argued that there is a cosmological basis for the rejection of sexuality by both the Buddhist and the Shintō clergy. In response to a question from a fictional interlocutor about why the Buddhists alone place emphasis on celibacy, he pointed out that those who serve the kami also must be continent, at least for a limited period of time. He argued that there is considerable agreement between the foundational myths concerning the kami and the Buddhist emphasis on sexual purity, referring to the preface of the *Kojiki*, in which Ō no Yasumaro (d. 723) writes, "when heaven and earth were first divided, the three deities became the first of all creation. The Male and Female here began, and the two spirits were the ancestors of all creation."[51] Nishiari attempted to connect his argument against clerical marriage to Shintō doctrine by alluding to the asexuality of the three creator deities (*zōka sanshin*), Ame no Minaka Nushi, Takami Musubi, and Kami Musubi. He claimed that, according to the foundation myths of the *Kojiki*, the universe ultimately is based on purity rather than corruption, and he pointed out that the cosmos begins with asexual kami. The three creator deities were all single deities (*dokushin*) that hid their bodies, and, as Nishiari noted, even the first male and female kami did not have sexual relations.[52] Only with the beginning of yin and yang, that is, the appearance of Izanagi and Izanami, does the "defilement of Heaven and Earth" take place, which results in the creation of people and all other phenomena.[53]

Based on the purported original purity of the cosmos, Nishiari argued that even if the people arise from sexual impurity, this does not mean the ultimate nature of the cosmos is impurity. Some people believe that sexual activity is not impure because they forget the original nature of the cosmos. Such people are like insects that are born in stagnant water and therefore believe the ultimate nature of the world to be stagnation. The foundational mythological description of creation is in agreement with Buddhist cosmology because in the Buddhist universe, as one moves into the higher levels of existence, sexual desires disappear altogether. Therefore, if the kami viewed human sexual relations with disgust, how much more so must the Buddhas who have transcended the three realms?[54]

In a clear attempt to counter the claim made by Ōtori and Ugawa that allowing the clergy to marry would invigorate the government promulgation campaign, Fukuda and Nishiari attempted to link the preservation of clerical purity with the success of the government's proselytization efforts

---

[51] Philippi (1969, 37); Aoki et al. (1982, 11).

[52] Aoki et al. (1982, 18). The three deities of creation were particularly important in early Meiji because, along with Amaterasu in the form of Tenshō Daijin, they were enshrined at the Daikyōin and, after its dissolution, at Ise. See Hardacre (1989b, 43); Haga (1984, 15–19).

[53] Uan (1879, 173).   [54] Ibid., 173.

and the preservation of order in the fledgling nation. In his petition to the Ministry of Doctrine and in his *Sessō tōmon*, Fukuda contended that having married clerics would confuse the laity and weaken the Buddhist community, which in turn would destroy the ability of the clergy to act as proselytizers and would throw the temples—which after all were teaching academies—into confusion. Nishiari took the argument one step further. In the true spirit of the defense of the Dharma literature, he yoked together the purity of the clergy and the fortunes of the realm:

> When those who serve the kami are pure the kami are delighted; when those who serve the Buddhas are pure the Buddhas are delighted. We know this is so because when the kami and the Buddhas are delighted they obey our prayers and always respond to our appeals. Since ancient times pure clerics have moved the virtuous spirits and kami of Heaven and Earth; we know this by the extraordinary fashion in which their prayers were realized. Therefore those who have respect and faith for the Buddhas and the kami should love pure clerics. The kami and the Buddhas take pleasure in an abundance of pure clerics. When the kami and the Buddhas rejoice then their protection grows stronger. Thus we can say when pure clerics are numerous, those who protect the nation are numerous.
>
> The fate of the Tokugawa family is a recent example of this. At the beginning of the Tokugawa's reign, the clergy's rules were upheld, in the middle the rules gradually slackened, and by the end the rules were in great disorder. This gave rise to the "abolish the Buddhas" movement of Lord Mito. Is it not the case that the vigor and weakness of the pure clerics corresponded with the prosperity and decline of the Tokugawa family?
>
> If you love your nation you should support the celibate schools and you should pray that those who uphold the precepts will increase daily. You should not favor those who break the precepts.[55]

FILIAL PIETY AND THE ATTACK ON CLERICAL MARRIAGE

In the "Refutation of Clerical Marriage," Nishiari directly addressed several specifically Confucian criticisms concerning Buddhism. Confucian critics frequently attacked the Buddhist clergy for not producing heirs, an act that Mencius claimed is the greatest act of unfilial behavior.[56] The Confucians also argued that the Buddhist clergy were unfilial because home-leaving entails abandoning one's father and mother to fend for themselves in their old age. The complaints about the unfilial nature of Buddhist

[55] Ibid., 173–74; Uan (1999, 85).

[56] See Mencius (1970, 127). "Mencius said, 'there are three ways of being a bad son. The most serious is to have no heir. Shun married without telling his father for fear of not having an heir. To the gentleman, this was as good as having told his father'" (Book IV, Part A, 26).

ordination were not new. Similar attacks had been leveled against the Buddhist clergy almost since its first appearance in China, and the same arguments were used again in Japan during the Edo period as Neo-Confucian and Nativist attacks on Buddhism became more prominent.[57] Such important Edo period scholars as Itō Jinsai (1627–1795), Dazai Shundai (1680–1747), Yamagata Bantō (1748–1821), Yoshikawa Koretari (1616–94), and Hirata Atsutane (1776–1843) vigorously condemned Buddhism for undermining filial piety. Dazai, for example, criticized Buddhism for its overwhelming emphasis on home-leaving and ordination.[58] Hirata, who saw no contradiction with his attacks on Jōdo Shin clerics for sexual profligacy, denounced Buddhism because the celibate clergy failed to provide for the continuity of the family, which was crucial if there were to be descendants to undertake that which Hirata deemed the ultimate act of filiality, ancestor worship.[59] Ogyū Sorai (1666–1728) claimed that the Buddhists had stressed monastic life and concerned themselves with only the salvation of the individual, thereby abandoning human moral relations.[60]

Concern over filiality remained prominent in the Meiji literature defending Buddhist monastic practice. In response to the Confucian-style attacks, Nishiari drew from a rich mine of apologetic literature that had been developed in response to the criticisms against Buddhism in both China and Japan. One of the most extensive Buddhist defenses against the charge of unfiliality is found in the *Yudao lun* by the Chinese Buddhist Sun Chuo (ca. 300–380). Sun argued that Buddhism teaches the ultimate filial piety because the Buddhist cleric, by realizing supreme enlightenment, comes to be revered by all beings. Because "father and son are of one body, united by the same fate," the great achievement of the son also raises the status of the parents. Sun also asserted that Confucian ethics was incomplete, due to the contradiction between two of the virtues it most vigorously advocated: filial piety and loyalty. Finally Sun stressed that home-leavers make the ultimate repayment for their debt to the family by converting their parents to Buddhism and assuring their salvation.[61]

The same counterarguments were adduced by a series of Japanese Buddhists much closer to Nishiari chronologically. During the Tokugawa period, the Ōbaku monk Chōon Dōkai (1628–95) defended Buddhism from the volley of Confucian-inspired attacks. Chōon, like Sun Chuo, contended that Buddhism is superior to Confucianism because Buddhism is a teaching for the three times (past, present, and future) in the three realms, not just the current human existence. Therefore, unlike the Confu-

[57] Discussions of the debate over filiality are contained in (Ch'en, 1973, 14–50); and Zürcher (1972, 13–14; 281–85). See also Keenan (1994, 83–90).

[58] Furuta (1981, 1:151–80).

[59] Harootunian (1988, 201–7; 221).

[60] Ogyū Sorai, *Bendō*, cited in Furuta (1981, 1:156).

[61] Zürcher (1972, 282).

cians, the Buddhists do not kill other sentient beings for food. Again, after achieving enlightenment Buddhist saints make the ultimate repayment of their debt to their family by returning to the world to save their parents and all other sentient beings. This, according to Chōon, is great compassion that dwarfs the narrow morality of the Confucians.[62]

The rich tradition of Buddhist defense provided Nishiari with a set of ready answers to those who criticized the monastic emphasis in Buddhism. To the question, "what can you say about 'home-leavers' leaving their parents and traveling far away, thereby not giving filial care to their father and mother?" Nishiari replied,

> the Buddha stated, "all sentient beings are my children." Thus the people of the world should all be considered our siblings. If one's siblings have difficulty, how can one not help them? For example, suppose one's sister marries into another family. If there is a fire or flood, even if one's parents are on their sickbed, one should do what is necessary to go to help her. Not only will one's father and mother not reprimand one for this, but their illnesses will be soothed by such action. If the flood or fire is said to be severe and one does not help because one's parents are ill, then parents' illness will only worsen. Is this not human nature?
>
> In the defiled world the difficulties posed by the three poisons and the four devils are even graver than those from flood or fire.[63] The difficulties arising from a fire or flood are temporary and do not affect negatively one's future rebirths, but the three poisons and the four devils will eternally affect this and future lives. If that is not frightening then what is? If one is always diligent and leaves one's home and parents in order to devote oneself to the amelioration of difficulties caused by the three poisons and the four devils, ultimately there will be no time to worry about not having descendants. Therefore although people who engage in such activities are called "home-leavers," in fact they are "debt-repayers."[64]

In claiming that filiality toward one's parents was overshadowed by other more important virtues, Nishiari was aligning himself with an important segment of Japanese Confucian scholars who had argued in the Tokugawa period for the prioritization of loyalty over filial piety. In this respect the Japanese Confucian scholars broke with the Chinese Confu-

---

[62] Furuta (1981, 1:162–63). Two of Chōon's important defenses of Buddhism were *Jubutsu benron* and *Shigetsu yawa*.

[63] The four devils (*shima*) are (1) the evil passions that torment one's mind and body (*bonnōma*); (2) the five skandhas that are produced due to the concatenation of the 108 evil passions (*onma*); (3) death (*shima*); and (4) the evil prince of attachment to the world who prevents one from following the Buddhist path, sometimes referred to as the king of devils in the Paranirmitavaśavartin heaven who tries to thwart one's attempts to do good (*takejizaiten-shima*). Based on DJBT, 297, with emendations by the author.

[64] Uan (1879, 172).

cians, who had tended to value filiality over loyalty when conflicts arose between these two responsibilities. Like Sun Chuo, Nishiari played on the potential for conflict between filiality and loyalty to bolster his claim that the benefits derived from the monastic life supersede those to be won by ordinary filial behavior.[65] Equating the entrance into the clergy with giving up one's life for one's lord, Nishiari wrote,

> for example, a loyal retainer loses his life for the sake of his lord—how can we dare say that he has been unfilial? If that is taken to be a sin and can be construed as unfilial, then it will not do to laud Kusunoki Masashige and the retainers of Akō.[66] Now, home-leaving is done for the sake of the Way. The Way is undertaken in order to save sentient beings from their delusions and thereby to cause them to escape eternal suffering in the future. How can this not be "Great Mind"?[67] Do you suppose that for one who has put forth this Great Mind there is room to harbor a thought of one's own descendants?
>
> Confucius said, "Serving one's father and mother is the beginning of filial piety; achieving fame is the culmination of filial piety."[68] Although home-leaving is not done in order to achieve fame, those individuals whose pure name and world-saving skill is transmitted to all future generations are the most filial individuals of all. It goes without saying that the filiality of those petty individuals who merely raised children is insignificant by comparison. In regard to the superiority of the home-leaver's filial piety you should study fully Myōkyō Daishi's discussion on filial piety. I will not discuss it in detail here.[69]

Nishiari concluded his main antimarriage tract by linking the inability of the Buddhist clergy to keep the precepts with broader social problems that he believed were rampant in Meiji Japan. In this manner he hoped to

[65] An excellent discussion of the conflict between loyalty and filiality in Japanese Confucianism is found in McMullen (1987, 56–97).

[66] Kusunoki Masashige (?–1336) was a leading supporter of Go-Daigo and the loyalist cause and helped to restore Go-Daigo to power. He met what was considered a glorious death, defending the imperial cause at the Battle of the Minato River in the summer of 1336. In Japanese literature he is often portrayed as the paragon of loyalty. Clearly identifying and wanting to use the memory of Masashige as an example of true loyalism, in 1872 the Meiji government deified him and established the Minatogawa Shrine at the site of his grave. See KDJ, 13:398. The "retainers of Akō" were the famous Forty-seven Rōnin who gave their lives to avenge the death of their lord.

[67] *Daishin* is one of the three types of mind that should be manifested by the head cook of the monastery, as described by Dōgen in *Tenzo kyōkun*. It is an impartial, pliable mind, which Dōgen likens to a great mountain or ocean. See DZZ, 2:302.

[68] See the *Xiao jing*, trans. James Legge (1900, 1:393): "Our bodies—to every hair and bit of skin—are received from our parents, and we must no presume to injure or wound them: this is the beginning of filial piety. When we have established our character by the practice of the filial course, so as to make our name famous in future ages, and thereby glorify our parents: this is the end of filial piety."

[69] Uan (1879, 172). Myōkyō Daishi was the posthumous name of Qisong (1007–72), a Chinese Chan cleric of the Yunmen branch.

counter the charge that standards of clerical purity are out of keeping with modernity. When Nishiari responded to the charge that if the Buddhists persisted in clinging to their outmoded standards of behavior they would meet the same decline in fortunes that had befallen the unmarried Roman Catholic clergy, he called into question the entire agenda of modernization. The focus had been exclusively on material improvement, not spiritual progress, and this devotion to materiality had severe repercussions. Nishiari attributed a host of problems—ranging from disloyalty to social dislocation—to the overwhelming concentration on material progress and modernization at the expense of spiritual cultivation. The inability of the Buddhist clergy to keep their vows was symptomatic of a more fundamental ill that plagued Japan. It was inner development, not material progress, that marked true "enlightenment and civilization."

> I am old-fashioned and there are things I do not understand about "civilization and enlightenment." Should what is happening in Japan today be seen as progress or decline? The most striking things about the so-called progress of civilization are such external manifestations as machinery, tiled roofs, Western clothes, Western literature, and Western language. However, when we examine the disposition of those who are adolescents or younger, we find that those with flippant, servile, and resentful voices are numerous, but those with a sense of integrity are extremely few.
>
> Precept violation by the clergy, the business enterprises of the nobles, and ex-samurai pulling rickshaws are not considered contemptuous. A woman is not embarrassed about being a consort or a geisha, and things have reached the state where it is considered foolish to be a "virtuous woman and a good wife." Deceit is a natural occurrence. It is difficult to loan and borrow money without collateral, even among fathers and sons or brothers. If this trend continues for a few more years, what will become of the nation, let alone the Buddha Dharma? When compared to the generations in which celibate clerics were valued and virtuous women were admired, is the current state of affairs beautiful or ugly, progress or decline? Ultimately my grieving over the decline of the Buddha Dharma results in my grieving for the nation.[70]

DEBATING THE MINISTERS: UNSHŌ'S VISIT TO THE MINISTRY OF JUSTICE

Fukuda's first petition to the Ministry of Doctrine was unanswered by the ministry officials. Efforts on the part of the leading clerics of most of the Buddhist schools—Jōdo, Shingon, Sōtō, and Nichiren—continued during the next few years. Petitions from other clerics were sent to the various organs of government in the hope of gaining some concessions on the

[70] Ibid., 174.

Figure 3. Shaku Unshō, Age 80

decriminalization of *nikujiki saitai*. Almost a year after Fukuda had submitted his petition, Shaku Unshō appealed to members of the Sain to repeal the decriminalization. Unlike Fukuda's petition, the two petitions from Unshō—dated November 2 and November 12, 1873—drew an immediate response from several members of the Sain's Criminal Law

Department. On November 13, the Sain sent a letter of summons to Unshō, ordering him to appear before a committee of its members.[71]

Like Fukuda, Unshō was a central figure in the precept restoration movement of early Meiji who hoped to revive the fortunes of Buddhism through the advocacy of the ten good precepts and the Threefold Training.[72] Unshō based his view of the universal importance of the ten good precepts on the writings of Jiun, particularly *Jūzen hōgo*, and sought to counter the claim that Buddhism was a world-abnegating philosophy by stressing the applicability of the precepts in daily life. In light of what he considered to be the particularly close relationship between the court and the Shingon school, Unshō believed that the support of the court was essential for the revival of Buddhism. At the same time he emphasized the necessity of strict adherence to the precepts as the sole means by which the Shingon school might preserve its function as an effective protector of the throne and nation. Unshō, like Fukuda, believed that the failure of the Buddhist clergy to abide by the precepts had resulted in the laity's general disdain for Buddhism and the growing anti-Buddhist furor in the Bakumatsu and early Meiji periods.

Unlike the vast majority of his contemporary Buddhist clerics, Unshō strictly adhered to the 250 precepts and is reputed to have refrained for much of his later life from drinking liquor, carrying money, eating after noon, and taking life. He is said even to have avoided pouring hot water on the ground for fear of injuring the countless sentient beings that live in the soil.[73] Unshō's uncompromising advocacy of the precepts placed him at odds with many of the members of the Buddhist reform movement, who viewed his approach as unnecessarily world-abnegating. Unshō's traditionalism also alienated many members of his own Shingon school. He vigorously fought the Meiji government's lifting of the ban on women at Mt. Kōya, much to the embarrassment of many colleagues who judged his view old-fashioned. His recalcitrance and vociferousness with regard to the issue eventually caused temple officials to remove him from Mt. Kōya; they believed him to be a madman endangering the welfare of the school by directly challenging the government.[74] Unshō, again like Fukuda,

[71] Shaku Unshō, *Nichiji zakki*, SUS, 3:23–27. Kusanagi Zengi, the editor of the collection of Unshō's writings, is unsure of the dating for the diary and suggests it was written in 1872. Unshō submitted the petitions in November 1873, however, indicating that the diary, which describes their submission on November 2 and November 12, was also written in 1873. For the petitions, see the MKP, 2: 917–19; 945–47.

[72] In addition to the information on Unshō in the SUS, see Ikeda (1976b, 58–80); Ikeda (1976a, 52–68).

[73] Tsunemitsu (1968, 1:89–91).

[74] Ibid., 1: 84. The policy of *nyonin kinsei* was ended on May 4, 1872, about a month before the decriminalization of *nikujiki saitai*. For the edict lifting the prohibition against women at shrines and temples, see NSRK, 620.

retired from the Shoshū Dōtoku Kaimei because he felt that the organization devoted too much energy to advocating the worldly interests of Buddhism—for example, the Buddhist role in the maintenance of the census system—rather than addressing the more pressing matter of spiritual renewal.[75]

Unshō's November 2 petition concerning clerical marriage specifically called for the revamping of the sect law of the various Buddhist schools in order to end such abuses as fornication, drinking, and eating meat. He observed that the heads of the Buddhist schools had remained indolent in the face of the government edict calling for reform of sect law and an end to all clerical abuses. The passage of the *nikujiki saitai* law had made matters even worse because decriminalization had resulted in flagrant disregard for sect law. Speaking from personal experience, Unshō complained that those clerics so bold as to admonish the wayward clerics became the object of scorn and vilification. The brief petition ended with a call for the government to pass a law that would require strict adherence to sect law.[76]

In the November 12 petition, Unshō called attention to inconsistencies in government regulations governing the clergy. The Grand Council of State, for example, had issued a proclamation on Meiji 3/12/25 (February 15, 1871) that blamed the Buddhist leadership for the corruption of the Buddhist clergy and called for the reform of sect law and strict adherence to the precepts.[77] The *nikujiki saitai* law clearly contradicted the spirit of the earlier edict. Unshō pointed out that the cleric repaid his debt to society through his teaching, not by caring for his family, having descendants, or practicing a trade. He noted that the precepts are the core of Buddhist practice, and committing any one of the four *pārājika* offenses that results in expulsion from the Buddhist sangha is referred to as *danzuzai*, literally, a crime that results in beheading, because as surely as decapitation causes a person's death, such infractions spell the end to one's status as a member of the clergy. A cleric guilty of precept violation, Unshō declared, is not fit to drink the water or to stand upon the soil of the realm.[78] As he elaborated in a note to Kuroda Kiyotsuna, the vice minister of the Ministry of Doctrine, the precepts of the Buddha must not, indeed cannot, be modified in any way. And like Nishiari and Fukuda, he tied the fate of Buddhism to

[75] Ikeda (1976b, 66). For Unshō's description of the debate over the *koseki* and the clergy, see *Tōzai ryōkyō hinami dairyaku*, SUS, 3, *Nikki shū*: 13–14.

[76] Shaku Unshō (1873a, 917–18).

[77] Miyachi (1988, 436); NSRK, 601.

[78] Shaku Unshō (1873b, 945). The four offenses for monks that result in expulsion from the sangha are unchastity, stealing, destruction of life, and falsely claiming supernatural powers. In the *Mahāvagga* it says, "It is prohibited for a monk to have sexual intercourse, even with a female animal. A monk who has sexual intercourse is not a monk anymore, nor a son of the *Sākyans*. As a man who has been beheaded cannot live with only a body, so a monk who has had sexual intercourse is not a monk anymore." The translation of that passage comes from Wijayaratna (1990, 91–92). See also OBD, 1185c.

the nation's welfare. Citing the *Mahāparinirvāṇa Sūtra*, Unshō wrote, "if we do not rectify the sectarian regulations, we will not be able to guide people. We tens of thousands of clerics vainly will assume the name of Doctrinal Instructor and will provide no benefit to the state. This will quickly result in the incursion of Christianity. Therefore, my petition is not solely for the sake of Buddhism, but is also concerned with the national polity."[79]

In the November 12 petition, Unshō went on to argue that those members of the Buddhist clergy who violate the Buddhist proscription against sexual relations should be subject to the same punishments meted out for the sexual improprieties—adultery or incest—of the laity. If the government was going to punish those who destroy Buddhist images, Unshō asked, should it not also hold those guilty of demolishing the absolute body of Buddhism, that is, the precepts, equally accountable? He also requested that clerics guilty of actions that are unbecoming of a Buddhist monk be expelled from their temples and their names be struck from the clerical registry, just as a lay person who is a peer or samurai would be demoted to commoner status if found guilty of extraordinarily shameful behavior.[80]

While blaming the clerical leadership for the laxity of practice, Unshō also recognized the ineffectiveness of the head temples in forcing the clergy to abide by sect law, and we must conclude that he believed that, ultimately, enforcement of sect law required access to some means of physical violence. This necessitated state support for the sectarian regulations. Therefore, Unshō was asking for the government to intervene on behalf of the head temple establishments when lower-ranking clerics refused to abide by the punishments assigned to them. He recalled that "Japanese Buddhism had flourished with the support of the imperial court. So long as there was no faith at the imperial court, it would be impossible to revive Buddhism."[81] Unshō was not the only advocate of limited state support; Fukuda clearly was asking the government to stand behind the head temples in their effort to enforce the ban on *nikujiki saitai*. The inability of these reformers to enforce a strict code of behavior without the support of the government demonstrates the extent to which Buddhism was dependent on the state after the late medieval period, when the state destroyed the military power of the Buddhist monasteries and left the Buddhist establishment without a means of maintaining internal discipline.[82]

[79] Shaku Unshō, *Nichiji zakki*, SUS 3:24.   [80] Shaku Unshō, (1873b, 946).

[81] Ikeda (1976b, 65); SUS, 2:250.

[82] Ilana Silber's comment concerning the maintenance of standards for clerical conduct in Theravāda monasteries is germane in this regard: "Since the Sangha wielded no temporal authority and power of its own, it came to depend on external forces and especially on the willingness, ability and even initiative of the political center to ensure its internal cohesion and purity." Silber (1981, 171).

Four government officials responded in person to Unshō's petitions on November 17. According to his detailed diary entry for the meeting, they began by reading a formal response explaining why they were unable to follow the suggestions laid out in his petition. While admiring the stringency of his standards, they noted that the clerics of each school and not the government were responsible for the health of their religious organizations. "Is this new era of enlightenment and civilization to be an era in which we cling to old habits (*kyūshu*)?" the officials asked in regard to the *nikujiki saitai* measure. "That is the reason we lifted the ban."[83] As far as the officials were concerned, the fate of Buddhism did not hinge on continued enforcement of the outmoded ban on marriage. Unshō carefully recorded in his diary the exchange that followed between himself and the officials. The dialogue not only gives us the clearest statement of the government policy concerning sectarian regulations and state law but also demonstrates how far apart the worldview of such conservative clerics as Unshō was from that of the officials—the difference in cosmological assumptions approached comical dimensions at times. Here follows a portion of the exchange. It begins with Takasaki's assertion that marriage does not necessarily entail the extinction of Buddhism; one need only to look at the prosperous Jōdo Shin denomination to see that is the case. Unshō retorted that "they are laymen (*ubasoku*). Pure clerics (*seisō*) make the precepts fundamental" (26). Takasaki responded that the clerical regulations should conform to the age and that if Śākyamuni were alive today, he would modify the precepts accordingly. Unshō, however, refused to accept this hypothetical statement and, in accordance with Buddhist eschatological predictions, countered that there will be no Buddha until Maitreya appears. What is more, he continued,

> Even if the Buddhist teaching undergoes various changes, the precepts do not change. The precepts were advocated in the same manner by Aśvaghoṣa, Nāgārjuna, the monks of China, [the teachers of] 1,300 years ago in Japan, 1,000 years ago by Kūkai and Saichō, and after, until around 900 years ago, in the decrees from the patriarchal teachers to the Dajōkan. Next there were Eisai's *Kōzen gokokuron*, Dōgen's *Shōbōgenzō*, Hōnen, and others; even 500–700 years ago, at the time of the samurai government, there were people advocating the precepts and reviving the true teaching. If we do not advocate these precepts today, the true teaching will disappear. Whatever Buddha exists, he will attempt to revive these precepts. (29–30)

According to Unshō, the precepts are immutable. For us to change them to accord with the spirit of the times would be extremely foolhardy because we lack the wisdom of the Buddha. "The precepts are the body of the

---

[83] Shaku Unshō, *Nichiji zakki*, SUS, 3:27. Further references to this work will be cited as page numbers in the text.

sangha. They are the basis of the transmission of the true teaching. Because the Buddha was omnipotent, if we were to make various mistaken discriminations using our ordinary intelligence, we would destroy the Buddhist teaching" (40). Takasaki, however, stated that although he agreed with Unshō that Buddhism in Japan has reached its nadir, he did not believe it is the government's responsibility to guarantee the preservation of the precepts. In all other nations, there is separation of church and state. Only the imperial government of Japan continues to support religion through the establishment of the Great Teaching Academy and the Chief Priest system. Beyond that the fate of Buddhism rests with clergy who, in Takasaki's words, "must make enormous efforts" in order to revive Buddhism.

Unshō questioned Takasaki about the government's lack of involvement in the matter of clerical celibacy by raising the example of state laws governing fornication. He asked, "Is there not a [charge of] improper sexual relations (*bonkan*) in the secular law?" After Takasaki agreed that there are regulations governing such matters, Unshō then claimed,

> therefore, when [a cleric] takes a wife, the parishioners and villagers will be extremely scornful of them. What should be done about this?
>
> TAKASAKI: There is no prohibition in the secular law against publicly marrying.
>
> UNSHŌ: In that case, Buddhism will eventually disappear.
>
> TAKASAKI: Even if Buddhism disappears, that is of no concern to the court. The secular law has nothing to do with the prosperity or disappearance of Buddhism. [Deep reflection.] Buddhism is [a matter of] inner disposition (*Buppō wa shinjutsu nari*), it does not have anything to do with the Kingly Law, nor should it depend on Kingly Law. Furthermore it should not be regulated [by Kingly Law]. (34–35)

Unshō went on to state that although it is the responsibility of the clergy to preserve the precepts, they need the help of the state to discipline those "obdurate evil clerics" who ignore their superiors. He then asked the following of Takasaki:

> The Kaitei Ritsu contains a law that one must not destroy a statue of the Buddha. When a cleric openly violates the precepts, the parishioners and villagers strongly vilify him, because he is doing something that one who is a cleric should not do. I only ask of you that a regulation be adopted that a cleric must not violate the precepts.[84]
>
> TAKASAKI: [Quiet for a time.] Relations between men and women are natural (*tennen no shō*). It is impossible to forgo them.

---

[84] The Kaitei Ritsu is a reference to the Kaitei Ritsurei promulgated by the Meiji government in 1873. The new legal code was a modification of the earlier Shinritsu Kōryō that had been issued in 1870. See KDJ 3: 78–79.

UNSHŌ: There is nothing of the kind among such kami, as Amaterasu and the others. Also, such individuals as Yamato Hime no Miko, who were devotees of the kami also abhorred such things.[85]

TAKASAKI: Although people are capable of remaining pure for seven days prior to a festival, to do so for a lifetime is impossible. If Śākyamuni were to appear today he would allow such things.[86] (36)

Takasaki thus defended the decriminalization of clerical marriage in the same manner as Ōtori, who argued that the Buddhist precepts had long ago ceased to conform to the times and were in need of correction. Unshō, on the other hand, hoping to renew strict adherence to the precepts, expressed the fear that the Buddhist leadership would be unable to do so without the direct support of the state.

In a telling exchange, Takasaki argued that "if you rectify the precepts, the Buddhist clergy will disappear." Unshō retorted, "the Buddha said that neither kings, ministers, nobles, or laymen can destroy the true teaching. Only my disciples in the Last Age can extinguish it" (32) According to Unshō, true destruction of Buddhism is caused by corrupt clerics, not outside forces. In addition, clergy who do not abide by the canons of Buddhist discipline are useless to the sangha or the nation. Unshō, citing the words of the Buddha, likened such individuals to vicious bandits or fleas on a lion and suggested that it would be far wiser to make these wayward clerics rice threshers or mailmen than to allow them to remain in the temples. At least then they could be of some use to the nation. Like Fukuda, Unshō urged the government to allow the head temples to expel those clerics who did not meet the standards set by the clerical leadership. He demanded that the secular law support Buddhist law, according to which "a cleric is a cleric because he upholds the precepts. One who violates the precepts is not a cleric. Therefore forcing them to be returned to the secular *koseki* and laicized is in accordance with the Buddhist precepts. The laws of the ruler should be the same" (31).

Takasaki did not agree to act quickly to correct the criminal code, as Unshō suggested, but he did consent to investigate further the matter of the clerical status of those who flagrantly violated protocols of behavior. The discussion of this particular point reveals that the government was flexible on some issues and willing to act on suggestions from the clergy. At least in this specific regard, the government adopted a position in line

---

[85] Yamato Hime no Mikoto was the daughter of Emperor Suinin who, according to the *Nihon shoki*, served as medium (*mitsueshiro*) for Amaterasu and became the head priestess at Ise. See the *Nihon shoki*, "Sujin Tennō" Year 6, "Suinin Tennō," Year 25, for a partial description of these events.

[86] In a subsequent visit to Kuroda Kiyotsuna, Unshō adds that the kami of the sun, the kami of the moon, and Yamato Hime no Mikoto all observed ritual purity for their whole lives. Shaku Unshō, *Nichiji zakki*, SUS, 3, *Nikki shū*: 40.

with Unshō's position. When, the following year, the Ministry of Justice received an inquiry from Yamagata Prefecture asking whether those clerics guilty of shameful behavior should lose their status as clerics, be demoted from *shizoku* to *heimin* and returned to their original permanent domicile, or, if already *heimin*, simply lose their clerical status and be returned to their original domicile, the officials answered—as Unshō had urged them to do in his petition—in the affirmative.[87]

[87] NSRK, 678–79. The same inquiry is contained in the *Sōryo hikkei*, MBSS, 5:341, but the editor, himself a Buddhist cleric, has added an interlinear note that *harenchi hanahadashii* means such violations as illicit sexual relations (*kantsū*), stealing, and gambling.

CHAPTER 7

Denominational Resistance and the
Modification of Government Policy

THE FEROCIOUS protest that arose following the promulgation of the *nikujiki saitai* law caught the officials in the Ministry of Doctrine by surprise. In spite of much serious resistance from leading Buddhist clerics, however, ministry officials refused to rescind the new order. During the next six years, Buddhist leaders tested the government's resolve to stay the course and tried to maintain control of the clergy in the absence of government intervention on their behalf. Although eventually accepting that enforcement of clerical regulations regarding marriage and meat eating were no longer a state concern, clerical leaders continued to claim that they, rather than individual clerics, could set the standards for the deportment of clergy in their denomination. A number of Buddhist denominations made skillful use of the ambiguities of the *nikujiki saitai* law, particularly the meaning of "voluntary" clerical marriage. As discussed earlier, many Buddhist intellectuals also attacked the law from this standpoint. Resistance to ministry intervention in denominational affairs was facilitated by turning the government's own newly created rhetoric about the disestablishment and independence of Buddhism and religious freedom against those who attempted to force sect leaders to relax clerical standards. Resistance to the measure thus crossed sectarian lines and, as was so common during the early Meiji, alliances of sect leaders wrote and submitted petitions to ministry officials.

It appears that the Buddhist response to the decriminalization was split. The accounts of Fukuda Gyōkai, Kuroda Kiyotsuna, and Matsumoto Mannen, the author of *Inaka hanjōki*, all noted the confusion and strife that followed the promulgation of the new law.[1] Although the clerical elites at first uniformly were opposed to the decriminalization, many clerics seem to have been far less distressed by the measure. Kitagawa Chikai noted, for example, that "since the lifting of the ban on eating meat and clerical marriage due to the promulgation of Grand Council of State Edict 133 in Meiji 5, precept-breaking clerics have been thrilled. The ignorant, without understanding the difference between state law and Buddhist law,

---

[1] Matsumoto's account of the debate over *nikujiki saitai* within the Daikyōin is cited by Tsuji (1949, 245).

eat meat, marry, and abandon the precepts. They rob Buddhism of its life and condemn it to destruction."[2] Similarly, Hattori Masao argued that the majority of the Buddhist clergy were pleased by the promulgation of the law decriminalizing *nikujiki saitai*.[3]

One of the earliest organized responses to the ministry's new regulation came from the leaders of the Sōtō sect, who disseminated two edicts to their subordinates just two months after the adoption of the law. Sōtō leaders were firm supporters of the movement to end the decriminalization measure. Not content with merely appealing to the Meiji bureaucracy for modification of the law, the Sōtō leadership also warned the clergy at branch temples to continue to adhere to the precepts that they had received at their ordinations. On Meiji 5/6/2 (July 7, 1872) the leaders of the Sōtō head temples, Eiheiji and Sōjiji, sent a directive to all Sōtō clerics who were lecturing doctrinal instructors. Noting that the government had "entrusted" to the clergy the matter of adhering to the precepts, the authors of the directive warned, "If one does not strictly adhere to the precepts, then it is difficult to practice the Buddhist teaching (*kyōhō*). If the violence of human emotions is not constrained by the precepts, then one cannot distinguish right and wrong." The letter admonished all of the Sōtō doctrinal instructors to unfailingly continue to teach the rank-and-file clergy at the branch temples in accordance with the precepts of the Buddhas and Patriarchs.[4]

Just three days later, on Meiji 5/6/5 (July 10, 1872), a more detailed and forceful statement was issued to all Sōtō branch temples. The new announcement claimed that many clerics had misconstrued—perhaps deliberately—the decriminalization measure as a government order to marry. For this reason the Sōtō leadership intended to clarify the new law. The authors of the directive acknowledged the complaint of such critics as Ōtori that a only a small minority of the Buddhist clergy maintained the discipline expected of a cleric, writing that, "of every ten monks, eight or nine of them feign liberation in public, but embrace fettering thoughts when out of view."[5] The authors claimed that the decriminalization measure was a government strategy for separating true disciples of the Buddha from the false by giving them the freedom to choose between adhering to or violating the precepts. The intent of the measure, the authors stated, was not to abolish the precepts for the clergy, but to end government involvement in enforcing clerical rules. The Sōtō leaders exhorted their subordinates that

---

[2] Kitagawa (1933, 284).   [3] Hattori (1938, 63–64).

[4] *Sōtōshū Ryōhonzan futatsu zensho*, vol. 1 (M. 5/11), 3v–4r. See also Tanaka Keishin (1984a, 132); Morioka (1986, 125); Kuriyama (1917, 60).

[5] *Sōtōshū Ryōhonzan futatsu zensho* vol. 1 (Meiji 5/11), Proclamation of Meiji 5/6/5, 4 verso–5 recto.

a decree now has entrusted the Buddhist precepts to the monks [the meaning of "voluntary" (*katte tarubeki*) is that it is "entrusted" (*makaseru*)], so it is up to the clergy to ensure that the precepts are strictly followed. If at this time disciples of the Buddha do not "return the light to illumine the source" (*ekō henshō*), correct previous infractions of the rules, rouse themselves to protect and uphold the True Law, and repay their debt to the nation, then when will they?[6]

In urging all clerics to continue to obey the precepts—specifically, those concerning fornication and meat eating—the leadership of the Sōtō denomination did not go further than calling on each cleric to rely upon his or her own conscience. The Sōtō directive therefore did not contradict the letter of the *nikujiki saitai* decriminalization measure, which had rendered adherence to Buddhist behavioral norms voluntary. The authors of the directive interpreted the law in a manner that justified their continued control of clerical behavior. According to the Sōtō leadership's gloss on the new law, the government devolved control of Buddhist affairs to the sects but stopped short of advocating clerical marriage and other violations of sect law. As with Fukuda's interpretation of the measure, the Sōtō leaders glossed the phrase *katte tarubeki* as "to entrust." Following this rather strained interpretation of the law, they concluded that each denomination was empowered to ensure adherence to the precepts. It did not mean that each cleric was free to do as he or she chose. According to the directive, during the Edo period the Buddhist precepts had been conflated with secular law, a mistake that needed to be rectified. Ultimately standards of clerical behavior were rooted in the Buddhist precepts, not the secular law. Although firmly opposed to the decriminalization measure, at this juncture the Sōtō leaders went no further than a cautious appeal to the clergy to adhere to the precepts and avoid sullying the Buddhist teaching.

The leaders of other denominations gave even more stringent warnings to their subordinates. Shortly after the promulgation of the decriminalization measure, Rinzai Zen leaders issued a joint directive to the clergy of the Gozan temples that called for the expulsion of clerics who unrepentantly flaunted the proscription against sexual activity. The leadership of both the Jōdo (1872; 1874) and Nichiren (1875) denominations also warned their clerics to continue to adhere to the precepts.[7]

Despite the official hard-line attitude toward *nikujiki saitai*, it appears that the Sōtō leadership was aware that full enforcement of its standards would be all but impossible in the wake of the new decriminalization law. Even as some leaders were promulgating stringent restrictions concerning clerical marriage, steps were being taken within the denomination to deal

---

[6] Ibid., 4v.
[7] See Sakurai (1954, 261); Ōhashi (1987, 80; 93); Nichirenshū rokuji (1878, 2–3).

with the married clerics. Kumamoto Einin has pointed out that a document recently discovered at the Sōtō temple Myōōji indicates that as early as 1873 some denominational leaders advised turning a blind eye toward those clerics who, in accordance with local customs, chose to ignore sect law and marry. The document, which was signed by the abbots of Eiheiji and Sōjiji, stated that the debate over the *nikujiki saitai* decriminalization measure would be heated and warned clerical leaders to respect the traditions of the various local temples and not to be overly rigid in their attempts to enforce sectarian discipline.[8]

The degree of flexibility in the government's position concerning the amount of control held by head temples over the subordinate clergy at the branch temples was ambiguous at best. Although the Sōtō officials managed to avoid drawing the attention of the bureaucrats at the Ministry of Doctrine, the leadership of one branch of the Shingon sect, the Omuro-ha, proved to be less adept at walking the fine line between the voluntary and the mandatory. The events surrounding the Omuro-ha leadership's efforts to suppress clerical marriage within their sect are recorded in detail in the *Shaji torishirabe ruisan* and have been discussed at length by Morioka Kiyomi.[9] The Omuro-ha case, discussed in the following pages, will serve to clarify the government's interpretation of the new law.[10]

In the wake of Edict 133, the leadership of the Omuro-ha's head temple, Ninnaji, disseminated, via the administrative temple, Saifukuji, a message concerning the standards for clerical behavior. It began by citing the *nikujiki saitai* law and then noted that, despite the government's passage of the law, the violation of the precepts was not appropriate behavior for a true disciple of the Buddha. The purpose of the decriminalization edict, the authors explained, was to cause "the true relationship between sovereign and subjects, enlightened civilization, and true teachers of Buddhism to flourish." For this to occur it was important to destroy all stubborn adherence to the evils of the past. The Buddhist clergy therefore should act in a manner appropriate to its station and adhere to the Buddhist law

---

[8] Kumamoto (1996, 18).

[9] Morioka (1986, 126–30).

[10] STR 182, "Myōdō-ken yori sōryo nikujiki saitai no gi ni tsuki ukagau," Meiji 5/11/5. Morioka (1986, 126–29). The STR file includes the following documents: Meiji 5/10 Ministry of Doctrine cover letter; Meiji 5/10/5 letter of complaint from the Myōdō government to the Ministry of Doctrine; Meiji 5/11 letter from the Kyoto government to the Ministry of Doctrine; Meiji 5/5/17 letter from Ninnaji to the Kyoto government; Meiji 5/5/21 letter from Ninnaji to the Kyoto government; Meiji 5/5/28 letter from Ninnaji to the Kyoto government; Meiji 5/7/25 letter from Myōdō government to the Kyoto government; copy of the directive circulated by Ninnaji; Meiji 5/7/25 copy of same submitted to the Myōdō government by Ninnaji; Meiji 5/8/3 letter from Kyoto to Myōdō government; Meiji 5/8/5 letter from Ninnaji to Kyoto government; Meiji 5/8 letter from Myōdō to Kyoto; M 5/8/27 letter from Kyoto to Myōdō; Meiji 5/11 Ministry of Doctrine response to the inquiry.

and precepts. The document concluded that those who wished to marry, eat meat, grow their hair, or wear ordinary clothing were to submit a document to the head temple testifying to that effect. Sect clerics were not free to engage in any of the aforementioned activities without first receiving explicit permission from the head temple. If those in charge at the branch temple agreed with the proposal, they were to sign a statement to that effect and return it to the head temple. In effect, the head temple would determine who could break their Buddhist vows and would keep track of whether a cleric was "pure."[11]

Interestingly, the Omuro-ha leadership had not acted unilaterally in this matter. Prior to circulating the petition, it had duly applied to the Kyoto prefectural government for permission to send the document to all branch temples. In the request the authors had stated that the purpose of the petition was to investigate the spiritual disposition of the sect's members to see whether "they would eat meat, marry, grow their hair, and so on, or if they will, as in the past, practice in accordance with the teachings and prohibitions of the Buddhas and Patriarchs." A second letter to the Kyoto government, dated Meiji 5/5/28 (June 10, 1872), and signed by the Archbishop (Sōjō) Kaimyōji Shōtsū, expressed several reasons why the sect should be allowed to establish some means of controlling the behavior of its subordinate clerics. Shōtsū, echoing Fukuda's petition, wrote that if the sect did not take steps to distinguish between those who adhere to the precepts and those who live like laypeople, then the impostors, who would continue to look like clerics, would be able to deceive the ignorant masses, causing confusion and dissension. These false teachers would not only be able to distort the meaning of the Buddhist teachings, but would also cause the people to misinterpret the laws issued by the government. Shōtsū also emphasized that clerical discipline was equally important for the success of the new imperial government. If the Ninnaji leadership was not allowed to enforce the patriarchal rules and regulations, then clerics would profoundly misinterpret the meaning of the teachings.[12]

The officials at the Kyoto prefectural level gave their imprimatur to the proposal, allowing the Omuro-ha leadership to send functionaries to the various branch temples to solicit local compliance with the sect law in spite of the decriminalization edict. When a document from the Saifukuji temple was circulated in Myōdō-ken, which, according to Morioka, contained 10 percent of the Omuro-ha branch temples, Myōdō officials appealed to the Kyoto government in a letter dated Meiji 5/7/25 (August 28, 1872). They requested that the order be rescinded because, in that the sect leaders had attempted to privately discipline their clerics, they had contradicted the intent of the *nikujiki saitai* law.

[11] STR, 182, "Myōdō-ken yori sōryo nikujiki saitai no gi ni tsuki ukagau."
[12] Ibid.

On September 6 the Kyoto officials responded to the Myōdō letter. They denied that the actions of the Omuro-ha leadership contravened government policy because the law did not mean that the Buddhist clergy *had to* marry or eat meat; it meant only that it was acceptable if they did so. Shōtsū's letter did not specifically state that the clerics at branch temples could not marry if they wished to do so, and, in light of their sect law, the sect leaders correctly asserted that those who do not engage in *nikujiki saitai* should be treated as "true monks" (*shōsō*), while those who do should be regarded as laymen (*ubasoku*). The sole intent of the letter was to ensure the correct practice of the Buddhist teaching, the officials concluded, and therefore Myōdō officials had no reason to ban the circulation of the document in question.[13]

Myōdō officials refused to accept these arguments, however. In their opinion, the decriminalization measure did not allow distinctions to be made between pure, celibate clerics and impure laymen. After failing to receive an appropriate response from the Kyoto government, the Myōdō officials then appealed for direct intervention from the Ministry of Doctrine.[14]

In their response, the officials at the Ministry of Doctrine tried to clarify the underlying intent of the decriminalization edict. Finding in favor of the Myōdō position, they wrote, in language that echoed Ōtori's second petition:

> the purpose of the decree that makes meat eating, marriage, growing the hair, and the wearing of ordinary clothing voluntary for the Buddhist clergy is to preserve Heavenly Principle (*tenri*), to support humaneness (*jindō*), and to eliminate all evil customs in the past sect law. For the clerics at Ninnaji to cling to their old regulations and, based on their own opinion, to set up distinctions among their clerics and issue proclamations to the clergy of their branch temples is absolutely contrary to the will of the court and hinders the education of the public.[15]

The Ministry of Doctrine therefore ordered the objectionable letter calling for the registration of "impure" clerics to be retracted. With that, the Omuro leadership finally was forced to end its tour of inspection of the branch temples and to allow clerics at the branch temples to marry without informing the head temple. The finding from the Ministry of Doctrine clearly reflects the language of Ōtori Sessō's petition to the government and demonstrates the solidification of that view of celibacy and other clerical customs into official policy.

[13] Ibid., letter from Kyoto to Myōdo government.

[14] STR, 182.1, "Myōdō-ken yori sōryo nikujiki saitai no gi ni tsuki ukagau," letter from Myōdō to Kyoto, Meiji 5/8.

[15] STR, 182, "Ninnaji sō no Myōdō-ken junkai ni tsuki tatsuan"; also cited in Morioka (1986, 128).

The struggle between the Kyoto government and the Ministry of Doctrine over the Ninnaji case was ironic given the Kyoto position in a debate that had erupted between Kyoto officials and ministry bureaucrats immediately after the ministry was formed in late spring 1872. An anonymous letter denouncing the mandate of the new Ministry of Doctrine was sent from the Kyoto government to the central government. In it, Kyoto officials criticized the central government for incorporating the Buddhist clergy into its program of popular education, the Great Promulgation Campaign, as doctrinal instructors. The central government was wasting both time and money because the "preservation of a deceptive religion and the control of each and every priest should not be an urgent concern of the ministers of our nation."[16] As Sakamoto has observed, Kyoto officials believed that granting the Ministry of Doctrine jurisdiction over elements of public education through the teaching academies and proselytization campaign was supererogatory. These measures conflicted with existing efforts by the Ministry of Education to establish a system of public education and, what was even worse, employed the ignorant clergy to accomplish that task. In that the Kyoto government officials felt that the ministry was treading on their territory by legislating to the religious institutions in their sphere of influence, they may have used the Ninnaji affair to test the resolve of the Ministry of Doctrine. By giving a loose interpretation of the *nikujiki saitai* law and allowing the Omuro-ha leadership to decide how to apply the law to its own branch temples, Kyoto government officials attempted to undercut whatever control the ministry might have had over the clergy. The response of the Ministry of Doctrine was harsh and definitive. But although the Kyoto government was overruled on this point of legal interpretation, the arguments it advanced would, in just a few years, come to be adopted as the official central government position on the issue of state versus sect law.

The problem of clerical marriage in the Shingon and Tendai denominations was complicated by the forced absorption of former Shugendō clergy, many of whom were married, into their ranks when the Meiji government disbanded Shugendō in 1872.[17] The edict abolishing Shugendō orders forced all clerics formerly associated with that school to join either the Shingon or the Tendai establishments.[18] The leadership of the Shingon and Tendai denominations rapidly established a two-tiered ranking system for the clergy and forbade the former Shugendō clerics from wearing Shugendō robes or performing Shugendō ceremonies. In addition, the

---

[16] Ketelaar (1990, 100). See also Sakamoto (1983, 54–60).

[17] The starting date of open acceptance of clerical marriage in the Shugendō sects is not entirely clear, but Hikita Seishun speculates that in the Tōzan sect, marriage existed during the first part of the Heian period. See Hikita (1991a, 102–3).

[18] NSRK, 662.

Shugendō clergy were relegated to second-class status within the schools, prevented from moving beyond a relatively low level of initiation and barred from officiating at high-level ceremonies.[19]

In the case of the Shingon denomination, for example, Chief Priest Sasaki Gihan issued in 1876 a strictly worded directive to the branch temples delineating the division between "pure" and "impure" assemblies (*seishu/zasshu*). Members of the pure assembly were defined as those who were well versed in doctrine and worked zealously to protect Buddhism. They did not engage in meat eating, marriage, abandoning tonsure, or wearing secular clothing. Members of the impure assembly were classified as those whose disposition toward doctrinal matters and the protection of the teaching was weak, and who succumbed to *nikujiki saitai* and related activities. Only members of the pure assembly would be considered as candidates for the abbacy of the more important temples and allowed to attend esoteric initiations or other important ceremonies.[20]

The former Shugendō clergy did not passively accept their relegation to second-class status. As early as 1874 the clerics protested to the Ministry of Doctrine about the harsh treatment they were receiving. On August 25, 1874, for example, two former Shugendō clerics from Shimane Prefecture, Kurihara Chijō and Date Shingi, filed a petition with the Ministry of Doctrine in which they complained about the visit to Shimane of Yamauchi Zuien, the representative of the Shingon chief priest. Yamauchi informed the Shugendō clergy in the region of the differences between their regulations and those of the Shingon school and also disseminated news of an agreement that had been reached between the Shingon and Tendai chief priests concerning the status of the Shugendō clergy who had been incorporated into those denominations.[21] According to the accord, the former members of the Shugendō denominations were to be subordinate in status to the "pure" clergy of the Shingon and Tendai denominations because the Shugendō clerics were laymen, not true home-leavers.[22] Kurihara and Date stated that they could not abide such terms, and—as with the petitions submitted by Ōtori and Ugawa—they complained that such arbitrary discrimination would hinder proselytization efforts and give rise to popular suspicions about the clergy. They argued that adherence to the precepts depends solely on one's inner disposition (*shinjutsu*) and has no effect on one's status as a member of the Buddhist clergy. The key to Japan's wealth

---

[19] Miyake (1978, 71–72).   [20] Shingonshū rokuji (1876, 1–2).
[21] Kurihara and Date (1874, 3:475–76).
[22] According to Hikita (1991a, 141–46), from the founding of their denominations, the Shugendō clergy were frequently referred to as *ubasoku*. A number of sources also indicate that they did not draw a rigid distinction between groups of clerics on the basis of marriage or the tonsure. It was even permissible for members of the Shugendō denominations to bear arms.

and strength is to teach Buddhism to the people effectively. If the subjects are patriotic and loyal, then whatever the strength of foreign powers, Japan will not be subdued. Given the urgency of such a task, the authors asked, should they be wasting their time clinging to "trivial old practices of our school"?[23]

Kurihara and Date attempted to use the arguments concerning national welfare to further their own sectarian goal—that is, to circumscribe Shingon and Tendai control over Shugendō and the relegation of the Shugendō clergy to second-class status within those schools based on their status as laymen. At least some Shugendō clerics therefore supported the proselytization effort as a strategy in their struggle for autonomy from the Tendai and Shingon establishments. Shugendō clerics also found the emerging definition of religious practice as a matter of inner intention and private conscience to be another useful weapon in their struggle. The somewhat curious use of the term *shinjutsu* to characterize religious, specifically Buddhist, practice, which appears in Takasaki Goroku's dialogue with Unshō, is also found in Kurihara and Date's petition. These clerics trumpeted the characterization of Buddhism as a private concern to free themselves from Tendai and Shingon control.

Kurihara and Date's petition did not prevent the official adoption of the two-tiered system by the Shingon and the Tendai chief priests, but low-ranking clerics continued to express strong resentment about their relegation to second-class status. For example, several years after the publication of a detailed account of the two-tiered Shingon system in *Meikyō shinshi*, Minami Danzō submitted a critique of that system to the same journal. Minami described himself as "a lay believer (*koji*) who eats meat and is married, and who, by nature, is unable to free himself from the passions of the world. I am a member of the lowest class of what in our school is called the *zasshu*."[24] He was, therefore, in the same low stratum of the Shingon school as Kurihara and Date. Minami complained that very few of the thousands of clerics in the Shingon school were capable of meeting the rigorous standard of behavior established by the leadership, and that overly severe standards would result in outward conformity and hidden violation—which would only further incite opponents of Buddhism to criticize the clergy. Minami, like Kurihara and other proponents of clerical marriage, further asserted that, given the severity of the crisis facing Buddhism, it was entirely necessary to make use of talented clerics as soldiers in the defense of Buddhism even if they were married or ate meat. He maintained that the traditional precepts were out of keeping with the age, and he asked rhetorically whether Śākyamuni would order people to

[23] Kurihara and Date (1874, 3: 475–476).
[24] Minami (1878, 1). The letter is summarized in Tanaka Keishin (1984b, 263).

follow such precepts in an age when meat eating, prostitution, and illegitimacy were rampant. "The pressing matter today is not the prohibition of meat eating or marriage, it is education. We must abandon trivialities and strengthen the fundamentals." Minami concluded by expressing his confusion over the proclamation of the system from the head temple and asked for clarification. The editors of *Meikyō shinshi* commented that, although they did not agree completely with Minami's approach to the problem of clerical marriage, they had published his letter because the Buddhist clergy were increasingly distressed by the decriminalization of *nikujiki saitai*, which had become one of the most crucial problems of the day.[25]

The example set by the institution of the two-tiered system in the Shingon and Tendai schools apparently influenced the Sōtō school as well. Kuriyama Taion described an attempt by one faction of the Sōtō leadership to resolve the problem of clerical marriage by establishing two distinct groups within the school, practitioners (*bendōshi*), who were "pure," unmarried clerics, and evangelists (*shōdōshi*), who were allowed to marry. According to Kuriyama, the division of the Sōtō clergy into two classes was proposed during the period of 1888 to 1889.[26] As in the Shingon school, only the practitioners would be able to act as teachers and serve as abbots of the head temples. Kuriyama traced the origin of the two-tiered system to the Tendai denomination, in particular to the noted Tendai cleric Murata Jakujun (1838–1905), who, according to Kuriyama, advocated the division of the Tendai school into unmarried clerics (*gedatsusō*) and married clerics (*gonjisō*).[27] In trying to date when the Tendai leaders might have initiated the system, we know that Kurihara had described an 1874 agreement between the Shingon and Tendai chief priests about the disposition of the Shugendō clergy within those two schools. In any case, because Murata died in 1905, the Tendai school must have begun the system prior to that time.

Kuriyama vehemently opposed the two-tiered system because he believed it would eventually lead to the total segregation of the two types of clerics and to disunity within the school. Kuriyama, a partisan of the Sōjiji faction of the Sōtō denomination, may have feared that such a policy would relegate more Sōjiji temples to permanent second-class status and thus was another attempt by the Eiheiji proponents to weaken the Sōjiji faction. No doubt many others also opposed the plan, because it was never adopted by the Sōtō school.[28]

[25] Minami (1878, 4).

[26] Kuriyama (1917, 66). Taion does not name those responsible for the proposal, perhaps because of his caustic criticism of the plan. Yokozeki Ryōin (1938, 1) suggests that Hara Tanzan (1819–1892) made this proposal for the Sōtō denomination.

[27] *Gonji* is a translation of the Sanskrit word for a lay Buddhist, *upāsaka*.

[28] Kuriyama (1917, 71–73).

MODIFICATION OF THE GOVERNMENT POSITION AND THE
RESPONSE OF THE CLERICAL LEADERSHIP

Although the clerical leadership received no positive response to their first wave of petitions, they did not desist in their attempt to pressure the Sain to issue a regulation that would either rescind the *nikujiki saitai* law or at least strengthen their hand in enforcing sect law. In September 1877, Fukuda wrote another petition to the government, much more urgent in tone than the earlier one. Stating that, as a result of the new law, "Unmarried clerics rapidly have set up their wive's quarters and the pure place of practice quickly has become a butcher shop where meat is consumed," Fukuda once again pleaded with officials to either abolish the decriminalization measure or issue a new one forbidding *nikujiki saitai*.[29] Again the petition was signed by the chief priests of all the Buddhist denominations.

The government was more receptive to Fukuda's second petition than his first, primarily due to the government's significantly shifting attitude toward the Buddhist clergy. As described in chapter 4, by the mid-1870s the attempt to orchestrate the proselytization effort through a joint Buddhist-Shintō organization, the Ministry of Doctrine, had proved a monumental failure. Christians and some Buddhists made increasingly vocal calls for at least limited freedom of religion as the nation prepared to draft its first constitution. In 1877, bowing to pressure from within and without, the government abolished the Ministry of Doctrine and assigned management of sectarian affairs to the Shrine and Temple Bureau within the Home Ministry. Each denomination was to handle the matter of proselytization as it saw fit, and matters of sect law and discipline were to be handled solely by the sectarian establishments.

In the context of the changes in religious policy, officials at the Home Ministry were more accommodating to the requests of the Buddhist leadership. Several months after receiving Fukuda's second petition, in February 1878 officials issued a terse proclamation in an attempt to mollify the coalition of leading clerics that formed the core opposition to the decriminalization. The modification, addressed to the chief priests of the various denominations, stated, "Edict 133, which states that the clergy are free to eat meat and marry, only serves to abolish the state law that had prohibited such activities. In no way does the law have anything to do with sectarian regulations."[30]

Although a step in the right direction as far as the opponents of *nikujiki saitai* were concerned, the modification to the law was still far less than they had hoped to receive. The sectarian leadership did, however, inter-

---

[29] Fukuda Gyōkai, *Sōfū risei no kengen*, GSZ, 456–457.
[30] Ibid., 454. NSRK, 720.

pret the new addendum as permission to issue more stringent regulations concerning clerical marriage and meat eating. A flurry of activity by the various denominations followed. The leadership of the various schools again attempted to proscribe clerical marriage, but without the added support of state enforcement.

The Sōtō school, for example, acted rapidly to discipline the clergy at the branch temples. One month after officials at the Home Ministry issued the clarification, the Sōtō denomination leaders sent a strongly worded message to the clergy at all branch temples that, in light of the new government regulation, from now on they should "make greater efforts to reflect on themselves and should take care not to violate any of the sectarian regulations (*shūki*)."[31]

The leadership of the Jōdo, Nichiren, Ji, Rinzai, and Shingon denominations also reacted swiftly.[32] In an attempt to shore up their defense of stringent precept practice among the Jōdo clergy, less than a month after the Home Ministry issued its new ruling those in charge at the Chion'in in Kyoto proclaimed to the clergy at the branch temples that the decriminalization of clerical marriage had no effect on current sect law.[33] On February 13, 1878, the heads of the Nichiren denomination likewise published a directive to their clergy that described the change in state policy and urged them not to violate the Buddhist precepts. Similar in tone to the brief directive issued from the Sōtō school, the document reminded the Nichiren clergy that

> the basis of Buddhism is achieving enlightenment and liberation from attachments. Therefore, there is no abandoning of one's obligations and entering the unconditioned unless one takes the tonsure, dons Buddhist robes, ceases sexual relations, and stops eating meat. That which is the most difficult to abandon is abandoned; that which is the most difficult to endure is endured. The names for laity and home-leavers are different from each other; their actions are also distinguished from each other. Furthermore, above, seek unlimited awakening, below, benefit the sentient beings of the nine realms. We should call those who transcend the masses, rise above the secular, impartially abandon conventional emotions, and earnestly avoid sullying their reputation "Buddhist monks" (*sō*).[34]

The new government policy also provided the Shingon leadership a chance to clamp down on the rapidly increasing group of married clerics within its ranks. The two-tiered system of pure and impure clergy had been instituted with the intent of limiting the influence of openly married Shugendō clerics within the school, but some members the regular Shingon

---

[31] *Sōtōshū Ryōhonzan futatsu zensho*, 3:120.
[32] See Hikita (1991a, 178–82).
[33] Ōhashi (1987, 93).
[34] Nichirenshū rokuji (1878, 2–3).

clergy had chosen to marry as well. Therefore, on February 8, 1878, just days after the Home Ministry directive was disseminated, the Shingon chief priest issued an edict to the clergy that demanded that all clerics, except for those who were formerly Shugendō clerics, strictly observe the regulations of the Shingon school. In addition, all clerics were to submit a signed statement to their Middle Teaching Academy acknowledging that they had received and would abide by the directive.[35]

These individual measures proved insufficient to stop the spread of clerical marriage and other associated practices, however. As a result, denominational leaders continued pan-sectarian efforts to curtail the spread of *nikujiki saitai*. In February 1883 the chief abbots (except those from the various Shin denominations) convened in Osaka to draft another petition concerning the problem. In May they met again, this time in Kyoto to declare that although *nikujiki saitai* was legal according to state law, from a religious perspective Buddhist clerics who married were criminals (*zainin*). They also discussed how to prohibit *nikujiki saitai* for all Buddhist clerics. Just one month later, more than three hundred Tendai clerics signed a pledge in which they agreed to the ban against clerical marriage.[36]

Buddhist leaders were given further impetus to crack down on the infraction of sectarian regulations following the abolition of the Doctrinal Instructor system in 1884. As part of the new relationship between the government and the various religious organizations subsequent to the end of that system, each denomination was required to submit its sect law to the Home Ministry for approval, which led the leadership of several denominations to attempt to spell out clearly their attitude toward clerical marriage. As the leadership wrote regulations that would be uniform for their denomination, the new rules became points of controversy for contending factions within each school. One of the most stringent anti-marriage measures incorporated into the new, state-approved sect laws was that of the Sōtō denomination, issued in June 1885. The introduction to the new Sōtō regulations made clear that because of the abolition of the Doctrinal Instructor system, the control of abbatial appointments, advancement and demotion, and other matters were no longer the direct concern of the government. Responsibility for all such concerns now was to be entrusted to the head temple, specifically the chief priest. The sectarian regulations had received the approval of the head of the Home Ministry, and it was imperative that all clerics at the branch temple abide by those regulations. The regulations also stressed that the Sōtō leadership henceforth was free to disseminate sectarian teachings without any interference from the government.[37]

---

[35] "Shingonshū rokuji" (1878, 2). Also cited in Tanaka Keishin (1984b, 264).

[36] MNJ, 3:449–50.

[37] Sōtōshū Shūmukyoku (1899, 1).

The new rules for the Sōtō denomination further stressed the implications of the nascent separation of religion and the state in the following article, which dealt specifically with the problem of clerical marriage:

> Women may not be lodged in temples: Although Proclamation 133 of 1872 stating that the government will not prevent the marriage of Buddhist clerics has been issued, the Additional Proclamation of 1878 from the Home Ministry makes clear that this law has no bearing on sect law. Therefore, the sect law, as before, forbids the marriage of the clergy. The separation of religion and the state has now been demarcated. We are free from further government involvement and may conduct our affairs independently. The above sect law shall be adhered to strictly. The same applies to the lodging of men in convents.[38]

Despite the strong language of the article, just how seriously did the Sōtō leaders take the regulation? Some clearly viewed the passage of the provision as a complete ban on clerical marriage. On October 3, 1885, the *Tōkyō Yokohama mainichi* newspaper, for example, reported that as of the first of that month, all Sōtō clerics were strictly prohibited from engaging in *nikujiki saitai*.[39] At least one Sōtō critic of the policy, however, questioned whether the Sōtō leaders were sincerely trying to extirpate clerical marriage. In a major work advocating the open acceptance of marriage in the Sōtō denomination, *Sōryo kazoku ron*, Kuriyama Taion retrospectively raised doubts about the intentions of the Sōtō leadership. Kuriyama sarcastically noted, for one thing, that the regulation said nothing about liaisons with a woman outside of the temple, adding that the Buddhist precepts make no distinction between inside and outside of the temple precincts as far as fornication is concerned. Kuriyama also mentioned that, unlike most prohibitory laws, which state penalties for their infraction, the prohibition of lodging women in temples had none. Nor was a specific punishment set forth for clerical marriage. Kuriyama concluded that the authors had "vainly embellished [the regulations] with idle words about upholding the precepts," and that in the end such strong language without the threat of punishment would be inefficacious.[40] It may well be that the same hesitation expressed by the abbots of Eiheiji and Sōjiji about enforcing sect laws that contradicted local custom, mentioned above, tempered the actions of those who drafted the new Sōtō sect law in 1885. As will be discussed in chapter 9, the stringent prohibition against clerical marriage remained in effect until the first Sōtō denomination constitution was adopted in 1906. At that time the ban on clerical marriage was removed from the sect regulations without any comment from the Sōtō leadership.[41]

[38] Ibid., 21.   [39] MNJ, 3:442.   [40] Kuriyama (1917, 65).
[41] Ibid., 67; Gendai Kyōgaku Kenkyūkai (1990, 12).

CONCLUSIONS

A number of patterns that transcend sectarian boundaries may be detected in the first responses to the decriminalization of *nikujiki saitai*. Initially the leadership of the various Buddhist schools responded in concert to resist the measure. Visible statements about the matters dealt with by the new law were overwhelmingly opposed to the new direction in the government's policy toward the clergy. From the passage of the measure in 1872 until 1886 there was little open support for allowing *nikujiki saitai* among clerical leaders or Buddhist intellectuals. Yet at first clerical leaders were constrained by the Ministry of Doctrine to asking their subordinate clerics to obey their consciences and to observe the precepts that they had taken upon ordination. With the Home Ministry's emendation of the law in 1878, however, the clerical leaders again argued that they were free to set standards of clerical deportment. From their perspective, the decriminalization of *nikujiki saitai* meant only that the government would no longer interfere in sectarian matters.

Clerical leaders thus stood in opposition to not only ministers like Takasaki, who viewed the precepts as a private matter, but also many of their own clerics. Although such clerics as Fukuda and Unshō continued to argue that things should be otherwise, proponents of government policy and clerics who supported clerical marriage construed the matter of precept adherence as an individual decision that should not be dictated by the denominational leadership. Although much of the language expressing this interpretation is imprecise, I believe the attempt to internalize the precepts is visible in the petition of Ugawa Shōchō, where he argues that the clergy are overly concerned with their own personal morality (*nairin*) at the expense of attention to the great matters facing the Japanese nation. A similar understanding of the precepts is seen in the arguments advanced by Takasaki Goroku and in the Shugendō petition where the authors define Buddhism or precept adherence as a matter of *shinjutsu*, that is, "inner disposition."[42] Although the government backtracked on this position with the promulgation of the addendum to the *nikujiki saitai* law in 1878, for the first few years after the decriminalization measure was adopted, adherence to the precepts could not be mandated by the denominational leadership. Immediately after the decriminalization, any attempt by the chief priests to ban marriage was blocked by the Ministry of Doctrine. The struggle among the Omuro sect, the Kyoto and Myōdō prefectural author-

[42] Literature by clergy that was written after Meiji reflects this internalization of the struggle to adhere to the precepts. This may be glimpsed in Takeda Taijun's novel *Igyō no mono*, in which the protagonist, a young cleric, struggles with sexual desire. The only restraining force for his sexual passion is his sense of shame as a cleric. Takeda Taijun was himself ordained as a cleric before becoming a writer.

ities, and the officials at the Ministry of Doctrine bears witness to the lengths that the ministry was willing to go to allow the clergy to marry and eat meat "voluntarily."

Setbacks like the one suffered by the Omuro-ha hierarchs did not deter the sectarian leadership from continuing to pressure the government to rescind the new law. Reports make clear that the depth and persistence of the pressure that was brought to bear by the clergy was much stronger than the government had expected. The established Buddhist denominations remained a powerful lobbying bloc and were able through steady pressure to win at least minor concessions from the government. The speed with which the officials at the Ministry of Justice and the Ministry of Doctrine usually responded to the petitions of the clerical elite demonstrates that those at the pinnacle of the Buddhist establishment had not completely lost access to the corridors of power.

As a result of continual shifts in state religious policy and waffling on the part of Buddhist leaders, regulations concerning precept adherence were hopelessly compromised, particularly with the dissolution of the Doctrinal Instructor system. As I have noted, while on the one hand the Home Ministry refused to withdraw the *nikujiki saitai* law, which made adherence to some precepts voluntary, it also issued directives calling on all clerics to abide by the sect law that the ministry approved for each denomination. (See chapter 4.) In response to the change in Home Ministry policy, the leadership of almost every denomination other than Jōdo Shinshū restated their adamant opposition to *nikujiki saitai*. Thus clerics were ordered to follow sect law at the same time that all state penalties for clerical meat eating, marriage, abandonment of tonsure, and wearing secular clothing were eliminated. It is no wonder that there was so much confusion surrounding the standards for clerical deportment.

Although there was undoubtedly resistance at other levels of the Buddhist community, the petitions opposing clerical marriage that I have uncovered are almost universally written by those at the upper levels of the institutional hierarchy. Among those condemning clerical marriage were Arai Nissatsu, Morotake Ekidō, Shaku Unshō, Fukuda Gyōkai, Takaoka Zōryū, Murata Jakujun, and Nishiari Bokusan. All of those men served as abbots of the most important temples of their denominations, and many served as chief priests of their schools at some point in their careers.

But the petition system (*kenpaku seido*) and the numerous Buddhist journals of early Meiji also preserved the letters, essays, and petitions of those who were in favor of the decriminalization edict.[43] Although such

---

[43] The *kenpaku seido* was an organized system for the public to submit petitions to the Meiji government. Numerous petitions, along with the government responses, have been preserved. A varied selection of the documents is now being published in MKP. For more on how the *kenpaku seido* operated, see Sakamoto (1986, 1–4).

sources are also weighted toward those at the upper levels of the Buddhist establishment, they fail to record much early support for open clerical marriage at those levels. With the exception of Ōtori Sessō, few Buddhist intellectuals or leaders rallied behind the government's plan to modernize the clergy by ridding the state of laws upholding the Buddhist precepts. Support for the measure was limited until the late 1880s, and until that time it came almost exclusively from the ranks of the lesser-known, lower-ranking clerics. As described earlier, support for clerical marriage came from such figures as Ugawa Shōchō of the Tendai school, Kurihara Chijō and Date Shingi of the Shugendō denomination, and Minami Danzō of the Shingon denomination.

The attacks on clerical marriage bore many points in common, no matter to which denomination the author of the tract belonged. As we have seen, there was a good deal of cooperation between the leaders of the various denominations. The chief priests of the Buddhist denominations were in close contact with each other and, through the Shoshū Dōtoku Kaimei, tried to coordinate the effort to have the decriminalization measure retracted. Even the works addressed specifically to the clergy of a particular denomination are similar. Unshō, Fukuda, Nishiari, and others expressed grave concern over preserving sectarian discipline after the state ceased enforcing the precepts. Every author complained that the subordinate clergy, or the young clergy, or the ignorant country clergy would be incapable of upholding the precepts in the absence of penalties for behavior unbecoming of a cleric. The potential for infraction was, more often than not, out there somewhere, away from the head temple's sphere of dominance, among the ignorant or young clerics and the untutored country clergy.

The plaintiveness of the pleas for renewed government enforcement of the ban on clerical marriage reveals the growing strains within the head-branch temple system, which had been systematized during the Tokugawa period and was becoming even more uniformly hierarchical during early Meiji with the introduction of the Chief Priest system and the application of uniform sect law in each denomination. As the leadership of each denomination began to compose sect law for the entire school, various tensions within the school were highlighted. Prominent areas of contention included the ban on meat eating, the prohibition of clerical marriage, and standards of clerical dress. Despite challenges from dissenting clerics, for almost three decades after the adoption of the *nikujiki saitai* law the opponents of clerical marriage remained in control of the mechanisms for drafting sect law. As a result, they were able to continue the ban against those practices, at least on paper. As I will show in the next two chapters, however, their control over actual clerical behavior was much less solid.

CHAPTER 8

Tanaka Chigaku and the
Buddhist Clerical Marriage:
Toward a Positive Appraisal of Family Life

> Carnal desire is innate. This is a truth of Buddhism. Criti-
> cizing [sexual desire] and abhorring it as filthy and evil is
> Buddhist skillful means. Carefully using this skillful
> means, the truth is made to shine; using this means, the
> true light is put forth. This is said to be the teaching path
> of skillful means and the absolute truth each serving its
> own function. It is difficult to use that *upāya* and to avoid
> falling into error. Today, in dealing with the problem of
> human carnal desire, Buddhism has, in progressing, killed
> the skillful means; in retreating, it has poisoned the truth.
> *Tanaka Tomoenosuke (Chigaku) 1930*

ALTHOUGH the first wave of responses to the decriminalization of *nikujiki saitai* were overwhelmingly negative, by the 1880s some Buddhist intellectuals began openly to criticize the position taken by the leaders of the Buddhist denominations. One of the earliest, most radical responses to the problem of clerical marriage was propounded by Tanaka Chigaku (1861–1939). Tanaka was a Nichiren denomination ex-cleric and the founder of the Nichirenist (*Nichirenshugi*) movement, which was an important influence upon the originators of such prominent Nichiren-based new religions as Reiyūkai.[1] After leaving the Buddhist clergy, Tanaka founded a series of lay Nichirenist new religions, culminating in 1914 with the creation of the ultra-nationalist Kokuchūkai (National Pillar Society). Seeing in the rise of the modern Japanese state the concrete fulfillment of the *Lotus Sūtra*, Tanaka fervently believed that righteousness and peace would prevail once Japan had unified the whole world. If necessary, even violence and military action were justified in the pursuit of this goal.[2]

---

[1] Tanaka Chigaku frequently used his secular given name, Tanaka Tomoenosuke, in his writings. For a brief description of Tanaka's influence on the founder of Reiyūkai, Kubo Kakutarō (1892–1944), see Hardacre (1984, 11–13). For a brief description of Tanaka's influence on the founder of Reiyūkai, Kubo Kakutarō (1892–1944), see Hardacre (1984, 11–13).

[2] Tanabe (1989, 199–206).

Although several Western authors have examined the jingoistic aspects of Tanaka's teaching in some detail, his ideas concerning the reformulation of Buddhist practice for the modern age, the creation of lay Buddhism, and the problem of *nikujiki saitai* have been relatively ignored by non-Nichiren scholars. This component of Tanaka's thought was central to the organizations he founded and, as Edwin Lee has noted, was linked intimately with his political vision of a Lotus empire.[3] Tanaka vigorously advocated removing control of Buddhism from the clergy in order to construct a Buddhism that would extend beyond the narrow confines of the temple and prove to be more suitable for married householders. Unlike such previous defenders of clerical marriage as Ugawa Shōchō, Ōtori Sessō, and members of the Shugendō sects, Tanaka attempted to provide a positive rationale for clerical marriage and labored to find scriptural support for his notion of the Buddhist couple. He believed that true Buddhism—the very essence of the teaching as presented in Nichiren's interpretation of the *Lotus Sūtra*—provided the basis for the acceptance of the spiritual potential of women and supported the married couple. In his attempt to reform Nichiren Buddhism and create a vigorous lay organization, Tanaka attacked the established Buddhist schools, including the Nichiren school, and Christian missionaries. Tanaka's solution to the problem of clerical marriage and the general weakening of Buddhism in Meiji was revolutionary: he called for the total replacement of the old parishioner-temple system, which had been the pillar of Buddhist institutional organization, with a Nichiren lay Buddhist organization that would provide the religious support for eventual world unification under Japanese imperial rule. By the turn of the century Tanaka had reached the extreme conclusion that the whole debate over clerical marriage was actually irrelevant because there could be no true home-leavers in the Last Age of the Teaching.

As Helen Hardacre has noted in her study of the use of the *Lotus Sūtra* in modern Japan, the trend toward lay centrality was particularly vigorous in the Nichiren denomination and was grounded in novel interpretations of the *Lotus Sūtra*.[4] In her discussion of Butsuryūkō, a lay Nichirenist new religion founded by the ex-Nichiren cleric Nagamatsu Nissen (Seifū) (1817–90), Hardacre has shown the importance of such problems as clerical marriage, lay participation, and women's religious roles to the members of that group. Like Nagamatsu, Tanaka turned to the *Lotus Sūtra* to find a doctrinal solution for the problem of *nikujiki saitai* in the modern age.

The study of Tanaka's approach to the problem of *nikujiki saitai* provides us with a valuable example of the centrality of doctrinal issues in the formation of one early new religious organization in Japan. One of the

[3] Lee (1975, 24–26).
[4] Hardacre (1989a, 209–10).

prime reasons for Tanaka's break with the Nichiren denomination was his radical perspective on marriage and the family. At a time when such issues as conjugal relations, domesticity, and the home (*katei*) had become increasingly prominent in Japanese intellectual circles, Tanaka attempted to reformulate Buddhism as a domestic religion. These doctrinal and practical issues remained central to him until well into the twentieth century and help explain his departure from the Nichiren clergy to found a lay religious group.

By examining Tanaka's response to the problem of clerical marriage and his understanding of the relationship between Buddhism and the family, I aim to understand the origin of one stream of Buddhist-based new religions in light of its broader Buddhist doctrinal and institutional context. Robert Sharf and James Hubbard have observed that all too often studies of the new religions have focused on social, economic, and practical aspects of the organizations at the expense of doctrinal concerns specific to the groups in question.[5] Such studies have also tended to emphasize the current organizational structure of these groups rather than the genealogy of these new religions. Sharf has written that in part this has occurred because most studies of the new religions in Japan have been conducted by anthropologists and sociologists rather than specialists in the history of Buddhism, whose work has almost entirely centered on premodern Buddhism. As a result of this unfortunate division of labor, many studies of the new religions have failed to examine how these groups arose in part as responses to significant doctrinal and institutional problems within the established Buddhist denominations. Sharf has commented that consequently there has been a "noticeable lack of ethnographically textured and anthropologically sophisticated studies of the older Buddhist schools and practices as they survive in the modern period. The other side of the coin is the paucity of 'theologically' nuanced studies of the Buddhist New Religions, or studies sensitive to the historical and scriptural precedents for modern reforms."[6] As I show in this chapter, it was precisely doctrinal disagreements with the Nichiren establishment that spurred Tanaka to leave the clergy and found his first lay-centered organization. It is in the context of the *nikujiki saitai* problem that we can best appreciate the trend toward lay centrality in such organizations as Tanaka's Kokuchūkai, as well as such other Nichiren-based new religions as Butsuryūkō, Reiyūkai, and Risshō Kōseikai.

The son of Tada Genryū (d. 1870), a physician and convert to Nichiren Buddhism, and Wakabayashi Rinko, Tanaka entered the Nichiren clergy

---

[5] Sharf (1995, 452–453); Hubbard (1998, 59–62). In a similar vein, Daniel Métraux (1995, 6–7) has written that Buddhist "new religions" should be viewed as reform movements within Buddhism, not as sui generis new traditions. See Métraux (1995, 6–7).

[6] Sharf (1995, 453).

shortly after his father's death.[7] Following his entrance into the Nichiren Daikyōin (Nichiren Great Academy), which later became Risshō University (Risshō Daigaku), he began to question various aspects of clerical Nichiren Buddhism and the wisdom of remaining within the established sectarian organization. One of his main doubts concerned what he perceived to be an increasingly accommodationist attitude toward other Buddhist schools by the followers of Nichiki (1800–59, a. k. a. Udana-in), the most prominent of whom was Arai Nissatsu, the head of the Daikyōin for the Nichiren school. As George Tanabe has observed, Tanaka particularly took issue with the Nichiren establishment's meek interpretation of "subduing evil" (*shakubuku*), that is, the practice of criticizing other Buddhist schools for their deviation from the Nichiren denomination's interpretation of Buddhism as presented in the *Lotus Sūtra*. Tanaka believed that such lack of resolve had resulted in the distortion of Nichiren's teachings, including, for example, tolerance for the use of the wooden drum (*mokugyo*) in chanting the title of the *Lotus Sūtra* (*daimoku*) and even for certain alien Buddhist practices such as chanting the name of Amida Buddha (*nenbutsu*), which Nichiren vehemently and explicitly denounced during his lifetime. His essential belief was that the dawn of the new era heralded by the Restoration called for a reexamination of Buddhism, including the various sects of the Nichiren school, and the restoration of True Buddhism as propounded by Nichiren.[8]

Tanaka also became increasingly disenchanted with the manner in which Buddhism was practiced and organized. He believed that the parishioner (*danka*) system, in which families were bound to a particular temple more by family history than by faith, was outmoded in post-Restoration Japan. In the wake of such changes as the separation of religious doctrine and the state and freedom of religion (that is, tolerance of Christianity), the old "feudal" relationship between the faithful and their family temples also demanded radical change. Tanaka envisioned the institution of a new relationship in which affiliation would be based on free election by the parishioner of his or her Buddhist affiliation. Tanaka hoped to shift the focus of lay Buddhists from the relatively passive reverence for the clergy

[7] Chigaku was his ordination name. He received the surname Tanaka in 1872 when in his absence he was accidentally registered with that surname in the new household registry by someone at his home temple and an unknowing local official. The incident is an indication of the massive confusion that must have accompanied the assumption of surnames by clerics, peasants, and others in the early Meiji period. Tanaka Hōkoku (1954, 23). Tanaka Hōkoku is the son of Tanaka Chigaku and Kirigaya Mine. For a brief biography of Tanaka Chigaku, see Lee (1975, 20–24).

[8] For more on Tanaka's attitude toward the Nichiren school's accommodationist positions, see Tanabe (1989, 193–96). See also, Tanaka Kōho (1981, 37–39). Later Tanaka was to adopt a "wooden bell," an instrument that closely resembles the *mokugyo* for use in religious ceremonies. The bell is still in use at Kokuchūkai today.

to the active manifestation of Buddhist practice in the parishioners' daily lives.[9]

Tanaka's increasingly aggressive approach to *shakubuku* and his deep dissatisfaction with the disengagement of Buddhism from everyday life, coupled with a bout of pneumonia, led him to leave the Nichiren Great Academy in 1876 for a period of independent study. After two years of intensive reading in Buddhist texts, Tanaka resolved to spread true Nichiren Buddhism among the Japanese people as a lay missionary. His departure from the clergy in 1879, at the age of nineteen, was prompted by his growing conviction that the Last Age of the Teaching required the establishment of a vigorous lay Buddhism outside of the temples that would serve as a support for the Japanese nation. He argued in his autobiography and many other writings that the confinement of Buddhism to temples had resulted in its obsolescence. He also expressed the fear that assuming the abbacy of a country temple would confine him solely to performing funerals and memorial services for the rest of his days.[10]

Soon after returning to lay life, Tanaka moved to Yokohama, and in 1880 he formed the lay association Rengekai in order to propagate the teachings of the *Lotus Sūtra* and Nichiren. About the same time, he also married, and his first wife, Kirigaya Mine (d. 1895), gave birth to his first child, a son who died several months later.[11] Ironically, for one who was strongly to advocate the importance of a healthy marriage, Tanaka eventually divorced Mine. His second marriage, however, in 1896 to Ogawa Yasuko (d. 1955), the daughter of the devout Nichirenshū supporter and scholar Ogawa Taidō (1814–78), proved more long-lasting.[12]

Tanaka began to lecture on marriage and the family several years after forming the Rengekai. The demands of running a lay organization and having his own family brought new, more quotidian concerns to the attention of the ex-cleric. In 1886, for example, he responded to the requests of his lay followers by creating a ceremony for conferring the *Lotus Sūtra* on newborn children (*tanji chōkyō shiki*). The following year, he wrote what is probably the first Japanese Buddhist wedding ceremony.[13] In his autobiography Tanaka wrote of the circumstances that led him to consider the related issues of marriage, family, and the Buddhist precepts for the clergy more carefully over the next several years. First and foremost in his mind was the need to create a new Buddhism that was involved not only with funerals, but also with all the essential activities of daily life. Buddhist temples had become, in Tanaka's judgment, funeral homes rather

---

[9] Tanaka Kōho (1981, 38).
[10] Tanaka Tomoenosuke (1936, 1: 350–51); Tanaka Hōkoku (1954, 40–44).
[11] Tanaka Kōho (1977, 52–54). Tanaka Kōho is a grandson of Tanaka Chigaku.
[12] Lee (1975, 21).
[13] Tanaka Hōkoku (1960, 15).

Figure 4. Tanaka Chigaku and Tanaka Yasuko

than a place where the quest for awakening (*bodai*) began. He complained
that the customary linkage between Buddhism and death had led to the
exclusion of Buddhism from all auspicious occasions; the Buddhist clergy
did not attend their parishioners' weddings, and no sutras were read at
the wedding ceremony for fear of tinging the event with associations of
death. In the eyes of most laypeople, the Buddhist clergy were little more
than undertakers. It was telling, wrote Tanaka, that during the New Year's
season the Buddhist clergy, like physicians, were not to visit their parishioners until after the third day of the New Year because they might stain
the year with death. It was to counter the tendency to exclude Buddhism
from the most important life events that Tanaka composed a Buddhist
wedding ceremony.[14] Constructing the wedding ritual as, in the words of
Laurel Kendall, a locus of "morality and of personal and national identity,"

[14] Tanaka Tomoenosuke (1936, 2: 3).

Figure 5. 1895 Risshō Ankokukai Buddhist Wedding Ceremony

he set about creating a uniquely Japanese Buddhist ceremony.[15] In his auto-biography Tanaka later wrote, "Because it is imperative to destroy this stupid condition and recreate a healthy religious consciousness and healthy religious customs, I created a religious (shūkyō) wedding ceremony."[16]

The ceremony was to be conducted in front of the Nichiren school's primary object of worship, the gohonzon, which bears the central calligraphic inscription "Homage to the Profound Lotus Sūtra" (Nam-myō-hō-ren-ge-kyō). In the course of the ceremony, Nam-myō-hō-ren-ge-kyō would be chanted, passages from the Lotus Sūtra would be read, and the couple would be ceremonially instructed in the essential teachings of Nichiren, the true object of worship, the true precepts, and the true title (honmon honzon, honmon kaidan, honmon daimoku). Most importantly, the couple was to affirm their faith in true Buddhism—the teachings of the Lotus Sūtra. During the ceremony the couple was presented with a certificate of marriage. In the ceremony the principal actors were the leader, the bride and groom, and the go-betweens. As one would expect

---

[15] Kendall (1996, 53). Kendall discusses how in Korea late-nineteenth- and early twentieth-century Christian missionaries and reformers catalyzed the development of new-style wedding rituals. The emergence of religious wedding ceremonies in Japan will be discussed further in chapter 9.

[16] Tanaka Tomoenosuke (1936, 2:3).

for a ceremony focusing on the conjugal family, the parents and relatives were nonparticipants who came to the *dōjō* to witness the event. The performance of a specifically Japanese religious wedding ceremony as early as 1887 makes Tanaka's ceremony probably the first indigenous religious wedding ceremony in Japan. (As I will discuss in the next chapter, the so-called traditional Shintō wedding was not invented until the late 1890s.) According to Tanaka's account, the ceremony proved to be a popular one. He claimed that clerics from the Jōdo Shinshū and Zen schools soon copied it. To further integrate Buddhist ritual with important rites of passage and to further link the religion to daily life, Tanaka subsequently created Buddhist rituals for such other events as joining Rengekai and entering military service. In addition, to give Buddhism a more festive spirit, he also created religious hymns for use at meetings and ceremonies.[17]

Tanaka's reformulation of Buddhism to include ceremonies centered on the individual and the family should be viewed in the context of growing interest in matters pertaining to the conjugal family in late-nineteenth-century Japan. Tanaka created his rituals for Rengekai members at a time when Christian missionaries, Japanese Christians, and intellectual members of the new middle class were popularizing the distinctively middle-class ideal of the Western-style home in Japan. Identified by the katakana term *hōmu* or by the Sino-Japanese word *katei*, the new domestic ideal was frequently contrasted with its antithesis, the *ie* (household; lineal family), in the numerous newspapers, magazines, and popular tracts where the notion was popularized. According to its proponents, the home consisted of the married couple and their children living as a self-contained unit in isolation from the extended family and such nonfamily members as servants and workers. While the *ie* was old-fashioned, Chinese, and anti-industrial, the *katei* was modern, Western, and the family unit best suited for Japan's industrial transformation.[18] One important change, according to Jordan Sand, was the novel conception of the home and "family life as a locus of moral meaning."[19]

Tanaka, reacting vigorously to the inroads being made by Protestant Christians in Japan, created a variety of new forms that he hoped would move Buddhism to the center of the home. In particular, his focus on the married couple marks a significant departure from the Edo pattern of Buddhist affiliation, which had primarily involved *ie*-centered funeral rituals. Although scholars of modern Japanese religions have stressed the importance of the *ie* in the rise of the new religions, Tanaka's efforts were clearly focused on a much smaller unit. One striking feature of the wedding

[17] Ibid., 2:5.
[18] Muta (1994, 58–61).
[19] Sand (1998, 192).

ceremony that he created is the extent to which the extended family is removed from center stage. The parents of the bride and groom have become members of the audience, along with more-distant relations and friends. Only the leader, the bride and groom, and the go-betweens actually are engaged in the ceremony. And the venue for the ceremony, which formerly had been the homes of the bride and groom's family, has shifted to the more neutral space of the *dōjō*.[20]

Tanaka provided a detailed theoretical defense of his family-centered lay Buddhism and an extended attack on world-abnegating tendencies in Buddhism several years later, on December 11–12, 1886, when he delivered a two-day series of lectures on the Buddhist couple (*fūfu*) to the Risshō Ankokukai (founded 1884), the successor organization to the Rengekai. The lectures were transcribed, revised, and published as *Bukkyō fūfu ron* the following year. In 1894 Tanaka presented a substantially revised and polished edition of the lectures to the imperial couple on the twenty-fifth anniversary of their marriage, which was celebrated that year.[21] Housed in a wooden chest, the brocade-bound commemorative edition was brought by a procession of Tanaka's followers to the imperial palace, receiving an official certificate of acceptance from the Imperial Household Agency on March 9, 1894, the day of the anniversary celebration. In this edition, Tanaka had tightened up the text, toning down some of the most vituperative language of the original lectures and eliminating repetition. In addition, reflecting his growing concern with the national polity (*kokutai*), he more explicitly stressed the interrelationship among the married couple, Nichiren Buddhism, and the Japanese state.

The tract on the "Buddhist couple" was one of the first extensive works written about marriage and the family from a Buddhist perspective. But it is much more than a discourse on marriage. The work was of crucial importance for Tanaka's attempt to reconnect Buddhism with the life of the laity and the state; if Buddhism were to have a role in daily affairs, it would have to address concerns that were central to daily life. Marriage, for Tanaka, was one of the foundations of human existence. He believed that the building of a successful, relevant Buddhism depended in part on overcoming the widespread, fundamental belief that Buddhism was world-abnegating and had little to teach about fundamental human interactions.

Edwin Lee characterized the *Bukkyō fūfu ron* as a watershed book in Tanaka's career. Lee, who wrote one of the few studies of Tanaka in English, astutely observed the intimate connection between Tanaka's vigor-

[20] Walter Edwards (1989, 143–45), discussing the nature of modern Japanese weddings has noted the close connection between the couple-centered ceremony and the nuclear family.
[21] Tanaka Tomoenosuke (1936, 3:137–45); Tanaka Hōkoku (1954, 111–12); Tanaka Kōho (1994, 7; 14).

ous nationalism and his advocacy of lay Buddhism, clerical marriage, and general support for family life.[22] In *Bukkyō fūfu ron*, Tanaka for the first time combined his concern with creating a lay Buddhism that would affect the practical, everyday affairs of the people with his conviction that Nichiren Buddhism—in particular the *Lotus Sūtra*—was the essential basis of the Japanese national polity.[23] He wrote that, like husband and wife, the teachings of Nichiren and the national polity were inextricably joined. The relationship of husband and wife becomes a microcosm of the larger relationship between the teachings of the *Lotus* as made manifest by Nichiren and the national essence.

> Śākyamuni established the teaching for the sake of the world. Nichiren spread the teaching for the sake of the country. I have heard that religious law and religious meaning have been established for the sake of the secular state (*sekken kokka*). I have never heard that the secular state exists for religious law and religious meaning. Therefore Nichiren wrote in the *Risshō ankoku ron*, "the country prospers through the Dharma, the Dharma is reverenced by people. If the country is destroyed and the people are extinguished, who will pay reverence to the Buddhas, who will believe the Dharma? [Therefore] first pray for the state, then you should establish the Buddha Dharma." In the very least, if it is going to be a doctrine that is established and taught for the sake of the secular state, then it must manifest its teaching function in a manner that addresses the path that holds the utmost power for the secular state. In other words, [the teaching] must provide the correct rules and correct support and protection for the husband-wife relationship, which is the most important matter in human life and the root of morality. Thereby, the first principle of teaching [Buddhism] (*kaidō*) must be the construction of the perfect secular state.[24]

As this passage indicates, Tanaka was not beyond creatively using Nichiren's writings to bolster his ultra-nationalistic interpretation of Nichiren. Jacqueline Stone recently observed that the image of Nichiren as a die-hard patriot is largely an invention of the Meiji and Taishō periods.[25] Tanaka's use of the *Risshō ankoku ron* in the above passage is a perfect illustration of the selective use of Nichiren's writings to highlight Tanaka's

[22] Lee (1975, 24–26).

[23] For an analysis of the linkage of the *Lotus Sūtra* and *kokutai*, see Tanabe (1989, 191–208).

[24] Tanaka (1930, 2–3). Unless noted otherwise, all citations come from the version of *Bukkyō fūfu ron* submitted to the court by Tanaka in 1894 and reissued by Kokuchūkai with headnotes written by Chiō Yamakawa Dennosuke. This edition of the text was issued to commemorate the marriage of Prince Takamatsu no Miya Nobuhito Shinnō (1905–87) on February 4, 1930. The 1894 version differs from the rougher, original 1886 edition of the lectures. See Tanaka Chigaku (1994, 17:15–63).

[25] Stone (1994).

support for the newly restored imperial government and the emperor and to underscore his belief in the primacy of the nation with regard to Buddhism. Tanaka used that quotation at two crucial junctures in the *Bukkyō fūfu ron*, in the first and last chapters. He thereby attempted to tie his assertion that the Buddhist Dharma exists for the sake of the nation to Nichiren himself. He did not, however, present the quotation in context. In the *Risshō ankoku ron*, this passage is voiced by a guest who questions his host about the reasons for the famines and disasters sweeping Japan. Nichiren is using the guest as a foil to present his own perspective, voiced by the host, on Buddhism and the crisis in Japan. The host asserts that the safety and security of the nation are important, but only because this will allow Buddhism to flourish fully. As recently argued by Satō, this passage is "encouraging readers to pray, first and foremost, for the peace and prosperity of the nation, as part of the very process of establishing and enhancing Buddhism."[26] Rather than advocating the supremacy of Kingly Law over Buddhist Law, as many prewar Nichirenists claimed, Nichiren saw all beings, including the emperor, as equally subject to the same ultimate standard of Lotus Buddhism. But in *Bukkyō fūfu ron* and numerous later texts, Tanaka tore the quotation out of context in order to ground his ultra-nationalistic interpretation of Buddhism in Nichiren's writings and to give primacy to the emperor and nation rather than to the Dharma.[27]

Tanaka asserted that misogyny and the denigration of marriage are not indigenous to Japan. Rather, the indigenous teachings, which he contended arose directly from human emotion, were fully supportive of the marital relationship. He wrote that the presence of such notable women as Ototachibana Hime and writers Murasaki Shikibu and Sei Shonagon was an indication of the high regard for women in ancient Japanese society. He saw Japanese history as a steady departure from the truths of the indigenous traditions. Like numerous proponents of the Western-style home, who partially blamed detrimental Asian and Confucian customs for the family problems they considered rampant in Japan, Tanaka viewed Chinese culture as one cause of the denigration of women.[28] Another pernicious force operating within Japan was provisional, that is, Hīnayāna or what Tanaka in the early version of *Bukkyō fūfu ron* had derisively called "Indian bumpkin Buddhism" (*yamadashi Bukkyō*).[29] With the importation of Chinese culture and the acceptance of the Confucian notion of the three subordinations of women and such provisional Buddhist doctrines as the

---

[26] Satō (1999, 311). Satō goes on to argue on pp. 315–18 that Nichiren even called into question the absolute authority of the emperor, something that was unthinkable for Tanaka.

[27] Ibid., 321–22. Mizuno Kōgen, in a discussion of the *Risshō ankoku ron*, notes that this quotation has been a favorite one for Nichiren nationalists. See BKJ, particularly 281.

[28] For more on this view of Chinese influence in the *katei* literature see Muta (1994, 58–59).

[29] See Tanaka Chigaku (1994, 29).

five hindrances, the freedom of women was destroyed.[30] In Tanaka's schematicization of Japanese history, during the medieval period the decline in female status was exacerbated by the growing bellicosity of Japanese life and the overall deterioration of learning and virtue. Tying the complete abandonment of indigenous virtue to the loss of imperial power, he wrote that, beginning with the Hōgen conflict in 1156, Japan entered a period of incessant warfare and a dark age of ignorance and immorality.

Tanaka contended that this period of growing violence forced Buddhism increasingly to espouse world abnegation—rebirth in the Pure Land was the only salvation that people could hope for in such a troubled world. The horrors of the age thus gave rise to the teachings of Hōnen and Shinran, with their exclusively otherworldly character, and led all the other schools of Buddhism to emphasize monastic withdrawal from the world. As a result, all of the established schools—Zen, Tendai, Shingon, and the Nara schools—"revered elevated and profound explanations, while ignoring the pressing matters of human existence. The [authorities] prattled on about the teaching as if it were cold ash. Their teachings for people concerned only death. Therefore in teaching women they solely [preached] that women were deeply sinful and exclusively [taught] that life and death should be feared. In this manner they constructed their method of teaching (13–14)."

Just as he had in his autobiography, Tanaka claimed in the *Bukkyō fūfu ron* that by ignoring basic human relationships and failing to provide rites of passage for major life events, the clergy had turned Buddhism into a religion of negativity and death. Beginning with the calligraphic frontispiece for the earliest version of the text, in which Tanaka wrote "Buddha is not a dead person" (*Hotoke wa shibito ni arazu*), Tanaka attacked the current state of Japanese Buddhist practice.[31]

> Buddhism has more and more become estranged and withdrawn from the most important aspects of the world. Laypeople simply see Buddhism as outside the realm of society and Buddhist clerics themselves submit to this, taking themselves to be beyond the world or of lofty nature. Thus they have transformed love of the Dharma into world abnegation. They talk about death but do not speak about life. They concentrate on funerals but do not teach about marriage. They abandon the most important period of human

---

[30] Tanaka Tomoenosuke (1930, 12–13). Further references to this work will be cited as page numbers in the text. The three subordinations (*sanjū*) are found in the *Li ji* (Book of rites). They are subordination to one's father, one's husband, and, if widowed, one's children. The five obstacles (*goshō*) are described and then refuted in the *Lotus Sūtra*. The teaching of the five obstacles holds that women are unable to attain the status of Bontennō (King of the Brahma Heaven), Taishaku (Indra), Maō (devil king of the sixth heaven of the desire realm), Tenrinnō (a *Cakravartin* king), or a Buddha. See IBJ, 274.

[31] Tanaka Hōkoku (1960, 8).

existence, life, and purposefully labor at explaining the silence after death. Truly this is an extremely major force in misleading the secular nation. (8–9)

From Tanaka's perspective such a world-denying teaching was fatally flawed. After describing the degeneration of Japanese Buddhism into a funereal religion, he noted that, "the Way of men and women, along with being the root of the multitude of misfortunes, is also the foundation of peace, good fortune, virtue, and decorum. Education, customs, finances, and government. On a small scale, one family. On a large scale, the nation. All of these things begin from the morality of the correct relationship between husband and wife. Therefore when this path is imperfect, it represents the imperfection of the state" (15). As we can see in this passage, despite lashing out at Sinocentricism, Tanaka remained indebted to the notions of governance expressed in such Confucian classics as *Da xue* (Great learning), whose author had written, "desiring to order the realm, they first ordered their states. Desiring to order the states, they first ordered their families."[32]

Tanaka claimed that Restoration had brought a decisive end to the period of chaos and confusion. With the restoration of imperial power, the Japanese people finally could recover from the insidious influences of Sinocentricism (*Shina shugi*) and provisional Buddhism.[33] "Now, as we attempt to recover we must give up the provisional teachings, ferret out heterodoxies, and exalt Japanese Buddhism (*Nihonteki Bukkyō*, that is, Nichiren Buddhism), thereby creating a Buddhist Japan (*Bukkyōteki Nihon*)" (18). According to Tanaka, the Restoration not only eliminated the chaos of feudalism; it also made the reconstruction of true Buddhism possible.

A significant section of *Bukkyō fūfu ron* is devoted to the defense of Buddhist attitudes toward marriage and women against Christian criticism. Tanaka, like other Buddhist writers of his day, was painfully aware of the growing Christian presence in Japan and of attacks on Japanese marital relations. No doubt he saw Protestant missionary activity as direct competition with his efforts to establish an active lay Buddhist organization and to redeem the Japanese image of Buddhism. Referring to the spread of the Christian-supported women's rights movement and notions of companionate, monogamous marriage into Japan, Tanaka argued that at its core, Christianity repudiated these ideals (34–35). He attempted to counter the claims by those foreign missionaries and Japanese Christians who argued that Christianity is more suited to the modern world than

---

[32] *Da xue* 1.

[33] Tanaka used the term *gonshō no hō butsu*, which Yamakawa glossed in the headnotes of the 1930 text as "provisional Hīnayāna teachings and Buddhas." See Tanaka Tomoenosuke (1930, 10, headnote). Tanaka believed that all teachings of the Buddha prior to the *Lotus Sūtra* were temporary, expedient doctrines taught to help sentient beings not yet ready to receive the ultimate teachings of Buddhism.

Buddhism, in part because it holds a more sanguine view of women and marriage. (For more on Christian critics of Buddhist attitudes toward women and marriage, see chapter 9.) He tried to demonstrate what he believed was the fundamental misogyny and illogicality of Christianity, which made it an unsuitable religion for the Japanese. Using a variety of Biblical quotations, he attempted in particular to show Buddhism's clear superiority to Christianity with regard to attitudes toward women and marriage.

Despite the common understanding that Christianity presented a more positive view of marriage than did Buddhism, Tanaka argued that the Christian tradition actually had a fundamentally scornful view of women and an inconsistent attitude toward women and marriage. He wrote, "People generally believe that when it comes to expounding about the path of men and women or husbands and wives, Buddhism is superficial and Christianity is profound. Although this may be true on the surface, in reality things are vastly different" (24). He cited Matthew 19:1–12 to prove that Jesus's approach to marriage was so severe that not even his disciples were capable of following his instructions. In that passage, Jesus delivered a strict injunction against divorce in response to a question from the Pharisees. Jesus concluded that "Whoever divorces his wife, except for unchastity, and marries another, commits adultery." To this Jesus's disciples remarked, "If such is the case of man with his wife, it is not expedient to marry."[34] Tanaka interpreted this remark as proof that Jesus's expectations were so unrealistic that he could not even convince his own disciples (25). He added that the Christian rejection of divorce is even more severe than the Confucian injunction that, once widowed, a virtuous woman is not to remarry for the rest of her life. Tanaka concluded that Jesus's attitude toward marriage as expressed in these passages comprised an extremely uncharitable doctrine.

In Tanaka's eyes, Christian marital doctrine was also self-contradictory. As proof of biblical inconsistency with regard to marriage, he cited Romans 7:1–4 and Corinthians 1 7:39, where Jesus states it is all right for a woman to remarry once her husband has died. How can it be, wrote Tanaka, that Jesus proclaims in one part of the New Testament (Matthew 19:6) that husband and wife are of one flesh eternally and that therefore "monogamy (*ippu ippu*) has been commanded by heaven, so people should not indiscriminately put it asunder" and then in another passage says that a woman can remarry once her husband dies? "To take this [marriage] as God's will (*tenmei*) and also to allow remarriage is at the very least to [say that] God's will is multiple. If this is not a superficial understanding of human nature, it is making light of it based on God's will" (26).[35] Christian

---

[34] All biblical citations are from the Revised Standard Version. I have used May and Metzger (1977).

[35] Matthew 19:6: "So they are no longer two but one flesh. What therefore God has joined together, let no man put asunder."

misogyny is not as explicit as attacks on women undertaken in numerous Buddhist texts, but in Tanaka's view, the disparagement of women takes place at the deepest level of the Christian faith, which is very unlike the nature of the phenomenon in Buddhism. Just as humanity is subordinate to God—a concept that Tanaka found abhorrent because he believed that the focal point of a religion should be humanity, not God—Christianity portrays females as by nature dependent upon males, because Eve was created in subordination to Adam (27). In addition, women are portrayed in Genesis as fundamentally evil: although created by God to serve man, the first woman seduced man into rebelling against God. Unlike Confucianism, which elevates men and subordinates women (*danson johi*) for the sake of order, or Buddhism, which ostracizes women (*nyonin haiseki*) in order to destroy delusions, in Christianity women are innately subordinated to men. Tanaka concluded that "their expounding on love and the married couple is nothing more than derisive laughter directed at the world." Even some Christians have rebelled against this underlying scorn for women. Such negative attitudes toward women and family were precisely what led Luther to rebel against Rome by ending the ban on clerical marriage and the Mormons to teach polygamy. No doubt, reasoned Tanaka, these radical breaks with previous Christian tradition presage future upheavals in Christian doctrine (27).

The reverse is true of Buddhism, claimed Tanaka. Unlike Christianity, which on the surface seemingly allows for marriage, Buddhism superficially denies all sexual relations and is unrelenting in its attack on women as the source of the most delusive of all the passions, sexual desire. Tanaka wrote that the denigration of women in Buddhism was a temporary strategy to smash attachments, nothing more. The problem with the predominant view of the Buddha's attitude toward women is that it does not distinguish between skillful means (Skt. *upāya*, *hōben*) and the central truths of Buddhism. The critical point to understand, he contended, is that, Śākyamuni never intended for his teachings that deny the spiritual potential of women to be the final one. Such teachings were offered during the first phase of his ministry—the first forty-two years after his enlightenment. This, according to the usual Nichiren school characterization of the ministry, was a preliminary period during which Śākyamuni responded to people who were incapable of fully putting into practice the "real Buddhism," that is, the teachings that were expressed in the *Lotus Sūtra*. And during that preliminary phase, Tanaka asserted, Śākyamuni spoke of women in disparaging terms as an indirect way of criticizing the delusions of men (34).

Tanaka further asserted that maintaining the distinction between the provisional and the ultimate teachings is essential for an accurate understanding of Buddhism and for the health of the nation. "If one's method is immature and if one carelessly applies the provisional teachings, then the teachings will be unfit for people—they will not be appropriate for people's spiritual capacities, they will contradict human emotions and the spirit of the times, and the vast array of teachings will become a tool injurious to the secular nation" (5).

According to Tanaka, the quintessential truth of Buddhism and the basic view of women is to be found in the *Lotus Sūtra*, which Śākyamuni preached during the most important phase of his ministry, forty-two years after his enlightenment (66–68). Ignorant clerics and laypeople had given rise to a host of errors with regard to Śākyamuni's provisional teachings about women, and the clergy continued to advocate provisional teachings that were no longer appropriate for the times. Even when Śākyamuni had attacked women as the source of sexual passion and delusion, Tanaka claimed, he had denied sexual relations to those who were clerics merely as a "special preparation for proselytization" (41). Neither were laity were without blame for the confusion, having made the dangerous error of taking the clergy as models for their own behavior and viewing continence as a universal virtue, when actually celibacy was appropriate only for a certain group of people at a particular time. More broadly, the laity, due to the complexity of Buddhist doctrine and practice, had abnegated all responsibility for practice to the clergy. Consequently, rather than having faith in the teaching, the parishioners had substituted faith in the clergy for true religious practice. Tanaka called this "turning people and the Dharma topsy-turvy" (44).

Adhering to the Nichiren school's traditional classification of the teachings, Tanaka held that the truth presented in the *Lotus*—as distilled in the five characters of the sūtra's title (*daimoku*)—is complete, final, and all-encompassing.[36] It includes within its depths acceptance of sexuality and the relationship between men and women: "The five characters *Myō-hō-ren-ge-kyō* are the storehouse of wisdom, the standard of virtue, the wellspring of goodness, the original beauty, the path of human life, and the principle for managing the nation; not one of these elements does not spring from [the *daimoku*]. How then could only masculinity and femininity, the husband-wife relationship, stand outside these five characters?" (57–58).

Prior to the teaching of the *Lotus Sūtra*, Tanaka explained, women, though they could be reborn in the Pure Land, could not, as women, become Buddhas (*nyonin jōbutsu*) (66).[37] The Buddha *had* to teach this

---

[36] Nichiren used the standard Tendai classification of the Five Periods and the Eight Teachings (*goji hakkyō*) and emphasized the exclusive appropriateness of the *Lotus Sūtra* for the Last Age of the Teaching. Nichiren's exposition of this classification may be found in *Kanjin no honzon shō*. See Tokoro and Takagi (1970, 132–58); NSJ, 95–96.

[37] According to the *Muryōjukyō* they would not even be reborn as women. The thirty-fifth vow of Dharmakāra Bodhisattva in the *Muryōjukyō* reads, "I, when I attain Buddhahood, women in the immeasurable and inconceivable Buddha-lands of the ten directions who, having heard my Name, rejoice in faith, awaken aspiration for Enlightenment and

doctrine because people were not ready for the most profound teachings. Ultimately, however, Śākyamuni set aside the provisional teachings about sexuality and women and expounded the *Lotus Sūtra*. Tanaka focused on the account of the dragon girl in the "Devadatta" chapter of the *Lotus Sūtra*, in which a dragon girl is transformed from her female form into a Buddha, much to the amazement of witnesses to the event.[38] Quoting from Nichiren, he emphasized that "the attainment of Buddhahood by the dragon girl was not the attainment of Buddhahood by just one woman. It was the attainment of Buddhahood by all women in the ten directions and in past, present, and future times" (67).[39]

According to Tanaka, in the *Lotus Sūtra* women cease to be treated with the disdain that one sees in earlier, provisional scriptures. In the sutra Samantabhadra speaks of the merit that will by gained by copying, reciting, and upholding the *Lotus Sūtra*, including rebirth in the Trāyastriṃśa Heaven where the faithful will be attended by heavenly courtesans.[40] In regard to this passage, Tanaka noted that in the *Lotus Sūtra* women had gone from being regarded as the root of all evil to being seen as the foundation of good fortune. He then propounded the standard Nichiren denomination view that the *Lotus Sūtra* sweeps aside all provisional teachings and complications, and that the teachings of Nichiren—in particular his positive attitude toward women—illuminate the darkness of the Last Age of the Dharma (68).[41]

Unlike those who sought a basis for clerical marriage in the doctrines of schools with a relatively weak emphasis on *mappō*, Tanaka and other Nichiren denomination figures found their school's doctrines much more congenial to arguments that called for ignoring the traditional ban on

---

wish to renounce womanhood, should after death be reborn again as women, may I not attain perfect enlightenment." Inagaki (1995, 247); T. 12:360.

[38] T. 9:34. *Scripture of the Lotus Blossom of the Fine Dharma* (1976, 200–201). "At that time the assembled multitude all saw the dragon girl in the space of an instant turn into a man, perfect bodhisattva-conduct, straightway go southward to the world-sphere Spotless, sit on a jeweled lotus blossom, and achieve undifferentiating, right, enlightened institution, with thirty-two marks and eighty beautiful features setting forth the Fine Dharma for all living beings in all ten directions." Tanaka ignores that the dragon girl first became a man before achieving Buddhahood.

[39] See Nichiren, *Kaimokushō* in SNS, 1:589. I would like to thank Jacqueline Stone for pointing out this reference.

[40] T. 9:61c. See *Scripture of the Lotus Blossom of the Fine Dharma* (1976, 334–35): "If he but copies it, that person at the end of his life shall be born in the Trāyastriṃśa Heaven. At that time, eighty-four thousand goddesses, making music with a multitude of instruments, shall come to receive him. That man shall straightway don a crown of the seven jewels, and among the women of the harem shall enjoy himself and be gay."

[41] In a later work, Tanaka asserted that women have a deep, special connection with the *Lotus Sūtra* because of the story of the dragon girl. Because Japan is the nation of Nichiren Buddhism and the *Lotus Sūtra*, women also have a unique tie with the Japanese nation. See Tanaka Tomoenosuke (1925, 30–31).

marriage. The powerful emphasis on *mappō* in the Nichiren school, combined with the *Lotus Sūtra*'s acceptance of potential Buddhahood for women, proved fertile ground for Nichirenist advocates of clerical marriage. Thus Tanaka, the first Nichirenshū-affiliated person in Meiji to argue for the acceptance of marriage by the clergy on the basis of the *Lotus Sūtra*, was soon joined by several other Nichiren clerics, including, by the turn of the century, Tanabe Zenchi and Nakazato Nisshō. Tanabe wrote that the *Lotus Sūtra* rendered all previous forms of the precepts obsolete. In contrast to the standards of behavior put forth in the Hīnayāna or Mahāyāna precepts, if a person sincerely receives and upholds the teachings of the *Lotus Sūtra*, then that person remains a true practitioner of the Lotus (*Hokke no gyoja*) even should that person eat meat or take a spouse. Tanabe went so far as to claim that "in the end those loathsome clerics in the Lotus school who do not permit meat eating or clerical marriage should be ranked with the vulgar upholders of the Hīnayāna precepts. Contrary to what one might think, they are evil people who slander the *Lotus Sūtra* and aim to violate its precepts."[42]

According to Tanaka, the importance of the husband-and-wife relationship was grounded in nature. At the root of the cosmos was the fundamental complement of male and female. The human couple was a symbol for the principle of complementarity that governed the whole universe. The interaction of male and female was visible in all realms of existence, both organic and inorganic (63–64). He concluded that "when we view things in this manner we see that the basis of society is truly men and women. The subtle function of the universe resides in the power of this husband-and-wife union." Using a typical Confucian-style argument, he further elaborated on the ontological importance of the male-female relationship.

> Father and son, lord and vassal. All human ethics arises from the husband-wife relationship. It is the beginning and end of human ethics. It is the basis of social interaction. If there is the Dharma, then there is the mystical. If there is form, then there is mind. If there is the cosmos, there are things. If, however male and female natures do not exist, then the Way is incomplete. If there are male and female but they are not combined together into a conjugal couple, then the vigorous and vital secret creative power of heaven cannot function. Men and women cannot be properly ordered. The mind cannot be pacified. The body cannot be subdued. The ordering of the family, the ruling of the nation, and the pacification of the realm cannot occur. That is to say, society cannot be maintained." (64–65)

If Buddhism was to reclaim its utility as an important tool for ensuring societal harmony and order, it would have to address seriously the conjugal relationship (65–66).

[42] Tanabe (1901, 17).

Tanaka concluded *Bukkyō fūfu ron* with an unambiguous affirmation of lay-householder life. Reiterating the intimate connection among the Buddhist teaching, ethics, and the state, he said that when one realizes the inseparability of these three elements, one can speak of the true teaching. As final proof of the world-affirming character of the Buddhist teachings, he turned one last time to the writings of Nichiren, citing at length Nichiren's 1276 letter (Kenji 2/6/27) to his devoted lay patron, Shijō Kingo (d. 1296?) (70). In the letter Nichiren stated that all that is necessary for true practice is recitation of the *daimoku*: "Just chant *Nam-myoho-ren-ge-kyo*, and when you drink saké, stay at home with your wife. Suffer what there is to suffer, enjoy what there is to enjoy. Regard both suffering and joy as facts of life and continue chanting *Nam-myoho-ren-ge-kyo*, no matter what happens. Then you will experience boundless joy from the Law. Strengthen your faith more than ever."[43]

Tanaka found the importance of the fundamental relationship among Buddhism, the family, and the state summarized in the Chinese ode cited by Mencius: "He set an example for his consort / and also for his brothers, / and so ruled over the state" (71).[44] Foreshadowing his later complete fusion of faith in the *Lotus Sūtra* with his ardent reverence for the emperor and the state, Tanaka closed *Bukkyō fūfu ron* with the two phrases that concisely summarize his core beliefs: "Homage to the Profound *Lotus Sūtra*" and "Imperial Japan Forever and Ever" (*Nippon teikoku banbanzai*) (71).

Just as Tanaka's Buddhist wedding ceremony was one of the earliest recorded religious marriage rituals created in Japan, he also seems to have given voice to growing national attention to the importance of the married couple and the *katei*. Much of the language that he used in *Bukkyō fūfu ron* resembles statements in the Japanese press on the occasion of the Meiji imperial couple's anniversary in 1894 and Crown Prince Yoshihito's marriage to Kujō Sadako on May 10, 1900. Celebrating the anniversary in 1894, one writer for the *Kokumin shinbun* commented that "the Way of Man and Wife is the Great Foundation of human ethics."[45] Several years later, announcing that the Shintō wedding of the crown prince "made the Way of monogamy clear," another reporter wrote, "We subjects, in keeping with the emperor's wish, should understand that the great foundation for governing one's family is the Way of Man and Wife; and in practicing this [Way], we must by all means strive not to err."[46] Although determining lines of influence is impossible given the information avail-

---

[43] Yampolsky (1990, 355–56); SNS, 2:1181–82.

[44] Mencius (1970, 56). I have used Lau's translation with slight modifications.

[45] *Kokumin shinbun*, March 9, 1894, cited in Fujitani (1996, 189). Fujitani discusses at length the importance of these imperial ceremonies for disseminating modern attitudes concerning monogamous marriage.

[46] *Kokumin shinbun*, May 10, 1900, cited in ibid., 189–90.

able at this time, clearly Tanaka's ideas concerning marriage resonated with the opinions of other intellectuals and writers.

Bukkyō fūfu ron may be seen as a companion volume to Tanaka's never-completed defense of Buddhist clerical marriage, *Bukkyō sōryo nikusai ron* (hereafter, *Nikusai ron*).[47] Tanaka finished about 25 percent of the ambitious work that he had outlined before abandoning it. He began working on *Nikusai ron* when in 1889 he was presented with the opportunity to use the Buddhist canon housed at the Shōtokuji, a Jōdo temple run by his friend, Chiba Shunrei. Wanting to take a careful look at various sūtras and commentaries in preparation for writing the work on clerical marriage, Tanaka spent a full month at Shōtokuji reading numerous texts.[48] The *Nikusai ron* was not published until 1891, when parts of the uncompleted manuscript were published in the Nichirenist journal *Shishiō*. Not until 1968 was the unfinished work published in its entirety, in the journal *Nichiren shugi kenkyū*.

In many respects, *Nikusai ron* is a more scholarly presentation of the ideas presented in the earlier *Bukkyō fūfu ron*. Scriptural citations are used throughout the text to bolster Tanaka's main conclusions, which he summarized later in his autobiography. Reiterating the distinction between provisional and ultimate teachings in Buddhism, Tanaka asserted that the precepts for the clergy, particularly those regarding *nikujiki saitai*, were provisional, not ultimate teachings. "[T]he reason why eating meat and clerical marriage are not necessarily violations of the precepts is that when we discuss the original idea and form of the Buddhist precepts and return to the original intention for the establishment of Buddhism, [we find that] the prohibitions against eating meat and clerical marriage are just provisional measures. They absolutely do not comprise the fundamental meaning of the Buddhist teaching."[49] As Tanaka claimed in *Bukkyō fūfu ron*, the ultimate teachings were contained only in the *Lotus Sūtra*, not in previous scriptures. In this manner, he greatly diminished the significance of the precepts for Buddhist practice.

Given Tanaka's own lay status and his vigorous advocacy of marriage in *Bukkyō fūfu ron*, one would expect him to be an ardent defender of clerical marriage. The *Nikusai ron* contains the seeds of his argument that in the current age of *mappō* in Japan, the Buddhist clergy had become "lay bodhisattvas" (*zaike bosatsu*). The marriage and childbearing of these lay bodhisattvas were not motivated by selfishness, however. Rather, they were part of their effort to protect the teaching and the nation.[50] The table

---

[47] Tanaka Kōho (1968, 2–9); Tanaka Chigaku (1968, 10–59). A good summary of the *Nikusai ron* may be found in Akabori (1992, 145–53).

[48] Tanaka Tomoenosuke (1936, 2:30–36); Tanaka Kōho (1977, 71–75).

[49] Tanaka Chigaku (1968, 59).

[50] Ibid., 49.

of contents for the projected portions of the work indicate that Tanaka wished to mount an elaborate defense of clerical marriage and to provide a schema for the open incorporation of women and families into Buddhist life (as the Shin denomination had done for centuries). The titles of proposed chapters included "Achievement of Buddhahood by Women," "Education of Women," "Marriage of the Clergy," and "On the Inclusion of Temple Wives in the Clerical Registries." As in the *Bukkyō fūfu ron*, Tanaka planned to attack the misogyny of provisional Buddhism and advocate an increased role for the wives of the clergy.

But Tanaka's examination and understanding of the Buddhist canon pushed him toward a conclusion more extreme than that formed by any of the other advocates of clerical marriage. Another look at the provisional table of contents for *Nikusai ron* provides hints of the outcome of Tanaka's research. The conclusion was to be called "The End of Home-Leaving," which included a chapter provocatively titled "The Monks of the Past are the Laymen of Today."[51] One of the completed chapters of the text, "Home-Leaver Bodhisattvas and Lay Bodhisattvas," foreshadows this argument. Claiming that during the Last Age of the Teaching, "rather than retreating in order to uphold a single precept, advancing to remedy heterodox views will be the urgent problem," Tanaka rejected the importance of the precepts in the modern world. He concluded,

> You should know that bodhisattvas are not necessarily monks and that following the precepts does not necessarily mean not eating meat or marrying. Furthermore, you should know that in terms of the clerical registry and rank, clerics today in our nation during the Last Age of the Teaching, are already included among the lay bodhisattvas. You should also know that lay bodhisattvas make a household and have a wife and children not out of their own selfish desire, but in order to protect the Buddhist teaching and the nation.[52]

Although this conclusion was never published during Tanaka's lifetime, he spelled out these ideas publicly in several of his later works. By the time he wrote *Shūmon no ishin* (1907) and his autobiography (1936), he had abandoned the attempt to defend clerical marriage per se in favor of the more radical position that all Buddhism in the Meiji period was lay Buddhism, and so the defense of clerical marriage was neither necessary nor possible. Unlike such contemporaneous authors as the Nichiren clerics

[51] Tanaka Kōho (1968, 4); Tanaka Chigaku (1968, 12–13). Tanaka later modified the chapter title from *Nikusai ron*. In Tanaka Kōho's article about the *Nikusai ron* and in the accompanying table of contents, the terms "*biku*" and "*ubasoku*" are placed so that the chapter title reads "*Mukashi no iwayuru biku wa ima no iwayuru ubasoku nari.*" In Tanaka Tomoenosuke (1936, 2:35), however, the words are transposed and the term *sōryo* is substituted for *biku*: "*Ima no sōryo to iu mono wa inishie no iwayuru ubasoku ni ataru mono.*"

[52] Tanaka Chigaku (1968, 49).

Tanabe Zenchi and Nakazato Nisshō, in his post-1900 writings Tanaka did not assert that there is a scriptural basis for clerical marriage. Reflecting on his earlier attempt while at the temple Shōtokuji to find a justification for clerical marriage, Tanaka wrote in his autobiography that his reading of the canon forced him to conclude that "eating meat and clerical marriage were not allowed by any of the Mahāyāna sūtras."[53] Agreeing with critics of clerical marriage like Nishiari Bokusan and Ueda Shōhen, he decided that the spread of marriage among the Japanese clergy did not necessitate a defense of *clerical* marriage because those who married were not really clerics at all. Unlike other critics of clerical marriage, however, he went on to argue that in the Last Age of the Teaching in Japan there are simply no more true "home-leavers." "Because a mendicant (*biku*) is not supposed to eat meat or marry, I reached the conclusion that the clergy of today corresponded to those who were called laypeople (*ubasoku*) in the past."[54] Even those who do not engage in clerical marriage are not really home-leavers: "Because the clergy today can no longer leave their mother and father or exempt themselves from the [jurisdiction of] the Kingly Law, they too are just laypeople. How can it be that they have a secular *koseki*, that they use their family name, but they comfortably have nonsecular status?"[55]

Tanaka elaborated on this conclusion in his blueprint for the total reformation of the Nichiren school, *Shūmon no ishin*, writing that marriage was entirely suitable for Nichiren clerics and that clerical marriage, coupled with familial inheritance of temples, would ensure the health of the Nichiren school. Rather than seeing clerical marriage as something to be justified or condemned, Tanaka interpreted the existence of married clerics as one more proof that the only valid Buddhism for modern Japan was lay Buddhism. Drawing on the unpublished portion of the *Nikusai ron* cited above, Tanaka wrote,

> We know that in the Last Age of the Teaching monks no longer leave home. They use their family names, they are subject to government taxation, they are drafted. They are subject to the draft, and there is no arguing that in reality they already have lost their status as home-leavers. Even if there are one or two clerics who actually are like home-leavers, for most of them there is no arguing about it. *There are almost none of them.* The majority (rather, all of them) have the name and appearance of a home-leaver but are in reality laypeople. The term "monk" means nothing more than that they are religious specialists. Therefore, I make a proposal that will resolve the [*nikujiki saitai*] issue in one stroke: "those who are called monks today are

[53] Tanaka Tomoenosuke (1936, 2:35).
[54] Ibid.
[55] Tanaka Chigaku (1968, 47).

[the same as] those who were called laymen in the past." Once we have determined that they are laymen, the thorny problem of eating meat and clerical marriage is like hairs on a turtle or horns on a rabbit. I have realized that the system of marriage is ultimately [suited to] the Last Age of the Teaching; furthermore it is [suited to] the Nichiren school.[56]

Tanaka determined in *Shūmon no ishin* that all of the practices from previous times will be useless in the Last Age of the Teaching. One cannot view the practitioners of the current epoch in the same way that one views the great monks of the past. To see them from that perspective is to

fail to understand the teaching, the spiritual disposition of those who receive the teaching, the time, the country, and the teachings that are in circulation (*go-ki-ji-koku-kyōhō rufu*).[57] It is the height of stupidity and superficiality. Virtue in the Last Age of the Teaching is not the Five Precepts or the Ten Good [Precepts]; it is not the five constant virtues (*gojō*), nor the three bonds (*sankō*); it is not the Four Noble Truths, nor the Six Pāramitās; it is not temperament, nor is it morality. [Virtue in the Last Age of the Teaching] is only faith, that is, the fundamental faith in the planting of the seeds by the original Buddha (*honge geshū no konpon shin*)."[58]

Thus, just as in *Bukkyō fūfu ron*, Tanaka concluded here that the only valid practice for the Last Age was faith in the *Lotus Sūtra*.

In *Shūmon no isshin*, Tanaka went on to argue that clerical marriage was extraordinarily valuable for the spread of Nichiren's teachings and for the preservation of the temples. If the Nichiren leadership did not recognize the legitimacy of marriage for the clergy, it would continue to squander the talents of not only the male clerics, but their wives, who also could be invaluable as Buddhist teachers. Citing as a precedent the lineage of Nichiren's disciple Toki Nichijō (1216–99), which controlled the Nakayama temple on Mt. Minobu, Tanaka claimed that from early on the denomination had allowed familial inheritance of temples. (We should remember here that Tanaka was not the first person to claim that clerical marriage and familial inheritance were practiced at Nichiren temples. Both Chikū and local officials also made such claims.) If put into practice univer-

---

[56] Tanaka Tomoenosuke (1907, 55).

[57] The so-called *gokō/gogi* (five guides/principles for propagation of the teaching) were propounded by Nichiren. See NJ, 62–67. Nichiren believed that an examination of these five factors made clear that the *honmon* portion of the *Lotus Sūtra* (the second half of the sūtra) contained the appropriate teachings for the Japanese people during the *mappō* period.

[58] Tanaka Tomoenosuke (1907, 54). The five constants are love, righteousness, propriety, wisdom, and good faith. The three bonds are the relationships between ruler and subject, father and son, and husband and wife. In Nichiren Buddhism the term *geshu* refers to the sowing of the seeds of Buddhahood—that is, the five characters *myō-hō-renge-kyō*—in the hearts of sentient beings. See NJ, 54–55; NSJ, 74–75.

sally, this would benefit the whole denomination. He went so far as to suggest that the denomination create a "Nichiren Laywomen's Academy" (Myōshū Ubai Rin), where temple wives would learn Nichiren doctrine, practice, history, temple management, and even nursing. To ensure that capable women entered Nichiren temples, Tanaka urged that women who had not graduated from the academy should not be permitted to marry Nichiren clerics.[59]

In effect, Tanaka reached the same conclusion as did the government concerning the status of the clergy. Just as the Ministry of Finance official Ōkuma Shigenobu in 1874 advocated the complete abolition of the ordination system ("because they [the clergy] are allowed to use a surname, eat meat, and marry, the law does not distinguish between monk and lay, so to continue to use the term *shukke tokudo* is meaningless"), Tanaka reached the radical conclusion that only lay Buddhism was a viable option in Meiji Japan. Instead of attempting to resolve the contradictions of clerical marriage by defending the validity of that practice, he solved the problem by redefining who was and who was not a home-leaver. He interpreted the existence of clerical marriage as crucial evidence that the only Buddhism possible was lay Buddhism, specifically, the kind of Buddhism promulgated by his own lay organizations. He accepted entirely the government position that one who had a surname, was drafted, and so on, by definition could not be a cleric. Concomitantly, clerical marriage was not something that one had to—or even could—defend. The investigation of clerical marriage thus helped Tanaka to justify his own rejection of clerical life and his efforts to found a new lay Buddhist organization that would bring about the total reformation of the temples and temple clergy.

Tanaka's resolution of the *nikujiki saitai* problem had led him to renounce clerical life and found a lay Buddhist organization. By reforming Nichiren Buddhism, he aimed to link Buddhist doctrines and ceremonies more closely with the life of each household. In effect, Tanaka had tried to domesticate Buddhism by bringing it into the home. At the same time, as part of his plan for reviving Nichiren Buddhism, Tanaka also recommended allowing clerics—who after all were only lay "religious specialists"—to marry and pass on their temple to their children. In so doing he was hoping to turn the temples themselves into homes. As I will show in the next chapter, this approach to reform was soon to be trumpeted not only by outsiders like Tanaka, but increasingly by clerical members of numerous denominations as well.

[59] Tanaka Tomoenosuke (1907, 72–73).

CHAPTER 9

The Aftermath:
From Doctrinal Concern to Practical Problem

Ah, yet again the *nikujiki saitai* problem? It is a problem
about which we and the reader are sick of hearing and
talking. Truly it remains an unresolved problem in every
school. Sooner or later, however, the *nikujiki saitai* problem will have to be resolved. Ultimately we will have only
baseless, empty discussions so long as the problem remains
unresolved, no matter how much we wish for the successful dissemination of the teaching and the renaissance
of scholarship or hope for the prosperity of the [Sōtō]
school. At its root, the matter of Buddhist morality is
connected with the *nikujiki saitai* problem. Linking the
cultivation of public morality and Buddhism depends on
the prior resolution of the problem. Harmonizing Buddhism and society is related to this problem. Harmonizing Buddhism with philosophy and science is related to
this problem. Truly the reform of Buddhism depends
upon the prior resolution of this problem.
   "Nikujiki saitai mondai o kesseyo," 1901

Almost a generation had elapsed since the decriminalization of clerical
marriage, when the editors of the Sōtō-affiliated journal *Wayūshi* published the editorial above in 1901. The leadership of the Tendai, Sōtō,
Shingon, Nichiren, and Jōdo denominations had drawn up numerous
plans to resolve the problem of clerical marriage, but, if this editorial is to
be believed, it had only worsened with the passage of time. The combination of the prohibition of clerical marriage by the sectarian establishments
and its decriminalization by the government was extremely volatile. With
the sons of the first cohort of legally (as far as the state was concerned)
married clerics coming of age and assuming the abbacy of their family's
temple, it is easy to see why *nikujiki saitai* became so pressing an issue at the
turn of the century. The hard-line stance taken by the leaders of most denominations when, as ordered by the Home Ministry, they compiled their

sectarian regulations for government approval after 1884 appears to have done little more than drive ever more married clerics into a double life. In effect, the government's attempt to end covert marriage only made that phenomenon more prevalent. The editorial from *Wayūshi* demonstrates how intractable the debate had become. According to the editorial, the number of Buddhist clerics who spoke of the precepts in public while breaking them in private had multiplied. The teaching of the Sōtō school, the editors argued, emphasized that the receiving of the precepts was the greatest good for a householder. The problem, however, was that the cleric who granted the precepts while exhorting the recipient to refrain from adultery and liquor more often then not broke those precepts himself.

> More than ignorance and incompetence, the disparagement of the Buddhist clergy by those in the world today is due to their [the clergy's] immoral and shameful behavior. The immorality and shamefulness are due to the inability of the clergy to openly marry and eat meat. Because they attempt to be extremely secretive and vague about eating meat and marrying, they keep a woman, they carry on furtive affairs with other men's wives or with widows in order to satisfy their desires. Or they visit the pleasure quarters, thereby incurring the criticism of others.[1]

The authors then described the hellish suffering of those in the clergy who must learn how to "eat meat while appearing not to eat meat and marry while appearing not to marry."

The editors at *Wayūshi* did not venture an answer to the problem that they believed was plaguing Buddhism, particularly the Sōtō school. The point of the editorial, they asserted, was merely to reveal the nature of the problem confronting Buddhism. Noting with admiration that the Jōdo school had agreed on an order of succession for candidates for abbacy of a temple that included the blood son of the abbot, they called for the speedy resolution of the problem. Until that happened, the Sōtō and other schools would remain paralyzed.

A chronology of the literature concerning the *nikujiki saitai* problem reveals the changing tide of the debate. During the first two decades after decriminalization, few extensive defenses of clerical marriage were published. During the mid-1880s Tanaka Chigaku issued the first comprehensive defenses of marriage—first Buddhist marriage and, subsequently, clerical marriage. By the turn of the century a number of other tracts devoted to the defense of clerical marriage were published, and the subject received increased attention in the Buddhist press throughout the Taishō period. Listed below are the dates for the main defenses of clerical marriage during the Meiji, Taishō, and Shōwa periods.

---

[1] Nikujiki saitai mondai o kesseyo (1901, 2).

Tanaka Chigaku	*Bukkyō fūfu ron*	1886
Inoue Enryō	*Nikujiki saitai ron*	1898
Nakazato Nisshō	*Sōfū kakushin ron*	1899
Tanaka Chigaku	*Bukkyō sōryo nikusai ron*	1899
Tanabe Zenchi	*Nikujiki saitai ron*	1901
Maruyama[2]	*Sōryo saitai ron*	1911
Kuriyama Taion	*Sōryo kazoku ron*	1917
Furukawa Taigo	*Sōryo saitai ron*	1938

In marked contrast to the initial period following the 1872 decriminalization measure, after the 1880s there were no prominent attacks on *nikujiki saitai*. The last extensive attack on clerical marriage that I have been able to uncover was the Shingon cleric Ueda Shōhen's (1828–1907) *Sōhiron*, which was published in 1879. Opposition to clerical marriage at the head temple and denomination headquarters levels remained vigorous in some schools, however. The Sōtō leadership, for example, passed the most stringent antimarriage sect law in 1885. Likewise, in 1886 Imakita Kōsen, the head of the Engakuji branch of Rinzai Zen, continued to warn his disciples against abandoning traditional standards of behavior.[3]

In much of the pro–*nikujiki saitai* literature from the 1890s forward, there is a shift in emphasis from discussing clerical marriage as a doctrinal problem to addressing the practical problems that were increasingly associated with that practice. As the forces opposing clerical marriage grew silent, the voices of those who viewed the problem in terms of bringing an end to hypocrisy and granting freedom to the married clerics and their children came to control the Buddhist press. Ikeda Eishun has observed the shift in the nature of the discussion, pointing out that, whereas during the early Meiji the problem of clerical marriage was viewed primarily as a matter of precept violation and purging the clergy of corrupt elements, by mid-Meiji the focus had shifted to issues of clerical reformation and modernization.[4]

The transformation of the debate over clerical marriage and the identification of temple families as the source of a "social problem" must be viewed in light of what some scholars have recently described as the creation of the sphere known as the "social" in Meiji Japan. According to David Horn, this sphere, which encompasses portions of civil society, private family life, and the state, is

a new terrain, a "particular sector" in which, in the course of the nineteenth century, a wide variety of problems came to be grouped together, a "sector comprising specific institutions and an entire body of qualified personnel"

[2] The personal name of Maruyama is not clear. He is simple identified as Mr. Maruyama.
[3] Sawada (1998, 127–28).   [4] Ikeda (1976b, 265–66).

(Deleuze 1979). In Italy as elsewhere, these personnel came to include not only "social" assistants and "social" workers, but also a whole range of scientists and technicians of the social, who on the basis of a particular training (most often in medicine and statistics) constituted themselves as experts able to offer diagnoses, assess risks, and construct norms.[5]

From the 1880s onward, we see the growth of this sphere in Japan as the newly forming middle class tried to establish itself in contradistinction to the upper and lower classes and the government attempted to solve problems arising in the wake of massive social dislocations caused by industrialization, urbanization, and the mobilization of the populace for the wars with China and Russia. In response, a host of government bureaucrats, Japanese Christians, intellectuals, journalists, and other social reformers worked to identify and ameliorate such social problems as lack of education, poverty, juvenile delinquency, and crime. As the Japanese government embarked on a variety of "moral suasion" campaigns to resolve these social crises, numerous individuals formed groups and proposed reforms with that same end in mind.[6] Together, these forces created the social in Japan.[7] It is in this context that more and more Buddhist leaders, intellectuals, and clerics came to view the resistance to clerical marriage in terms of its social costs—impoverished temples, dispossessed temple wives, and illegitimate children.

There is little doubt that by the turn of the century the forces opposed to clerical marriage were losing ground. As mentioned in the editorial quoted above, a steady flow of petitions to the sectarian leadership proposing the adoption of protection laws for the temple wives and children kept the issue of clerical marriage alive at the annual congresses of the various Buddhist denominations. Other sources indicate that although at the end of the 1800s the leadership of most denominations continued to ban open clerical marriage and other related practices, they were under increased pressure to modify their position.

Attempts to curb the spread of marriage among the clergy or to ignore the problem had failed miserably. At the 1891 pan-sectarian conference of Buddhist clerics in Nagoya, abolition of the sectarian prohibitions against *nikujiki saitai* was placed on the agenda but never came to the floor.[8] By 1901 the Jōdo school leadership tacitly recognized the right of

---

[5] Horn (1994, 11). I would like to thank David Ambaras for pointing out this reference.

[6] Garon (1997, 7) describes the extension in meaning of the term *kyōka*, which literally referred to the dissemination of Buddhist teachings, to the more general sense of "moral suasion." According to Garon, during the late nineteenth and twentieth centuries in Japan, "Elaborate bureaucracies sprang up, devoted to running moral suasion campaigns, coordinating local moral suasion groups, disseminating 'social education,' and effecting 'spiritual mobilization.'"

[7] Ambaras (1999, 68–74). See also Garon (1997, 8–15).

[8] MNJ, 4:653.

the clergy to marry by allowing agnatic and nonagnatic sons to register as candidates for succession to the abbacy of their father's temple.[9] In a similar vein, Kita Sadakichi noted that in 1897 discussion of the *nikujiki saitai* issue was commonplace at the Shingon school headquarters, and in the summer of 1906 the prohibition against *nikujiki saitai* was lifted on Mt. Kōya.[10] By the turn of the century, petitions requesting the acceptance of clerical marriage were being submitted regularly to the annual Tendai and Nichiren denominational congresses.[11] One can only conclude that by the turn of the century the defense against *nikujiki saitai* was crumbling.

THE EVIDENCE FROM STATISTICS

The increasingly exasperated tone of the literature concerning clerical marriage is one indication that the practice was spreading. Even given the spotty nature of the information available, it is apparent that the actual increase in the number of married clerics helped force the clerical leaders to moderate their open hostility to clerical marriage and to take measures to accommodate their new constituency.

Gauging the spread of clerical marriage and such concomitant practices as patrimonial inheritance of temples in the non-Shinshū denominations is not an easy task. Although we know from anecdotal evidence that clerical marriage was practiced by a significant number of clerics prior to the Meiji period, we do not know the size of that population. In addition, few statistics concerning the spread of clerical marriage for the Meiji and the Taishō periods are available. The earliest denomination-wide censuses date only from the early Shōwa period, when nationwide surveys were made in both the Jōdo (1934) and Sōtō denominations (1937). Prior to that, figures concerning the number of married clerics are almost nonexistent.

A glimpse of the number of married clerics at the time of the decriminalization can be gained from government census figures for the years 1872 through 1876. The census recorded the number of family members for each class of Japanese subject, including the Buddhist clergy. In 1872 the census recorded 98,585 family members for a total population of 113,261 male clerics.[12] The census does not break down the total according to denomination, however, so it is difficult to assess the meaning of those figures. The census figures for that short period also show a steady decline in the number of family members that corresponds with the precipitous decline in the total number of Buddhist clergy. As indicated in chapter 4, the decreasing trend is in part due to laicization of the clergy,

[9] Nikujiki saitai mondai o kesseyo (1901, 4).

[10] Kita (1933, 143–44).

[11] "Sugimura (1901, 418). Also cited in Ikeda (1994, 407–8).

[12] See NJTS, vol. 1; Collcutt (1986, 162).

TABLE 1. Buddhist Clerical and Temple Family Populations, 1872–76

	1872	1873	1874	1875	1876
Male Clerics	75,925	73,875	69,256	64,881	19,490
Disciples of Male Clerics	37,336	36,422	33,745	26,918	14991
Female Clerics	6,068	5,632	4,248	3,509	1067
Disciples of Female Clerics	3,553	3,694	3,694	2,672	646
Total Clerical Population	122,882	119,623	110,943	97,980	36,194
Family Members of Male Clerics	98,585	97,372	95,434	90,230	38,711
Male Family Members (calculated)*	38,416	38,510	38,389	35,938	14,991
Female family members	60,169	58,862	57,045	54,292	23,720
Family Members of Female Clerics	0	0	0	0	0
Total Temple Population	221,467	216,995	206,377	188,210	74,905
Number of Temples	89,914	88,423	79,120	74,784	71,962

Source: Census figures from NJTS, vol. 1.
*The number of male family members was calculated by subtracting the number of female family members from the total number of family members of male clerics.

but to a large extent it is a result of the 1876 redefinition of who was legally a Buddhist cleric. It would appear that, because primarily lower-ranking clerics lost the right to be called *sōni*, the decrease in the number of family members of Buddhist clerics from 90,230 in 1875 to 38,711 in 1876 was a result of the low-ranking clerics being reclassified as students. The remaining family members were those associated with 19,490 clerics ranked Kyōdōshoku *shihō* or higher. (See table 1.)

Although at first glance the large number of family members in the 1872 census is surprising, it is entirely possible that almost all of them lived at temples of denominations that openly had allowed clerical marriage during the Edo period: Jōdo Shinshū and Shugendō. If we assume an average family size of 4.5 people per temple (according to sectarian surveys from the Shōwa period, on average approximately 5 family members lived in each Jōdo temple and 4 in each Sōtō temple), that would mean there were married clerics at approximately 24 percent of the temples. If one assumes an average family size ranging between 4 and 6 people, then the percentage of temples with families would be between 18 and 27 percent.[13]

[13] Morioka Kiyomi has used the census figures for the total number of family members and the numbers of female family member in temples to estimate the number of male children in the temples. Morioka has subtracted the number of male temple children from the number of female family members to figure the number of wives. In so doing he has arrived at a percentage of 28.7 percent married clerics for 1872. The percentage of married clerics remains fairly stable for the next three years, fluctuating from 27.5 to 28.3 percent in 1875. According to Morioka, in 1876 the percentage rises to 44.8 percent, but he does not take into account

Tamamuro Fumio has calculated that approximately 31 percent of all temples at the start of the Meiji period were Jōdo Shinshū temples.[14] That would mean there were almost 28,000 Jōdo Shin temples left in 1872. If 80 percent of them had a family, that would mean an average family size of approximately 4.4 people, which is well within the realm of possibility. It is therefore conceivable that most if not all of the family members recorded in the early Meiji censuses resided at Jōdo Shinshū temples.

Anecdotal evidence, primarily the journal articles and editorials noted earlier, indicate that after 1872, the male Buddhist clergy married rapidly. This picture is supported by the limited statistical data available for the mid-Meiji, Taishō, and Shōwa periods. Taishō University sociologist Hikita Seishun has arrived at some very partial figures concerning the diffusion of patrimonial inheritance of temples, a practice that assumes clerical marriage. In his 1965 study of the Shingon Buzan sect, Hikita used records at the sect headquarters to determine when patrimonial inheritance began at 150 sect temples in the Niigata region.[15] According to those figures, by the end of the Meiji period patrimonial inheritance of temples had occurred at 23 (15 percent) of the temples. Therefore the percentage of married clerics was at least 15 percent by that time, if not higher, despite the fact that the sect leadership still strongly discouraged the marriage of non-Shugendō clergy.

According to Hikita's research, the largest growth in the number of Buzan sect temples took place between 1911 and 1926, after the leadership had at least tacitly accepted the right of the clergy to marry. During that period patrimonial inheritance began at another 35 of the Niigata temples, bringing the total number to 58 (39 percent). At the end of the Taishō period a number of temples were already in the second or third generation of patrimonial inheritance, which suggests that at least some of them had begun that practice before reporting it to the sect headquarters. By 1955 patrimonial inheritance had taken place at 71 temples (47 percent). Hikita adds that at an additional 38 temples either a true son, an adoptive son, or some other family member was registered as the successor to the current abbot, making patrimonial inheritance a possibility at 109 (73 percent) of the temples. Many of the remaining 41 temples were extremely isolated, impoverished temples that were jointly managed with another temple, which made the likelihood of patrimonial inheritance very improbable at those locations.

---

the massive reduction in clerical numbers due to the redefinition of *sōni* by the government. Just how that change affected the percentage is an open question, but it seems curious that the percentage of married clerics would remain almost constant for four years and then in one year jump by more than 16 percent. See Morioka (1995, 8).

[14] Tamamuro (1994).

[15] Hikita (1965, 101–2).

The Jōdo and the Sōtō denominations performed denominational censuses during the 1930s. According to the census authors, the surveys were undertaken in response to the massive changes in society and economy that had drastically altered the context for temple management. The compilation of accurate information regarding the temples of the denomination was viewed as a first step in formulating an effective response to those societal changes. As Horn has observed, the emergence of statistics as a means for apprehending the nature of poverty, mental illness, disease, and other social phenomena was an important element in the creation of the social in modern societies. According to Horn, the use of statistical information helped transform problems like poverty that had been attributed to individual failings—drunkenness, poor planning, dissipation—into normal features of social life that were amenable to correction by experts.[16] In the case of the clergy, surveys conducted by the denominational leaders demonstrated scientifically the presence of that which had always been present to a certain degree, clerical marriage. But by rendering that knowledge statistically, clerical experts changed clerical marriage from a transgression of the precepts into a social problem ameliorable through particular policy measures—insurance for temple families and systematization of abbatial succession at the local temple level.

The statistics contained in those surveys give us a sense of how far clerical marriage had spread in the Jōdo and Sōtō schools by the 1930s. Although both censuses contain information concerning the number of temple families, only the census for the Sōtō school gives a figure for the percentage of the clergy that were married. The Jōdo census, which was primarily concerned with the conditions of economic hardship for its clergy, contains only information concerning the average number of family members per temple, figured with the assumption that all temples contained families.[17] For this reason, the information provided in the 1934 Jōdo survey, is not as specific as the 1936 Sōtō survey with regard to the percentage of temple families in the school. According to the Jōdo survey, in a total of 1,261 temples there were 5,864 family members. The overall average family size was approximately five per temple. Therefore, it is possible to calculate roughly the percentage of temples with families— approximately 93 percent. By comparison, the Sōtō survey revealed that on average there were 3.7 family members per temple and that more than 80 percent of the temples contained families.[18]

The Sōtō census also added the interesting statistic that the middle-ranked temples, not the largest or the smallest, contained the majority of the temple families. The authors of the survey found that the spread of

[16] Horn (1994, 11–12).
[17] Shimano (1934, 10–11).
[18] Taniguchi (1937, 13–22).

temple families had occurred in greatest numbers in those regions where the influence of the head temples had traditionally been the weakest. Less remote areas, for example, Kyoto, and regions under the control of the head temples—Fukui and Ishikawa prefectures—had the largest number of temples without temple families.[19] The Sōtō survey is discussed in more detail later in this chapter.

CHRISTIAN CRITICISMS OF BUDDHISM AND THE CHANGING PERSPECTIVE ON THE FAMILY

The growing number of married clerics was but one source of pressure on the Buddhist schools to accept clerical marriage. Christian criticism of Buddhist attitudes toward marriage and traditional disparagement of women also played a role in stimulating the Buddhist establishment to respond to the crisis. We have seen that Tanaka Chigaku, aware of the Christian attacks, attempted to demonstrate the importance of Buddhism to family life and the "true" Buddhist position on the salvation of women. He was not the only Buddhist writer to view with hostility the claims of Japanese Christians and foreign missionaries about the superiority of Christian teachings concerning women and family life. Nor was he the only Buddhist writer to offer a more positive view of women and to promote the benefits of marriage for both the laity and the clergy.

Beginning in the 1880s and continuing into the Taishō period, in general there was a growing concern in Buddhist circles with the family, education of women, and women's rights. In part the growth in awareness of and sensitivity to the welfare of temple wives and children in the promarriage Buddhist literature may have been catalyzed by more positive evaluations of family life and marriage in Japanese society as a whole. As I noted in chapter 8, during the last decades of the nineteenth century there was increasing attention to the *katei* or home as the primary site of moral education. Buddhists like Tanaka Chigaku responded to this trend by arguing for the centrality of Buddhism to domestic life.

The new attention to marriage and family life in the *nikujiki saitai* literature was a departure from the tracts of the Edo and early Meiji period. The authors of the Edo defenses of Shin practice and the early Meiji proposals in favor of clerical marriage, despite their advocacy of that practice, had been almost exclusively silent or even negative about women and marriage. Such earlier advocates of clerical marriage as Ōtori Sessō and Ugawa Shōchō had argued that ideally the clergy were to be celibate, however, given the circumstances—Japan's race to catch up with the West, the threat of Christianity, the conditions during the Last Age of the

[19] Ibid., 16.

Teaching, and so on—the clergy had to marry. It was seen as a practice demanded by geopolitical circumstances. But by the 1880s there was a definite shift toward a more positive evaluation of marriage in general and, by extension, of clerical marriage as well.

No doubt the growth in concern for domestic issues by Buddhist writers was partially spurred by the spread of newer attitudes concerning marriage and women in society as a whole during the Meiji period. The new concentration on domestic issues was found both among reformers and their organizations and at the governmental level. The Meiji Civil Code, adopted in 1898, for example, required that all marriages and divorces now be registered in order to be legally acknowledged.[20] As noted by Sharon Nolte and Sally Hastings, "in the two decades between 1890 and 1910, the Japanese state pieced together a policy toward women based on two assumptions: that the family was an essential building block of the national structure and that the management of the household was increasingly in women's hands." The growing consensus among bureaucrats and reformers that "Japan would not be able to equal the West until it provided proper respect for the institution of marriage" may account for the almost total absence of public attacks on clerical marriage after the late 1870s.[21]

In addition, along with many intellectuals and government leaders, Japanese Buddhists were put on the defensive by critiques of Japanese conjugal life, which ranged from gentle chiding by such observers of the Japanese scene as L. W. Küchler of the British consular services to more strident diatribes by Japanese Christians and foreign missionaries against Japanese marital customs and the place of women in Japanese society. From mid-Meiji through the Taishō period, the criticisms of Buddhism by domestic and foreign Christians made the recasting of Buddhist attitudes toward marriage, women, and family life imperative.[22]

As I discussed in the previous chapter, during the last several decades of the nineteenth century, marriage, the family, and the *katei/hōmu* had become important issues for a wide spectrum of reformers and civil servants. Sheldon Garon has observed that by the late 1880s, although few in number, Japanese Christians, particularly the Japanese branch of the Women's Christian Temperance Union (Nihon Kirisutokyō Kyōfūkai, WCTU) and such Christian educators as Naruse Jinzō (1858–1919) had become influential in challenging long-standing attitudes toward women and mar-

---

[20] Fujitani (1996, 188).

[21] Nolte and Hastings (1991, 171).

[22] Küchler in 1885 wrote a description of Japanese marriage ceremonies and the position of women within marriage: He disparagingly concluded: "until important and radical changes are effected in the whole marriage system—changes, especially, which will give to wives greater security against the possible tyranny or caprice of their husbands—the position of woman must continue to remain far below that of her sisters in nations laying claim to civilization." See Küchler (1885, 127–28).

riage.[23] These reformers waged a vociferous campaign against prostitution and drinking and also tried to raise the status of women and to promote marriages in which the woman was a companion and partner as well as bearer of children. As noted by Garon with reference to the WCTU, "these Protestant women endeavored, above all, to elevate the married woman from a lowly member of the early modern Japanese family to a Western-style household manager and mother who enjoyed the love and respect of her husband."[24]

The uproar concerning *The Japanese Bride*, a book by Tamura Naomi (1858–1934), is illustrative of the competition and tension between Buddhists and Christians as they raced to become the arbiters of feminine virtue and domestic vitality. In 1893—the same year as the convening of the World Parliament of Religions in Chicago—the American-educated Japanese Protestant minister published in the United States this English-language tract that criticized customary Japanese attitudes toward women and implicitly blamed Buddhism for the harsh treatment of Japanese women.[25] When Tamura distributed his complimentary copies of the book to his friends in Japan, he was met with a storm of protest from both Buddhist and Christian apologists, who, in the words of an American observer, were outraged that Tamura had "in cold type compared the condition of his mother and sister and wife with that of women in other lands."[26] The subsequent clamor over Tamura's writings and activities abroad reveals the extreme sensitivity of the Buddhists and other Japanese to even a hint of foreign criticism of Japanese custom.

Critics were particularly piqued that Tamura had chosen to publish the work in America for the edification of the American public. Tamura claimed that Japanese home life was something "which foreigners never penetrate, and which most Japanese hesitate to reveal, feeling it to be a shame to open the dark side of our home life in public."[27] He explicitly stated in the preface his underlying disdain for Buddhism: "If any one who reads this book is able to catch a glimpse of our [i.e., Japanese] home life, and is thus led to compare the homes under Buddhist influence with the homes under the influence of Christianity, I shall be greatly rewarded" (v).

Although Tamura did not dwell at any length on the Buddhist attitude toward women, he did blame Buddhism for the poor position of women

---

[23] For information about Naruse, see Sitcawich (1997, 36–88). On the WCTU, see Sheldon Garon (1993b, 710–32); Garon (1994, 346–66).

[24] Garon (1994, 359).

[25] Thelle (1987, 126) provides a short description of the uproar surrounding the publication of Tamura's book.

[26] Curtis (1896) 1:242–44.

[27] Tamura (1900, v). The book was copyrighted in 1893 and responses in the Japanese press were published the same year, so I assume the first edition of the book was published that year. Further references will be cited as page numbers in the text.

in the Japanese home and society: "Public sentiment places love for a woman very low in the scale of morals. Probably this is the outcome of the teaching of the Buddhist religion, which says that, 'woman is impure, and a scape-goat [*sic*].' This false doctrine has had a very harmful influence in moulding our opinions" (2–3).

Tamura was highly critical of the subordinate place of the woman in the Japanese home, noting that the "wife's position in our home is that of mistress rather than queen" (68). He also accused Japanese men of mistreating their wives because they so freely engaged in extramarital affairs:

> Our bride may have a great grief and heart-breaking which your bride may not meet in her life: The husband may do anything he wishes with absolute freedom. He may stay out a week or a month if he does not choose to come home. He may have a concubine in his own house or in a private house, and the wife has no right to oppose her husband's wishes. If she does oppose and say disagreeable things to him, what is the result of it? The consequences will be more trouble than ever in her life. Therefore a Japanese wife will allow her husband to do whatever he wishes, and will treat him as lovingly and pleasantly as possible, though her heart is full of a grief and sorrow like death. (72)

In the autumn of 1893, just after the publication of *The Japanese Bride*, a series of four editorial responses was published in the influential Buddhist journal *Meikyō shinshi*.[28] In extraordinarily harsh language, the editors accused Tamura of being a traitor to Japan, an enemy of his countrymen, and a threat to the nation. They bore particular umbrage toward Tamura for asserting that the Japanese wedding ceremony did not demonstrate the sacrality of marriage,[29] and for choosing to reveal the ugly aspects of Japanese domestic life to Americans.[30] In an effort to demonstrate that their concerns were not parochial and that even foreigners viewed Tamura as a shameless mercenary, the editors also cited at length a translation of a highly critical English-language review from the *Kirisutokyō shinbun*, a Japanese Christian newspaper, that questioned Tamura's motivation for publishing such information in English in the United States. If Tamura had the best interests of the Japanese at heart, they argued, why did he not publish his criticisms in Japanese? Clearly he was only out to make a profit at the expense of his countrymen. The editorial concluded by accusing Tamura of having ridiculed Japanese customs before American audiences in order to receive lucrative honoraria and of having planned to parade a

[28] Baikokudo (1893, 7); Mura to mura no shōtotsu (1893, 7–8); Tamura Naomi (1893, 7–8). According to Thelle (1987, 292, n. 96), the fourth article was published in *MKS* 9/6/ 1893. It is unavailable to me at this time.

[29] Baikokudo (1893, 7).

[30] Tamura Naomi (1893, 7).

group of twelve Japanese women around the Columbian Exhibition in Chicago as if they were mere merchandise until the U.S. press accused him of being a phony minister and forced him put a stop to his plans.[31] In the end, so great was the uproar in the Japanese press that Tamura was stripped of his pastorate.[32] Such censure did not cow Tamura, however. Much of his congregation left the Presbyterian Church with him, and, according to William Eleroy Curtis, after the incident he was "much more prosperous than before."[33]

Given the high profile gained by the WCTU campaign and the ongoing competitive tensions between Buddhists and Christians, it is probably no coincidence that after 1886—the same year the WCTU was established in Tokyo—a number of Buddhist intellectuals and clerics began disseminating in the Buddhist press similar exhortations about marital relations. In fact, Buddhist attention to conjugal relations seemed to blossom in the late 1880s, around the same time that Japanese Protestants and foreign missionaries were lambasting the Japanese for their tolerance of prostitution and the unequal status of women in marriage. We have seen that in 1886, for example, Tanaka Chigaku delivered to his lay organization, Rengekai, a series of lectures extolling the virtues of the husband-wife relationship. The same year, the prominent Sōtō layman Ōuchi Seiran— who, like Tanaka, was an ex–cleric—wrote an essay, published in the Buddhist journal Kyōgaku ronshū, that described in straightforward fashion the numerous benefits of a more mutual husband-and-wife relationship. Ōuchi noted the recent proliferation of discussions concerning the rights of women in marriage and called for a break with the Japanese custom that dictated that it was improper for a wife to accompany her husband in public. That simple practice, being the basis for a healthy and productive marriage, would also benefit other families and the nation as a whole. "The benefit for the husband and wife will resuscitate that household. One family will affect 10,000 families and provide vast benefit to the nation," wrote Ōuchi.[34]

Not to be outdone by the Christians concerning the welfare of women and families, other Buddhist writers published articles and pamphlets describing their perspective on these issues and Buddhist remedies for reforming domestic life. Some tracts urged the modernization of attitudes toward women. Others defended Japanese customs and prescribed the various ways in which only Buddhist, not foreign or Christian, values could serve as the foundation of Japanese feminine virtue and healthy family life. During the last several decades of the Meiji era, Buddhist

[31] Ibid.
[32] KDJ, 10: 304; Thelle (1987, 292, n. 96).
[33] Curtis (1896, 1:244).
[34] Ōuchi (1886, 18–21).

writers produced a variety of works describing the creation of a "Buddhist home." The literature of this type was produced by clerics from several denominations and includes such tracts as *Futoku no kōryō* (Moral principles for women; Jōdo Shinshū); *Bukkyō no katei* (The Buddhist family; Jōdo Shinshū); *Bukkyō katei kyōkun* (Instructions for the Buddhist family; Sōtōshū), as well as an assortment of articles in Buddhist journals.[35] Like Tanaka Chigaku, the authors of these works considered the home to be the fundamental social unit, serving as the interface between the individual and society and as the site for moral training. As Mine Genko wrote in the introduction to his tract, *Instructions for the Buddhist Family*, "as for those individuals that the various religions of the world call moral, all of them have paid deep attention to the morality of the family."[36]

SEXUALITY AND THE IMPOSSIBILITY OF CELIBACY

The *Wayūshi* editorial contained a summary description of the arguments advanced by the advocates of clerical marriage, whom they labeled as "Buddhists of the New Buddhism Faction" (*Shin Bukkyōha Bukkyōto*). According to the editorial, the main argument advanced in favor of clerical marriage was that people, even those who have achieved liberation, are subject to ordinary human desires. The suppression of those desires is "inhumane, antinationalistic, antisociety, and unpsychological." As a result of such an unrealistic teaching, the new Buddhists contended, those nations where Buddhist thought flourished—India, Southeast Asia, and China—had fallen into ruin. Those who supported such stringent practices were disparagingly characterized as "deformed children, hypocrites whose actions differ from their words, cruel cold-hearted individuals who lack passion."[37]

During the late nineteenth and early twentieth centuries, pro–clerical marriage advocates increasingly argued that sexual abstinence was unnatural and potentially harmful to the body, psyche, and society. As new understandings of human biology, evolution, and heredity proliferated in Japan during the Meiji era, promarriage clerics proclaimed the biological necessity of human sexual activity and the medical and hereditary threats posed by mandatory celibacy.

These authors did not have to rely solely upon new knowledge of human biology and sexuality imported from the West to make their case. Rather,

---

[35] See, for example, Kyōto Fujin Kyōkai Jimusho (1891); Ishihara (1901); Koizumi (1927); Suzuki (1911). Along with the pamphlets and books, a number of new Buddhist women's journals also appeared, including *Bukkyō fujin* (Buddhist woman), *Fujin kyōkai zasshi* (Women's teaching assembly magazine), *Futoku* (Feminine virtues), and *Katei* (Home).

[36] Mine (1911, 1).

[37] Nikujiki saitai mondai o kesseyo (1901, 3–4).

advocates were able to link these new understandings of human sexuality with earlier, resonant promarriage arguments. It was not too difficult to shift from the Confucian argument of Ōtori and others that celibacy contradicted Heavenly Principle (*Tenri*) or the dispensationalist argument that the precepts could not be followed in the Last Age of the Teaching to these biologized understandings of human sexuality. By 1881, with the publication of the expanded Japanese translation of William Fleming's *Philosophical Dictionary*, the term *tenri* was already being used as a substitute for "nature."[38] The conflation of the older Confucian term with the new Western scientific notion of nature made it possible for anticelibacy proponents to argue that celibacy violated natural law and thus seem modern and scientific. But at the same time, their understanding of sexuality retained a distinctively Japanese resonance. The result of the influx of various Western understandings of medical science and biology and the modernization of Buddhist attitudes toward sexuality in Japan was thus something more complex than "Westernization." As Frank Dikötter has observed in the case of the modernization of sexual attitudes in early Republican China,

> The changes which occurred in the discursive field we analyze cannot be described as a conflict between two "systems," in which both would be seen as distinctive, integrated and self-determining "frameworks." Modernizing discourses of sex were not "hybrids" of "Chinese" and "Western" ideas, nor can they be interpreted as some sort of survival of "traditional" cultural values underneath a veneer of modern scientific ideas. What emerged was a type of "latticed knowledge," to borrow a term from the anthropologist David Parkin, a body of knowledge in flux, characterized by interactions, overlaps and echoes, by constant change and endless combinations.[39]

In much the same way, arguments in favor of clerical marriage developed in a discursive field in which older Japanese Confucian and Nativist critiques of celibacy became intertwined with newer notions of human biology, evolution, and sexuality.

Several advocates of marriage argued that marriage of the clergy should be allowed because sexual relations were natural and insuppressible. I showed in chapter 3 that in the eighteenth century the Jōdo Shin cleric Chikū indirectly asserted that those who in public decried *nikujiki saitai* inevitably would in private fall prey to their desires for meat and women.[40] Jōdo Shin clerics, he explained, would be better clergy because those basic needs would not trouble them and they would have clear consciences. Chikū's argument, however, was based on the assumption that sexual

[38] Hida (1979, *honbun* 57).
[39] Dikötter (1995, 12).
[40] Chikū, *Nikujiki saitai ben*, 42.

desire was overpowering because people were living during a period of spiritual decline, the *mappō* period. Thus, by marrying, the Jōdo Shin clergy were acting in accordance with the epoch—*saitai* was inevitable because it was the Last Age of the Teaching.

The early Meiji proponents of clerical marriage had advanced arguments containing the same sense of the inexorability of sexual desire, but by the 1880s they had abandoned the earlier reliance upon the Buddhist eschatological component of the defense, instead arguing that marriage was unavoidable because sexual relations between men and women were a fulfillment of Heavenly Principle—a position taken by Nativists, Confucians, and Shintoists as well. As we have already seen, Ōtori Sessō used this argument in his second petition to the government in 1872 when he complained that "the Buddhist clergy erects lofty goals and contradict Heavenly Principle. They establish rules that suppress human nature and are unsuitable for noble positions and superior vision."

By the 1880s, in the wake of more biological understandings of reproduction and sexuality, the "Heavenly Principle" argument against celibacy was transmuted in the light of novel political and scientific ideas. The Nichiren cleric Tanabe Zenchi, using the new language of rights and constitutionalism, argued in his *Nikujiki saitai ron* that prohibiting marriage of the Buddhist clergy amounted not only to a violation of biological laws; it also was an infringement of their basic human rights.

> If we appeal to reason in thinking about this matter, [we see that] although they are clerics, they are still human and they are members of the human family. As human beings living in the world they have an innate right (*tenpu no kenri*) to demand those things biologically essential and infringement [of those rights] by others is not permissible. To say that the Buddhist clergy alone are not permitted to eat meat and marry is clearly a suppression of human rights and is following the evil practices of the feudal period. It is nothing more than the words in the dreams of the Hīnayāna and provisional Mahāyāna teachings. In this enlightened age, should Buddhists [living in] this nation of constitutionalism contradict the teachings of Mahāyāna, destroy the vital Human Way, and follow the pigheaded annihilationist prohibition against eating meat and clerical marriage?[41]

Another Nichiren cleric and promarriage advocate, Nakazato Nisshō, shared Tanabe's view that human sexuality was a natural, essential desire, no different from the need for food or sleep. In Nakazato's book the novel interlacing of traditional Buddhist cosmology with biologized understandings of sexuality is clearly visible. Taking issue with the argument advanced by Nishiari, Fukuda, and others that according to Buddhist teachings sexu-

41 Tanabe (1901, 4).

ality is impure, Nakazato did not stress the asexual nature of the first kami or the lack of physical desires in the highest heavens. Instead, he asserted that Buddhist sutras and commentaries say that all beings born in one of the realms between the hells (*jigokukai*) and the six heavens of the world of desire (*rokuyokuten*) are subject to the three desires: food, sleep, and sex. To deny a person food or sleep would clearly lead to biological injury. Likewise, argued Nakazato, complete sexual abstinence would result in bodily harm to any being living in one of the realms where the three desires prevail. Without citing a source for his evidence, Nakazato claimed that statistics bore him out on this point: people who were married (and therefore were sexually active) were longer lived than those who remained single. Natural desires would be indulged no matter what the consequences. If, like the Tokugawa regime, the government or the head temples refused to allow the Buddhist clergy to fulfill their desires, the result would be the same as during the Edo period, when, in Nakazato's view, harsh anti–clerical fornication laws had warped natural sexual desire into homosexuality.[42]

Not all Buddhists, even more progressive ones who held that the sex drive was natural, agreed with the conclusions reached by Nakazato and Tanabe. Suzuki Daisetsu (a.k.a. D. T. Suzuki, 1870–1966), for example, writing from the United States in 1900, contributed an article (entitled "Seiyokuron") on sexual desire to the journal *Nihonjin*. Suzuki accepted the general notion that sexual desire was a natural biological instinct rather than a deluded, harmful passion. But he also maintained that a balance had to be struck between giving free reign to one's instincts and spiritual cultivation. Pointing to the behavior of a number of animals, ranging from social insects to trout, Suzuki argued that the sex drive and the urge to procreate were strong enough to cause animals to sacrifice their own lives for the sake of reproduction.[43] But, he added, humans could not be reduced to mere animals; they also had a spiritual destiny to fulfill.

Citing with agreement the theories of Joseph Ernest Renan (1823–92) as presented in *L'Irréligion de l'avenir* by the French philosopher Marie Jean Guyau (1854–88), Suzuki posited an inverse relationship between sexual

---

[42] Nakazato (1899, 56–58). In *Nikujiki saitai ben*, 315, Chikū also asserted that those who defamed *saitai* satisfied their sexual desires in a much more reprehensible practice—same-sex intercourse. "In the *Matokurokuga ritsu* [Sarvāstivādin Vinaya *mātṛkā*], Chapter 3, page 18 it warns, 'if a monk should penetrate another's anus, it is a *pārājika* offense.' What do they [critics of clerical marriage] make of this passage? The monks of other schools keep young boys and child servants. What do they make of this Vinaya citation? There is no graver sexual transgression than this one." The passage from the *Matokurokuga* is found at T. 23:582. John Boswell (1980, 216–17) has noted that in the West in the twelfth century, the pro–clerical marriage priests in the Catholic Church also accused antimarriage priests of homosexuality.

[43] Suzuki (1900, 26–27).

activity and the energy available for intellectual or spiritual endeavors.[44] Although Suzuki felt Renan was perhaps excessive in his praise of the virtues of celibacy, he agreed that it was a "physiological fact" that an intimate connection existed between sexual relations and intellectual life. Suzuki wrote,

> be it in Buddhism or Christianity, the rejection of marriage by the clergy was [undertaken not because] acting on sexual desire was seen as a hindrance to the chaste life; it was undertaken because the clergy perceived a profound relationship between the mindless fulfillment of sexual desire and the clarity of consciousness. When one devotes one's individual vitality to the elevation of religious consciousness, certainly sexual desire—that is, the depletion of vitality—must be stopped. I believe that superficially the prohibition of meat eating and clerical marriage has a religious significance, but in fact, it is an unconscious response to this physiological principle.[45]

Given the relationship between sexual energy and higher intellectual pursuits, future spiritual virtuosi are physiologically required to limit or even forgo entirely sexual activity. But clearly this was not the path for everybody—Suzuki himself was a lay Buddhist and believed that the rigors of celibacy were appropriate only for a small minority of gifted individuals. Most people, including clerics, were incapable of living the celibate life and so, Suzuki concluded, they should not be compelled to do so. He thus determined that, though society has no reason to be critical of those who devote themselves entirely to religious or scientific pursuits, "to make this into a law that unreasonably demands the submission of others is wrong. Temple-shrine laws or regulations that unreasonably require celibacy of the clergy of a particular denomination or sect are terribly wrong. One should not interfere in this matter."[46]

[44] Guyau (1962, 328–29). (Guyau's book was translated into English in 1897, but the translator is not listed in the above edition of the work.) Of particular interest to Suzuki may have been Guyau's notion of *fecondité morale*, that is, that life strives to express itself through the creative process. Unlike Renan and Suzuki, who defended celibacy for physiological reasons, Guyau, like many of the pro-*saitai* Buddhist writers, viewed sexuality as a form of sacrifice for the preservation of the species and celibacy—particularly enforced celibacy—as self-centered. "It is to be regretted that Catholicism . . . should have come to consider absolute continence superior to marriage, contrary to all physiological and psychological laws." Like many Japanese political economists and Nativists, Guyau saw celibacy as a wasteful drain of human energy and fecundity. Suzuki seems to have been intrigued by the attempts by such French positivists as Renan and Guyau to establish rational, scientific bases for religious ideas, that is, "religion" without superstition.

[45] Suzuki (1900a, 23). It is interesting that even when clearly focusing on sexuality, Suzuki uses the phrase *nikujiki saitai*. His attitude toward meat consumption was inconsistent. In another letter from the United States that was published in *Chūō kōron* in 1900, Suzuki argued that the Buddhist clergy should be allowed to eat meat because this would give them more vitality. See Suzuki (1900b, 415–18).

[46] Suzuki (1900a, 23–24). In his conclusions, Suzuki called for an end to licensed prostitution and all forms of contraception.

PRACTICAL COMPLICATIONS:
WOMEN, CHILDREN, AND TEMPLE INHERITANCE

More than any of the theoretical arguments concerning clerical marriage, it was the practical problems that arose in conjunction with that practice that spurred clerical leaders toward partial acceptance of married clergy. Without doubt, such issues as dispossessed widows, illegitimate children, and impoverished families must have always existed in areas where covert clerical marriage had been the custom. But beginning in the 1880s, increased attention to social matters by a growing corps of reformers and experts, including Buddhist journalists and statisticians, shed a different light on these phenomena, transforming them from the inevitable consequences of transgression of the precepts into problems that could be resolved with insurance, education, institutional reform, and financial restructuring.

The editors of *Shin Bukkyō* noted that as clerical marriage became the rule rather than the exception, practical problems replaced doctrinal concerns.[47] From the 1880s the *nikujiki saitai* debate was transformed into a debate over temple families. Simultaneously the focus moved from the issue of fornication to problems related to the status and welfare of the women and children living in temples. The associated problems of eating meat, drinking liquor, tonsure, and appropriate clerical dress were gradually disengaged from the issue of marriage. Discussion of those peripheral issues continued, but what had been known as the *nikujiki saitai* debate became simply the *saitai* debate or, even more significantly, the problem of temple families (*jizoku mondai*).[48]

In an article about women in modern Buddhism, Uchino Kumiko has suggested that it was the growing number of temple wives and children, more than any other cause, that forced the Buddhist leaders to resolve the *nikujiki saitai* problem. Kuruma Tatsu, one of the few temple wives to have published in the Buddhist press, wrote that by the early 1880s 40 to 50 percent of the clergy had wives and families. Despite widespread acceptance by the clergy, however, the status of an abbot's wife and children remained vague due to parishioner disapproval and continued resistance from the clerical leadership.[49] Attempts to suppress clerical marriage continued in most schools until the end of the century. The children of such marriages were considered illegitimate and related to their father more as his disciples than as his children.[50]

[47] Gyūsen (1901, 417).

[48] Buddhist journals from late Meiji to Taishō are filled with articles discussing these diverse aspects of clerical life. Some examples of this literature are Miura (1897); Takashi (1907, 5–6); Watanabe (1920, 76–85) (a lecture originally delivered in 1919).

[49] Kuruma Tatsu (1933, 260–65).

[50] Uchino (1990, 328–29).

The shadowy nature of turn-of the-century temple life for married couples is conveyed in a firsthand account of temple conditions by the well-known historian Kita Sadakichi (1871–1939). His account demonstrates the continued circumspection of the married clergy, even in regions where marriage was no longer strictly taboo. Although by 1889 the openness with which some members of the clergy, particularly those living in urban centers, conducted their family life shocked even the well-educated, young Kita, it appears that many of the marriages remained unregistered. When Kita moved to Kyoto, he lodged for a time at a Jōdo temple. He was surprised to see the temple wife, referred to as *obasan* (auntie), greeting parishioners and, just like the woman of the house in any lay family, openly feeding her infant and preparing fish in the kitchen. Kita, a native of Kyūshū, noted that although a woman referred to as "Daikokusan" lived at the Sōtō temple patronized by his family, the temple abbot frequently spoke of the precepts and remained discreet about his private laxity with regard to them. Kita soon realized that *nikujiki saitai* among the Kyoto clergy was commonplace, and he lost his repulsion for those who engaged in such practices. Nonetheless, he noted that, despite the openness with which the Jōdo temple wife conducted her affairs, she was not a legitimate wife. Rather, her relationship with her husband was unregistered and informal according to civil law. The children were registered in the *koseki* as illegitimate and referred to their father as *oshō-san*, as would any disciple.[51]

Other anecdotal accounts of temple marriages echo Kita's description of unregistered wives. In his biography of the Sōtō Zen cleric Suzuki Shunryū (1904–71), for example, David Chadwick discusses how Suzuki's teacher, Gyokujun So-on (1877–1934), had lived with a woman at his Shizuoka temple, Rinsōin, for many years. The parishioners accepted the woman's presence at the temple because she and the abbot remained unmarried. However, when Suzuki assumed the abbacy of the temple and openly married in 1935, his wife was forced to live at a smaller branch temple rather than the head temple because of parishioner resistance to having an openly married cleric living with his family at the temple.[52]

The growing concern with family life, domesticity, and the ideal of the home among new middle-class intellectuals and social reformers inevitably held implications for discussions of clerical marriage. In a pro–clerical marriage article in the Sōtō-affiliated journal *Wayūshi*, an author identified only as Mr. Maruyama directly addressed the issue of the place of women in the temple and the unhealthy environment in which they lived. Maruyama argued that the time had come to accept temple women as legitimate wives and allow the creation of true home life in Buddhist temples.

[51] Kita (1933, 138–40).
[52] Chadwick (1999, 81; 87).

What do we mean by a wife (*tsuma*)? A wife is not a mistress (*jōfu*), she is not a concubine, and of course she is not a mechanism for the satisfaction of all our sexual desires. When we speak of marriage (*saitai*) the concept of the *katei* is necessarily included. Or rather, marriage implies the formation of a *katei*.

Therefore, the debate over marriage is a debate over the *katei*. That is to say, the marriage of the Buddhist clergy is the creation of the *katei* by the Buddhist clergy, it is nothing other than the temple *katei*. But in fact are there actually homes in today's temples? In the end do the Buddhist clergy create a home (*hōmu*)? Those who advocate clerical marriage frequently debate whether one should have a wife, but they have not yet touched on whether one should have a home. Although some speak of the necessity of allowing a woman in the temple, those who speak of the need for a home are few.[53]

According to Maruyama, the lack of a true home in most temples could be attributed in large part to the precarious state in which temple families lived. Rivaling the exposés of other social reformers, Maruyama described the plight of the temple family in pathetic terms.

Most of those who are members of the temple household are miserable individuals. They are wretched old maids forced into marriage. Or they are former licensed prostitutes who serve as Daikoku (wife of a monk)? The temple household is an ephemeral thing. The temple wife is not a legal wife taken through proper procedures, she is a de facto wife (*naien no tsuma*) or she is manipulated as if she were a mistress. The temple household is a pitiable, sad thing. If the abbot were to die, his wife and children would not be given the means to provide for themselves. The worst thing is that outsiders will gang up on the family and forcibly transfer all of the so-called temple possessions to the next abbot. If he should despise the female successor, then that especially is the end, for he will happily find an excuse to dismiss her, naked and barefoot. It was that way in the past, it is that way now, and it will probably be that way in the future.[54]

In his brief article, Maruyama identified two important problems that by the end of the Meiji period had increasingly become associated with the practice of clerical marriage. First, the opprobrium of the various Buddhist schools and societal disapproval of clerical marriage ensured that temple wives would be of low status. Second, the economic and social security of the temple family was extremely precarious.

Maruyama was not alone in his concern with these issues. As marriage of the clergy became more prevalent, the low status of the temple wives appears to have been a growing embarrassment for Buddhists. Concern

[53] Maruyama-sei (1911, 848–49).
[54] Ibid., 851.

about the quality of the clergy and temple wives in the "celibate" denominations prompted an exchange between the Jōdo Shin reformer-clerics Inoue Enryō and Shimaji Mokurai in the journal *Nihonjin*. Like many others writing about clerical marriage in late Meiji, both Shimaji and Inoue were worried about the problems facing clerical families and the effect those problems were having on the quality of the clergy. The arguments marshalled by these late-Meiji critics of celibacy again reveal the convergence of the older political-economic anticlericalism of Nativists, Shintōists, and some Buddhist reformers with scientistic discourses imported from the Western powers. In their articles, Inoue and Shimaji synergistically merged the scientistic discourses of eugenics and evolutionism with the older fecundist arguments in favor of clerical marriage exemplified by the petitions of Ōtori and others. Through the strategic addition of the authority of "science" in the form of evolutionism to the anticelibacy argument, Inoue and Shimaji were able to characterize the advocates of celibacy as antimodern and opposed to science.

In an 1890 letter to the heads of the celibate denominations (he lists the Tendai, Shingon, Zen, Jōdo, and Nichiren establishments), Inoue expressed concern about the deterioration of the biological quality of the candidates for clerical ordination. He wrote that, unlike Jōdo Shinshū, which drew the majority of its clerics from temple families, the celibate denominations depended for their continued existence on the recruitment of new clerics from outside the clergy. Therefore the fate of those schools hinged on the quality of the newly recruited ordinands. According to Inoue, the leaders of those schools had not paid enough attention to the hereditary character (*idensei*) of the ordinands, a factor of critical importance for the future success of Buddhism. Contrasting the quality of current clerical candidates with that of candidates in an idealized past, Inoue argued that formerly only the finest candidates had been allowed to enter the clerical registry. The result was a vigorous clergy composed of many brilliant individuals. But by the Meiji period, Inoue claimed, the schools no longer attracted men and women of talent. Accepting the eugenic notion that intellectual potential and character were inherited, he concluded that because only people of poor hereditary quality now joined the "celibate" denominations, it was impossible for them to become clerics of character. Inoue urged the heads of those denominations that continued to ban clerical marriage and familial succession at the denominational temples to investigate carefully the family histories of potential ordinands to ensure that the Buddhist clergy were of the finest hereditary stock.[55]

---

[55] Inoue (1890, 587–88). Curiously, despite providing a clear model of a married clergy for the other Buddhist denominations, the Jōdo Shin clergy largely remained aloof from the debate over *nikujiki saitai*. Apart from the exchange of letters between Inoue and Shimaji discussed here and an 1898 essay by Inoue advocating meat eating and clerical marriage,

Shimaji Mokurai responded to Inoue by extending Inoue's eugenic concern for the ordinands to the covert wives of clerics in the "celibate" denominations. Shimaji agreed with Inoue that clerics who were truly celibate needed only to follow Inoue's suggestion that they use caution in choosing a disciple—but Shimaji was well aware that many "celibate" clerics were actually covertly married and were passing on their temples to their biological sons, who posed as their disciples. Therefore, an additional warning was required for the majority of "ordinary teachers" in the schools where marriage was still banned. In the past, Shimaji wrote, because of the strict ban on clerical marriage, the Buddhist clergy in the "celibate" schools would clandestinely marry women of very poor background and character (that is, women past the age considered optimal for marriage, destitute widows, and former prostitutes). There was no reason for such a harmful practice to continue now that the government had allowed the clergy to marry freely. It was particularly important, Shimaji wrote, that clerics be free to use eugenic criteria in the selection of their future wives. Those clerics who would marry had to consider "of course the merits and demerits of their wife's character and whether she was educated, but most importantly they should pay attention to the hereditary quality of her family line."[56]

The second social problem identified by Maruyama was the extremely precarious economic and social position of temple wives and children. The often unofficial and unregistered position of the temple family meant that the wife and children truly were one monk removed from destitution and homelessness. As an example of the instability of their situation, Maruyama raised the issue of family security following the death of the abbot-husband-father. With the death of her husband, the temple wife was placed at the mercy of the next abbot, the parishioners, and the head temple. Other journals and newspapers circulated similar tales concerning the tribulations of temple families. A 1901 account by Sugimura Juō described the fate of a married abbot of a Zen temple, his wife, and their two children. Unfortunately, sometime after the birth of two children, the cleric had died from a sudden illness, leaving his widow and children to fend for themselves. For a time after the demise of the father the family

---

there is relatively little direct comment on the controversy by Jōdo Shin clerics. See Inoue (1898).

[56] Shimaji (1890, 636–37). Shimaji, like Maruyama, asserted that most temple wives were not desirable marriage partners. It is worth reserving final judgment on this accepted understanding until more information concerning early temple wives is examined. Anne Barstow (1983) has argued that despite a similar received wisdom concerning the first generation of women who married Anglican clerics, historical sources demonstrate that many of these women were of the same background as the men they took as their spouse. Thus high-ranking clergymen married women with affluent backgrounds, and poor clerics married women of similar station.

had remained at the temple. However, when the parishioners subsequently selected a candidate who was renowned for his strict adherence to traditional standards of clerical deportment to succeed the deceased abbot, the potential successor refused the position, complaining, "How could I live in an impure temple like that?" This response to their offer of the abbacy only confirmed for the parishioners that this cleric was the man for the job. To get the candidate to accept the abbacy, the parishioners banished the widow of the former abbot and her two children from the temple, leaving them homeless and without any means of support.[57]

Similarly, in 1925 the Sōtō journal *Kōsei*, which had taken a stance in favor of the adoption of a family protection law for temple families, published a letter that a temple widow had written to her father. The woman, who had three children ranging in age from under one year to thirteen, had been expelled from the temple by her husband's successor. She described how the committee of parishioners for the temple had decided to rent the temple fields and had ordered the woman off the land by the end of the year. Because the children were not just hers alone, she had no choice but to turn them over to her husband's family to be raised. Having nowhere else to turn, the woman had asked the parishioners for permission to rent the temple fields as a sharecropper, but at the time she wrote her father, she had not yet received a reply.[58]

In addition to the problems concerning the security and livelihood of temple wives and children, the spread of temple families placed a financial strain on small temples that prior to Meiji had frequently supported only one person. Now the same income (or even less, given that much income-producing land had been stripped from temples during the early Meiji land reforms) often had to support four or five people.[59] Not only was the temple family in a precarious position—the successor to the abbot was financially burdened by the temple family. Assuming the abbacy of the temple already required substantial costs for the new abbot. When a cleric formally became abbot of a temple, he was required to pay a large sum of money, which often placed an enormous strain on his personal finances. It is no wonder the new abbot would be unwilling to take on the added burden of his predecessor's wife and family. In addition, the increased burden that a family placed on already insufficient temple finances often meant crushing poverty for an abbot and his family. As the problems of poverty and succession disputes affected a growing percentage of clerics, the head temple establishments were forced to provide some

[57] Sugimura (1901, 452–55).

[58] Jizoku no hiai (1925, 2).

[59] A Jōdo survey taken in early Shōwa indicates that on average urban temples contained five family members in addition to the abbot; farm village temples, four people; and fishing village temples, six people. See Shimano (1934, 10–11).

protection for temple families and clarify the order of succession to the abbacy.[60]

The identification of such phenomena as temple poverty, illegitimacy, and dispossession of widows as social problems forced several major Buddhist denominations to adopt family protection laws for temple families by the end of the Meiji and the beginning of the Taishō periods. In the adoption of these protections for the temple families there was a shift from apportioning blame for transgression of the precepts by individual clerics to acceptance of clerical marriage as an inevitable social circumstance. Although many clerical leaders continued to frown upon clerical marriage, punishment for this moral failing was no longer an option. The best that the clerical leaders could do was to make sure that the social consequences of clerical marriage and temple families did not damage the denomination in some way.[61]

Temple succession was one of the thorniest problems to emerge as a result of the spread of clerical marriage. With the retirement of the first generation of legally married abbots came an increase in patrimonial inheritance of temples. In much the same manner as the taking of surnames and *koseki* registration had been seen as endangering the status of temple property, patrimonial inheritance was viewed by some as a threat to the preservation of the communal character of temples. An unsigned editorial in *Chūgai nippō* in 1902, for example, expressed the fear that when a woman was lodged in a temple, it ineluctably came to be considered the cleric's private property. As the temples were passed on to the abbots' children they changed in character from public assembly places to private property. The editors commented that the temple wife phenomenon was accompanied by two problems: clerics selfishly regarding temple property as their own, and the willful violation of the school's traditional precepts. The best course for the clergy who wished to marry, the editors concluded, was for them to join a denomination that did not prohibit clerical marriage. The hypocrisy of remaining in a school that banned such practices would only mean the destruction of that denomination.[62]

Acceptance by the head temples of regulations governing the rights of temple families was tantamount to tacit acceptance of clerical marriage and the patrimonial inheritance of temples. A new term, *jizoku*, was coined to identify the wife of the abbot and her children who lived in the temple.[63]

---

[60] Kawamura (1933, 5–6).

[61] On the relationship among the rise of insurance, social assistance, and the changing perception of such social problems as poverty and industrial accidents in Italy, see Horn (1994, 34–42).

[62] "Daikoku ron" (1899, 1).

[63] For a history of the term *jizoku*, which was first used by the Jōdoshū in 1919, see Kumamoto (1995, 316–21).

Thus at the very least the new regulations accepted the presence of temple families. For the non-Shin denominations it was (and still remains) the closest they have come to acknowledging and accepting clerical marriage.

The temple family protection laws (*jizoku hogo hō*) that were adopted beginning in 1919 had several common features. Most important, these laws publicly recognized and provided a system of registration for the temple family along with the teacher and his disciples. In effect that aspect of the regulations clearly delineated the scope of the temple family. The laws also clarified what was to happen to the temple family in the event of the abbot's death. If the family included a person who was recognized by the school as a potential abbot, a temporary abbot from a nearby temple would be appointed to oversee temple affairs and train the successor. If there was no potential successor in the family and the temple family had to leave the temple, then neighboring temples and those affiliated with the temple were to provide appropriate help to the family. Finally, these laws spelled out various mechanisms for resolving disputes over temple succession and the disposition of temple families. Listed below are the years in which various schools adopted regulations that, to a lesser or greater extent, served as temple family protection laws and tacitly recognized the right of the Buddhist clergy to marry.[64]

1919   Jōdo temple family protection law
1921   Shingon Buzan sect temple family protection law
1924   Sōtō law allowing registration of abbatial successors
1927   Kogi Shingon temple family protection law
1930   Rinzai Myōshinji sect regulations governing the appointment and dismissal of abbots
1930   Shingon Chizan sect regulations governing the appointment and dismissal of abbots
1937   Sōtō temple family protection law

In some cases, tacit acceptance of temple families and clerical marriage preceded the adoption of an actual family protection law. In particular, regulations governing the rules for abbatial succession and rules concerning insurance for the families of Buddhist clergy often allowed for succession by the abbot's own son. Kawamura, the author of a study on family protection laws, noted that the schools that adopted such laws took two different approaches. One method of protecting temple families was to allow family members to register as candidates for the abbacy of the temple. The other way was to ensure family member's financial security in the event of the abbot's untimely death. The Shingon sects—Kogi, Chizan, and Buzan—adopted regulations that combined both means of helping

---

[64] Kawamura (1933, 8; 7). The information concerning the Sōtō family protection law comes from Gendai Kyōgaku Kenkyūkai (1991, 12).

temple families. The Sōtō (until 1937), Jōdo, and Rinzai denominations used the abbatial registration method alone.[65] In either case, such rules amounted to indirect recognition of the right of the clergy to marry. By the early 1930s the schools that provided financial aid to temple families and allowed blood sons to register as successor to the abbot were in the majority. Despite the gains made by the married clerics, no Buddhist school issued a regulation that directly stated that it was permissible for the clergy to marry.

PARTIAL RESOLUTION:
THE EXAMPLE OF THE SŌTŌ DENOMINATION

If the course of events in the Sōtō school is any indication of a general pattern among the various Buddhist denominations, the passage of temple family protection laws did not occur without a struggle. Although advocates viewed temple family protection regulations as solutions to practical problems, the sectarian leadership of some schools bitterly resisted adopting the laws because the regulations amounted to an end to the doctrinal prohibition against sexual relations. In some cases the laws were also opposed on practical grounds, for example, that they were financially unsound or unsuitable for such public institutions as temples. As noted in the journal *Shin Bukkyō*, the attempt to pass these regulations took multiple attempts over a period of years before sectarian congresses finally adopted the measures.[66]

The battle over the adoption of family protection laws in the Sōtō denomination was particularly rancorous.[67] By the late Meiji period, at least some prominent members of the Sōtō denomination began to challenge the adamant resistance to *nikujiki saitai*. One of the most eloquent early Sōtō advocates for clerical marriage was the young graduate of the Sōtōshū Daigakurin, Kuruma Takudō (1877–1964). Kuruma was himself the eldest son of a Sōtō cleric, Kuruma Ryūdō, who at the time of Takudō's birth in 1877, long before the Sōtō leadership accepted clerical marriage, was abbot of the temple Banryūji in Tokyo. Kuruma was ordained at his father's

[65] Kawamura (1933, 9).

[66] Sugimura (1901, 418). Also cited in Ikeda (1994, 407–8).

[67] I have chosen to present the material concerning the Sōtō denomination for several reasons. Although my research was not limited to Sōtō materials, in the course of study at numerous libraries and archives in Japan, I have uncovered far more documents pertaining to the Sōtō denomination than to any other. Contemporary Sōtō scholars and clerics have also paid more attention to the history of modern clerical marriage than their counterparts in other denominations. Over the last decade they have produced more secondary research on the history of modern clerical marriage and the status of temple families than almost any other denomination. These conditions have allowed me to document more fully the gradual acceptance of clerical marriage in the Sōtō denomination.

Figure 6. Kuruma Takudō. Kuruma Takudō, ed. *Gaito no Bukkyō*

temple at the age of six and remained there until he entered middle school in 1889. He went on to study at the Sōtōshū Daigakurin and eventually succeeded his father, becoming the abbot of Banryūji in 1900. Like his father, Kuruma Takudō married. In 1902 he was united with Satomi Tatsu in a Buddhist wedding ceremony that Kuruma devised and later disseminated among Buddhists.[68]

It was from his vantage as editor of two important Buddhist journals in which the debate over marriage was being waged—*Wayūshi* and *Bukkyō*—and as the son of a cleric and abbot of a small Sōtō temple that Kuruma joined the debate over clerical marriage. In a series of articles published in *Bukkyō* in 1901, the year before his own marriage, he rebutted the objections to clerical marriage and, more positively, described the benefits of marriage for Buddhism and how married clerics were to support their families.

[68] Kuruma (1917, 1).

Like other advocates of clerical marriage, Kuruma argued that applying old standards to Japanese Buddhism was a fruitless endeavor. Such critics of marriage as Fukuda Gyōkai, Ueda Shōhen, and the hierarchs of the Sōtō denomination responsible for the official antimarriage position of the denomination had argued that celibacy was the rule at the time of Śākyamuni and therefore should remain the rule for the Buddhist clergy in the Meiji era. As Kuruma summarized their argument, "at the time of the Buddha, there were no married clerics. There is no reason why clerics should marry today." But for Kuruma, the argument of these Buddhist fundamentalists missed the point entirely. Describing how different circumstances were for the Buddhist clergy in Meiji Japan, he compared their lot to that of idealized, early Buddhist monks.

> This is a criticism made by everybody. However, at the time of the Buddha there also were no abbots (*jūshoku*). Nor were there temples (*jiin*). Nor was there any need for clerics to perform bill keeping, run a guest house, etc. Those who were clerics wandered throughout the realm and slept under a tree or on a rock. If today's clerics were to return completely to this former state, leaving their temples, becoming mendicants, and true wanderers, then of course they would live with three robes and one bowl and would feel no need for a wife.[69]

For Kuruma, Meiji temple life, which required continual activity—preaching, raising funds for the temple, and so on—by the cleric outside the temple necessitated that someone stay at home to tend to chores. Drawing on the increasingly powerful ideal of the married woman as "good wife, wise mother" (*ryōsai kenbo*), Kuruma concluded that "the cleric who tries to support the temple, stay free from debt, and to be active outside the temple, should look for a good wife (*ryōsai*) and rely upon her assistance." Ultimately,

> clerics who are frantic abbots, kept busy with domestic chores, and who, when they occasionally venture out to disseminate the teaching, are pursued at the gate by creditors, are not those who possess the spirit of the Buddha. Rather, the one who has sought a wife and entrusted to her domestic matters and is active in the world is the cleric that is in harmony with the spirit of the Buddha. This is the one who should be called a noble, eminent cleric.[70]

In light of the fundamental importance of having an assistant at the temple to free the cleric for proselytization and active engagement in society, Kuruma argued that it was crucial for the Buddhist clergy to resolve the practical problems mentioned by critics of clerical marriage.

---

[69] Kuruma (1934, 479). The article cited, *Zenko iori mango*, first appeared in *Bukkyō* in August 1901.
[70] Ibid.

To this end he suggested several ways in which married clerics could separate their private family lives and finances from their public function as temple abbot. Pointing to the Protestant church where frequently the minister had a private residence or parish house on church property, Kuruma suggested that some type of separate private family residence quarters be constructed on temple grounds. He also wrote that the finances raised for specific temple purposes, for example, money donated for the head temple or for the building of a lecture hall, not be used for supporting the family. However, money gathered from giving lectures, ceremonies, sermons, sūtra readings, and painting or calligraphy was not necessarily off limits for private use by the cleric. If that income should not be used to support the cleric's family, then it also should not be used to purchase shoes, clothing, or other personal effects either.[71]

Like Tanaka Chigaku, Kuruma was interested in legitimizing marriage on the ritual as well as the theoretical level by creating a specifically Buddhist marriage ceremony. Between the time Tanaka created his Buddhist wedding ceremony and the turn of the century, the pressures to create Buddhist wedding ceremonies had grown considerably. During the 1890s both Shintō and Christian religious wedding ceremonies became even more visible. In 1898 one of the earliest Shintō weddings (*shinzen kekkonshiki*) was performed at the Hibiya Daijingū in Tokyo. More significantly, the imperial wedding between Crown Prince Yoshihito and Kujō Sadako on May 10, 1900 (Meiji 33), which took place in front of the worship hall for Amaterasu (*kashikodokoro*) on the imperial palace grounds, was widely publicized. As Fujitani has observed, the religious nature of the imperial wedding was unprecedented. "No religious ceremonies, let alone ceremonies before the Sun Goddess, had ever accompanied the marriage of any member of the imperial household." The imperial wedding, which mimicked European court marriage ceremonies, further piqued public interest in religious weddings and catalyzed the spread of a new "tradition," the Shintō wedding.[72] Within just one year the Shintō-affiliated Imperial Women's Association (Teikoku Fujin Kyōkai) had offered at Hibiya Shrine a public demonstration of the proper ritual procedures for a Shintō wedding.[73]

Although he was unmarried at the time he wrote the articles advocating clerical marriage, Kuruma married Satomi Tatsu (b. 1879), the daughter

[71] Ibid., 116–17.

[72] Along with the wedding of Crown Prince Yoshihito on May 10, 1900, the celebration of the silver anniversary of the Meiji imperial couple did much to stimulate public interest in wedding ceremonies and monogamous conjugal life. On these two public spectacles, see Fujitani (1996, 111–21; 185–90).

[73] Uejima (1990, 523).

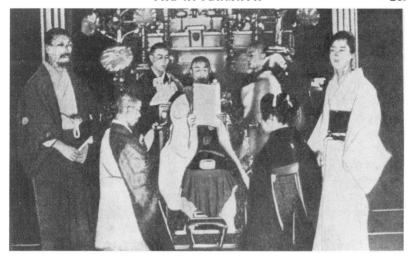

Figure 7. Kuruma Takudō and Satomi Tatsu's Wedding Ceremony. Kuruma Takudō, ed. *Gaito no Bukkyō*

of a Jōdoshū family, on May 18, 1902, in a public ceremony that he had devised.[74] Kuruma later wrote that the creation of the Buddhist ceremony was his response to the growing popularity of Shintō wedding ceremonies.[75] Like Tanaka, he argued that such a crucial ritual as the marriage ceremony could not be left up to the Shintō or Christian clergy.

As described by Kuruma in the journal *Bukkyō* in 1902, the key elements of his wedding ceremony were confession of one's past karmic actions and the taking of the threefold pure precepts (*sanjujōkai*).[76] The earliest version of Kuruma's ceremony included a procession through the main temple hall by the husband and wife. According to Fukase, the procession was modeled after the installation ceremony for a new abbot (*shinsanshiki*) and thus helped symbolize the role of husband and wife as co-abbots of the temple.[77]

The 1902 ceremony also included the singing or playing of what was the de facto national anthem, *Kimiga yo*, a ceremonial act that linked the marriage to the nation. The connection between the couple whose mar-

---

[74] Unlike most of the first and second generations of temple wives, there is some biographical information available about Kuruma Tatsu. See the short biography of Kuruma Takudō's family members in Kuruma (1934, 538).

[75] Kuruma (1917, 1). On the creation of Shintō weddings, see Uejima (1990, 519–542).

[76] Hikita (1991, 256–59). The threefold pure precepts are not to do any evil actions; to do all beneficial, good actions; and to benefit all sentient beings.

[77] Fukase (1997, 31).

riage began with a Buddhist ceremony and the prosperity of the nation was rendered more explicit by Kuruma in his introduction to a slightly modified ceremony that was presented in *Chūgai nippō* in 1917. Kuruma wrote, "marriage is one of the great issues of human existence. It is no exaggeration to say that the success or failure of a life depends on this event . . . because a vow taken before the Buddha must not be broken, performing this solemn ceremony before the Buddhas will without doubt promote the prosperity of the family and the elevation of humankind. It will be a cause for contributions to the nation and the world."[78]

By late Meiji pressure on the Sōtō leadership to acknowledge the depth of the clerical marriage problem within the denomination began to sway or at least silence even the staunchest celibacy advocates. At the Fifth Sōtōshū Congress in 1901, a group of eight assembly members submitted a petition requesting that the leadership abolish the sect law banning clerical marriage.[79] In response to the petition, the members of the Committee of the Two Head Temples (Ryōhonzan Iin) asked that the matter of the ban on marriage be entrusted to a committee charged with reforming Sōtō sect law. In an effort to placate the promarriage faction and at the same time to avoid admitting the failure of their policies, the committee members disingenuously predicted that—because in a denomination that transmits the Great Dharma of the Buddhas and Patriarchs, explicit restriction of clerical marriage is unnecessary—the regulation prohibiting clerical marriage would probably be abolished when the new "enlightened sect law" (*bunmeiteki shūsei*) was completed.[80] As the committee members predicted, five years later the Sōtō leadership abolished the strict regulation that prohibited the housing of women in temples. Without a word of public comment, the ban was deleted from sect law when the First Sōtō Constitution (Sōtōshū shūken) was issued in 1906.

In 1917, as Kuruma was disseminating a modified version of his Buddhist wedding ceremony in the Buddhist press, Kuriyama Taion (1860–1937) began a scathing attack on the Sōtō establishment for its continuing disparagement of clerical marriage. Kuriyama was an influential Sōtō cleric who began working at the Sōtō headquarters in 1889 and eventually became the director (*sōmu*) of that organization.[81] In 1934 he became abbot of Sōjiji. Kuriyama wrote, published, and distributed his main work on clerical marriage and temple families, the three-hundred-page book *Sōryo kazoku ron*, in 1917.[82]

---

[78] Kuruma (1917, 1). For more on various Buddhist weddings, including Kuruma's, see Hikita (1991, 253–76). On changes in Kuruma's ceremony and its adoption by the Sōtō school as a primarily lay-centered ceremony, see Fukase (1997, 31–41).

[79] Kumamoto (1994, 18).

[80] Ibid., 18–19.

[81] Matsura (1976, 4–9); Kumamoto (1991, 102–3).

[82] Kuriyama (1917). References to this work will be cited as page numbers in the text.

Sōryo kazoku ron was the most extensive defense of clerical marriage ever published. In addition to its importance in the debate over clerical marriage, the detailed information it contains about the conditions of temple life and regional differences in practice make it a rich source of information about Meiji and Taishō Buddhism. In Kuriyama's work we see a further shift away from the argument about the doctrinal correctness of clerical marriage to the discussion of problems caused by the growing number of married clerics. The book reiterates a number of arguments that were made in the defense of clerical marriage by the Jōdo Shinshū clergy and the various proponents of *nikujiki saitai* that preceded Kuriyama. Like his predecessors, Kuriyama stressed the need to modify the Buddhist teaching in accordance with the age. In a manner unusual for a Sōtō cleric, however, given the Sōtō school's relatively indifferent attitude toward *mappō* thought, Kuriyama emphasized the impossibility of fully following the precepts during the Last of the Teaching. He even signed the work "disciple of the Buddha in the Last Age of the Teaching, Raiju Taion" (*mappō Butsu deshi, Raiju Taion*) (1). He also devoted two of the last sections to explaining the importance of the decline of the teaching as the underlying cause for the spread of clerical marriage. To fight the nature of the times, Kuriyama wrote, would be like trying to make water flow uphill (264–68).

Kuriyama's book was unique in its emphasis on the human cost that the suppression of clerical marriage entailed. The tacit acceptance of clerical marriage that resulted when overt prohibitions disappeared from Sōtō sect law were not sufficient as far as Kuriyama was concerned. He believed that in fact, by allowing clerics to marry while refusing to affirm their marriages in a positive manner, the leadership had heightened the crisis, and he raised examples of the pain that was caused by forcing married clerics to hide their family life. In a chapter devoted to describing the attempts by temple parents to conceal their children's origins, Kuriyama energetically directed the reader's attention to the difficulties encountered by the wives and children of the clergy. Commenting on an article in a December 1916 issue of *Chūgai nippō* that had disparagingly referred to the sons of clerics as "Venerable Rāhula," Kuriyama wrote, "the children born at temples are called Venerable Rāhula (Ragora sonja). The temple wife and mother of the children is called Princess Yaśodharā (Yashudara hime). Or it is common to call her Daikoku or Bonsai. They endure vehement reproaches that truly are the extremes of insult. Are they not unavoidable phenomena during the transitional period in which the problem of clerical marriage remains unresolved?" (24).

Much as the editors of *Wayūshi* did, Kuriyama emphasized the importance of finding a permanent answer to the problem of temple families and clerical marriage. "Proselytization is important, education is important, and the method for administering the school is also important. In the [Sōtō] school today, however, more than proselytization, more than education, more than the method for administering the school, it is essential to resolve the problem of clerical marriage, which involves the foundation of each cleric's moral behavior and the societal policy of the [Sōtō] school" (25). The resolution of the marriage problem was essential, Kuriyama argued, because the very biological-genetic fiber of the clergy was at stake. Borrowing the argument that had first been advanced by the two Shinshū intellectuals Inoue Enryō and Shimaji Mokurai in 1890, he claimed that the antimarriage attitude of the Sōtō school had forced the clergy to marry women who were largely undesirable—ex-prostitutes, older women, and low-class women. He concurred with Shimaji's claim that because of the need to hide one's married status from others, clerics were forced to marry women unfit to bear and raise children. Therefore, the very quality of the next generation of clerics and, as a result, Buddhism were being jeopardized.

In the conclusion to *Sōryo kazoku ron*, Kuriyama carefully summarized the necessity for openly accepting clerical marriage. The aim was to revitalize Buddhism and the Sōtō school, and to do so it was essential to improve the moral quality of the clergy. The largest stumbling block in that effort, however, was the prohibition of clerical marriage, and so the rebuilding of Buddhism depended on the successful resolution of that problem. Kuriyama believed that in attempting to solve the clerical marriage issue, the actions of the majority of the clergy were what mattered. "In this sense, I conclude that not getting married is the exception and that clerical marriage is the rule," he wrote, proceeding to call for either taking only part of the bodhisattva precepts or a relaxing of the bodhisattva precept prohibiting sexual activity and an end to all Sōtō school prohibitions of such activity (258).

The sympathy Kuriyama expressed for the plight of the married clergy and their families is probably unmatched among the writings of the period on the subject. The closing words of *Sōryo kazoku ron* were addressed not to the abbots of the temples, but to their wives. In one of the most emotional sections of the work Kuriyama wrote,

> At the temple where you are now living, do you have a public grave site where your remains will be interred? The answer is probably, again, "not yet." "Not yet" is probably the truth. If you have no grave site for when you die, can you live at peace? When you die, will your coffin be publicly visited by your family, by the parishioners and clerics, and accompanied to the grave site? Probably not. Although all of you now have, in fact, a husband-wife relationship, it lacks that all-important component of being together "for better or for worse." If you are not together "for better or for worse," it is not a husband-wife relationship, but rather just a physical relationship. Is

that not wretched? Even though you are now married, you bear an uneasiness that you cannot talk about even with your chosen. You are already uneasy in your marriage and will again embrace uneasiness at your death—all of you are caught between these two worries. Do you not pass your days unable to be at peace? (268–70).[83]

Kuriyama concluded by asserting that he wanted the temple wives to be at peace and that, in fact, his intention was to ensure their peace in life and after death. "Along with being an ally of your husbands, I am your ally. From now on please live with the intention of openly being a splendid 'Mrs.' before all the world" (270). Clearly he had embraced the notion of the wife as companion and friend, and he demanded that the temple wives be allowed openly to achieve that kind of relationship.

In spite of his sympathy for the plight of temple women, by no means did Kuriyama transcend the standard view of women as polluting and marriage as an evil necessitated by the degenerate nature of the era. To counter arguments that the presence of women would vitiate the spiritual efficacy of the temples, he suggested that women actively pray to Jizō bodhisattva. By relying on Jizō's power, they would be able to counteract the negative effects of their polluting presence and avoid vitiating the power of the temple's protective deities (229).

Although the battle lines in the Sōtō school had not changed much in the fifty years since the decriminalization of clerical marriage, by the late Taishō period the antimarriage proponents were increasingly on the defensive. The passage of a temple family protection law became the proxy issue for those in favor of clerical marriage. Most opponents of the family protection law saw it as a complete betrayal of the principles of the Sōtō school and struggled to prevent its adoption.[84] The first proposal for the temple family protection law was submitted to the Twenty-third Sōtō Congress in 1919 by a large number of abbots from Ōita and Fukuoka, led by Nagayama Kōryū. It did not pass. The measure was submitted at the Twenty-fourth, Twenty-fifth, and Twenty-sixth meetings, each time drawing a growing body of supporters, but it failed each time.[85] In 1922 the Twenty-sixth Sōtō Congress ended with the bill shelved for further consideration. Supporters of the measure continued to press for its

[83] In a recent article, Kawahashi Noriko has observed that one of the complaints from Sōtō temple wives today is that their remains are not usually interred with those of their husbands. See Kawahashi (1995, 161–83).

[84] A very detailed compilation of source materials related to the Sōtō denomination's debate over the adoption of a family protection law has recently been published by Kumamoto Einin (1994, 99–112). I would like to thank Professor Kumamoto for generously sharing with me many of the documents he gathered.

[85] Okumura (1925, 2).

adoption, however, and the following year the school did adopt a law concerning the registration of abbatial candidates for a temple. The regulation in effect allowed an abbot to register his son as the successor to the abbacy of the temple, which gave the temple families a greater measure of security than they had possessed in the past.[86]

By the time of the Twenty-eighth Sōtō Congress in 1925, the debate over the adoption of the temple family protection law had reached a fever pitch. Proponents of clerical marriage called for recognition of the legitimacy of the temple families.[87] Those who favored the family protection measure argued that their opponents were denying the obvious—the Sōtō clergy was overwhelmingly married. One advocate of adoption, Takita Chinsui, speculated that some 70 percent of Sōtō temples would be passed on through patrimonial inheritance if the temple family protection law were adopted and temple families were given official recognition. The days of celibate practice were over, but the conservative clerics clung to their hard-line opposition to clerical marriage and, therefore, the temple family protection law.

In the end, despite considerable pressure in the Buddhist press in favor of adopting a regulation guaranteeing limited security for temple families, the forces opposed to a family protection law remained in control.[88] The regulation was withdrawn from consideration at the Twenty-eighth Congress and failed each time it was resubmitted at the three subsequent meetings.[89] During those years, however, the circumstances surrounding the Sōtō school continued to change in ways that impelled the leadership inexorably toward tacit recognition of the married clergy and approval of a family protection measure. Without doubt demographics was one of the most important reasons why the Sōtō leaders finally gave temple wives official recognition. By the time of the Fortieth Sōtō Congress in 1936, continued economic and social changes had so disrupted traditional patterns of practice that delegates to the meeting adopted a measure to begin a complete census of Sōtō temples. The goal of the project was to determine the circumstances of the school so that appropriate responses to the new conditions could be successfully constructed.[90]

The Sōtō survey, which was mentioned earlier in this chapter, obtained information from more than 95 percent of Sōtō temples in Japan, a total of 13,043 temples. The census provides detailed information concerning the distribution of age, sex, educational status, and temple inheritance for the temple family members. According to the survey, in 1936 families lived in more than 81 percent of the temples, which made the Sōtō school

[86] Kumamoto (1991, 108).
[87] Takita (1925, 2); Okumura (1995, 2).
[88] Okumura (1995, 2).
[89] Hosaka (1926, 1). See also Kumamoto (1991, 108).
[90] Taniguchi (1937, 1).

an overwhelmingly married order by early Shōwa, despite ongoing resistance from the leadership of the school. Leaving little room for doubt about what comprised a "family," the survey authors noted that all but a tiny fraction of the temple families included a wife, thus excluding the possibility that "family" might be construed as the clerics' aged parents or infirm siblings. The authors concluded that unmarried practice took place in only 18 percent of the temples and added that it was not difficult to predict the rapid shrinkage of that number in the future.[91]

In late 1936, just before the survey results were published, the Sōtō school finally adopted the temple family protection law, which was put into effect on January 1, 1937. The editor of the census, Taniguchi Kozan, could not hide his disdain for those who had for so long ignored reality by failing to approve the measure, which had been first submitted to the Sōtō congress eighteen years earlier. Noting the percentage of married clerics in the Sōtō school, Taniguchi prefaced the section of the survey on temple families as follows:

> Let us set aside, for the time being, the debate over whether [the high percentage of married clerics] is lamentable. I would like to demonstrate statistically that this is the actual condition of our denomination. Today, when we have put the Temple Family Protection Law into effect, there probably no longer is any way we can twist things to question whether there are temple families in the Sōtō school. Our verification through the survey that their existence is a fact in a sense may be nothing more than a confirmation of common knowledge, but I believe it should be held up as an example of the effectiveness of the survey. It goes without saying that whether one likes the fact or not, we must completely abandon our idle fantasies and create a policy that conforms to fact.[92]

Statistical analysis thus helped move the debate over clerical marriage outside the realm of doctrinal debate and personal preferences. The existence of married clerics was according to the Sōtō census a social fact that demanded appropriate policies, not moral exhortation.

The new Sōtō Temple Family Protection Regulation (*Sōtōshū jizoku hogo kitei*) defined the *jizoku* as a temple abbot's wife and children who had been formally registered with the Sōtō denomination. According to the sect law, the *jizoku* were to register their names, dates of birth, permanent domicile, and dharma or familial relationship with the abbot. The abbot was to register one member of the *jizoku* as the family representative. If there was an appropriate successor amongst the *jizoku*, that person could apply to the Sōtō headquarters for recognition as abbot. If the designated successor was not mature enough to assume that position but had

[91] Ibid., 13–14.
[92] Ibid., 14.

already been ordained, the temple would be placed under the care of an appropriate cleric until the successor could assume the abbacy. If no successor were present, the *jizoku* could be asked to leave the temple, but an appropriate sum of money for family support would be provided by the temple. The regulation also made provisions for the resolution of disputes over the protection of the family and for the removal of family members from their status as *jizoku*. Although various drafts of the proposal cursorily had specified the duties of the *jizoku*, the final law made no mention of their roles. The law also completely avoided saying anything about how the *jizoku* got into the temple in the first place—at no time was the problem of clerical marriage addressed.[93]

The editors of *Chūgai nippō* approvingly noted that at long last the Sōtō leadership had resolved this vexatious problem. At the same time, the Sōtō leadership remained wary of consigning all temples to the caprices of patrimonial inheritance. Reflecting the concerns of those like Kuruma Takudō who feared that the protection measure and patrimonial inheritance would spell an end to the promotion of talented clerics to positions of power at major temples, the Sōtō leadership expressly excluded the head temples and influential regional temples from the regulation. The abbacy of those temples was to be decided by the recommendations of the head temples. In effect, the Sōtō temples were divided into those that would henceforth be familial temples where succession took place by patrimonial inheritance and those that were not inherited by a family member.[94]

Uchino Kumiko has suggested that the affirmation of temple families by the Sōtō leadership was in part a product of the war mobilization that became more prominent by end of the 1930s.[95] Although Uchino gives little evidence for her claim, events both within and outside the Buddhist world at the time lend credence to it. With the increased tensions and mobilization during the late 1930s, men and women in many areas of Japanese society were forced to rethink their position concerning the traditional roles of women. The combined forces of the draft and the pressures of a wartime economy may have had a similar impact on the Buddhist world. As the wartime economy drained manpower away from every segment of Japanese society, women were pressured to step into positions normally denied them.[96] A broad spectrum of the Japanese women's movement also availed themselves of the opportunity presented by mobilization to press for the adoption of the Mother-Child Protection Law (*Boshi hogo hō*), which would provide aid to fatherless families.[97] Their effort proved

[93] Mio (1937, 90–91).

[94] Sōtōshū katoki no ōnō (1936, 2).

[95] Uchino (1990, 330); Uchino (1983, 190).

[96] For a look at the effects of war mobilization on various segments of Japanese society, see, for example, Havens (1975, 913–34).

[97] Garon (1993, 37).

successful and the law was adopted in 1937. Sheldon Garon has observed in a recent article that the government bureaucrats stood behind the efforts of the reformers because they saw the law as a means of ensuring the quality of future recruits.[98]

It may well be that the broader debate over protecting fatherless families added cogency to the arguments of those within the Sōtō and other denominations who pressed for similar sectarian guarantees for temple families in the absence of the abbots who normally ran the temples. As more Buddhist clerics were drafted, the Sōtō school leadership also must have been forced to rely more heavily on the temple wives to administer the temples and help train the child who would be the abbot's successor. By the height of the war in 1943 the leaders not only tolerated temple wives but encouraged them. An unprecedented special seminar for temple wives was held at Eiheiji in conjunction with a meeting for Sōtō nuns. It ended with an ordination ceremony and the granting of a Buddhist surplice (*kara*) to each participant. The following year, the Sōtō leadership also allowed temple wives to be ordained as nuns. In her husband's absence, a temple wife could become a nun if she attended a special seminar. As a report on the Eiheiji meeting made clear, these measures were on a par with emergency measures enacted by the central government.[99] In the span of just a few years the Sōtō leadership had gone from not even acknowledging the existence of the *jizoku* to relying on the wives and children for the maintenance of the temples. The Sōtō leadership stopped short of condoning clerical marriage, however.

[98] Garon (1994, 361).
[99] Uchino (1990, 331); Uchino (1983, 190).

CHAPTER 10

Almost Home

Sooner or later, however, the *nikujiki saitai* problem will
have to be resolved.
Wayūshi, 1901

That the debate over [clerical] marriage has not yet been
completely resolved is because the marriage system has
not yet been completely put out in the open.
Yamauchi Shun'yū, 1957

Those who wish to maintain the ideals of world renunciation and celibacy regard it as a sign of degeneracy that
the temple family (*jitei*) resembles more and more the lay
family (*katei*). The proponents of world-renouncing life-
style do, of course, have their own quite valid standpoint,
particularly within a tradition like Zen, which has its
roots in contemplative monasticism. It makes little sense,
however, to force this worldview upon the ordinary
temple, where clerical marriage has been the norm for
several generations now. Attempts to do so simply hinder
efforts to come to terms with the reality of life in the vast
majority of temples today.
Kawahashi Noriko, 1995

It is said that Japanese Buddhism is lay Buddhism, but
ultimately do the clergy themselves really think that? They
shave their heads or sport short crew cuts and wear Buddhist robes and a surplice. Superficially they look the
same as monks from Taiwan or Korea. In fact, when they
meet [their foreign counterparts] don't the Japanese
clerics relate with them as if they were equals?
Chūgai nippō, 1991

THE STRUGGLE over *nikujiki saitai*, which continues to this day, was prolonged and exacerbated by several important trends in the history of
modern Japanese religious institutions. As part of the government's effort

to modernize social life, Meiji officials abolished government enforcement of such status-based legal strictures as the prohibitions against meat eating, marriage, or abandonment of the tonsure by ordained Buddhist clerics. In effect, the end to these restrictions transformed the mandatory patterns of behavior that had signified the assumption of clerical status into voluntary practices that the clergy were free to reject. Although exactly who was to decide the standards of clerical behavior remained ambiguous and the subject of heated discussion, by the middle of the Meiji era it was clear that state penalties for specifically religious infractions had ended.

This trend, in which state crimes are distinguished from moral and religious ones, is clearly a by-product of the differentiation of religious and state institutions that is one of the hallmarks of secularization. Simply stated by Casanova, who has done a fine job of distinguishing the controversial and flawed prescriptive elements associated with the term secularization from the core sociological, descriptive sense of the term, "the core and the central thesis of the theory of secularization is the conceptualization of the process of societal modernization as a process of functional differentiation and emancipation of the secular spheres—primarily the state, the economy, and science—from the religious sphere and the concomitant differentiation and specialization of religion within its own newly found religious sphere."[1] In Japan part of the differentiation involved ending state enforcement of the precepts and allowing control of clerical behavior to devolve to the religious sphere, that is, that complicated space in which parishioners, clerics, and denominational organizations interacted.

Naturally taking specifically Japanese twists and turns during the course of early modern and modern Japanese history, the decision to end state intervention into what many government leaders considered to be matters of "private morality" was part of the process of differentiation that occurred in a number of modernizing nations. Particularly during the first quarter of the Meiji era, one can detect an effort to define religion—using the neologism *shūkyō* as the Japanese translation of that term—precisely as an activity that lay outside the bounds of state jurisdiction. Both Meiji officials, who wished to end their involvement in the exceedingly contentious realm of sectarian doctrine, and a wide variety of Buddhists, who wished to free themselves from the control of denominational hierarchs, used the public/private distinction to justify their actions. Officials like Takasaki Goroku described Buddhism as *shinjutsu*, an inner concern, and therefore something best left to the individual. Similarly, clerics like Ugawa Shōchō viewed the precepts as a matter of inner morality, and some *yamabushi* argued that they should not be subject to Shingon and Tendai control because Buddhism involved inner concern, not sect law. Additionally, clerics like Tanabe Zenchi attacked mandatory celibacy as an infringe-

[1] Casanova (1994, 19–20).

ment of individual rights. Ultimately, the debate over *nikujiki saitai* centered on precisely who was responsible for controlling clerical behavior: the state, denominational leaders, temple parishioners, or individual clerics. When Meiji officials ended their involvement in enforcing the precepts, the fight over *nikujiki saitai* became a battle between the heads of the denominations, who wished to set standards for clerical behavior, and individual clerics, many of whom wished to decide for themselves whether to follow sectarian regulations.

Although the leaders of the modern Japanese state washed their hands of direct involvement in sectarian affairs, they simultaneously enacted measures that furthered the centralization of the Buddhist institutions and unified denominational identity, trends that can be traced back to the beginning of the Edo period. As government officials moved from a policy of direct intervention in sectarian matters to one of indirect control of the denominations through the creation of the Chief Priest system, they required the adoption of government-approved sect laws universal for all clerics of each denomination and demanded that rank-and-file clerics obey the rules adopted by their leadership. Thus at the same time that secularization and societal change weakened the ability of Buddhist leaders to control their subordinates, the government called on those leaders to codify an institutional structure, sect law, and an overarching formal sectarian identity. Even as such figures as Fukuda Gyōkai, Nishiari Bokusan, and Shaku Unshō called for a return to true Buddhism, that Buddhism was changing under the influence of the massive institutional transformation that was occurring. Eliding the regional, sectarian, and hierarchical variations in practice that had existed in the past, the leaders of various Buddhist denominations adopted uniform rules and institutional arrangements for all clerics of their school. Just as decriminalization, social differentiation, and changing social mores made open clerical marriage a possibility, many denominational leaders tried to make the acceptance of monasticism and the rejection of *nikujiki saitai* an important component in the formulation of their respective denominational identities.

The tension between the emphasis on monastic, celibate practice as part of sectarian identity and the growing number of visible temple families was exacerbated by a variety of social trends, for example, the valorization of the home, the movement to improve the position of Japanese women, the biologization of sexuality, and the redefinition of such phenomena as illegitimacy and poverty as social problems. Pressed to act by lay and clerical reformers, denominational leaders enacted such measures as insurance programs and succession policies, thereby alleviating the social crises.

NIKUJIKI SAITAI AND THE LAY-CLERICAL DISTINCTION

Despite the spread of clerical marriage after Meiji, the established Japanese Buddhist denominations have continued to make a persistent distinction between lay and clerical roles. As Hubert Durt has noted in passing in an extended discussion of the lay-cleric distinction in early Mahāyāna, "In today's Japan, monks are secularized but are far from being laymen."[2] The durability of this distinction suggests that within the established Buddhist denominations the laicization of the modern Buddhist clergy was far from complete. I noted in chapter 8 that scholars have observed that one of the central features of Japanese religion since the late nineteenth century has been the trend toward "lay centrality," that is, the tendency for the laity to take on increasingly important religious roles and the decay of the lay-clerical distinction.[3] Certainly that observation is true for the various Nichiren-based New Religions that have followed the anticlerical model first proposed by such figures as Tanaka Chigaku and Nagamatsu Nissen.

The answer to the problem of clerical marriage suggested by Tanaka and Nagamatsu stands in marked contrast to the solutions offered by most other Buddhist figures of the day. By the time he wrote his blueprint for the reform of the Nichiren school, *Shūmon no ishin*, Tanaka had completely abandoned his attempt to provide doctrinal justification for allowing the clerical practice of *nikujiki saitai*. Instead, he observed that true clerical practice was impossible under current conditions and that all Buddhists, even those who were nominally "home-leavers," were lay Buddhists. One would imagine that as the ordained clergy became more laicized they would encounter difficulties in maintaining their distinctive clerical role. Like many Meiji government officials, Tanaka viewed the loss of clerical names, special registries, and celibacy as signs that there were no more true clerics and called for an end to the lay-clerical distinction entirely. In place of the traditional monastic clergy or married clerics, Tanaka built a succession of purely lay organizations. In his calls for complete devotion to the *Lotus Sūtra* while remaining totally immersed in the world, Tanaka advocated a very devout lay Buddhism. He frequently condemned the restriction of Buddhist practice to monastery-bound clerics and instead called for lay religious practice in the world. No formal clergy existed in the various lay organizations headed by Tanaka, and the laity performed all the ceremonies conducted by the organization, including weddings and funerals. It is this sort of devout lay centrality that characterizes those Japanese Buddhist groups (i.e., New Religions) that trace their intellectual lineage back to Tanaka's Nichirenshugi. Kokuchūkai, Reiyūkai, and Risshō Kōseikai could all be included in this category. Many

---

[2] Durt (1991, 15). See also Robinson (1966, 25–56).
[3] Hardacre (1989a, 209–24).

other Buddhist New Religions, like Agonshū and Shinnyoen, as well as such independent lay Zen organizations as the Sanbōkyōdan clearly demonstrate the same rejection of traditional Buddhist monasticism.[4]

The established Buddhist denominations, however, have not succumbed to the trend toward lay centrality. Despite the de facto acceptance of *nikujiki saitai* by the majority of the Buddhist clergy, there has been no concomitant dissolution of the lay-clerical distinction in the established denominations. Even in the wake of the acceptance of clerical marriage, the Buddhist clergy still undergo the rite of passage known as *tokudo*, which gives them power and access to the education and ritual purity necessary for them to perform rituals—most important, funerals—that a nonordained person cannot perform. Most married clerics primarily function as priests, carrying out the role of ritual specialist for their parishioners. As Gombrich has noted, this has become the most important function of the Buddhist clergy in contemporary Japan; there exists very little demand for them to be "moral exemplar, let alone religious virtuoso."[5] The impetus to distinguish between clerics and the laity in the established Buddhist denominations has been so persistent and influential that it has even affected the fundamentally anticlerical Jōdo Shin, which developed its own distinctive clerical ordination ritual and differentiation between *sōryo* and ordinary parishioners, with the *sōryo* taking on the role as ritual specialists for their lay supporters.[6] Such promarriage clerics as Nakazato Nisshō, Tanabe Zenchi, Ōtori Sessō, and Ugawa Shōchō all vigorously advocated increased involvement of the clergy in worldly affairs. Marriage, these writers argued, would ensure the fuller participation of the clergy in proselytization, spreading state doctrine, and even the military, much to the benefit of the nation. None of these advocates suggested that the clergy abandon their clerical status, however. The persistence of the lay-clerical distinction in the mainstream Buddhist denominations is one characteristic that distinguishes them from most of the lay-Buddhist New Religions.

The spread of *nikujiki saitai* highlights the need for a more nuanced understanding of the notion of "laicization." In a discussion of householder bodhisattvas, Richard Robinson has pointed out that "laicizing is often used ambiguously to mean enhancing the importance of the laity, imparting lay characteristics to the monastic community, or coloration of doctrine by typically lay values."[7] From this perspective, we can say that the acceptance of *nikujiki saitai* has been laicizing in the sense that it has

---

[4] Sharf (1995) has gone so far as to argue that, in fact, lay Zen groups like Sanbōkyōdan should be classified as New Religions.

[5] Gombrich (1994, 21).

[6] For an overview of the Shin ordination ceremony, see Tatsuguchi (1983, 18–42).

[7] Robinson (1966, 25–56). The same passage is cited at length in Durt (1991, 5).

imparted lay characteristics to the clergy. It has not, however, been accompanied by a concomitant heightening of the importance of the laity within the established Buddhist denominations, particularly with regard to their assuming sacredotal functions. The existence of married, meat-eating Buddhist clerics has forced modern Japanese authors to make the rather awkward, but illuminating, terminological distinction between *seisō* (pure clerics) or *shukkesō* (home-leaving clerics) and *zaikesō* (at-home clerics) or *zaizokusō* (secular clerics).[8] The use of such terms continues a long tradition within Japanese Buddhism of distinguishing pure clerics from so-called common clerics (*bonsō*), that is, married ones, a practice that was often hotly contested by elements of the clergy.

The 1991 schism between the Nichiren lay movement Sōka Gakkai and its parent organization, the cleric-centered Nichiren Shōshū, is a prime example of the tension that can arise between organizations favoring complete laicization and those where a married priesthood still wields institutional control. Although the alliance between Sōka Gakkai and Nichiren Shōshū has always been uneasy, since the end of the Pacific War they have worked together, with the ordained Nichiren Shōshū clergy carrying out essential sacerdotal functions—dispensing the primary object of denominational worship (*gohonzon*), performing funerals, and caretaking temples—for the massive and devout lay organization. But over time the laicization of the clergy became a point of contention for Sōka Gakkai members. Complaining that corrupt Nichiren Shōshū priests held licentious parties, had mistresses, and were involved in pornography, Sōka Gakkai members called into question the right of the overwhelmingly married, laicized clergy to oversee their religious lives. Although certainly not the only point of contention between the two factions, the married life-style of the clergy has loomed large in attacks on clerical privilege leveled by Sōka Gakkai members against the Nichiren Shōshū clergy. In a series of editorials and articles in the pro-Gakkai *Chūgai nippō* newspaper, the editors raised the defacto spread of *nikujiki saitai* and patrimonial inheritance of Nichiren Shōshū temples as one of the major underlying causes for a lack of trust by Sōka Gakkai members toward the Shōshū clergy. Noting in particular the extravagant life-styles of some Nichiren Shōshū temple wives, the editors lashed out at what they considered the misuse of temple funds by so-called secular clerics (*zokusō*) and the nepotism of the chief priest.[9]

---

[8] Nihon Bukkyō ni okeru shō to zoku, (1991, 3).

[9] "Nichiren Shōshū to Sōka Gakkai no konpon mondai" (1991, 3). An exposé detailing the extravagant shopping habits of the Nichiren Shōshū chief priest's wife was published in the same newspaper on January 17, 1991, p. 8.

NIKUJIKI SAITAI AND THE MONASTIC IDEAL

The power of the Buddhist head temples was weakened by the withdrawal of the state, but it was not entirely broken. Despite the massive social changes of the Meiji period and the subsequent practice of marriage by the overwhelming majority of the Buddhist clergy, to this day most established Buddhist denominations have not explicitly recognized the right of the clergy to marry. Although such marriage advocates as Tanaka Chigaku, Nakazato Nisshō, and Kuriyama Taion proposed doctrinal interpretations that would allow the embrace of clerical marriage, their suggestions have been largely ignored by establishment Buddhism, at least on the formal level. The restructuring of Buddhism according to those arguments represents a road not taken by the established Buddhist traditions. Buddhist doctrine has proven far less malleable than Buddhist practice.

The most powerful argument in favor of clerical marriage proved to be demographic, not doctrinal: By 1937, the majority of the Buddhist clergy had married. But that fact was not enough to convince those clerics in charge of the denominations that clerical marriage was acceptable; in the end clerical marriage became a tolerated but still undesirable practice. Even today, many Buddhist clerics are apt to view their marriages more as a sign of their own human frailty than anything else.

The de facto acceptance of clerical marriage was undertaken without concomitant changes in ritual and doctrine in most denominations—in effect, the leaders refused to acknowledge the doctrinal legitimacy of *nikujiki saitai*. Kanaoka Shūyū, in an article concerning the meaning of ordination in contemporary Japan, has noted that despite the massive changes in Buddhist institutions and life-style during the modern era, there have been almost no changes in the precepts taken during ordination.[10] Because there is little comprehensive pan-sectarian information in any language regarding the ritual conduct and interpretation of ordination in contemporary Japan, it is difficult to assess fully the accuracy of Kanaoka's assertion. However, information I have gathered suggests that he is correct, particularly about some of the largest denominations, for example, Sōtō. In both the Sōtō and Ōbaku denominations the prohibition against sexual activity (*futon'in/fuin'yoku*, respectively) remains among the precepts taken by all ordinands. In the case of the Ōbaku denomination, vows of abstaining from eating meat and drinking alcoholic beverages are also taken.[11]

---

[10] Kanaoka (1990, 4). Kanaoka has suggested that the most appropriate set of precepts for the modern Japanese clergy are the *jūzenkai*, which prohibit wrong sexual conduct (*jyain*) but not all sexual relations or the use of alcohol.

[11] See, for example, Sōtōshū Shūmuchō Kyōgakubu (1989, 246); Umino (1979, 12–13). It must be noted that in several smaller denominations, some changes in ordination proce-

In an effort to explain the contradiction between the precepts received at ordination and the actual life led by the majority of clerics, members of the Buddhist clergy have resorted to a variety of arguments. Some Jōdo scholars, for example, have argued that the precepts simply cannot be followed completely by human beings. Nonetheless, by taking the precepts we are reminded of human frailty and thereby are impelled to perform the *nenbutsu* with even greater sincerity. Other members of the Jōdo clergy have argued that the precepts serve an important function symbolizing the perfection of the absolute in this imperfect world. According to James Dobbins, some contemporary Jōdo clerics hold that, "Viewed as specifics, the precepts constitute a collection of rules and injunctions which, when followed scrupulously, yield a life of desisting from evil and cultivating good. Viewed as ideal, however, the precepts represent a palpable expression of the impalpable Buddhist absolute. When analyzing the precepts in this way, the Jōdoshū considers it possible to uphold them as ideal without necessarily upholding them as specifics."[12]

In a similar vein, one Sōtō cleric has attempted to explain the contradiction between practice and precept by invoking such Mahāyāna antinomian notions as the transcendence of and nonattachment to the precepts. Andō Yoshinori writes, "The bhiksus (practitioners) of the Southern school of Buddhism of Sri Lanka and Thailand are required to observe 227 different rules of conduct. Japanese monks, meanwhile, are sure to feel a prick of conscience when they recall the precepts about eating meat, marrying or drinking alcoholic beverages. Nevertheless, we must be careful to avoid an overly literal, 'the precepts for the sake of the precepts' attitude."[13] Andō's comments express the ambivalence that many clerics continue to feel about clerical marriage and are one attempt to rationalize the abandonment of monastic discipline.

---

dures have occurred. In the ordination for the Hossō denomination at the Kōfukuji, where the ten novice precepts (*shami jikkai*) are taken, clerical ordinands receive the precept prohibiting *illicit* sexual relations (*fujyain*). They do not receive the third precept banning all sexual relations (*fuin*), which Fukuda Gyōkai argued was the correct third precept for novices. In addition, since the start of the Meiji period, both the Ōbaku and Hossō denominations have ceased to use the full 250-rule *Shibunritsu* ordinations for clerics, many of whom are married and have children. Whether these shifts in ordination procedures were conscious responses to the spread of clerical marriage is an open and interesting question. Information about the Hossō denomination is based on an unpublished manuscript of the Hossō manual used at the clerical ordination ceremony performed at Kōfukuji on December 16, 1986. Thanks to Robert Sharf for sharing a copy of the text with me. Information about the ordination procedures in the Ōbaku and Hossō denominations is based on interviews with Tanaka Chisei, director of the Ōbaku Bunkaden at Manpukuji, the head temple of the Ōbaku denomination, and with Tagawa Shun'ei, chief priest of the Hossō denomination. I would like to thank Revs. Tanaka and Tagawa for their generous help.

[12] Dobbins (1995, 27–28).
[13] Andō (1994, 14).

The measures enacted in many Buddhist denominations during the Taishō and Shōwa eras alleviated many of the social problems associated with clerical marriage. However, these institutional changes have failed to satisfy successive generations of postwar clerics and temple wives. Although the debate over *nikujiki saitai* and the role of temple wives temporarily was quelled by the exigencies of war and recovery, eventually denominations that had resisted giving even partial recognition to temple wives and families prior to the war began to issue revised sect constitutions granting legitimacy to clerical marriage. In 1961, to cite one prominent example, after much debate, the leaders of the Myōshinji sect of Rinzai Zen added a series of articles concerning temple families to the new sect law. The new articles set forth the responsibility of the temple wife to aid the temple abbot in protecting the graves of the temple's former abbots, to make offerings on behalf of the parishioners' ancestors, and to help manage the temple. The new sect law also stipulated that unless a justifiable reason was offered, a member of the temple family would succeed the deceased abbot. According to an article in *Chūgai nippō*, the leaders had finally agreed to modify the sect law in this manner because, among other things, almost all abbots of branch temples were married, and to ignore in sect law the right to marry when that right had been allowed by state law was "nonsense." In adopting the new articles, the leaders overrode the objections of those who argued that recognition of temple wives would dilute the purity of the Rinzai teachings and would lead to patrimonial inheritance of branch temples.[14]

Despite the general postwar trend toward recognizing clerical marriage and acknowledging the rights of temple families, some Japanese clerics and temple wives have remained unhappy about the contradiction between the official teachings of their denomination and the married family life that most Buddhist clergy lead. By 1959 the Sōtō cleric Yamauchi Shun'yū once again called attention to the contradiction between Sōtō doctrine and actual practice and proposed changes to eliminate the gap between the two.[15] In the last decade, temple wives also have increasingly expressed dissatisfaction with such contradictions, which they view as the source of continued discrimination against them and lack of recognition for the important role they play in the maintenance of their home temples. Though today *nikujiki saitai* is almost universal among the Buddhist clergy of the established Buddhist denominations, many clerics and temple wives continue to feel that the clerical leadership fails to acknowledge the realities of local temple life. These individuals argue that the gap between doctrine

[14] Myōshinji-ha, Shin shūsei shikō e (1961, 4). Thanks to Professor Nishimura Eishin of Hanazono University for pointing out the date of this debate to me.

[15] Yamauchi Shun'yū published a three-part article on this problem in 1959. See Yamauchi (1990, 14–23).

and practice must be narrowed further and that temple women must become fully equal partners with their abbot-husbands.[16]

A 1995 article by Kawahashi Noriko, a Sōtō-denomination temple wife and scholar, provides an excellent summary of some of the social contradictions that still surround clerical marriage. Although most of the Sōtō clergy are married and the laity seem not to mind that fact—a recent survey even shows that the majority of Sōtō parishioners prefer a married cleric to an unmarried one—temple wives remain largely unrecognized by the Sōtō leadership.[17] In the mid-Taishō period Kuriyama Taion plaintively wrote that because clerical marriage was unrecognized, the *jizoku* could not be buried with their husbands.[18] More than three-quarters of a century later, Kawahashi observes that, still,

> one example of the irreconcilability of the principle of world–renunciation and the existence of the *jizoku* is the matter of *jizoku* graves. Unlike the case of lay believers, where the wife and husband are buried together, the *jizoku* has up until now been buried separately from the priest, as the priest is supposedly a world-renouncer. This issue was one of the concerns for the New Study Group for Doctrinal Studies. The institution is now showing a rather lenient attitude toward this restriction, as gradually more *jizoku* women are seeking to be buried with their husbands.[19]

One temple wife, distraught over the poor treatment that the *jizoku* receive, remarked, "once we die, we are treated miserably. The priest has a marvelous grave for himself, but what about us? We only have a small and miserable-looking grave."[20] Clerical marriage and temple families remain ambiguous and unrecognized in contemporary establishment Japanese Buddhism. What has changed is that the *jizoku*—both the temple wives and the new generation of clerics—are vocally protesting the status quo.

The attempt by a new generation of temple families to effect even small changes in articles related to this contentious issue in denominational constitutions has given rise on occasion to prolonged debate among various factions of the clergy. When, for example, the Sōtō leadership began drafting its new constitution, which was adopted in 1995, one important area of concern was the place of *jizoku* within the denomination. After much

---

[16] Particularly notable in this regard are Tanaka Keishin (1984a); Kumamoto (1995); Nakano (1994, 127–39); Kawahashi and Kumamoto (1998, 196–205).

[17] Kawahashi (1995, 162). In an article with Kumamoto Einin, the authors point out that the problems facing temple wives are not restricted to the Sōtō denomination. See Kawahashi and Kumamoto (1998, 203, n. 1).

[18] Kuriyama (1917, 269).

[19] Kawahashi (1995, 174, n. 25).

[20] Sōtōshū Shūmuchō Kyōgakubu, ed., *Dai-jūgokai jizoku chūōshūkai hōkokusho*, 58, cited in ibid., 175.

debate the denomination adopted an article specifying that "Those who are not priests, but believe in Sōtō Buddhism's teachings and reside in the temple, are called *jizoku*."[21] Although after years of study and consultation the drafters of the new Sōtō Constitution were able to agree on such a definition of temple wives and families, as Kawahashi has acerbically noted, the new articles failed to provide any positive affirmation of clerical marriage: the final articles made no mention of the sex of the *jizoku*, thus superficially maintaining the pretense of a celibate, monastic tradition. A more controversial amendment, which read, "The clerics are to practice Buddhist training through social activities, which may include marriage," was never adopted.[22] Thus, although now openly tolerated, clerical marriage still lacks official support from the denominational leadership.

Not all clerics in the established monastic denominations have disregarded the ban on sexual relations. Almost no Buddhist nuns (*nisō*) have married, even though since 1873 they, like male clerics, have been permitted to do so. According to Paula Arai, in 1985 less than 1 percent of the nuns in the Sōtō denomination were married. There are several reasons why so few nuns have ignored the prohibition against *nikujiki saitai*. One possible explanation for this difference, noted by Arai, is that relatively few nuns, even today, come from a temple family. The nuns have chosen to "leave home." As a result of coming to their clerical vocation as a calling rather than as a family responsibility, which is frequently the case with male clerics from temple families, nuns may be more stringent in their adherence to the precepts.[23] Although this is certainly a factor, based on my personal experience in Japan, most male clerics who did not come from temple families married nonetheless. A statistical comparison between male and female clerics from nontemple families would help clarify the extent to which this factor influences a cleric's tendency to marry.

Another more important factor, also noted by Arai, is succession pressure. Many of the male clerics that come from temple families marry in order to have children—hopefully male—who can succeed them as abbot. Many male clerics today work hard to "keep the temple in their family," an effort that frequently entails marriage or adoption. Nuns, by contrast, have controlled far fewer temples than the male clerics. As a result, succession pressures have been far less acute for the nuns. It is telling that as it has become more and more difficult to find successors for temples headed by nuns, more nuns have voiced support for marriage as well.[24]

---

[21] Kawahashi (1995, 162).   [22] Ibid., 173.   [23] Arai (1999, 138–39).

[24] Ibid., 139–40. For an interesting fictionalized account touching on the succession pressures facing one female abbot of a Zen temple, see Miura (1996). According to the translator, the novel is based on the actual experiences of the author.

Within the various denominations a tiny minority of male clerics also continue to practice as unmarried monastics. In what amounts to a de facto two-tier system, most of the abbacies of the training temples of the Rinzai Myōshinji sect continue to be held by unmarried clerics. Some members of the Rinzai clergy, for example, Morinaga Sōkō, continue to advocate celibacy as the best option for Buddhist clerical life. In a brief essay on the subject, Morinaga states that, at least for him, the best way to practice Buddhism and to help others is to remain free from family entanglements. Criticizing the overwhelmingly domestic character of life at most Japanese Buddhist temples today as a symptom of societal dysfunction, Morinaga writes,

> Wanting to contribute to world peace and well-being, Japanese Buddhism shows an increasingly strong tendency to this worldly benefit. At the same time, it acquires more and more the character of a lay community rather than that of a monastic one. In particular, the a-religious tendency of modern civilization—and along with it the loss of family ethics, the contempt for life, and the anthropocentric resources and worldwide destruction of the environment—has led to an extreme situation which ultimately cannot be dealt with in terms of superficial this-worldly profit thinking. It is true that the home-leavers, too, tend to strive more for secular fortune than for the faith arising from the self-awakening of the three treasures. They view the monastic community that ought to be their basis lightly and disregard its rules, and they are drawn into the secular world with a household and private property before having finished their own spiritual quest.[25]

In the Sōtō denomination as well, small numbers of clerics continue to reject clerical marriage. And while there are vocal critics of the ambiguous place held by temple wives and children within the denomination, it appears that many temple wives are relatively content. In 1994 a survey of approximately 1,600 temple wives showed that 67 percent were not troubled by the vagueness of their status. Although many of these women expressed concern about finding a successor and about their lack of knowledge of Buddhism, they did not seem to mind not having a more formal position in sectarian life.[26]

The continued struggle over clerical marriage in the Sōtō and other denominations is a convincing example of the resiliency and persistence of the monastic ideal in the face of tremendous pressures toward laicization. It also demonstrates how sectarian doctrine has determined the parameters within which adaptations to such new conditions as the decriminalization of clerical marriage may occur. Today, the clergy of the Sōtō and other denominations continue to wrestle with the implications

[25] Morinaga (1993, 157–58).
[26] Jizoku: Hyakunen no kiseki (1994, 10:29–31).

of clerical marriage, the existence of which has been ignored for the most part by the leadership of their denominations. The monastic orientation of such denominations as Tendai, Sōtō, Rinzai, and Hossō may have made the acceptance of clerical marriage particularly difficult in comparison to such denominations as Nichiren and Jōdo. For example, the Sōtō doctrinal options available to Kuriyama Taion for defending clerical marriage were more limited than those in the repertoire of the Nichiren or Jōdo clergy. That is to say, the relative unimportance of dispensationalism in Sōtō doctrine and Dōgen's emphasis upon "home-leaving" and the monastic life, particularly in his later writings, have made an embrace of clerical marriage without turning away from its emphasis on Dōgen's teachings extremely difficult for the Sōtō leadership. By contrast, the task of adapting Jōdo doctrine to allow for clerical marriage has been less troublesome because in the past it has been more ambiguous about the place of the precepts in Buddhist practice. Thus in monastic denominations like Sōtō, doctrine has helped ensure the survival of an ideal that stands in stark relief to the lived practice of their clerics.

To label the discord between practice and the ideal that endured in the wake of the nearly universal acceptance of clerical marriage as hypocrisy, however, is a facile assessment. Such judgments disregard the historical presence of many covertly married clerics and overlook the possibility that precepts may retain their importance for practitioners who violate them. James Laidlaw, writing about the relationship of ascetic values and actual practice in lay Jainism, has pointed out that simply to dismiss the demand of standards that conflict with actual behavior as somehow not being part of "true Jainism" or, in the case at hand, "true Buddhism" is to miss the point. To do so also means injecting oneself into a theological debate over whether, in spite of what Japanese clerics appear to think, they are "really" clerics at all. For many individuals an important part of being a Buddhist cleric in Japan today is accepting that one *should* observe standards of monastic deportment, even if one cannot actually do so. As Laidlaw notes in a comment on Martin Southwold's attempt to demarcate true and ideal Buddhism in his ethnography of local practice in Sri Lanka, "What [Southwold's] villagers say they ought to do and think, is part of what they do, observably, do and think. Their thinking and saying it is part of what they do. However much it may offend Southwold's sensibilities, notions of religious authority are central facts about a religious tradition—in life as much as in texts."[27] In the same way, one important thing that many contemporary Japanese Buddhist clerics do at times is to reflect that there are precepts—prohibiting sexual relations, for example— that they do not, for a variety of reasons, follow. What they have not done, although many forces are pushing them in that direction, is to follow

[27] Laidlaw (1995, 11).

the lead of many of the Buddhist New Religions and entirely dismiss the monastic ideal. Any ethnographic study of contemporary established Buddhist temple life will need to take the continuing force of the monastic standard seriously.

Despite their marriages and the imperative to find an abbatial successor, most non-Jōdo Shin Japanese Buddhist clerics continue to view ascetic monasticism as the desired, if unattainable, way of life. Even while marrying, the Buddhist clergy largely have maintained, at least for ceremonial occasions, their distinctive dress and tonsure. Although such practices may be viewed as superficial, they are gestures that also represent continued respect for the ideal those forms represent. The ongoing emphasis on the lives and teachings of the founders of the established Buddhist denominations reinforces this monastic nostalgia and stands as a normative critique of both local temple and householder life. More than a century after the decriminalization of *nikujiki saitai* by the Meiji government, many Japanese Buddhist clerics and their families continue to live amidst the tensions arising from the contradiction between the idealization of monastic, celibate practice that remains at the heart of their sectarian identity and the practical reality of family life at their temples, which have become almost home.

Glossary

Agui	安居院	Butsuryūkō	仏立講
Akamatsu Renjō	赤松連城	*Butsuzōkyō*	仏蔵経
Akizuki Tanetatsu	秋月種樹	Buzanha	豊山派
Amano Sadakage	天野信景	*chakuza*	着座
Ame no Murakumo	天叢雲剣	Chiba Shunrei	千葉春嶺
no Tsurugi		Chiji	知事
Anjōji	安祥寺	*chikyō*	治教
Aokage Sekkō	青蔭雪鴻	Chikū	智空
Arai Nissatsu	新居日薩	Chinzei	鎮西
baishin	陪臣	Chiō Yamakawa	智応山川伝之
baka	馬鹿	Dennosuke	助
Banryūji	万隆寺	Chion'in	知恩院
bendōshi	弁道師	Chizan	智山
Benkei	弁慶	*chō*	町
biku	比丘	Chōheirei	徴兵令
bō	坊	Chōkan	長官
bodai	菩提	Chōkan	澄憲
bodaiji	菩提寺	*chokuninkan*	勅任官
bōmori	坊守	Chōon Dōkai	潮音道海
bonkan	犯姦	*Chosŏn Pulgyo*	朝鮮仏教維新
Bonmōkyō	梵網経	*yusillon*	論
bonnōma	煩悩魔	Chūgen	中源
Bonsai	梵妻	*chūjakumon*	中雀門
bonsō	凡僧	*chūkō no daidō*	忠孝ノ大道
Bontennō	梵天王	*chūkyōsei*	中教正
bosatsu	菩薩	Chūsonji	中尊寺
Boshi hogo hō	母子保護法	*Da xue*	大学
bugyōdokoro	奉行所	Dai/Chū/Shō Kyōin	大・中・小教
Bukkiryō	服忌令		院
Bukkōji	仏光寺	*Daibon hannyakyō*	大品般若経
Bukkyōteki Nihon	仏教的日本	*Daichidoron*	大智度論
Bukkyō fujin	仏教婦人	Daihannyaji	大般若寺
bunmei	文明	*Daihannyakyō*	大般若経
bunmeiteki shūsei	文明的宗制	Daijōin	大乗院
Buppō	仏法	*Daijōin jisha zatsu jiki*	大乗院寺社
Buppō wa shinjutsu	仏法は心術		雑事記
nari	なり	*daikōgi*	大講義
Busshi	仏子	*daikyōsei*	大教正

daimoku	題目	*fuin'yoku*	不婬欲
Dainihon kōtei	大日本校訂大	Fujiidera	藤井寺
daizōkyō	蔵経	*Fujin kyōkai zasshi*	婦人教会雑誌
daishigō	大師号	*fujinkata*	婦人方
Daishin	大心	Fujiwara no Sadanori	藤原貞憲
Daishūkyō	大集経	*fujyain*	不邪婬
Daitokuji	大徳寺	Fuke	普化
Dajōdaijin	太政大臣	*fukko*	復古
Dajōruiten	太政類典	Fukuba Bisei	福羽美静
danka	檀家	Fukuda Gyōkai	福田行誠
danson johi	男尊女卑	*fukuden*	福田
danzuzai	断頭罪	Fukui	福井
Daoan	道安	*fukyō*	富強
Dazai Shundai	太宰春台	Fukyoraian	不去来庵
dochō	度牒	*furegashira*	触頭
dōjō	道場	Fushimi no Miya	伏見の宮貞成
dokushin	独神	Sadafusa Shinnō	親王
dōri	道理	Futo	浮屠
dōtoku	道徳	*Futoku*	婦徳
Ehime	愛媛	*futon'in*	不貧婬
Eikei	永継	*gakuryokata*	学侶方
Eikū	叡空	*gakusha*	学者
Eishō	永正	Gangōji	元興寺
ekō henshō	回光返照	Ge no bō	下の坊
Ekōin	回向院	*gedatsusō*	解脱僧
Ekū	慧空	Gekkan	月感
emyō kaitai	慧命戒体	Gen'na	元和
Enchō	円澄	Gendai Kyōgaku	現代教学研究
endonkai	円頓戒	Kenkyūkai	会
Engakuji-ha	円覚寺派	Genkaku-bō	玄覚坊
Enmei'in	延命院	Genna	元和
Ennō	円能	*genzoku*	還俗
Enoshima	江の島	Gion	祇園
entō/ontō	遠島	*go-ki-ji-koku-kyōhō*	教・機・時・
Entsū	円通	*rufu*	国・教法流
Erin	慧琳		布
Eshinni	恵信尼	*go-on*	呉音
eta /hinin	穢多・非人	Godenshō	御伝鈔
Etō Shinpei	江藤新平	*gogi*	五義
Fahu	法護	*gogyakuzai*	五逆罪
fūfu	夫婦	*gohō*	護法
Fuhōzō innen den	付法蔵因縁伝	gohonzon	御本尊
fuin	不婬	*gohōron*	護法論

goji hakkyō	五時八教	*hōben*	方便
gojō	五常	Hokekyōji	法華経寺
gojoku	五濁	*Hokke no gyoja*	法華の行者
Gokajō no seimon	五箇条の誓文	*hokoku*	保国
gokō	五綱	*hōkyō*	法教
gokumon	獄門	*hōmu*	ホーム
gon daikyōsei	権大教正	*hōmyō*	法名
gonjisō	近事僧	Hōnen	法然
gonkundō	権訓導	*Honganji no Shōnin*	本願寺聖人親
gon shōkyōsei	権少教正	*Shinran denne*	鸞伝絵
gonshō no hō butsu	権小の法仏	*honge geshu no*	本化下種ノ根
goshō	五障	*konpon shin*	本信
gosho	御所	*honmatsu seido*	本末制度
goyōgakari	御用掛	*honmon*	本門
guchi	愚痴	*honmon honzon,*	本門本尊・
gyakushu hōmyō	逆修法名	*honmon kaidan,*	本門戒壇・
gyōki	澆季	*honmon daimoku*	本門題目
Gyōki no Gangōji	行基ノ元興寺	*honsekichi*	本籍地
gyōnin	行人	*Hōshakukyō*	宝積経
ha	派	*hōshintan*	豊心丹
Hachijōjima	八丈島	*hōshuke*	法主家
haibutsu kishaku	廃仏毀釈・排	*hosshin no emyō*	法身ノ恵命
	仏棄釈	Hossō	法相
haihan chiken	廃藩置県	*Hotoke wa shibito ni*	仏は死人にあ
Han Yongun	韓龍雲	*arazu*	らず
Hanazono Sesshin	華園摂信	*Ichiwa ichigen*	一話一言
hanshi	藩士	*idensei*	遺伝性
haritsuke	磔	*ie*	家
Harunasan	榛名山	*Igyō no mono*	異形の者
Hayashiyama Bunko	林山文庫	Ii	伊井
heifū	弊風	*ikai*	位階
heimin	平民	Ikishima	壱岐島
Hibiya Daijingū	日比谷大神宮	*ikkyū*	一級
Higashi Honganji	東本願寺光勝	Imakita Kōsen	今北洪川
Kōshō		*in*	婬／淫
Higo	肥後	*in'yoku*	婬欲
hijiri	聖	*Inaka hanjōki*	田舎繁昌記
Hikone	彦根	*inbon*	婬犯
Hirakawa	平河	Inō Hidenori	伊能穎則
Hirata Atsutane	平田篤胤	Inoue Hōchū	井上豊忠
Hirosawa Saneomi	広沢真臣	Inoue Kaoru	井上馨
hishūkyō	非宗教	Inoue Kowashi	井上毅
hō	法	*ippu ippu*	一夫一婦

isha	医者	*jūmotsu*	什物
Ishin Sūden	以心崇伝	*junkai Kyōdōshoku*	巡廻教導職
isshin	一新	*junkei*	閏刑
Itō Jinsai	伊藤仁斎	*junshi*	殉死
Iwakura Tomomi	岩倉具視	*jūshoku*	住職
Iwamotoin	岩本院	*Jūzen hōgo*	十善法語
Izu Shichitō	伊豆七島	*jūzenkai*	十善戒
ji	時	*jyain*	邪婬
jigō	寺号	Jyunnyo	准如
jigokukai	地獄界	*Kagenki*	嘉元記
jihō	寺法	*kahō*	家邦
jiin	寺院	*kaidō*	開導
jiin hatto	寺院法度	*kaiken*	戒験
jiin meisaisho	寺院明細書	*Kaimokushō*	開目鈔
jiin no seitaikei	寺院の生態系	*kaimyaku*	戒脈
Jiinryō	寺院寮	*kaimyō*	戒名
Jiinshō	寺院省	Kaimyōji Shōtsū	皆明寺照通
jiki	時機	Kaitei Ritsurei	改定律例
Jikkai ryakutō	十戒略答	Kakunyo	覚如
Jiku	竺	Kamei Koremi	亀井茲監
jindō	人道	*kamidana*	神棚
jingi	仁義	Kan'eiji	寛永寺
jinin	神人	Kanbōji	看坊寺
jinrin	人倫	Kanbun	寛文
Jinshin	壬申	Kanchō	管長
jiseki	寺籍	*Kanjin no honzon shō*	観心の本尊抄
jisha bugyō	寺社奉行	*Kanmon gyoki*	看聞御記
jishu	寺主	Kanpō	寛保
jisō	寺僧	Kanrin	館林
jitei	寺庭	Kanshu	管首
Jizō	地蔵	*kantsū*	姦通
jizoku	寺族	*kara*	掛絡
jizoku hogo hō	寺族保護法	*kasa ippon*	傘一本
jizoku mondai	寺族問題	*kashikodokoro*	賢所
Jōdo fusatsu shiki	淨土布薩式	*katei*	家庭
Jōdo Shinshū	淨土真宗	*katte tarubeki*	勝手タルベキ
jōfu	情婦	*Kattō besshi*	葛藤別紙
Jōjuin	成就院	Kawachi	河内
Jōzō	淨藏	Kawajiri	川尻
Jubutsu benron	儒仏弁論	*kazoku*	華族
jūjūkai	十重戒	Kazusa	上総
jūjūkinkai	十重禁戒	*kegare*	穢
jukai	受戒	*Kegonkyō*	華嚴経

Keihōkan	刑法官	Kōshō	降承
kemosō	羯磨僧	Kōshōji	興正寺
Kenjitsu	憲実	*koshu*	戸主
Kenki	憲基	Kōshū Kaidō	甲州街道
Kenninji	建仁寺	*koyū no michi*	固有の道
kenpaku seido	建白制度	Kōzanji	高山寺
Kenshin	顕真	*Kōzen gokokuron*	興禅護国論
ki	機	Kōzushima	神津島
Kido Takayoshi	木戸孝允	*ku*	区
Kikyōshi	帰郷子	Kubo Hideshige	久保季茲
Kimiga yo	君が代	Kubo Kakutarō	久保角太郎
Kin'ei	瑾英	*kuchi ni seisen*	口に腥膻を啖
Kinpusenji	金峯山寺	*o kurau*	らふ
Kinshokuji	錦織寺	Kuiji	窺基
Kirigaya Mine	桐ヶ谷みね	*Kujikata osadamegaki*	公事方御定書
kisei Bukkyō	既成仏教	Kujō Kanezane	九条兼実
Kishū	紀州	Kumarajū	鳩魔羅什
kizoku	帰俗	(Kumārajīva)	
ko	戸	*kuni*	国
Kōbunroku	公文録	*Kunkai hachijō*	訓戒八條
kochō	戸長	Kuonji	久遠寺
Kōdō	皇道	Kuroda Kiyotsuna	黒田清綱
Kōfukuji (Nara)	興福寺	Kuruma Ryūdō	来馬立道
Kōfukuji (Kazusa)	高福寺	Kūsei	空誓
Kōgan	公巌	Kusunoki Masashige	楠木正成
Kogi	古義	*kusurigui*	薬食
Kogi Shingon	古義眞言	Kyōbukyō	教部卿
koji	居士	*Kyōbushō e kengen*	教部省へ建言
Kojimachi no toriya	麹町の鳥屋	Kyōdōshoku	教導職
kokka	国家	*kyōdōshoku shiho*	教導職試補
Kokkyō	国教	Kyōhō	亨保
koku	石	*kyōhō*	教法
Kokuchūkai	国柱会	*Kyōhō shihi*	教法私批
kokumin	国民	*kyōin*	教院
Kokuritsu	国立古文書館	*kyōka*	教化
Komonjokan		*kyōki*	教規
kokushigō	国師号	Kyōnyo	教如
kokutai	国体	*kyōwa seiji*	共和政治
Kōmori mōdanki	蝙蝠妄談記	Kyōze	教是
Konakamura Kiyonori	小中村清矩	*kyūshu*	旧株
kōsatsu	高札	*Li ji*	礼記
koseki	戸籍	*maisu*	売僧
Kōsen Mujaku	黄泉無著	*makaseru*	委

mamorifuda	守札
Manase Gensaku	曲直瀬玄朔
Manji	万治
Manpukuji	万福寺
Manpukuji monjo	万福寺文書
Manzan Dōhaku	卍山道白
Maō	魔王
mappō	末法
mappō Butsu deshi,	末法佛弟子雷
Raiju Taion	澍泰音
Mappō tōmyōki	末法灯明記
Matokurokuga ritsu	摩徳勒伽律
Matsudaira	松平
Matsudaira Yoshinaga	松平慶永
Matsumoto Mannen	松本万年
Matsuya hikki	松屋筆記
mekake	妾
mibun seido	身分制度
Mieidō	御影堂
miko	神子
Minamoto Yoshitsune	源義経
minkan jiin	民間寺院
Minobusan	身延山
mippu	密夫
Mishima Chūshū	三島中洲
Mitsu	三津
mitsueshiro	御杖代
mittsū	密通
Mizusawa-ken	水沢県
Mokuan Shōtō	木庵性瑫
mokugyo	木魚
momonji-ya	ももんじ屋
monshu	門主
monzeki	門跡
monzen machi	門前町
Mori Arinori	森有礼
Morotake Ekidō	諸嶽奕堂
Mt. Nikkō	日光山
Murata Jakujun	村田寂順
Muryōjukyō	無量寿経
mushikikai	無色界
Myōdō-ken	名東県
Myōhen	明遍

Myōhōji	妙法寺
Myōhōji monjo	妙法寺文書
Myōichi	明一
myōji	苗字／名字
Myōkyō Daishi	明教大師
Myōōji	妙応寺
Myōshū Ubai Rin	妙宗優婆夷林
Myōyūji	妙幽寺
Nagamatsu Nissen	永松日扇
(Seifū)	(清風)
Nagatani Nobuatsu	長谷信篤
Nagayama Kōryū	長山黄龍
Nagoya Gen'i	名古屋玄医
naien no tsuma	内縁の妻
Naikan Bunko	内館文庫
Naimukyō	内務卿
nairin	内倫
Nam-myō-hō-ren-ge-	南無妙法蓮華
kyō	経
namagusai	生臭い
nanshoku	男色
Naruse Jinzō	成瀬仁蔵
Nehangyō	涅槃経
nenbun dosha	年分度者
nenbutsu	念仏
Nichidō	日道
Nichiji zakki	日次雑記
Nichiki	日輝
Nichiren	日蓮
Nichirenshugi	日蓮主義
Nihon Kirisutokyō	日本キリスト
Kyōfūkai	教矯風会
Nihonteki Bukkyō	日本的仏教
Nikki shū	日記集
nikujiki	肉食
nikujiki saitai	肉食妻帯
Nikujiki saitai ben	肉食妻帯弁
Nikujiki saitai kikigaki	肉食妻帯聞書
Nikujiki saitai ron	肉食妻帯論
nikushoku	肉食
Nikushoku ron	肉食論
ninbetsuchō	人別帳
ninjō	人情

Ninnaji	仁和寺	oshikome	押込
Ninnōkyō	仁王経	Ōshio Heihachirō	大塩平八郎
Nippon teikoku banbanzai	日本帝国万々歳	oshō-san	和尚さん
		Ōtani Kōshō	大谷光勝
Nishi Tōshōgū	西東照宮	Ōtori Sessō	鴻雪爪
Nishiari Bokusan	西有穆山	Ototachibana Hime	弟橘媛
nisō	尼僧	Ōuchi Seiran	大内青巒
nōke	能化	Owari	尾張
nyobon	女犯	Qisong	契嵩
nyobon nikujiki	女犯肉食	Ragora sonja	ラゴラ尊者
nyonin haiseki	女人排斥	Rangaku	蘭学
nyonin jōbutsu	女人成仏	Reiō	霊昶
nyonin kinsei	女人禁制	Reiyūkai	霊友会
Nyozen	如善	Rengekai	蓮華会
Ōbō	王法	Rengeōin	蓮花王院
Oda Nobunaga	織田信長	Rennyo	蓮如
Ōgaki	大垣	renza	連座
Ogawa Taidō	小川泰堂	risei	釐正
Ogawa Yasuko	小川泰子	Risshō ankoku ron	立正安国論
Ōgimachi Sanjō Sanenaru	正親町三条実愛	Risshō Ankokukai	立正安国会
		Risshō Daigaku	立正大学
Ogino Dokuon	荻野独園	Risshō Kōseikai	立正佼成会
Ogyū Sorai	荻生徂徠	Risshōkaku	立正閣
Ōhara Shigetomi	大原重徳	ritsuryō	律令
Ohara Tesshin	小原鉄心	rōju	老中
Okamoto Yasutaka	岡本保孝	Rokkakudō	六角堂
Okinoshima	隠岐島	rokukyū	六級
Ōkubo Toshimichi	大久保利通	Rokuon nichiroku	鹿苑日録
Ōkuma Shigenobu	大隈重信	rokuyokuten	六欲天
Ōkuninushi no Mikoto	大国主命	rōshū	陋習
Ōkurakyō	大蔵卿	Ryōbu Shintō	両部神道
okusan	奥さん	Ryōgae	楞伽会
Omuro-ha	御室派	Ryōgakyō	楞伽経
Onkō Jiun	飲光慈雲	Ryōgongyō	楞厳経
onma	陰魔	Ryōhonzan Iin	両本山委員
Ono Jusshin (Sekisai)	小野述信 (石斎)	Ryōken	亮賢
		ryōsai kenbo	良妻賢母
Ontakegyōja	御岳行者	Ryōshō	良勝
Ontakekō	御岳講	Ryūshō	隆承
Ontakekyō	御嶽教	Ryūzen	柳全
Ōoku	大奥	Saeki	佐伯
Osadamegaki hyakkajō	御定書百箇条	Saidaiji	西大寺
		Saifukuji	西福寺

Saigin	西吟	Seiwa'in	清和院
Saijin ronsō	祭神論争	Seizanha	西山派
saijyo	妻女	*seken uro no kai*	世間有漏の戒
saikyō itchi	祭教一致	*sekken kokka*	世間国家
Sain	左院	*Sendai Sengakuin*	仙台仙岳院文
saisei itchi	祭政一致	*monjo*	書
saishi	祭祀	Senjuji	専修寺
saitai	妻帯	Senkōji	千光寺
saitai (Chūsonji)	妻躰	Senkyōshi	宣教師
saitai jikiniku	妻帯食肉	Sensōji	浅草寺
San'ei-chō	三栄町	*seshū*	世襲
sanbu no yokogami	三武のよこが	*sesshō kindan*	殺生禁断
	み	Sesshū Naniwa Zuiryū	接州難波瑞竜
sangai	三界	Tetsugen Zenji	鉄眼禅師
sangaku	三学	*Setsuyōshū*	節用集
sangi	参議	*Shakashi*	釈迦子
Sanjo	三助	Shaku	釈
Sanjō no Kyōsoku	三条の教則	Shaku Kōnen	釈興然
Sanjō Sanetomi	三条実美	Shaku Ryūtō	釋隆燈
sanjū	三従	Shaku Shugu	釈守愚
sanjujōkai	三聚浄戒	Shaku Sōen	釈宗演
Sanjūsangendō	三十三間堂	Shaku Unshō	釈雲照
sankō	三綱	*shakubuku*	折伏
sanma	秋刀魚	*Shakumon shinki*	釈門新規三策
sanpatsu dattō rei	散髪脱刀令	*sansaku*	
sanshu no jingi	三種神器	*shami jikkai*	沙弥十戒
sanshu no jōniku	三種ノ淨肉	*shamon*	沙門
Sanzen seigyō	三善清行	*Shamon seishi ben*	沙門姓氏弁
sarashi	晒	*shaseki*	社籍
Sasaki Gihan	佐々木義範	*shasō*	社僧
Satomi Tatsu	里見たつ	*Shibunritsu*	四分律
Seiin	正院	*Shichikajō no*	七箇条起請文
Seikaku	聖覚	*kishōmon*	
seikei	正刑	*shido*	私度
seikyō bunri	政教分離	*Shigetsu yawa*	指月夜話
Seiryōji	清涼寺	*shihō*	嗣法
seisatsu	制札	Shijō Kingo	四条金吾
Seishi	勢至	*shikan*	祠官
seishu	清衆	Shikiburyō	式部寮
Seishū Shusetsu	蜻州守拙	*shikikai*	色界
seisō	清僧	Shikitei Sanba	式亭三馬
seisōji	清僧寺	*shima*	死魔
Seiun	清雲	*shima*	四魔

Shimada Mitsune	島田蕃根	shokesō	所化僧
Shimaji Mokurai	島地黙雷	Shōkokuji	相國寺
shimin byōdō	四民平等	Shoku Nihongi	続日本紀
shimin dōitsu	四民同一	Shōrui awaremi no rei	生類憐れみの令
Shimin shukke no gi ni tsuki ukagau	四民出家ノ儀二付伺	shōrui bugyō	生類奉行
Shin Bukkyōha Bukkyōto	新佛教派佛教徒	Shoshū Dōtoku Kaimei	諸宗道德会盟
		Shoshū jiin hatto	諸宗寺院法度
Shina shugi	支那主義	shōsō	正僧
Shinbun zasshi	新聞雑誌	Shōtokuji	正徳寺
shinbutsu bunri rei	神仏分離令	shō	少輔
shinjutsu	心術	Shōzan	正山
shinkoku	神国	shū	宗
Shinkyō	神教	Shūgiin	集議院
shinmei	神明	shūki	宗規
shinmin dōitsu	臣民同一	shukke	出家
shinmin ippan	臣民一般	shukke datsuzoku	出家脱俗
shinni	瞋恚	shukkesō	出家僧
shinōkōshō	士農工商	shukke tokudo	出家得度
Shinran	親鸞	shukke tokudo no sei o haishi	出家得度之制ヲ廃シ
Shinran jagi ketsu	親鸞邪義決		
Shinran muki	親鸞夢記	Shukusatsu daizōkyō	縮刷大蔵経
Shinran Shōnin denne	親鸞聖人伝絵	shūkyō	宗教
Shinran Shōnin shōtoden	親鸞聖人正統伝	shūkyō mibun	宗教身分
		shūmon aratame ninbetsu chō	宗門改人別帳
Shinritsu kōryo	新律綱領		
shinsanshiki	進(晋)山式	Shūmon tefuda aratame jōmoku	宗門手札改條目
Shintō	神道		
shinzen kekkonshiki	神前結婚式	shūsei	宗制
Shinzenkōji	新善光寺	shūshi	衆仕
shishi	志士	shūto	衆徒
Shishido Tamaki	宍戸璣	sō	僧
Shishiō	獅子王	sō ni arazu zoku ni arazu	非僧非俗
shizai	死罪		
shizoku	士族	Soejima Taneomi	副島種臣
shizoku keitō	民族系統	sōgya	僧伽
Shōbōgenzō	正法眼蔵	sōgyaya	僧伽耶
Shōchūzan	正中山	Sōjiji	総持寺
shōdōshi	唱道師	Sōjō	僧正
Shōgenji	正眼寺	Sōmu	総務
shōjin ryōri	精進料理	sōni	僧尼
Shōjōkōji	清浄光寺	Sōniryō	僧尼令
shōjōzai	正浄財	Sonpi bunmyaku	尊卑分脈

Sōrinji	宗林寺	Teikoku Fujin Kyōkai	帝国婦人協会
sōryo	僧侶	*tenmei*	天命
sōseki	僧籍	Tenna	天和
Sōtōshū Daigakurin	曹洞宗大学林	*tennen no shō*	天然の性
Sōtōshū jizoku hogo kitei	曹洞宗寺族保護規程	Tennōji	天王寺
		tenpu no kenri	天賦の権利
Sōtōshū shūken	曹洞宗宗憲	*tenri*	天理
Sōtōshū Shūmuchō	曹洞宗宗務庁	Tenrinnō	天輪王
sotsu	卒	Tenshō Daijin	天照大神
sotsuzoku	卒族	*Tenzo kyōkun*	典座教訓
Sun Chuo	孫綽	Tetsugen Dōkō	鉄眼道光
Suwa Jinja	諏訪神社	Tetsuran Mutei	鉄藍無底
Suzuki Kiichi	鈴木喜一	Toda	戸田
T'aego chong	太古宗	Tōeizan	東叡山
Tada Genryū	多田玄龍	Tōji	東寺
tai	体	*Tōjō zaike shūshōgi*	洞上在家修証義
taiki seppō	対機説法		
Tairyū Bun'i	泰龍文彙	Toki Nichijō	富木日常
Taisanji	大山寺	*tokudo*	得度
Taishaku	帝釈	Tokugawa Iemitsu	徳川家光
taitō kinrei	帯刀禁令	Tokugawa Ienobu	徳川家宣
Takada kaisan Shinran Shōnin shōtō den	高田開山親鸞聖人正統伝	Tokugawa Ietsuna	徳川家綱
		Tokugawa Ieyasu	徳川家康
Takada Tomokiyo	高田与清	*Tokugawa jyūgodai shi*	徳川十五代史
Takada-ha	高田派		
Takagi Hidenori	高木秀臣	Tokugawa Tsunayoshi	徳川綱吉
Takamatsu no Miya Nobuhito Shinnō	高松宮宣仁親王	Tokugawa Yoshimune	徳川吉宗
		Tokuhon Gyōja	徳本行者
Takaoka Zōryū	高岡増隆	*ton'yoku*	貪欲
Takeda Katsuyori	武田勝頼	*torii*	鳥居
Takeda Shingen	武田信玄	Tōshōgū	東照宮
takejizaitenshima	他化自在天子魔	Toyotomi Hidetsugu	豊臣秀次
		Toyotomi Hideyoshi	豊臣秀吉
takuhatsu	托鉢	*Tōzai ryōkyō hinami dairyaku*	東西両京日並大略
Tamahi	玉妃		
Tamajo	玉女	Tōzan-ha	当山派
Tan'an	澹菴	*tsuien*	退院
Tanaka Chigaku	田中智学	*tsuiin*	追院
Tanba	丹波	*tsuma*	妻
tanji chōkyō shiki	誕児頂経式	*tsuma o motsu koto*	妻を持つこと
tanjun no shūkyōsha	単純の宗教者	*tsuya*	通夜
Tayū	大輔	Tsuzureko Jinja	綴子神社
tefuda	手札	Uan Rōnin	有安老人

ubasoku	優婆塞	*yoriki*	与力
Udana-in	優陀那院	*Yōrō Ritsuryō*	養老律令
Ugai Tetsujō	養鸕徹定	*yōshi*	養子
Ugawa Shōchō	宇川照澄	Yoshikawa Koretari	吉川惟足
ujidera	氏寺	*Yudao lun*	喩道論
ujiko aratame	氏子改	*Yuishinshō*	唯信鈔
Ukiyo no arisama	浮世乃有様	*Yuishinshō mon'i*	唯信鈔文意
Ukiyodoko	浮世床	*yūrai saitai*	有来妻帯
wa	羽	Yushin	庾信
wagōshū	和合衆	*zaike*	在家
wagōsō	和合僧	*zaike bosatsu*	在家菩薩
Wakabayashi Rinko	若林凛子	*zaikesō*	在家僧
wakō dōjin	和光同塵	*zainin*	罪人
Xiao jing	孝経	*zaizokusō*	在俗僧
Yakushiji	藥師寺	*zasshu*	雜衆
yamabushi	山伏	*Zenko iori mango*	前古庵漫語
yamadashi Bukkyō	山ダシ仏教	Zenkōji	善光寺
Yamagata Aritomo	山県有朋	*zenkoku shokyō*	全国諸教
Yamagata Bantō	山片蟠桃	Zenshin	善信
Yamato Hime no Miko	大和姫皇女	*zenshū*	禅衆
Yamauchi Zuien	山内瑞円	Zhu	竺
Yasakani no Magatama	八坂瓊曲玉	*zōbō*	像法
		zōgyō	雜行
Yashudara hime	耶須陀羅姫	*Zoichi agongyō*	増一阿含経
Yata no Kagami	八咫鏡	Zōjōji	増上寺
yō	用	*zōka sanshin*	造化三神
yokkai	欲界	*zokuseki*	族籍
Yokoi Shōnan	横井小楠	*zokusō*	俗僧

Bibliography

Abe Yoshiya. 1968–69. Religious Freedom under the Meiji Constitution. *Contemporary Religions in Japan* 9–10 (December 1968): 268–338; (March–June 1969): 57–97; (September–December 1969): 181–203.

Akabori Shōmyō 赤堀正明. 1992. Nichirenshū wo chūshin to shita "nikujiki saitai rei" no kōsatsu 日蓮宗を中心とした「肉食妻帯令」の考察. *Gendai shūkyō kenkyū* 26 (March): 127–57.

Ambaras, David Richard. 1999. Treasures of the Nation: Juvenile Delinquency, Socialization, and Mobilization in Modern Japan, 1895–1945. Ph.D. dissertation, Princeton University.

Amstutz, Galen. 1997. *Interpreting Amida: History and Orientalism in the Study of Pure Land Buddhism*. Albany: State University of New York Press.

Andō, Yoshinori. 1994. The World of the Yuikyōgyō. *Zen Quarterly* 6 (2): 10–14.

Anjōji Ryūtō kengonsho shintatsu tensho 安祥寺隆燈建言書進達添書, STR, 155.

Aoki Kazuo 青木和夫 et al., eds. 1992–94. *Nihonshi daijiten* 日本史大事典. Tokyo: Heibonsha.

Aoki Kazuo 青木和夫 et al., eds. 1982. *Kojiki* 古事記. *Nihon shisō taikei*. Tokyo: Iwanami Shoten.

App, Urs. 1997. St. Francis Xavier's Discovery of Japanese Buddhism: A Chapter in the European Discovery of Buddhism (Part 1: Before the Arrival in Japan). *The Eastern Buddhist* 30 (1): 53–78.

Arai, Paula. 1999. *Women Living Zen: Japanese Sōtō Nuns*. New York: Oxford University Press.

Arakawa Genki 荒川元暉. 1989. *Jitei fujin hyakka* 寺庭婦人百科. Tokyo: Sansei Shobō.

Asao Naohiro 朝直弘, ed. 1992. *Mibun to kakushiki* 身分と格式. Tokyo: Chūō Kōronsha.

Baikokudo 売国奴 (1893). MKS, August 30, 7.

Baroni, Helen J. 1994. Bottled Anger: Episodes in Ōbaku Conflict in the Tokugawa Period. *Japanese Journal of Religious Studies* 21 (2–3): 191–210.

———. 2000. *Obaku Zen: The Emergence of the Third Sect of Zen in Tokugawa Japan*. Honolulu: University of Hawaii Press.

Barstow, Anne Llewellyn. 1983. The First Generation of Anglican Clergy Wives: Heroines or Whores? *Historical Magazine of the Protestant Episcopal Church* 52 (1): 3–16.

Bloom, Alfred. 1968. *The Life of Shinran Shōnin: The Journey to Self-Acceptance*. Leiden: E. J. Brill.

Bodiford, William M. 1993. *Sōtō Zen in Medieval Japan*. Honolulu: University of Hawaii Press.

Bond, George D. 1996. Theravāda Buddhism's Two Formulations of the *Dasa Sīla* and the Ethics of the Gradual Path. In *Pāli Buddhism*, ed. F. J. Hoffman and Deegalle Mahinda, 17–42. Richmond, Surrey: Curzon.

Boswell, John. 1980. *Christianity, Social Tolerance, and Homosexuality: Gay People in Western Europe from the Beginning of the Christian Era to the Fourteenth Century*. Chicago: University of Chicago Press.

Botsman, Dani V. 1992. Punishment and Power in the Tokugawa Period. *East Asian History* 3:1–32.

Breen, John. 1996. The Imperial Oath of 1868: Ritual, Politics, and Power in the Restoration. *Monumenta Nipponica* 51 (4): 407–429.

Bunkachō 文化庁, ed. 1999. *Shūkyō nenkan: Heisei jyūnenban* 宗教年鑑－平成十年版. Tokyo: Gyōsei.

Buswell, Robert E., Jr. 1992. *The Zen Monastic Experience: Buddhist Practice in Contemporary Korea*. Princeton: Princeton University Press.

Casanova, José. 1994. *Public Religions in the Modern World*. Chicago: University of Chicago Press.

Chadwick, David. 1999. *Crooked Cucumber:The Life and Zen Teaching of Shunryu Suzuki*. New York: Broadway Books.

Ch'en, Kenneth K. S. 1964. *Buddhism in China*. Princeton: Princeton University Press.

———. 1973. *The Chinese Transformation of Buddhism*. Princeton: Princeton University Press.

Chiba Jōryū 千葉乗隆. 1977. *Kōzanji Sōboku no shōgai* 宏山寺僧樸の生涯. Kyoto: Kōzanji.

Chikū 智空. *Nikujiki saitai ben* 肉食妻帯弁. SZS, 59: 293–318.

———. *Nikujiki saitai kikigaki* 肉食妻帯聞書. Unpublished manuscript. Ryūkoku University Library Catalog #1502-183-1.

Collcutt, Martin. 1986. Buddhism: The Threat of Eradication. In *Japan in Transition*, edited by M. Jansen and G. Rozman. Princeton: Princeton University Press.

Confucius. 1979. *The Analects*. Translated by D. C. Lau. New York: Dorset Press.

Curtis, William Eleroy. 1896. *The Yankees of the East: Sketches of Modern Japan*. 2 vols. New York: Stone and Kimball.

Daikoku ron 大黒論. 1899. *Chūgai nippō* (March 29): 1.

Date Mitsuyoshi 伊達光美. 1930. *Nihon jiinhō ron* 日本寺院法論. Tokyo: Ganshōdō Shoten.

———. 1981. *Nihon shūkyō seido shiryō ruiju kō* 日本宗教制度史料類聚考. Kyoto: Rinsen Shoten. Original edition 1930.

Davis, Winston. 1989. Buddhism and the Modernization of Japan. *History of Religions* 28 (4): 304–39.

Deleuze, Gilles. (1979). The Rise of the Social. In *The Policing of Families*. Jacques. Donzelot, ix–xvii. New York, Pantheon.

Dikötter, Frank. 1995. *Sex, Culture, and Modernity in China*. Honolulu: University of Hawaii Press.

Dobbins, James C. 1989. *Jōdo Shinshū: Shin Buddhism in Medieval Japan*. Bloomington: Indiana University Press.

———. 1990. The Biography of Shinran: Apotheosis of a Japanese Buddhist Visionary. *History of Religion* 30 (2): 179–96.

———. 1995. Buddhist Precepts in the Jōdoshū. Paper read at The Practice of Vinaya in East Asian Buddhism, Taipei, Taiwan.

Dumoulin, H. 1990. *Zen Buddhism: A History*. Vol. 2, Japan. New York: Macmillan.

Durt, Hubert. 1991. Bodhisattva and Layman in the Early Mahāyāna. *Japanese Religions* 16 (3): 1–16.

Edamatsu Shigeyuki 枝松茂之, et al., eds. 1994. *Meiji Nyūsu Jiten* 明治ニュース事典. 9 vols. Tokyo: Mainichi Komunikēshonzu Shuppanbu.

Edwards, Walter. 1989. *Modern Japan Through Its Weddings: Gender, Person, and Society in Ritual Portrayal*. Stanford: Stanford University Press.

Eiheijishi Hensan Iinkai 永平寺史編纂委員会, ed. 1982. *Eihiheijishi* 永平寺史. 2 vols. Eiheiji: Daihonzan Eiheiji.

Endo Hajime 遠藤一. 1989. Bōmori izen no koto 坊守以前のこと. In *Shinjin to kuyō* 信心と供養, edited by Ōsumi Kazuo 大隅和雄 and Nishiguchi Junko 西口順子, 41–79. Tokyo: Heibonsha.

Erin 慧琳. *Shakunan Shinshū sōgi* 釈難真宗僧儀. SZS, 59:339–50.

Faure, Bernard. 1998. *The Red Thread: Buddhist Approaches to Sexuality*. Princeton: Princeton University Press.

Foulk, T. Griffith. 1988. The Zen Institution in Modern Japan. In *Zen: Tradition and Transition*, edited by Kenneth Kraft, 157–77. New York: Grove Press.

Francis, Xavier. 1992. *The Letters and Instructions of Francis Xavier*. Translated by M. J. Costelloe. St. Louis: Institute of Jesuit Sources.

Fujii Jintarō 藤井甚太郎, ed. 1934. *Iwakura Tomomi kankei monjo* 岩倉具視関係文書. Tokyo: Nihon Shiseki Kyōkai.

Fujii Sadafumi 藤井貞文. 1974. *Meiji kokugaku hassei shi no kenkyū* 明治国学発生史の研究. Tokyo: Yoshikawa Kōbunkan, 1974.

Fujii Yoshio 藤井嘉雄. 1987. *Osadamegaki hyakkajō to keibatsu tetsuzuki* 御定書百箇条と刑罰手続. Tokyo: Kōbundō Shuppansha.

Fujitani, Takashi. 1996. *Splendid Monarchy: Power and Pageantry in Modern Japan*. Berkeley: University of California Press.

Fukase Shunji 深瀬俊路. 1997. Girei no hensen to kindai tōmon 儀礼の変遷と近代洞門. *Nihon kindai Bukkyōshi kenkyū* 4:31–41.

Fukuda Gyōkai 福田行誡. 1878. *Shumisen ryakusetsu* 須彌山略説. In MBSS, 6:90–93.

Fukushima Masao 福島正夫, ed. 1959a. *"Ie" seido no kenkyū, shiryō hen* 「家」制度の研究、資料編. 2 vols. Tokyo: Tōkyō Daigaku Shuppankai.

———, ed. 1959b. *Koseki seido to "ie" seido* 戸籍製度と「家」制度. Tokyo: Tōkyō Daigaku Shuppankai.

———. 1967. *Nihon shihonshugi to "ie" seido* 日本資本主義と「家」制度. Tokyo: Tōkyō Daigaku Shuppankai.

Fung Yu-lan. 1953. *A History of Chinese Philosophy*. Translated by Derk Bodde. 2 vols. Princeton: Princeton University Press.

Furukawa Taigo 古川碓悟. 1938. *Sōryo saitai ron* 僧侶妻帯論. Tokyo, Chūō Bukkyōsha.

Furuta Shōkin 古田紹欽. 1958. Kamakura Bukkyō ni okeru jiritsushugi to hanjiritsushugi: Hōnen no baai 鎌倉仏教における持律主義と反持律主義─法然の場合. *Indogaku Bukkyōgaku kenkyū* 6 (1): 94–103.

———. 1981. Bukkyō haiseki shisō ni taisuru gohō shisō no hanpatsu 仏教排斥思想に対する護法思想の反撥. In *Furuta Shōkin chosakushū* 古田紹欽著作集, ed. Furuta Shōkin, 1:151–180. Tokyo: Kōdansha.

Garon, Sheldon. 1993a. Women's Groups and the Japanese State: Contending Approaches to Political Integration, 1890–1945. *Journal of Japanese Studies* 19 (1): 5–41.

———. 1993b. The World's Oldest Debate? Prostitution and the State in Imperial Japan, 1900–1945. *American Historical Review* 98 (3): 710–32.

———. 1994. Rethinking Modernization and Modernity in Japanese History: A Focus on State-Society Relations. *Journal of Asian Studies* 53 (2): 346–66.

———. 1997. *Molding Japanese Minds: The State in Everyday Life*. Princeton: Princeton University Press.

Gendai Kyōgaku Kenkyūkai 現代教学研究会, ed. 1991. *1990 Kenkyū hōkoku* 研究報告. Tokyo: Sōtōshū Shūmuchō Kyōgakubu.

Genkaku 玄覚. *Shinran jagi ketsu no kogi ketsu* 親鸞邪義決之虚偽決. SZS, 59:1–21.

Gombrich, Richard. 1994. A Buddhologist's Impression of Japanese Buddhism. In *Japanese New Religions in the West*, edited by P. B. Clarke and J. Somers. Sandgate, Folkstone, Kent: Japan Library (Curzon Press).

Gorai Shigeru 五来重. 1975. *Kōya hijiri* 高野聖. Tokyo: Kadokawa Shoten.

———. 1985. *Nihon no shomin Bukkyō* 日本の庶民仏教. Tokyo: Kadokawa Shoten.

Grapard, Allan G. 1984. Japan's Ignored Cultural Revolution: The Separation of Shintō and Buddhist Divinities in Meiji (*shinbutsu bunri*) and a Case Study: Tonomine. *History of Religions* 23 (February): 240–65.

Groner, Paul. 1984. *Saichō: The Establishment of the Japanese Tendai School*. Berkeley: Berkeley Buddhist Studies Series.

Guyau, M. (Jean-Marie). 1962. *The Non-Religion of the Future: A Sociological Study*. New York: Schocken Books.

Gyūsen 牛涎. 1901. Sōryo saitai o ronzu 僧侶妻帯を論ず. *Shin Bukkyō* 新佛教 9 (2): 417–21.

Haga Noboru 芳賀登 and Matsumoto Sannosuke 松本三之助, eds. 1971. *Kokugaku undō no shisō* 国学運動の思想. Vol. 51, *Nihon shisō taikei*. Tokyo: Iwanami Shoten.

Haga Shōji 羽賀祥二. 1981–82. Meiji Jingikansei no seiritsu to kokka saishi no saihen 明治神祇官制の成立と国家祭祀の再編. *Jinbun gakuhō* 49:27–84; 51:51–100.

———. 1984. Shintō kokkyōsei no keisei 神道国教制の形成. *Nihonshi kenkyū* 264:1–31.

———. 1985. Meiji kokka keiseiki no seikyō kankei—Kyōdōshokusei to kyōdan keisei 明治国家形成期の政教関係—教導職制と教団形成. *Nihonshi kenkyū* 271:114–38.

———. 1994a. "Meiji ishin to 'seihyō' no hensei" 明治維新と「政表」の編成. *Nihonshi kenkyū* 388: 49–74.

———. 1994b. *Meiji ishin to shūkyō* 明治維新と宗教. Tokyo: Chikuma Shobō.

Hall, John Carey. 1979. *Japanese Feudal Law*. Washington, DC: University Publications of America. Original edition 1906.

Hanazono Sesshin 花園摂信. 1974–83. Sesshin Shōnin kinnō gohō roku 摂信上人勤王護法録. In *Shinshū shiryō shūsei* 真宗史料集成, edited by Kashiwahara Yūsen et al., 11:82–239. Kyoto: Dōbōsha.

Hane, Mikiso. 1986. *Modern Japan: A Historical Survey*. Boulder: Westview Press.

Hanley, Susan B. 1991. Tokugawa Society: Material Culture, Standard of Living, and Life-Styles. In *The Cambridge History of Japan: The Early Modern Period*, edited by J. W. Hall, 4: 660–705. Cambridge: Cambridge University Press.

———. 1997. *Everyday Things in Premodern Japan: The Hidden Legacy of Material Culture*. Berkeley: University of California Press.

Harada Nobuo 原田信男. 1988. Shōjin ryōri to Nihon no shoku seikatsu 精進料理と日本の食生活. In *Gairai no shoku no bunka* 外来の食の文化, edited by Kumakura Isao 熊倉功夫 and Ishige Naomichi 石毛直道. Tokyo: Domesu Shuppan.

———. 1989. *Edo no ryōri shi* 江戸の料理史. Tokyo: Chūkō Shinsho.

———. 1993. *Rekishi no naka no kome to niku* 歴史のなかの米と肉. Tokyo: Heibonsha.

Hardacre, Helen. 1984. *Lay Buddhism in Contemporary Japan: Reiyūkai Kyōdan*. Princeton: Princeton University Press.

———. 1989a. The Lotus Sutra in Modern Japan. In *The Lotus Sutra in Japanese Culture*, edited by G. J. Tanabe, Jr., and W. J. Tanabe, 209–24. Honolulu: University of Hawaii Press.

———. 1989b. *Shintō and the State, 1868–1988*. Princeton: Princeton University Press.

Harootunian, H. D. 1970. *Toward Restoration: The Growth of Political Consciousness in Tokugawa Japan*. Berkeley and Los Angeles: University of California Press.

———. 1988. *Things Seen and Unseen: Discourse and Ideology in Tokugawa Nativism*. Chicago: University of Chicago Press.

Hattori Masao 服部荘夫. 1938. *Ōtori Sessō ō* 鴻雪爪翁. Tokyo: Kokyōkai.

Havens, Thomas R. H. 1975. Women and War in Japan, 1937–1945. *American Historical Review* 80 (4): 913–34.

Hendry, Joy. 1981. *Marriage in Changing Japan*. Rutland, VT: Charles E. Tuttle.

Hida Yoshifumi 飛田良文, ed. 1979. *Tetsugaku jii: Yakugo sōsakuin* 哲学字彙—訳語総索引. Tokyo: Kasama Shoin.

Hikita Seishun 疋田精俊. 1965. Jiin no seshūka jiki ni tsuite 寺院の世襲化時期について. *Shūkyō kenkyū* 186:101–2.

———. 1975. Bukkyō ni okeru hakai sō no shiteki kōsatsu 仏教における破戒僧の史的考察. *Taishō Daigaku kenkyū kiyō* 61:459–74.

———. 1991a. Shugendō shūdan no sezokusei 修験道集団の世俗性. *Taishō Daigaku kenkyū kiyō* 76:101–121.

———. 1991b. *Bukkyō shakaigaku kenkyū* 仏教社会学研究. Tokyo: Kokusho Kankōkai.

Hirata Atsushi 平田厚志. 1979a. Saigin kyōgaku no shisōshiteki igi 西吟教学の思想史的意義. *Dendōin kiyō* 22–23: 44–65.

———. 1979b. Eishōji Saigin cho "Kyakushō mondō" 永照寺西吟著『客照問答』. *Kinsei Bukkyō* 4 (1): 22–50.

———. 1996. Kinsei Honganji kyōdan ni okeru "shinzoku nitai" shisō no keisei 近世本願寺教団における「眞俗二諦」思想の形成. In *Shinshū to shakai* 真宗と社会, edited by Yamasaki Ryūmei 山崎龍明, 103–40. Tokyo: Daizō Shuppan.

Hori Ichirō 堀一郎. 1966. Sō no saitai to jiin no sezokuka 僧の妻帯と寺院の世俗化. In *Waga kuni minkan shinkō no kenkyū* 我国民間信仰の研究, edited by Hori Ichirō 堀一郎. Tokyo: Tōkyō Sōgensha, 1966.

Horn, David G. 1994. *Social Bodies: Science, Reproduction, and Italian Modernity*. Princeton Studies in Culture/Power/History. Princeton: Princeton University Press.

Hosaka Shinsai 保坂真哉. 1926. Jizoku hogo ni kansuru ketsuron 寺族保護に関する結論. *Kōsei* 1926: 1.

Howell, David L. 1995. The Prehistory of the Japanese Nation-State: Status, Ethnicity, and Boundaries. *Early Modern Japan* 5 (2): 19–24.

Hubbard, Jamie. 1998. Embarrassing Superstition, Doctrine, and the Study of New Religious Movements. *Journal of the American Academy of Religion* 66 (1): 59–92.

Ienaga, Saburō. 1965. Japan's Modernization and Buddhism. *Contemporary Religions in Japan* 6 (1): 1–41.

Iinuma Masamori 飯沼賢司. 1988. Uji to myōji to sei 氏と名字と姓. *Rekishi hyōron* 457:16–21.

Ikai Hōryō 猪飼法量. 1911. *Bōmori no oshie* 坊守のをしへ. Kyoto: Hōzōkan.

Ikeda Eishun 池田英俊. 1976a. *Meiji no Bukkyō—sono kōdō to shisō* 明治の仏教ーその行動と思想. Tokyo: Hyōronsha.

———. 1976b. *Meiji no shin Bukkyō undō* 明治の新仏教運動. Tokyo: Yoshikawa Kōbunkan.

———. 1990. Kindai Bukkyō no keisei to "nikujiki saitai ron" o meguru mondai 近代仏教の形成と肉食妻帯論をめぐる問題. In *Sōtōshū ni okeru zaike shūgaku no teishō*, edited by Yamauchi Shun'yū, 338–48. Tokyo: Daizō Shuppan.

———. 1994. *Meiji Bukkyō kyōkai/kessha shi no kenkyū* 明治佛教教会・結社史の研究. Tokyo: Tōsui Shobō.

———. 1998. Teaching Assemblies and Lay Societies in the Formation of Modern Sectarian Buddhism. *Japanese Journal of Religious Studies* 25 (1–2): 11–44.

Inagaki, Hisao. 1984. *A Dictionary of Japanese Buddhist Terms*. Kyoto: Nagata Bunshodo.

———. 1995. *The Three Pure Land Sutras: A Study and Translation from Chinese*. Kyoto: Nagata Bunshodo.

Inoue Enryō 井上円了. 1890. Saitai kinseishū shoshi ni nozomu 妻帯禁制宗諸師に望む. *Nihonjin* 41 (February 18): 587–88.

———. 1898. Nikujiki saitairon 肉食妻帯論. *Zenshū* 35:25–29.

Inoue Nobutaka 井上順孝 and Sakamoto Koremaru 坂本是丸, eds. 1987. *Nihon-gata seikyō kankei no tanjō* 日本型政教関係の誕生. Tokyo: Daiichi Shobō.

Irokawa Daikichi 色川大吉 and Gabe Masao 我部政男, eds. 1986–. *Meiji kenpakusho shūsei* 明治建白書集成. Tokyo: Chikuma Shobō.

Ishida Mizumaro 石田瑞麿. 1995. *Nyobon* 女犯. Tokyo: Chikuma Shobō.

Ishihara Giken 石原宜賢, ed. 1901. *Bukkyō no katei* 仏教の家庭. Kyoto: Hōzōkan.

Ishii Ryōsuke 石井良助, ed. 1959. *Kinsei hōsei shiryō sōsho* 近世法制史料叢書. 3 vols. Tokyo: Sōbunsha.

———. 1964. *Edo no keibatsu* 江戸の刑罰. Tokyo: Chūō Kōronsha.

———. 1981. *Ie to koseki no rekishi* 家と戸籍の歴史. Tokyo: Sōbunsha.

———. 1990. *Hitogoroshi/Mittsū* 人殺・密通. Tokyo: Meiseki Shoten.

Ishikawa Rikizan 石川力山. *Kinsei Bukkyō ni okeru nikujiki saitai ron* 近世仏教における肉食妻帯論. Manuscript.

———. *Sōtōshū ni okeru nisō no ichi to sono gendaiteki kadai* 曹洞宗における尼僧の位置とその現代的課題. Manuscript.

———. 1989. *Shinshū to Zenshū no aida* 真宗と禅宗の間. *Zengaku kenkyū* 67:79–109.

———. 1993. *Chūsei Bukkyō ni okeru ni no isō ni tsuite: toku ni shoki Sōtōshū kyōdan no jirei o chūshin to shite (Part 2)* 中世仏教における尼の位相について―特に初期曹洞宗教団の事例を中心として(下). *Komazawa Daigaku Zen Kenkyūsho nenpō* 4:63–80.

———. 1996. *Naikan Bunko shozō shiryō no kenkyū (2): Kōmori bōdanki/Jōkōki ni tsuite* 内館文庫所蔵資料の研究 (2)―『蝙蝠忘談記』・『攘蝗記』について. *Komazawa Daigaku Bukkyō Gakubu kenkyū kiyō* 54:57–46.

Izuya Denpachi Bunka Shinkō Zaidan 伊豆屋伝八文化振興財団, ed. 1999. *Henkaizan Fukyoraian* 遍界山不去来庵. Shizuoka: Izuya Denpachi Bunka Shinkō Zaidan.

Jaffe, Richard. 1990. Buddhist Clerical Marriage in Japan: Origins and Responses to the 1872 Nikujiki Saitai Law. Paper read at Fo Kuang Shan International Buddhist Conference, Gaohsiung, Taiwan.

———. 1991. *Ōtori Sessō to nikujiki saitai mondai* 鴻雪爪と肉食妻帯問題. *Shūgaku kenkyū* 33:89–92.

Jingū Shichō 神宮司庁, ed. 1977. *Kojiruien* 古事類苑, *Shūkyōbu* 宗教部. 4th ed. 4 vols. Tokyo: Yoshikawa Kōbunkan. Original edition 1896.

Jizoku hogo de momu 寺族保護でもむ. 1936. *Chūgai nippō* 11,041 (October 9): 2.

Jizoku—Hyakunen no kiseki 寺族―百年の軌跡. 1994. *Sōtōshū shūhō* 9:10–28; 10:2–35.

Jizoku no hiai 寺族の悲哀. 1925. *Kōsei*, November 3: 2.

Jōdoshū Daijiten Henshū Iinkai 浄土宗大辞典編集委員会, ed. 1980. *Jōdoshū daijiten* 浄土宗大辞典. 4 vols. Tokyo: Sankibō.

Jones, Charles Brewer. 1999. *Buddhism in Taiwan: Religion and the State, 1660–1990*. Honolulu: University of Hawaii Press.

Kamo Gi'ichi 加茂儀一. 1976. *Nihon chikusan shi: shokuniku/nyūraku hen* 日本畜産史―食肉・乳酪篇. Tokyo: Hōsei Daigaku Shuppan Kyoku.

Kanaoka Shūyū 金岡秀友. 1990. *Gendai "shukke" kō* 現代「出家」考. *Bukkyō taimusu*, March 25: 4; April 5: 4; April 15: 4.

Kashiwahara Yūsen 柏原祐泉. 1969. *Nihon kinsei kindai Bukkyōshi no kenkyū* 日本近世近代仏教史の研究. Kyoto: Heirakuji Shoten.

———. 1980. *Jiun "jūzenkai" no rekishiteki yakuwari* 慈雲「十善戒」の歴史的役割. *Indo tetsugaku Bukkyōgaku kenkyū* 29 (1): 83–88.

———. 1990. *Nihon Bukkyōshi: kindai* 日本仏教史―近代. Tokyo: Yoshikawa Kōbunkan.

Kashiwahara Yūsen 柏原祐泉 and Fujii Manabu 藤井学, eds. 1973. *Kinsei Bukkyō no shisō* 近世仏教の思想. *Nihon shisō taikei* 日本思想大系. Tokyo: Iwanami Shoten.

Katō, Shōshun. 1998. "A Lineage of Dullards": Zen Master Tōjū Reisō and His Associates. *Japanese Journal of Religious Studies* 25 (1–2): 151–65.

Katō Totsudō 加藤咄堂. 1933. Meiji jidai no zaike Bukkyō 明治時代の在家仏教. *Gendai Bukkyō*. Special issue devoted to Meiji Buddhism: 132–37.

Katsuki Jōkō 香月乗光. 1974. *Hōnen jōdokyō no shisō to rekishi* 法然浄土教の思想と歴史. Tokyo: Sankibō Busshorin.

Kawahashi, Noriko. 1995. Jizoku (Priest's Wives) in Sōtō Zen Buddhism: An Ambiguous Category. *Japanese Journal of Religious Studies* 22 (1–2): 161–83.

Kawahashi Noriko 川橋範子 and Kumamoto Einin 熊本英人. 1998. Jakusha no kuchi o karite nani o kataru no ka: Bukkyōkai no "josei no jinken" no katari o megutte 弱者の口を借りて何を語るのか—仏教界の「女性の人権」の語りをめぐって. *Gendai shisō* 26–27: 196–205.

Kawamura Seiji 川村精治. 1933. Jizoku hogo ni tsuite 寺族保護に就いて *Shūkyō gyōsei* 5:1–14.

Keenan, John. P. 1994. *How Master Mou Removes Our Doubts : A Reader-Response Study and Translation of the Mou-tzu Li-huo lun*. Albany: State University of New York Press.

Keimu Kyōkai 刑務協会, ed. 1943. *Nihon kinsei gyōkei shi kō* 日本近世行刑史稿. 2 vols. Tokyo: Gyōsei Kyōkai.

Kendall, Laurel. 1996. *Getting Married in Korea: Of Gender, Morality, and Modernity*. Berkeley: University of California Press.

Ketelaar, James Edward. 1990. *Of Heretics and Martyrs in Meiji Japan*. Princeton: Princeton University Press.

Kido Takayoshi 木戸孝允. 1932. *Kido Takayoshi nikki* 木戸孝允日記. 3 vols. *Nihon shiseki kyōkai sōsho* 日本史籍協会叢書. Tokyo: Tōkyō Daigaku Shuppankai.

Kishimoto, Hideo. 1956. *Japanese Religion in the Meiji Era*. Translated by J. F. Howes. Tokyo: Ōbunsha.

Kita Sadakichi 喜田貞吉. 1925. Sōni onju no ben 僧尼飲酒の弁. *Rekishi chiri* 46 (6): 512–20.

———. 1926. Nikujiki saitaishū no kenkyū 肉食妻帯宗の研究. *Rekishi chiri* 47 (1): 11–21; (5): 365–80.

———. 1933. Meiji Bukkyō ni okeru nikujiki saitai 明治仏教に於ける肉食妻帯. *Gendai Bukkyō*. Special issue devoted to Meiji Buddhism: 138–50.

Kitagawa Chikai 北川智海. 1933. Meiji Bukkyō to kairitsu 明治仏教と戒律. *Gendai Bukkyō*. Special issue devoted to Meiji Buddhism: 283–86.

Kitagawa, Joseph M. 1966. *Religion in Japanese History*. New York: Columbia University Press.

Kobayashi Masamori 小林正盛, ed. 1936. *Ōtori Sessō ō san'urō shibunshō* 鴻雪爪翁山雨樓詩文鈔. Tokyo: Shin no Nipponsha.

Kodama Kōta 児玉幸多. 1963. Mibun to kazoku 身分と家族. In *Iwanami kōza Nihon rekishi* 岩波講座日本歴史, edited by Ienaga Saburō 家永三郎 et al. Tokyo: Iwanami Shoten.

Kōdansha, ed. 1993. *Japan: An Illustrated Encyclopedia*. 2 vols. Tokyo: Kōdansha.

Koizumi Ryōtai 小泉了諦. 1927. *Mondō kaisetsu Shinshū katei kōwa* 問答解説眞宗家庭講話. Kyoto: Kendō Shoin.

Kokugakuin Daigaku Nihon Bunka Kenkyūsho 国学院大学日本文化研究所. 1994. *Shintō jiten* 神道事典. 1st ed. Tokyo: Kōbundō.

Kokuritsu Kokkai Toshokan 国立国会図書館. 1983. *Shaji torishirabe ruisan* 社寺取調類纂. 68 microfilm reels. Tokyo: Yūshōdō Fuirumu Shuppan.

Kokushi Daijiten Henshū Iinkai 國史大辭典編集委員会, ed. 1979. *Kokushi Daijiten* 國史大辭典. 15 vols. Tokyo: Yoshikawa Kōbunkan.

Kosekiryō 戸籍寮, ed. 1874. *Meiji gonen Nihon zenkoku kosekihyō* 明治五年日本全国戸籍表. Tokyo: Kosekiryō.

Küchler, L. W. 1885. Marriage in Japan: Including a Few Remarks on the Marriage Ceremony, the Position of Married Women, and Divorce. *Transactions of the Asiatic Society of Japan* 13:114–37.

Kuga Etsugan 陸鉞巖. 1907. Sōryo kinshu ron 僧侶禁酒論. *Shūkyōkai* 宗教界 3 (11): 5–6.

Kumagai Kaisaku 熊谷開作. 1987. *Nihon no kindaika to "ie" seido* 日本の近代化と「家」制度. Kyoto: Hōritsu Bunkasha.

Kumamoto Einin 熊本英人. 1991. Kuriyama Taion cho "Sōryo kazoku ron" ni tsuite 栗山泰音著「僧侶家族論」について. *Sōtōshū Shūgaku Kenkyūsho kiyō* 4:101–10.

———. 1994. Sōtōshū gikai ni miru "jizoku" mondai: Shōwa 11 nen "Sōtōshū jizoku hogo kitei" happu made 曹洞宗議会にみる「寺族」問題―昭和十一年「曹洞宗寺族保護規程」発布まで. *Sōtōshū Shūgaku Kenkyūsho kiyō* 8: 99–112.

———. 1995. Sōtōshū ni okeru "jizoku" no go ni tsuite 曹洞宗における寺族の語について. *Shūgaku kenkyū* 37:16–32.

———. 1996. Sōtōshū Gikai ni miru kindai Sōtōshū no shikō—shukke kyōdan no kattō (1) 曹洞宗議会に見る近代曹洞宗の志向―出家教団の葛藤（一）. *Sōtōshū Shūgaku Kenkyūsho kiyō* 10:15–24.

———. 1997 *Tōjō kōron to Kōsei* 『洞上公論』と『公正』. *Sōtōshū Shūgaku Kenkyūsho kiyō* 11:251–58.

Kurihara Chijō 栗原智静 and Date Shingi 伊達信毅. 1874. Kyūshugen ki'nyū kisoku kaisei no gi 旧修験帰入規則改正の議. MKP, 3:475–76.

Kurita Mototsugu 栗田元次. 1976. *Edo jidai shi* 江戸時代史. 2 vols. Tokyo: Kondō Shuppansha.

Kuriyama Taion 栗山泰音. 1917. *Sōryo kazoku ron* 僧侶家族論. Tokyo: Ōju Gedō.

———. 1918. *Shūmon zaisei ron* 宗門財政論. Tokyo: Ōju Gedō.

Kuroda Toshio 黒田俊雄. 1980a. Chūsei jisha seiryoku ron 中世寺社勢力論. In *Iwanami kōza Nihon rekishi: Chūsei 2* 岩波講座日本歴史―中世 2, 6: 245–95. Tokyo: Iwanami Shoten.

———. 1980b. *Jisha seiryoku* 寺社勢力. Tokyo: Iwanami Shoten.

———. 1981. Shinto in the History of Japanese Religion. *Journal of Japanese Studies* 7 (1) (Winter): 1–21.

———. 1983. *Ōbō to Buppō* 王法と仏法. Kyoto: Hōzōkan.

Kuruma Takudō 来馬琢道. 1917. Butsuzen kekkon shikiji oyobi shikai 仏前結婚式次及私解. *Chūgai nippō* (May 11): 1.

———. 1925. Iwayuru jizoku mondai 所謂寺族問題. *Tōjō kōron* 2 (February 10): 1–2.

———, ed. 1934. *Gaitō no Bukkyō* 街頭の仏教. Tokyo: Bukkyōsha.

———. 1956. *Zenmon hōkan* 禅門宝鑑. Tokyo: Kōmeisha.

Kuruma Tatsu 来馬たつ. 1933. Meiji Bukkyō to fujin undō 明治仏教と婦人運動. *Gendai Bukkyō* 105:260–65.

Kusanagi Zengi 草繁全宜, ed. 1913. *Shaku Unshō* 釈雲照. 3 vols. Tokyo: Toku-kyōkai.

Kyoto Fujin Kyōkai Jimusho 京都婦人教会事務所, ed. 1891. *Futoku no kōryō* 婦徳の綱領. Kyoto: Kyōto Fujin Kyōkai Zōhan.

Laidlaw, James. 1995. *Riches and Renunciation: Religion, Economy, and Society among the Jains*. Oxford Studies in Social and Cultural Anthropology. Oxford: Clarendon Press.

Lee, Edwin B. 1975. Nichiren and Nationalism: The Religious Patriotism of Tanaka Chigaku. *Monumenta Nipponica* 20 (1): 19–35.

Legge, James. 1900. *The Sacred Books and Early Literature of the East*. Vol. 11, *Ancient China*. New York: Parke, Austin, and Lipscomb.

McMullen, I. J. 1987. Rulers or Fathers? A Casuistical Problem in Early Modern Japanese Thought. *Past and Present* 116:56–97.

McMullin, Neil. 1984. *Buddhism and the State in Sixteenth-Century Japan*. Princeton: Princeton University Press.

———. 1989. Historical and Historiographical Issues in the Study of Pre-Modern Japanese Religions. *Japanese Journal of Religious Studies* 16 (1): 3–40.

Maruyama-sei 丸山生. 1911. Sōryo saitai ron 僧侶妻帯論. *Wayūshi* 15 (10): 848–53.

Masutani Bun'yū 増谷文雄. 1942. *Gyōkai shōnin* 行誡上人. Tokyo: Hōnen Shōnin Sankōkai.

Matono Hansuke 的野半介. 1968. *Etō Nanpaku* 江藤南白. Vol. 73, *Meiji hyaku-nenshi sōsho*. Tokyo: Hara Shobō.

Matsura Eibun 松浦英文. 1976. Kuriyama Taion Zenji 栗山泰音禅師. *Chōryū* (March): 4–9.

May, Herbert G., and Bruce M. Metzger, eds. 1977. *The New Oxford Annotated Bible*. New York: Oxford University Press.

Meiji Bukkyō Shisō Shiryō Shūsei Henshū Iinkai 明治仏教思想資料集成編集委員会, ed. 1982. *Meiji Bukkyō shisō shiryō shūsei* 明治仏教思想資料集成. 8 vols. Tokyo: Dōbōsha Shuppan.

Mencius. 1970. *Mencius*. Translated by D. C. Lau. Harmondsworth, England: Penguin Books.

Métraux, Daniel A. 1995. *The Soka Gakkai Revolution*. Lanham, MD: University Press of America.

Minami Danzō 南断三. 1878. Shingonshū rokuji o yomu 真言宗録事を読む. *MKS* 291: 1–4.

Mine Genkō 峯玄光 1911. *Bukkyō katei kyōkun* 仏教家庭教訓. Tokyo: Kōmeisha.

Mio Tōkan 三尾透関, ed. 1937. *Shinsen Sōtōshū jūyō hōkishū* 新撰曹洞宗重要法規集. Tokyo: Kōseisha.

Miura Gorō 三浦梧楼. 1897. *Sōfuku kaisei ron* 僧服改正論. Tokyo: Miura Gorō.

Miura, Kiyohiro. 1996. *He's Leaving Home: My Young Son Becomes a Zen Monk*. Translated by J. Shore. Rutland, VT: Charles E. Tuttle.

Miyachi Masato 宮地正人. 1988. Shūkyō kankei hōrei ichiran 宗教関係法令一覧. In *Shūkyō to kokka*, edited by Yasumaru Yoshio and Miyachi Masato. Tokyo: Iwanami Shoten.

Miyagi Kimiko 宮城公子. 1977. *Ōshio Heihachirō* 大塩平八郎. Tokyo: Asahi Shinbunsha.

Miyake Hitoshi 宮家準. 1978. *Shugendō* 修験道. Tokyo: Kyōikusha.

Miyazaki Eishū 宮崎英修, ed. 1978. *Nichiren jiten* 日蓮辞典. Tokyo: Tōkyōdō Shuppan.

Mizuno Kōgen 水野弘元, ed. 1987. *Butten kaidai jiten* 仏典解題事典. 2d ed. Tokyo: Shunjūsha.

Mochizuki Shindō 望月信道, ed. 1942. *Gyōkai shōnin zenshū* 行誡上人全集. Tokyo: Daitō Shuppansha.

Mochizuki Shinkō 望月信亨, ed. 1957. *Bukkyō daijiten* 仏教大辞典. 10 vols. Revised and enlarged edition. Tokyo: Sekai Seiten Kankō Kyōkai.

Morinaga, Sōkō. 1993. Celibacy: The View of a Zen Monk from Japan. In *For Love Alone: Reflections on Priestly Celibacy*. Middlegreen, UK: St. Pauls.

Morioka Kiyomi 森岡清美. 1978. *Shinshū kyōdan to "ie" seido* 真宗教団と「家」制度. Kyoto: Sōbunsha.

———. 1984. Mibun kara shokubun e—Meiji ishinki no hōsei kaikaku ni miru sōni no sezokuka 身分から職分へ—明治維新期の法制改革にみる僧尼の世俗化. In *Shūkyō bunka no shosō* 宗教文化の諸相, edited by Takenaka Shinjō hakushi shōju kinen ronbunshū kankōkai 竹中信常博士頌寿記念論文集刊行会, 371–87. Tokyo: Sankibō.

———. 1986. Ichigenteki mibunsei no seiritsu—Meiji ishinki ni okeru sōni mibun no kaitai ni tsuite 一元的身分制の成立—明治維新期における僧尼身分解体について. *Nihon jōmin bunka kiyō* 日本常民文化紀要 12 (February): 123–38.

———. 1995. Meiji shoki ni okeru sōni no kaitai ni tsuite 明治初期における僧尼の解体について. *Nihon kindai Bukkyōshi kenkyū* 2: 1–22.

Morohashi Tetsuji 諸橋轍次, ed. 1955–60. *Dai kanwa jiten* 大漢和辞典. 13 vols. Tokyo: Taishūkan Shoten.

Mura to mura no shōtotsu 村と村の衝突. 1893. *MKS*, October 2: 5–6.

Murakami Shigeyoshi 村上重良. 1976. *Butsuryū kaidō Nagamatsu Nissen* 仏立開導長松日扇. Tokyo: Kōdansha.

———. 1980. *Japanese Religion in the Modern Century*. Translated by H. Byron Earhart. Tokyo: University of Tokyo Press.

Muta, Kazue. 1994. Images of the Family in Meiji Journals: The Paradox Underlying the Emergence of the "Home." *U. S.-Japan Women's Journal, English Supplement* 7:53–71.

Myōdō-ken yori sōryo nikujiki saitai no gi ni tsuki ukagau 名東県ヨリ僧侶肉食妻帯の儀に付伺. *STR*, 182.

Myōshinji-ha, Shin shūsei shikō e 妙心寺派、新宗制施行へ. 1961. *Chūgai nippō*, March 7: 4.

Naimushō 内務省, ed. 1992. *Nihon jinkō tōkei shūsei* 日本人口統計集成. 7 vols. Tokyo: Tōyō Shorin.

Nakajima Michio 中島三千男. 1972. Taikyō senpu undō to saijin ronsō 大教宣布運動と祭神論争. *Nihonshi kenkyū* 126:26–67.

Nakamura Hajime. 1960. *The Ways of Thinking of Eastern Peoples*. Tokyo: Japan Government Printing Bureau.

Nakamura Hajime 中村元, Fukunaga Mitsuji 福永光司, Tamura Yoshirō 田村芳郎, and Konno Tōru 今野達, eds. 1989. *Iwanami Bukkyō jiten* 岩波仏教辞典. Tokyo: Iwanami Shoten.

Nakamura Yukihiko 中村幸彦, Okami Masao 岡見正雄, and Sakakura Atsuyoshi 坂倉篤義, eds. 1982–99. *Kadokawa kogo daijiten* 角川古語大辞典. 4 vols. Tokyo: Kadokawa Shoten.

Nakano Yūshin (Yūko) 中野優信 (優子). 1994. Sōtōshū ni okeru sōryo no kon'in to seisabetsu 曹洞宗における僧侶の婚姻と性差別. *Sōtōshū Shūgaku Kenkyūsho kiyō* 8:127–39.

Nakazato Nisshō 中里日勝. 1899. *Sōfū kakushin ron: ichimei chikusai jōbutsu gi* 僧風革新論――一名蓄妻成仏義. Tokyo: Banjudō.

Nattier, Jan. 1991. *Once Upon a Future Time: Studies in Buddhist Prophecy of Decline*. Berkeley: Asian Humanities Press.

Nichiren Shōshū to Sōka Gakkai no konpon mondai 日蓮正宗と創価学会の根本問題. 1991. *Chūgai nippō*, January 14: 3; January 30: 3.

Nichirenshū Jiten Kankō Iinkai 日蓮宗事典刊行委員会, ed. 1981. *Nichirenshū jiten* 日蓮宗事典. Tokyo: Nichirenshū Shūmuin.

Nichirenshū rokuji 日蓮宗録事. 1898. *MKS*, 596:2–3.

Nihon Bukkyō Jinmei Jiten Hensan Iinkai 日本仏教人名辞典編纂委員会, ed. 1992. *Nihon Bukkyō jinmei jiten* 日本仏教人名辞典. Tokyo: Hōzōkan.

Nihon Bukkyō ni okeru shō to zoku 日本仏教における聖と俗. 1991. *Chūgai Nippō* 24,392 (February 4): 3.

Nihon Daijiten Kankōkai 日本大辞典刊行会, ed. 1979. *Nihon kokugo daijiten* 日本国語大辞典. 1972, 1st shukusatsuban ed. 10 vols. Tokyo: Shōgakkan.

Nihon Shiseki Kyōkai 日本史籍協会, ed. 1973. *Hyakukan rireki* 百官履歴. 2 vols. *Nihon Shiseki Kyōkai Sōsho*. Tokyo: Tokyo University Press. Original edition 1928.

Nikujiki saitai mondai o kesseyo 肉食妻帯問題を決せよ. 1901. *Wayūshi* 58 (2): 2–4.

Ninnaji sō no Myōdō-ken junkai ni tsuki tatsuan 仁和寺僧ノ名東県巡回ニ付達案. STR, 182.

Nishiari Bokusan 西有穆山 1875. Sōtōshū rokuji 曹洞宗録事. *MKS*, 150:1–2.

Nishiguchi Junko 西口順子. 1987. *Onna no chikara: Kodai no josei to Bukkyō* 女の力―古代の女性と仏教. Tokyo: Heibonsha.

Nitta Hitoshi 新田均. 1987. Meiji kenpō seiteiki no seikyō kankei—Inoue Kowashi no kōsō to Naimushō no seisaku o chūshin ni 明治憲法制定期の政教関係―井上毅の構想と内務省の政策を中心に. In *Nihongata seikyō kankei no tanjō*, edited by Inoue Nobutaka and Sakamoto Koremaru, 145–98. Tokyo: Daiichi Shobō.

Nolte, Sharon H., and Sally Ann Hastings. 1991. The Meiji State's Policy toward Women, 1890–1910. In *Recreating Japanese Women, 1600–1945*, edited by G. L. Bernstein, 15–74. Princeton: Princeton University Press.

Oda Tokunō 織田得能, ed. 1954. *Bukkyō daijiten* 仏教大辞典. Revised and enlarged edition. Tokyo: Daizō Shuppan. Original edition 1917.

Odawara Toshihito 小田原利仁, ed. 1993. *Toshi danshinto no shūkyō ishiki* 都市檀信徒の宗教意識. Tokyo: Sōtōshū Shūmuchō.

Ōhashi Shunnō 大橋俊雄. 1987. *Jōdoshū kindai hyakunenshi nenpyō* 浄土宗近代百年史年表. Tokyo: Tōyō Bunka Shuppan.

———, ed. 1971. *Hōnen Ippen* 法然一遍. Vol. 10, *Nihon shisō taikei* 日本思想大系. Tokyo: Iwanami Shoten.

Ōishi Shinsaburō 大石慎三郎. 1959. Edo jidai ni okeru koseki ni tsuite—sono seiritsu to seikaku no kentō 江戸時代における戸籍について―その成立と性格の検討. In *Koseki seido to "ie" seido*, edited by Fukushima Masao. Tokyo: Tōkyō Daigaku Shuppankai.

Okada Masahiko. 1997. Vision and Reality: Buddhist Cosmographic Discourse in Nineteenth-Century Japan. Ph.D. dissertation, Stanford University.

Okamura Shūsatsu 岡村周薩, ed. 1972. *Shinshū daijiten* 真宗大辞典. 3 vols. Kyoto: Nagata Bunshōdō.

Okitsu Daizō 沖津大象. 1925. Jiin kazokuhō ni tsuite 寺院家族法に就いて. *Kōsei* 1 (June): 3; 3 (August): 3; 4 (September): 4; 5 (October): 2.

Ōkubo Dōshū 大久保道舟. Meiji Bukkyō no saiken to koji no katsuyaku 明治仏教の再建と居士の活躍. *Kōza kindai Bukkyō* 2 (1961): 232–39.

———, ed. 1989. *Dōgen Zenji zenshū* 道元禅師全集. 2 vols. Kyoto: Rinsen Shoten. Original edition 1970.

Okumura Dōrin 奥村洞鱗. 1925. Jizoku hogohō ni tsuite 寺族保護法に就いて. *Kōsei* 10:2.

Ono Genmyō 小野玄妙. 1932–36. *Bussho kaisetsu daijiten* 仏書解説大辞典. 12 vols. Tokyo: Daitō Shuppansha.

Ontake gyōja kōkyo shinnyū jiken 御岳行者皇居侵入事件, in *Shūkyō to kokka*, edited by Yasumaru Yoshio and Miyachi Masato, 168–77. Tokyo: Iwanami Shoten.

Ōtori Sessō 鴻雪爪. 1891 *Shidankai sokkiroku* 史談会速記録, July 13.

———. 1903. *Sankō suichō zuki* 山高水長図記. Tokyo: Ōtori Setsunen.

———. 1936. Ōtori Sessō jijoden 鴻雪爪自叙伝. *Chūgai Nippō*. November 15: 8; November 17: 8; November 18; 8; November 19; 8; November 20: 8.

Ōtsuki Mikio 大槻幹郎, Katō Shōshun 加藤正俊, and Hayashi Yukimitsu 林雪光, eds. 1988. *Ōbaku bunka jinmei jiten* 黄檗人名辞典. Kyoto: Shibunkaku.

Ōuchi Seiran 大内青巒. 1886. Fūfu dōhan no riyaku o ronzu 夫婦同伴の利益を論ず. *Kyōgaku ronshū* 29 (May): 18–21.

Ozment, Steven. 1972. Marriage and the Ministry in the Protestant Churches. In *Celibacy in the Church*, edited by W. Bassett and P. Huizing. New York: Herder and Herder.

Phillipi, Donald L., tr. 1969. *Kojiki*. Tokyo: Tokyo University Press and Princeton University Press.

Reader, Ian. 1991. *Religion in Contemporary Japan*. Honolulu: University of Hawaii Press.

———. 1993. Buddhism as a Religion of the Family: Contemporary Images in Sōtō Zen. In *Religion and Society in Modern Japan: Selected Readings*, edited by M. R. Mullins, S. Shimazono, and P. L. Swanson. Berkeley: Asian Humanities Press.

Rhodes, Robert. F. 1980. Saichō's Mappō Tōmyōki: The Candle of the Latter Dharma. *Eastern Buddhist* n.s. 13 (1): 79–103.

Risshō Daigaku Nichiren Kyōgaku Kenkyūjo 立正大学日蓮教学研究所, ed. 1988. *Shōwa teihon Nichiren Shōnin ibun* 昭和定本日蓮聖人遺文. 4 vols. Minobuchō: Minobusan Kuonji. Original edition 1952–59.

Robinson, Richard H. 1966. The Ethic of the Householder Bodhisattva. *Bhāratī* (Bulletin of the College of Indology, Banaras Hindu University) 9: 25–56.

Ronsetsu 論説. 1875. *MKS*, 153:1–3.

Saigin 西吟. *Kyakushō mondō shū* 客照問答集. In Hirata (1979b).

Sakai, Robert K., ed. 1975. *The Status System and Social Organization of Satsuma: A Translation of the Shūmon Tefuda Aratame Jōmoku*. Tokyo: University of Tokyo Press.

Sakamoto Koremaru 坂本是丸. 1979. Kyōbushō setchi no ichi kōsatsu: Shintō kokkyōka seisaku no tenkai o chūshin ni 教部省設置の一考察—神道国教化制作の展開を中心に. *Kokugakuin Daigaku Nihon Bunka Kenkyūjo kiyō* 44:89–140.

———. 1981. Saisei itchi o meguru Sain no "seikyō" ronsō 祭政一致をめぐる左院の「政教」論争. *Kokugakuin zasshi* 82 (10): 15–31.

———. 1983. Meiji shoki ni okeru seikyō mondai—Sain/Kyōbushō to Shinshū kyōdan o chūshin ni 明治初期における政教問題—左院・教部省と真宗教団を中心に. *Shūkyō kenkyū* 57 (3): 47–68.

———. 1984. Ujiko shirabe to koseki hō/minpō 氏子調べと戸籍法・民法. *Kokugakuin zasshi* 85 (8): 26–44.

———. 1986. Meiji shoki no kenpaku seido to seiji jijō 明治初期の建白制度と政治事情. *Meiji kenpakusho shūsei geppō* 3:1–4.

———. 1987. "Nihongata seikyō kankei no keisei katei" 日本型政教関係の形成過程. In *Nihongata seikyō kankei no tanjō*, edited by Inoue Nobutaka and Sakamoto Koremaru, 5–82. Tokyo: Daiichi Shobō.

———. 1993. *Meiji ishin to kokugakusha* 明治維新と国学者. Tokyo: Taimeidō.

———. 1994. *Kokka Shintō keisei katei no kenkyū* 国家神道形成過程の研究. Tokyo: Iwanami Shoten.

———. 1996. Meiji ikō jinja saishi seido ni tsuite (1) 明治以降神社祭祀制度について (一). *Kyōgaku kenkyūjo kiyō* 1:1–40.

Sakurai Keiyū 桜井景雄. 1954. *Zoku Nanzenji shi* 続南禅寺史. Kyoto: Daihonzan Nanzenji.

Sakurai Shūyū 桜井秀雄. 1966. Kindai shūdan no ayumi (3) 近代宗団の歩み (三). *Shūhō* 371:46–48.

Samuel, Geoffrey. 1993. *Civilized Shamans: Buddhism in Tibetan Societies*. Washington, DC: Smithsonian Institution Press.

Sand, Jordan. 1998. At Home in the Meiji Period: Inventing Japanese Domesticity. In *Mirror of Modernity: Invented Traditions of Modern Japan*, edited by Stephen Vlastos, 191–207. Berkeley: University of California Press.

Sasaki Kunimaro 佐々木邦麿. 1967. Kinsei Tōhoku ni okeru Tendai kyōdan no dōkō 近世東北における天台教団の動向. *Tendai gakuhō* 10:64–66.

———. 1969. Kinsei jiin ni okeru saitaisō no toriatsukai ni tsuite 近世寺院における妻帯僧の取扱について. *Tendai gakuhō* 12:141–44.

Sasaki Makoto 佐々木真. 1970. Jiin hatto to Honganji 寺院法度と本願寺. *Shigaku* 43 (1–2): 191–201.

Satō, Hiroo. 1999. Nichiren's View of Nation and Religion. *Japanese Journal of Religious Studies* 26 (3–4): 307–23.

Sawada, Janine. 1998. Political Waves in the Zen Sea: The Engaku-ji Circle in Early Meiji Japan. *Japanese Journal of Religious Studies* 25 (1–2): 117–50.

Scripture of the Lotus Blossom of the Fine Dharma (The Lotus Sūtra). 1976. Translated by L. Hurvitz. New York: Columbia University Press.

Seshū kōtei no gotoki: Myōshinji zokurei seitei hōan 世襲肯定の如き一妙心寺族例制定法案. 1937. *Chūgai Nippō* 11,196 (December 16): 4.

Shaku Unshō 釈雲照. 1873a. Sōfū risei kengen 僧風釐正建言. MKP, 2: 917–18.

———. 1873b. Sōritsu no gi 僧律の議. MKP, 2:945–46.

Sharf, Robert H. 1993. The Zen of Japanese Nationalism. *History of Religions* 33 (1): 1–43.

———. 1995. Sanbōkyōdan: Zen and the Way of the New Religions. *Japanese Journal of Religious Studies* 22 (3–4): 417–58.

Shidankai 史談会, ed. *Shidankai sokkiroku* 史談会速記録. 1972. 46 vols. Tokyo: Hara Shobō. Originally published 1892–1938.

Shihōshō yori sōryo no gi ni tsuki kakariai 司法省ヨリ僧侶之儀ニ付掛合. In STR, 150.

Shimaji Mokurai 島地黙雷. 1890. Inoue Enryō shi ga "saitai kinseishū shoshi ni nozomu" no bun o yonde sara ni kinseishū shoshi ni nozomu 井上円了氏が「妻帯禁制宗諸師に望む」の文を読んで更に禁制宗諸師に望む. *Nihonjin* 42:636–37.

———. 1871. *Kyōbushō kaisetsu seigansho* 教部省開設請願書, in *Shūkyō to kokka*, edited by Yasumaru Yoshio and Miyachi Masato, 231–43. Tokyo: Iwanami Shoten.

Shimano Teishō 島野禎祥. 1934. *Jōdoshū jiin keizai chōsa hōkoku gaiyō* 浄土宗寺院経済調査報告概要. Tokyo: Jōdo Shūmusho Shakaika.

Shimoda Masahiro 下田正弘. 1989. "Sanshu no jōniku" saikō—buha ni okeru nikujiki seigen no hōkō「三種の浄肉」再考一部派における肉食制限の方向. *Bukkyō bunka* 22 (25): 1–21.

———. 1990. Higashi Ajia Bukkyō no kairitsu no tokushoku: nikujiki kinshi no yurai o megutte 東アジア仏教の戒律の特色一肉食禁止之由来をめぐって. *Tōyō gakujutsu kenkyū* 29 (4): 98–110.

Shimonaka Yasaburō 下中弥三郎, ed. 1939. *Shintō daijiten* 神道大辞典. 3 vols. Tokyo: Heibonsha.

Shin'yō 真陽. *Kindan Nichiren gi* 禁断日蓮義. Manuscript in the Ryūkoku University Library, Catalog #2812/8/11.

Shingonshū rokuji 真言宗録事. 1876. MKS, 251 (March 7): 1–2.

Shingonshū rokuji 真言宗録事. 1878. MKS, 592 (February 10): 2.

Shinmura Izuru 新村出, ed. 1991. *Kōjien* 広辞苑. 4th ed. Tokyo: Iwanami Shoten.

Shinshū Shōgyō Zensho Hensanjo 真宗聖教全書編纂所, ed. 1940–41. *Shinshū shōgyō zensho* 真宗聖教全書. 5 vols. Kyoto: Kōkyō Shoin.

Shintō jinmei jiten 神道人名辞典. 1986. Tokyo: Jinja Shinpōsha.

Shūkyōshi Kenkyūkai 宗教史研究会, ed. 1964. *Shaji torishirabe ruisan mokuroku* 社寺取調類纂目録. Tokyo: Shūkyōshi Kenkyūkai Shūmukyoku.

Silber, Ilana Friedrich. 1981. Dissent Through Holiness: The Case of the Radical Renouncer in Theravåda Buddhist Countries. *Numen* 28 (2): 164–93.

Sitcawich, Sumiko Otsubo. 1997. Eugenics in Modern Japan: Some Ironies of Modernity, 1883–1945. Ph.D. dissertation, The Ohio State University.

Sōboku 僧樸. *Bōmori saisoku no hōgo* 坊守催促の法語. Manuscript in the Ryūkoku University Library, 1775, Catalog no. 024.3/511/1.

Solomon, Michael. 1974. Kinship and the Transmission of Religious Charisma: The Case of Honganji. *Journal of Asian Studies* 33 (3): 403–13.

―――. 1997. *Rennyo and the Rise of Honganji: Shin Buddhism and Society in Medieval Japan*. Los Angeles: Pure Land Publications.

Sommerville, C. John. 1992. *The Secularization of Early Modern England: From Religious Culture to Religious Faith*. Oxford: Oxford University Press.

Sonoda, Kōyū. 1993. Early Buddha Worship. In *The Cambridge History of Japan, Ancient Japan*, edited by Delmer. M. Brown, 359–414. Cambridge: Cambridge University Press.

Sōryo henseki ken Seiin gian. 僧侶編籍件正院議案. STR, 150.

Sōryo henseki no gi ni tsuki 僧侶編籍之儀ニ付. STR, 150.

Sōryo myōji shintei no ikken 僧侶苗字新定の一件. 1913. *Bukkyō shigaku* 3 (4): 56–58.

Sōryo saitai mondai 僧侶妻帯問題. 1917. *Chūgai nippō* (October 6–9): 1; 1; 1.

Sōtōshū katoki no ōnō 曹洞宗過渡期の懊悩. 1936. *Chūgai nippō* 11,046 (October 15): 2.

Sōtōshū Shūmuchō Kyōgakubu 曹洞宗宗務庁教学部, ed. 1989. *Sōtōshū gyōji kihan* 曹洞宗行持軌範. Tokyo: Sōtōshū Shūmuchō.

Sōtōshū Shūmukyoku 曹洞宗宗務局, ed. 1899. *Genkō Sōtōshū seiki taizen* 現行曹洞宗制規大全. Tokyo: Kōmeisha.

Staggs, Kathleen. 1979. In Defense of Buddhism. Ph.D. dissertation, Princeton University.

Stone, Jackie. 1985. Seeking Enlightenment in the Last Age: Mappō Thought in Kamakura Buddhism. *Eastern Buddhist* 18 (1): 28–56; (2): 35–64.

―――. 1994. Meiji Buddhism and the "Nationalizing of Nichiren." Paper read at Meiji Studies Conference, Cambridge, MA.

―――. 1995. Medieval Tendai Hongaku Thought and the New Kamakura Buddhism: A Reconsideration. *Japanese Journal of Religious Studies* 22 (1–2): 17–48.

Sugimura Jūō 杉村縦横. 1901. Sōryo no saitai o nanzu 僧侶の妻帯を難ず. *Shin Bukkyō* 10 (2): 452–55.

Suzuki Daisetsu 鈴木大拙. 1900a. Seiyoku ron 性欲論. *Nihonjin* 126:25–27; 127:22–25; 129:20–24.

―――. 1900b. Beikoku tsūshin (Sōryo no nikujiki ni tsukite) 米国通信 (僧侶の肉食に就きて). In *Suzuki Daisetsu zenshū* 鈴木大拙全集. Tokyo, Iwanami Shoten. 27:415–18.

―――. 1911. Katei no mondai 家庭の問題. *Shin Bukkyō* 12 (4) (1911): 307–13.

―――. 1968. *Suzuki Daisetsu zenshū* 鈴木大拙全集. 32 vols. Tokyo: Iwanami Shoten.

Suzuki Shin'ichi 鈴木晋一. 1985. Momonjiya ももんじ屋. *Dai hyakka jiten* 大百科事典. Tokyo: Heibonsha. 14:986.

Suzuki, Shunryu. 1970. *Zen Mind, Beginner's Mind: Informal Talks on Zen Meditation and Practice*. New York: Weatherhill.

Taishū no saitai mondai 台宗の妻帯問題. 1917. *Chūgai nippō* (August 2): 3.

Takagi Hiroo 高木宏夫. 1959a. Gōsha teisoku to koseki hō 郷社定則と戸籍法. In *Koseki seido to "ie" seido*, edited by Fukushima Masao, 320–38. Tokyo: Tōkyō Daigaku Shuppankai.

———. 1959b. Shūkyō hō 宗教法. In *Kōza Nihon kindai hō hattatsu shi* 講座日本近代法発達史, edited by Fukushima Masao et al., 1–36. Tokyo: Keisō Shobō.

Takakusu Junjirō 高楠順次郎 and Watanabe Kaigyoku 渡辺海旭, eds. 1924–34. *Taishō shinshū daizōkyō* 大正新脩大蔵経. Tokyo: Taishō Daizōkyō Kankōkai.

Takano Toshihiko 高埜利彦. 1989. *Kinsei Nihon no kokka kenryoku to shūkyō* 近世日本の国家権力と宗教. Tokyo: Tōkyō Daigaku Shuppankai.

Takaoka Zōryū 高岡増隆. 1871. Myōōin Zōryū shūhei kaisei kengen 妙王院増隆宗弊改正建言. NBK, 4:398–402.

Takashi Etsugan 陸鉞巌. 1907. Sōryo kinshu ron 僧侶禁酒論. *Shūkyōkai* 3 (11): 5–6.

Takeda Chōshū 竹田聴洲. 1976. *Nihonjin no ie to shūkyō* 日本人の家と宗教. Tokyo: Hyōronsha.

Takeda Taijun 武田泰淳. 1975. Igyō no mono 異形の者. In *Takeda Taijun shū* 武田泰淳集, 437–63. Tokyo: Chikuma Shobō.

Takeshima Kan 竹島寛. 1926. Jiin no shishi sōzoku to kettō sōzoku 寺院の師資相続と血統相続. *Shigaku zasshi* 史学雑誌 37 (12): 1128–72.

Takikawa Masajirō 瀧川政次郎. 1929. *Nihon shakai shi* 日本社会史. Tokyo: Tōe Shoin.

Takita Chinsui 滝田枕水. 1925. Jizoku hogo hōan ni tsuite 寺族保護法案に就いて. *Kōsei* 6: 2.

Tamamuro Fumio 圭室文雄. 1986. Edo jidai ni okeru sōryo no nikujiki saitai—shiron 江戸時代における僧侶の肉食妻帯―試論. *Fujisawashi shi kenkyū* 19: 1–7.

———. 1987. *Nihon Bukkyōshi: Kinsei* 日本仏教史―近世. Tokyo: Yoshikawa Kōbunkan.

———. 1994. Meiji shoki no shinbutsu bunri 明治初期の神仏分離. Paper read at the Meiji Studies Conference, Cambridge, MA.

———. 1997. On the Suppression of Buddhism. In *New Directions in the Study of Meiji Japan*, edited by Helen Hardacre and Adam L. Kern, 499–505. Leiden: E. J. Brill.

Tamamuro Taijō 圭室諦成. 1967. *Nihon Bukkyōshi: Kinsei kindai hen* 日本仏教史―近世・近代篇. Kyoto: Hōzōkan.

Tamura Naomi 田村直臣. 1893. *MKS*, 7–8.

Tamura, Naomi. 1900. *The Japanese Bride*. New York: Harper and Brothers.

Tanabe, George J. 1989. Tanaka Chigaku: The Lotus Sutra and the Body Politic. In *The Lotus Sutra in Japanese Culture*, edited by G. J. Tanabe and W. J. Tanabe, 191–208. Honolulu: University of Hawaii Press.

Tanabe Zenchi 田辺善知. 1901. *Nihon Bukkyō nikujiki saitai ron* 日本仏教肉食妻帯論. Tokyo: Sugino Ihei.

Tanaka Chigaku 田中智学. 1968. Bukkyō sōryo nikusai ron 佛教僧侶肉妻論. *Nichirenshugi kenkyū* 1:10–59.

——— 1994. Bukkyō fūfu ron 仏教夫婦論. *Nichiren shugi kenkyū* 17:15–63.

Tanaka Hōkoku 田中芳谷. 1954. *Tanaka Chigaku Sensei ryakuden* 田中智學先生略伝. Tokyo: Shishiō Bunko.

———. 1960. *Tanaka Chigaku sensei eifu* 田中智学先生影譜. Tokyo: Shishiō Bunko.

Tanaka Keishin 田中敬信. 1984a. "Meiji gonen Dajōkan fukoku dai 133 gō" kō—sono 2 「明治五年太政官布告第131号」考－その2. *Shūgaku kenkyū* 26 (March): 131–36.

———. 1984b. "Meiji gonen Dajōkan fukoku dai 133 gō" kō—sono 3 「明治五年太政官布告第133号」考－その3. *Indogaku Bukkyōgaku kenkyū* 33 (1): 262–65.

Tanaka Kōho 田中香浦. 1968. Bukkyō sōryo nikusai ron no kaidai 仏教僧侶肉妻論の解題. *Nichirenshugi kenkyū* 1 (March): 2–9.

———. 1977. *Tanaka Chigaku* 田中智学. Tokyo: Shinsekai sha.

———. 1981. Nichirenshugi no kindaiteki hatten to shite no Tanaka Chigaku koji no zaike Bukkyō 日蓮主義の近代的発展としての田中智学居士の在家仏教. In *Nichirenshugi no kenkyū* 日蓮主義の研究, edited by Tanaka Kōho. Tokyo: Shinsekai sha.

———. 1994. Tanaka Chigaku koji no zaike bukkyō: *Bukkyō fūfu ron* no kaidai o kanete, sono igi o tou 田中智学居士の在家仏教－『仏教夫婦論』の解題をかねて、その意義を問う. *Nichiren shugi kenkyū* 17:3–14.

Tanaka Tomoenosuke (Chigaku) 田中巴之助 (智学). 1907. *Shūmon no ishin* 宗門の維新. 4th ed. Tokyo: Shishiō Bunko. Original edition 1901.

———. 1925. *Nihon koku no fujin* 日本国の婦人. Tokyo: Tengō Minpō Sha Shuppanbu.

——— 1930. *Bukkyō fūfuron* 佛教夫婦論. Tokyo: Kokuchūkai Honbu.

———. 1936. *Tanaka Chigaku jiden* 田中智学自伝. 10 vols. Tokyo: Shishiō Bunko.

Tan'an 澹菴. 1643? *Nikushoku ron* 肉食論. Manuscript held by Kokkai Toshokan; bound with another didactic Confucian text by the same author, *Kunkai hachijō* 訓戒八條.

Taniguchi Kozan 谷口庸山. 1937. *Sōtō shūsei yōran* 曹洞宗勢要覧. Tokyo: Sōtō Shūmuin Shomubu.

Tatsuguchi Myōsei 龍口明生. 1983. Shinshū Honganji kyōdan no tokudoshiki 真宗本願寺教団の得度式. *Shūgakuin ronshū* 54:18–42.

Tauchi Kenkō 田内憲晃. 1877. Meiji shinrei sōryo hikkei 明治新令僧侶必携. In MBSS 5:328–372.

Tendai-shū no saitai mondai 天台宗の妻帯問題. 1917. *Chūgai nippō* (July 3): 3.

Tetsugen Dōkō 鉄眼道光.1996. *Kōmori mōdanki* 蝙蝠妄談記. In Naikan Bunkō shozō shiryō no kenkyū (2): *Kōmori bōdanki/Jōkōki* ni tsuite, edited by Ishikawa Rikizan, 83–96. *Komazawa Daigaku Bukkyō Gakubu kenkyū kiyō* 54.

———. *Kōmori bōdanki* 蝙蝠忘談記. Ōtani University Library, Catalog no. 宗大 9812 1.

Thelle, Notto R. 1987. *Buddhism and Christianity in Japan: From Conflict to Dialogue, 1854–1899*. Honolulu: University of Hawaii Press.

Tokoro Shigemoto 戸頃重元 and Takagi Yutaka 高木豊, eds. 1970. *Nichiren* 日蓮. Tokyo: Iwanami Shoten.

Tokoyo Nagatane 常世長胤. 1988. Shinkyō soshiki monogatari 神教組織物語. In *Shūkyō to kokka*, edited by Yasumaru Yoshio and Miyachi Masato, 361–422. Tokyo: Iwanami Shoten.

Tokuryū 德龍. 1898. *Bōmori kyōkai kikigaki* 坊守教誡聞書. Kyoto: Nishimura Kurōemon.

Tokushi Yūshō 禿氏祐祥. 1930. Bukkyō zasshi shinbun nenpyō 仏教雑誌新聞年表. *Ryūkoku Daigaku ronsō* 293:116–32.

Tonomura, Hitomi. 1995. Universalized Women among Classified Men: Body, Sex, and Blood. Paper read at Association of Asian Studies, Washington, DC.

Tonooka Mojūrō 外岡茂十郎, ed. 1967. *Meiji zenki kazokuhō shiryō* 明治前期家族法資料. Vol. 2. Tokyo: Waseda Daigaku.

Toshitani Nobuyoshi 利谷信義. 1959. Meiji zenki no mibunhō to chōhei seido—Mibunhō ni okeru shihōteki seikaku no keisei katei 明治前期の身分法と徴兵制度—身分法における私法的性格の形成過程. In *Koseki seido to "ie" seido*, edited by Fukushima Masao, 339–98. Tokyo: Tōkyō Daigaku Shuppankai.

Tōyō Keizai Shinpō Sha 東洋経済新報社, ed. 1983. *Meiji Taishō kokusei sōran* 明治大正国勢総覧. 3d ed. 1927. Reprint, Tokyo: Tōyō Keizai Shinpōsha.

Toyoda Takeshi 豊田武. 1943. *Kaitei Nihon shūkyō seidoshi no kenkyū* 改訂日本宗教制度史の研究. Tokyo: Daiichi Shobō.

———. 1971. *Myōji no rekishi* 苗字の歴史. Tokyo: Chūō Kōronsha.

Tsuji, Tatsuya. 1991. Politics in the Eighteenth Century. In *Cambridge History of Japan: Early Modern Japan*, edited by John. W. Hall, 425–77. Cambridge: Cambridge University Press.

Tsuji Zennosuke 辻善之助. 1949. *Meiji Bukkyōshi no mondai* 明治仏教史の問題. Tokyo: Ritsubun Shoin.

———. 1944–55. *Nihon Bukkyō shi* 日本仏教史. 10 vols. Reprint. Tokyo: Iwanami Shoten, 1982.

———. 1984. *Nihon Bukkyōshi kenkyū* 日本仏教史研究. 6 vols. Tokyo: Iwanami Shoten.

Tsukamoto Manabu 塚本学. 1998. *Tokugawa Tsunayoshi* 徳川綱吉. Tokyo: Yoshikawa Kōbunkan.

Tsumaki Jikiryō 妻木直良, ed. 1913–16. *Shinshū zensho* 真宗全書. 74 vols. Vol. 59. Tokyo: Zōkyō Shoin.

Tsunemitsu Kōnen 常光浩然. 1968. *Meiji no Bukkyōsha* 明治の仏教者. 2 vols. Tokyo: Shunjūsha.

Uan Dōnin 有安道人. 1879. Dan sōryo saitai ron 彈僧侶妻帯論. MBSS, 7: 171–75.

———. 1999. A Refutation of Clerical Marriage. Translated by Richard Jaffe. In *Religions of Japan in Practice*, edited by George Tanabe, Jr., 78–86. Princeton: Princeton University Press.

Uchino, Kumiko. 1983. The Status Elevation Process of Sōtō Sect Nuns in Modern Japan. *Japanese Journal of Religious Studies* 10 (1–2): 177–94.

———. 内野久美子. 1990. Kindai Bukkyō ni okeru josei shūkyōsha—Sōtōshū ni okeru nisō to jizoku no chii kōjō 近代仏教における女性宗教者—曹洞

宗における尼僧と寺族の地位向上. In *Sōtōshū ni okeru zaike shūgaku no teishō*, edited by Yamauchi Shun'yū, 313–37. Tokyo: Daizō Shuppan.

Uchiyama Junzō. 1992. San'ei-chō and Meat-eating in Buddhist Edo. *Japanese Journal of Religious Studies* 19 (2–3): 299–303.

Ueda Shōhen 上田照遍. 1879. Sōhiron 僧非論. MBSS, 7:228–32.

Uejima Toshiaki 上島敏昭. 1990. Shinzen kekkonshiki no seiritsu 神前結婚式の成立. In *Kindai shomin seikatsu shi* 近代庶民生活史, edited by Minami Hiroshi 南博, 9:519–42. Tokyo: San'ichi Shobō.

Uesugi Taidō 上杉泰道, ed. 1963. *Jitei no sho* 寺庭の書. Tokyo: Sōtōshū Shūmuchō.

Ugai Tetsujō 養鸕徹定. 1913. Shamon seishi ben 沙門姓氏弁. In Sōryo myōji shintei no ikken. *Bukkyō shigaku* 3 (4): 56–57.

Umeda Yoshihiko 梅田義彦. 1971. *Kaitei zōho Nihon shūkyō seido shi* 改定増補日本宗教制度史. 4 vols. Tokyo: Tōsen Shuppan.

Umino Korin 海野虎林, ed. 1979. *Shami tokudo gihan yōryaku* 沙弥得度儀範要略. Uji: Ōbaku Shūmu Hon'in Kyōgakubu.

Washio Junkyō 鷲尾順敬. 1987. *Nihon Bukkyō jinmei jiten* 日本仏教人名辞典. Tokyo: Tokyo Bijutsu. Original edition 1903.

Watanabe Baiyū 渡部楳雄. 1920. Sakana wa kutte warui ka 魚は食って悪いか. *Daiichigi* 24:76–85.

Watt, Paul Brooks. 1982. Jiun Sonja (1718–1804): Life and Thought. Ph.D. dissertation, Columbia University.

Weinstein, Stanley. 1973. The Concept of Reformation in Japanese Buddhism. In *Studies in Japanese Buddhism*, edited by Ōta Saburō, 75–86. Tokyo: P.E.N. Club.

Wijayaratna, Mohan. 1990. *Buddhist Monastic Life*. Cambridge: Cambridge University Press.

Yamauchi Shūn'yū 山内舜雄. 1990. *Sōtōshū ni okeru zaike shūgaku no teishō* 曹洞宗における在家宗学の提唱. Tokyo: Daizō Shuppan.

Yampolsky, Philip B., ed. 1990. *Selected Writings of Nichiren*. New York: Columbia University Press.

Yasumaru Yoshio 安丸良夫. 1979. *Kamigami no Meiji ishin* 神々の明治維新. Iwanami Shinsho. Tokyo: Iwanami Shoten.

Yasumaru Yoshio 安丸良夫 and Miyachi Masato 宮地正人, eds. 1988. *Shūkyō to kokka* 宗教と国家. Tokyo: Iwanami Shoten.

Yokozeki Ryōin 横関了胤. 1938. Tanzan Oshō no seisō zokusō funbetsuan ni tsuite 坦山和尚の清僧俗僧分別案について. *Chūgai nippō* (March 19):1.

Yoshimura Shinji 吉村真治, ed. 1889. *Sōryo seiken ron* 僧侶政権論. Tokyo: Yoshimura Shinji, 1889.

Yuasa Yoshimi 湯浅吉美. 1990. *Nihon rekijitsu benran* 日本暦日便覧. Tokyo: Hako Shoin.

Zengaku Daijiten Hensanjo 禅学大辞典編纂所, ed. 1985. *Zengaku daijiten* 禅学大辞典. 2d ed. Tokyo: Taishūkan Shoten.

Zürcher, E. 1972. *The Buddhist Conquest of China*. 2 vols. Leiden: E. J. Brill. Original edition 1959.

Page numbers followed by *f* refer to figures; by *t*, to tables.

/